Roland Perry's cricket books include biographies of Shane Warne and Steve Waugh, *Captain Australia* – which profiled Australia's forty-one Test captains – and two books with Sir Donald Bradman: *The Don*, his official biography, and *Bradman's Best*, which described his all-time best cricket team. His other books include biographies of characters as diverse as journalist Wilfred Burchett, espionage agent Lord Rothschild and actor Mel Gibson.

BRADMAN'S BEST ASHES TEAM

SIR DONALD BRADMAN'S
SELECTION OF THE
BEST ASHES TEAMS
IN CRICKET HISTORY

ROLAND PERRY

CORGI BOOKS

BRADMAN'S BEST ASHES TEAMS
A CORGI BOOK : 0 552 14946 2

Originally published in Great Britain by Bantam Press,
a division of Transworld Publishers
First published 2002 in Australia by Random House Australia Pty Ltd.

PRINTING HISTORY
Bantam Press edition published 2002
Corgi edition published 2003

1 3 5 7 9 10 8 6 4 2

Copyright © Roland Perry 2002

Set in Garamond by
Falcon Oast Graphic Art Ltd.

Corgi Books are published by Transworld Publishers,
61–63 Uxbridge Road, London W5 5SA,
a division of The Random House Group Ltd,
in Australia by Random House Australia (Pty) Ltd,
20 Alfred Street, Milsons Point, Sydney, NSW 2061, Australia,
in New Zealand by Random House New Zealand Ltd,
18 Poland Road, Glenfield, Auckland 10, New Zealand
and in South Africa by Random House (Pty) Ltd,
Endulini, 5a Jubilee Road, Parktown 2193, South Africa.

Printed and bound in Great Britain by
Cox & Wyman Ltd, Reading, Berkshire.

To Tony and Joelle Maylam,
who love their French cricket

Contents

Acknowledgments

My thanks again go to Sir Donald Bradman for responding to my requests for his best Ashes teams, and for giving so generously on the project when time was so precious to him. Once he got down to the task of making his selections and explaining his reasoning, he enjoyed the exercise.

My appreciation goes to all those who helped in my research and the creation of this book. They include some players and their families in England and Australia. In particular, I am also most grateful for the assistance and hospitality shown to me by the Bedser brothers — Sir Alec and Eric — while I was in England doing research.

Gaining information on historic events, especially in areas before living memory, is sometimes difficult. Colin Clowes, honorary research librarian at the New South Wales Cricket Association, was most helpful here, as were the MCC Library, Thos Hodgson, Alan Young and Martin Ashenden.

This is my fifth book with Random House Australia and the association has been a happy one, not the least reason being the efficiency and creativity shown by the publishing team, including Benython Oldfield, who handles publicity. Special thanks for this book go to the editor, Jo Butler, who also worked on *Captain Australia*, and to the Head of Publishing, Jane Palfreyman.

As with *Bradman's Best*, some of the royalties from the sale of this book will go to the Bradman Memorial Fund. This is administered by the Bradman Museum and John Bradman.

Roland Perry
August 2002

BRADMAN'S BEST PERFORMANCES

S ir Donald Bradman was involved in watching, playing in or selecting Ashes cricket teams from the 1920–21 series until the last contest in the twentieth century between England and Australia in 1998–99. Before, during and after his playing days (1928–48), the biggest international contest in cricket was the Ashes. From the first Ashes in 1877 both England and Australia have had their separate periods of ascendancy. (Australia was seen as the easy-beats in the mid-1980s until captain Allan Border and coach Bob Simpson dragged the national team back from obscurity. Border's 1989 team began a seven-series winning streak that continued to 2001. But, before that, the two countries were close in terms of Test and series wins.) Only from the mid-1990s, when England's competitive edge seemed to have slipped more than temporarily, did other contests against the West Indies, South Africa, India and Pakistan seem more challenging for the Australians.

The Ashes tour of England (even in England's era of decline from 1989 to 2001) was the pinnacle for any aspiring Australian cricketer. The tour down-under was the ultimate challenge for an English player.

This long-running international sporting contest began in March 1877 when an England team led by James Lillywhite played Dave Gregory's 'Australian' combination – players from New South Wales and Victoria – at the MCG. Australia was almost a quarter of a century away from nationhood. Charles Bannerman made 165 retired hurt and Australia won by 45 runs. It sparked an unmatched enthusiasm for cricket throughout the colonies and the sport became a catalyst for forming a Commonwealth federal government. The Australian team was the only one to carry a national tag. Its success engendered a sense of nationalism. In England, the cricketing contest was not taken too seriously until three-and-a-half years later when the two countries played each other at The Oval. The game was of a high quality and closely fought. W.G. Grace made 152 in England's first innings and Will Murdoch made 153 not out in Australia's second innings. Although England was victorious by five wickets it was Australia that won respect at that game.

The interest was rekindled in Australia in 1881–82, where four Tests were played, the home team winning 2–0. Still, there was a snooty attitude to the colonials in 1882 when Murdoch took another team to England. But when Australia won by just seven runs in the first international 'thriller' – thanks to the superb bowling of Fred Spofforth – all of England now took notice. The colonials could not only challenge England's finest; they could literally beat them at their own game.

London's *Sporting Times* published a mock obituary for English cricket. At a time when England ruled the waves, won land wars and controlled over a quarter of the planet, defeat at the hands of another nation, even in sport, was a novelty. Suddenly, cricket matches between England and 'Australia' – until then looked upon as a rag-tag bunch of colonies – took on another dimension. They were a challenge.

Ivo Bligh took an England team on the long, arduous journey down-under for the 1882–83 season and managed a 2–2 result. In the spirit of the obituary notice that had been published in the *Sporting Times*, a group of young Melbourne women led by Florence Rose Morphy presented an urn containing burnt bails to Bligh. (Bligh took Morphy back to England and they married.) The ashes of the bails from then on represented the death of English cricket as depicted in the newspaper. The urn was eventually presented to English cricket's governing body, the Marylebone Cricket Club (MCC) at the spiritual home of the game, Lord's in North

London, and the urn has remained at the MCC ever since. The urn and the symbolic Ashes have been fought over by Australia and England in the Ashes competition ever since.

Murdoch sailed back to England in 1884 and after 16 years of dithering by England against touring Australian sides – beginning with Charles Lawrence's indigenous Australian team in 1868 – the competition got serious between England and Australia. There were three Tests. England won one and two were drawn.

The two countries had a more or less even fight for the symbolic Ashes for the next 46 years until 1930. Each country found it tough, but not impossible, to win 'away' while on tour. Then in 1930, the 21-year-old Australian, Don Bradman, showed himself to be so outstanding that he threatened to change the competition's equilibrium to such an extent that Australia seemed likely to dominate for as long as he was on the scene (ultimately two decades).

This prospect was too much for England's governors of the game. The Empire struck back in Australia in 1932–33 with Bodyline – fast bowling aimed at the batsman, with a close leg-side field – a tactic designed to injure or limit Bradman. For the first time the spirit of cricket, that had been so fierce but so fair since the thriller at The Oval in 1882, was in danger of being lost. The tactic reduced Bradman's average to 56.57, nearly half of what it had been. England won the Ashes by what most Australians saw as foul means rather than the fair means that had always characterised the competition. There were rumblings about a breakaway from the Commonwealth. Some even muttered the seditious word 'Republic'.

The 24-year-old Bradman, the son of a country carpenter from Bowral, New South Wales, was at the centre of the international controversy. The whole affair only served to heighten interest in the Ashes competition. Bodyline was effectively outlawed by the time Bill Woodfull's Australian team toured England in 1934. Bradman, as in 1930, was dominant. The Ashes returned to Australia. Bradman's penchant for the massive knock-out score of 300 or more when a series was at stake put him in a league of his own that no other cricketer even remotely approached for the rest of the twentieth century.

In the 1936–37 Australian Ashes competition after Bodyline, Bradman became both captain and a selector. Ultimately, he proved the most successful captain and player of the century, and retired from Test cricket in 1948. He continued on as a selector until 1971 and so played a hugely significant role in the selection of Ashes teams in essentially the middle third of the twentieth century. Bradman was heavily involved in Australian cricket long after giving up his national selector role and remained on the South Australian Cricket Association Board until 1986 when he was 78. From 1971 until his death in 2001, he was a keen observer and never missed seeing a series. His brilliant knowledge of cricket history meant that he had an unsurpassed comprehension of the game's finest players over the entire Ashes series from 1877 to 2000.

When Bradman first witnessed an Ashes match in 1920–21, several of the best players of the early twentieth century were still playing. This meant he only missed out on seeing a handful of the game's finest. An elephantine memory enabled him to recall the greatest players and their performances and compare them with each other down the decades. It was a favourite pastime of cricketers, fans, aficionados and cricket experts. Bradman's incisive mind, his ability to articulate and substantiate his judgments with clear-sighted technical observations, his command over the cricket figures and statistics, combined with his vast reading on the game, made him the expert's expert.

Bradman drafted teams at State and national level for the best part of four decades. In that time, he saw his share of great, good and ordinary cricketers from which to choose South Australian and Test teams. He endured his share of dross and, over the decades, developed a definite penchant for entertaining and aggressive players – those who were conscious of the paying public that supported the game.

I first became aware of his hobby of drafting 'best elevens' when interviewing him in 1995 for the biography of him that I was writing, *The Don*. I happened to ask him if he had ever considered a no-restrictions world-best 'dream' team from all players since international competition began in 1877.

He grinned enigmatically and replied: 'Often.'

We had discussed scores of players from all of the major cricket-playing nations. I kept a file on his thoughts about all of them. Bradman had the practical experience in 1971 of selecting an international squad led by Garry Sobers to play Ian Chappell's Australian team. This had come about after Bradman stopped a South African side from touring Australia for the 1971–72 season. Then he rolled up his sleeves with Sam Loxton and Neil Harvey, national selectors and fellow members of his 1948 winning Ashes team, the Invincibles, and chose a powerful squad to tour Australia. It beat Chappell's youthful yet strong team 2–1 in a five-Test series.

The cricket played was outstanding. There were many fine individual efforts and Bradman witnessed what he considered the best bowling and batting performances ever in Australia. Dennis Lillee took eight for 29 in an inspired burst on a fast Perth wicket. Garry Sobers smashed 254 in an awesome display on the MCG.

This successful selection experience was the catalyst for

Bradman to occasionally draw up lists of 'dream teams' over the next 30 years.

In October 1998, after much prompting, he finally divulged to me his best-ever world team. In batting order, it was: Barry Richards (South Africa), Arthur Morris (Australia), Don Bradman (Australia), Sachin Tendulkar (India), Garry Sobers (West Indies), Don Tallon (Australia, wicket-keeper), Ray Lindwall (Australia), Dennis Lillee (Australia), Alec Bedser (England), Bill O'Reilly (Australia), Clarrie Grimmett (Australia), with Wally Hammond (England) the 12th man.

The team contained seven Australians. Just another four names would give me his best-ever Australian XI. I asked him for this and he sent it to me in November 1998, along with his selection of a 12th man. I was then intrigued to know his dream England team, which would then give me his complete Ashes selections. He sent me his selections in February 1999.

He seemed to enjoy the experience which, at the end of his life, coinciding with the end of the twentieth century, consolidated his perspective on teams and performances.

In detailed discussions that followed on the 24 selections, Bradman disclosed what he considered were the five top performances with bat and ball in Ashes Tests that he witnessed in nearly eight decades of Ashes cricket. He also ranked what he thought were his own top five batting displays.

'I never saw Trumper and also missed [S.F.] Barnes at his best in Australia in 1911–12,' Bradman remarked. 'No doubt players like these performed well enough to be in these groups. But I am in no position to comment.'

Bradman's Best Five Ashes Performances: Batting

In Ashes batting Don Bradman considered the best five batting performances that he witnessed as being:

1: Stan McCabe, 232, Nottingham, First Test, 1938

England scored 658 and McCabe came to the wicket at two for 111. Before lunch on Day Three of the Test Australia was six for 194 and sinking when McCabe cut loose. He hooked paceman Ken Farnes for six and raced to 105 not out at lunch with Australia on six for 261. After the break McCabe took charge and attacked all bowlers with hooks and drives in a partnership of 56 with keeper Ben Barnett. When Barnett was caught off Farnes for 22 at 319, McCabe – left with tail-enders Bill O'Reilly, Ernie McCormick and 'Chuck' Fleetwood-Smith – proceeded to demolish the England attack, mixing upright grace with easy power. At one point he took four fours in one over from leg-spinner Doug Wright. Bradman was alone on the dressing-room balcony watching what he described as 'the best batting I ever saw or ever hope to see'. He asked his players in the dressing room to join him on the balcony.

'Come and look at this; you may never see anything like it again,' Bradman told them.

O'Reilly was dismissed at 319, then McCormick at 334. Ninth wicket down Fleetwood-Smith, the tail-ender's tail-ender, joined McCabe who farmed the strike, making 72 in a last-wicket stand of 77 in just 30 minutes. At 3.34 p.m. his masterful display ended when he was caught at cover by Denis Compton off left-hand spinner Hedley Verity for 232 out of Australia's score of 411. McCabe's innings took 235 minutes. He hit a six and 34 fours and gave no chance.

His second hundred took 84 minutes (the last 50 of it made in 24 minutes).

As McCabe came into the dressing room Bradman shook his hand and told him:

'I would give a great deal to be able to play an innings like that.'

The game was drawn.

2: David Gower, 123, Sydney, Third Test, 1990–91

Bradman placed this innings very close to the best he ever saw in Australia. Only Garry Sobers' 254 at Melbourne for a World XI versus Ian Chappell's Australians in 1971–72 ranked higher in Bradman's far-reaching memory.

Australia batted first and managed 518, which meant something big was needed from Gower, England's premier batsman. He didn't let his team down. He came to the wicket at three for 156 and joined Atherton. He signalled his intentions by beginning with a deliberate slash through the vacant third slip area. He was 33 not out at stumps. Gower began the next morning, Day Four, with three fours in the first over of the day. He kept up the brilliant performance with cover drives, delicate glances, back cuts, square cuts, on-drives and every other shot featured in Bradman's Art of Cricket, which Gower carried everywhere in his kit-bag.

Bradman described the innings as a 'masterpiece' and 'awe-inspiring'.

The game was drawn.

3: Wally Hammond, 240, Lord's, Second Test, 1938

Hammond came to the wicket on 24 June, the first day of the Lord's Test in 1938, with the score at two for 20.

Unperturbed, he launched into McCormick then Fleetwood-Smith. Hammond was 70 not out at lunch, with England three for 134. In the mid-session, he drove with exceptional power through the off-fields with shots through extra-cover, covers and mid-off. The late-cut was in evidence as he took complete command of the bowling.

'It was a throne-room innings,' leading English critic Neville Cardus wrote. 'He played greatly and deserved better bowling.'

Hammond added another 70 by tea, to be 140, and a further 70 by stumps when he was 210 not out. His partnership with Eddie Paynter (99) produced 222.

The next morning, injured and with a runner, he added 30 before McCormick bowled him. His 240 took 367 minutes and included 32 fours. It was the highest score by an Englishman in an Ashes Test at Lord's.

'It was a great innings,' Bradman commented. 'Wally Hammond was at the peak of his powers.'

The game was drawn.

4: Arthur Morris, 196, The Oval, Fifth Test, 1948

Saturday 14 August 1948 was an historic day in Ashes cricket. England was dismissed for 52, its lowest score of the twentieth century, with Ray Lindwall rampant, taking six for 20. Morris, a left-hander, opened with Barnes in a stand of 117 before Eric Hollies, the leg-spinner, had Barnes caught behind for 61. Bradman came to the wicket and lasted two balls before being bowled by Hollies for a duck in his last Test innings ever. Morris took charge and was 77 not out in Australia's two for 153 with Lindsay Hassett on 10 not out.

On Monday 16 August, Morris moved into top gear with a classic display of all the strokes possible in cricket from the hook and pull to cuts, glances and drives from both sides of the wicket. He was run out for 196.

'Arthur had been marvellous at Leeds,' Bradman remarked, 'but this innings (at The Oval) was outstanding. It was his peak performance for the 1948 season, which he dominated.'

Australia went on to win by an innings and 149 runs.

5: Charlie Macartney, 170, Sydney, Fifth Test, 1920–21

England batted first, scoring 204. In Australia's first innings, Macartney came to the wicket at one for 16 and produced attacking and, in Bradman's words, 'beautifully executed' shots all around the wicket. He drove, hooked and cut with power to be 32 not out at stumps on Day One, with Australia on two for 70. He came out the next day and continued his tour de force in a 198 stand with Jack Gregory (93).

This Test began on 25 February 1921, eighty years to the day before Bradman died. Aged twelve, young Bradman attended the first two days of the Sydney Cricket Ground game, the first Test he ever saw.

Bradman's Best Five Ashes Performances: Bowling

When assessing a bowler's performance, Bradman took into account a bowler's effort in both innings of a game. His thinking was based on the need to dismiss an opposing team twice to win a match. He also considered the weather and pitch conditions and the opposition batting line-up in his assessment of a bowler's performance.

Bradman considered the best five Ashes bowling performances that he witnessed as being:

1: Hedley Verity, fifteen for 104, Lord's, Second Test, 1934

England made 440, and Australia was two for 192 at stumps on Day Two. Verity, a slow left-arm spinner, had Bradman caught and bowled after a brilliant cameo of 36. The conditions were damp in the morning of Day Three, 25 June, which was to be Verity's day of glory. He took fourteen wickets on the day for 80 runs. Six of these wickets fell in the last hour and delivered England an Ashes win at Lord's for the first time since 1896. Verity's match figures were fifteen for 104, the best return until that point by an Englishman in an Ashes Test. (Only Jim Laker 22 years later did better with nineteen for 90.) The wicket was at first conducive to spin, but Bradman who, along with Stan McCabe, was dismissed twice by Verity in the game, said he had played on worse wickets. He put down Verity's performance more to his own ability to change pace, spin and direction than to the state of the pitch. Verity took seven for 61 and eight for 43.

England won by an innings and 38 runs.

2: Alec Bedser, fourteen for 99, Trent Bridge, First Test, 1953

Medium-pace swing bowler Bedser began England's quest to regain the Ashes after two decades by uprooting Hole's middle stump in his second over. It was an emphatic start and Bedser went on to take three for 26 on Day One, 11 June. Australia was three for 157. Rain on an uncovered wicket helped Bedser take seven for 55 off 38.3 overs and 16 maidens. Australia made 249. England's response was just 144. Carrying an instep injury caused by a Lindwall yorker, Bedser came out again and blasted out the first five Australians for just 22, and ended with seven for 44. Australia was rolled for 123, and the game finished in a draw. Bedser snared every Australian at least once in the match, except for number eleven Bill Johnston who remained not 0 and 4 in his two innings.

His scalps were Hole (twice), Morris, Hassett (twice), Harvey (twice), Miller, Benaud, Davidson, Tallon, Lindwall and Hill (twice).

The game was drawn.

3: Ray Lindwall, nine for 70, The Oval, Fifth Test, 1948

England batted first. Lindwall delivered what Bradman considered was the most brilliant, devastating spell of fast bowling he saw in any one Ashes innings, taking six for 20, which virtually sealed the game. England made just 52. Lindwall's victims included Hutton, Compton, Yardley and Evans. Australia replied with 389 and England made 188 in its second innings, in which Lindwall took three for 50. Australia won by an innings and 149 runs.

4: Jim Laker, nineteen for 90, Old Trafford, Fourth Test, 1956

Off-spinner Laker took nine for 37 out of a total of 84, and ten for 53 from 205, on a sharply turning, substandard Test pitch. No Australians, except for opener Colin McDonald (32 and 89) and Ian Craig (38 in the second innings), had any answer to Laker during this game and even McDonald and Craig were dismissed by him twice. His figures of nineteen for 90 were the best ever in Test history. England won by an innings and 170 runs.

The wicket made Laker nearly unplayable. He could extract spin even on hard Australian wickets, and was deadly with bite and turn on the Old Trafford wicket that, over the five days of play, was wet early on then on the last days was a dustbowl. His control of line and length was immaculate and he varied his pace and turn to bamboozle even Neil Harvey, one of the top half-dozen players of spin ever.

Laker's figures and performance were no fluke. Whether or not the wickets had been prepared for spin, Laker had taken all 10 Australian wickets playing for Surrey against the tourists. He had won the previous Test for England – the Third at Headingley – taking five for 58 and six for 55.

5: Bill O'Reilly, eleven for 129, Nottingham, First Test, 1934

Australia batted first, scoring 374. O'Reilly removed Hammond, Hendren, Ames and Verity in England's first innings of 268. O'Reilly took four for 75 on a good batting wicket, which remained good during Australia's second innings of eight declared for 273. The lead was 379. The pitch was still unhelpful to bowlers, and it took an hour before O'Reilly made inroads into the strong England batting line-up in its second innings. At 51 he had Sutcliffe caught. Over the next two hours, aided by Grimmett, he mowed down the English batting, which capitulated at 141. He took seven for 54. Australia won by 238 runs with just 10 minutes to spare.

Bradman ranked O'Reilly's ten for 129 at Melbourne in 1932–33 highly, but given the lasting state of the Nottingham wicket in 1934, he saw this as a superior performance against a very strong batting line-up.

Bradman's Own Best Five Ashes Innings

When I asked Bradman to rank his own best five batting performances in Ashes Tests he chose the following:

1: 254, Lord's, Second Test, 1930

This innings always remained special to Bradman. It was his first Test innings at Lord's, the home of cricket, and it was his first double hundred in Test cricket. He executed every shot in the textbook to perfection and gave no chance.

'Every shot went where it was intended,' he said, 'even the cover drive caught by Percy Chapman.'

Bradman judged his innings by the standard of his own performance regardless of the bowling strength. England batted first and scored 425. He came to the wicket mid-afternoon on Day Two, Saturday 28 June, with the score one for 162. There was a full house at Lord's as he stroked his way masterfully to 50 in 45 minutes. His hundred took 105 minutes and he was 155 not out at stumps, his last 101 coming in the final session. Australia was two for 404. His 200 took 234 minutes and his innings of 254 in all took 339 minutes. He hit 25 fours in what was then the highest score in a Test at Lord's. It remains the highest Ashes score there. Australia declared at six for 729 and went on to win by seven wickets.

2: 304, Leeds, Fourth Test, 1934

The night before this match, English writer Neville Cardus asked Bradman how many runs he thought he would get.

Bradman replied he needed to get at least 200 in order to give Australia a chance to win. Cardus told him there was no way he could do it.

'It's against the law of averages,' Cardus said, recalling that Bradman had made 334 in his last Test at Leeds in 1930.

'I don't believe in the law of averages,' Bradman replied.

He defied those laws during the Fourth Test at Leeds in 1934 as he did throughout his career, stroking a brilliant 304, with two sixes and 43 fours. He looked for boundaries at every chance, knowing that a mystery illness (later found to be peritonitis) would retard him if he ran too many ones, twos or threes.

He came to the wicket at three for 39 at the beginning of Day Two, after England had made 200. He began his innings with two drives for four off Bowes' first two deliveries and never looked back. He gave a tough catching chance to square leg on 72 and was 76 not out at lunch. He was 169 not out at tea, having hit 93 in the session. He reached 200 in 305 minutes and smashed 102 between tea and stumps to be 271 not out at stumps. Bradman and Bill Ponsford (181) had put on 388 for the fourth wicket. Bradman went on to score his second successive triple hundred at Leeds. His 304 took 430 minutes. The game was drawn.

Bradman ranked this innings above his 334 at Leeds in 1930, given his stroke-play, the condition of the series and his own battle against illness, which left him gaunt and dangerously underweight.

3: 334, Leeds, Third Test, 1930

Australia batted first and Bradman came to the wicket at one for 2 after five minutes. He carved his way to a scintillating century before lunch and another before tea to be 220 not out at the second break. In the final session he collected 89 to be 309 not out in a day's batting, which was the highest score ever in an Ashes Test at that time. He went on to 334 the next day. He batted against a strong England bowling line-up of Larwood, Tate, Geary, Tyldesley, Hammond and Leyland. Bradman was particularly severe on Larwood who took one for 139 off 33 overs. In all Bradman hit 46 fours and batted 383 minutes, and scored at close to a run a ball. His double century took 214 minutes and was the fastest ever in Test cricket to that point (as was his triple hundred).

The game was drawn.

4: 270, Melbourne, Third Test, 1936–37

Australia batted first on 1 January 1937 and made 200. England got caught on a glue-pot of a wicket, and captain Gubby Allen declared at nine for 76 so it could put Australia under pressure on the 'sticky'. Bradman countered by reversing his team's batting order. The tail-enders went in first and Bradman came to the wicket at 2.50 p.m. on Day Three when the score was five for 97.

At stumps he was 56 not out with Fingleton 39 not out. Australia was five for 194 with a lead of 318. On Day Four, 64,826 fans crowded the Melbourne Cricket Ground (the MCG) in the hope of a big Bradman performance. They got what they wanted. Gubby Allen set his fielders in a ring around the boundary in an attempt to tire Bradman. This slowed up Bradman's century that ended up taking 193 minutes. He reached 164 not out at tea. He stepped up his rate as England's bowlers and fielders, not he, tired.

Bradman reached 200 and took block again. He was 248

not out at stumps in 399 minutes. It was already the highest score by an Australian to that point in an Ashes Test in Australia. He was caught off Verity at 270. He faced 375 balls in his 458-minute stay and hit 22 fours. His innings included 110 singles in countering the ring field.

Australia won the match by 365 runs.

5: 244, The Oval, Fifth Test, 1934

The final Test at The Oval in 1934 was to be played out to the end, regardless of the time taken. With each team on one Test win, the final Test was the decider. Bradman came to the wicket at 21 and was 43 not out at lunch with the score at one for 100 (Ponsford 43 not out). Instead of digging in for the long haul after the break, Bradman reached 50 in 96 minutes and then went on the attack. Bradman reached his century in 170 minutes and hit 107 in the second session to be 150 not out at tea. After tea, he continued the calculated, precision onslaught with cuts, late-cuts, drives, leg-glances and the occasional hook and pull to reach 200 midway through the session. His second hundred had taken just 113 minutes and he was on a gradual path of acceleration that continued until 244 – his last 44 taking just 33 minutes. His innings had lasted 316 minutes. He faced just 272 balls at a strike rate of 89.87. He hit one six and 32 fours.

Australia reached 701 (Ponsford 266) and went on to win by 562 runs.

Bradman's selections for Australian and the English Ashes teams contained plenty of surprises, and perhaps one selection that he may have changed had he lived to the middle of 2002. That was the position of Australia's wicket-keeper. He chose Don Tallon as the best keeper he ever witnessed, and would not have changed his mind on this point. But he did remark, as outlined in the book *Bradman's Best*, that if Adam Gilchrist 'maintained his batting average above 50 and his form behind the stumps, he would be the most valuable keeper-batsman in history'.

This observation came in late 1999 after he had been 'enthralled' by Gilchrist's great 149 not out in 163 balls against Pakistan in the Hobart Test. In this game Australia scored six for 369 in the fourth innings of the Test to win – the third-highest winning score in the final innings of a Test.

Gilchrist went on over the next three years to play more than 30 Tests and average around 60. This ranked him behind Bradman himself (average 99.94) in a group of the game's greats, all averaging a tickle over 60 – Graeme Pollock (South Africa), George Headley (West Indies), Herbert Sutcliffe (England) and Eddie Paynter (England).

Yet it was the attacking way that he scored that 149 not out and his next five centuries that may have swayed Bradman towards his selection ahead of Tallon. Nevertheless, in late 2000, just a few months before he died, Bradman had not changed his mind on any player in either side. They remain his selections for the best Ashes teams – 1877 to 2000.

PART 1

THE ALL-TIME ASHES TEAM: AUSTRALIA

In batting order, Bradman's ideal Australian Ashes team is:

ARTHUR MORRIS (New South Wales)

BILL PONSFORD (Victoria)

DON BRADMAN (New South Wales and South Australia)

NEIL HARVEY (Victoria and New South Wales)

CHARLIE MACARTNEY (New South Wales)

KEITH MILLER (Victoria and New South Wales)

DON TALLON (Queensland)

RAY LINDWALL (New South Wales and Queensland)

DENNIS LILLEE (Western Australia and Tasmania)

BILL O'REILLY (New South Wales)

CLARRIE GRIMMETT (Victoria and South Australia)

RICHIE BENAUD (New South Wales) (12th man)

I received Bradman's list of his ideal Australian Ashes team in a letter in November 1998. Late in 2000, he confirmed that the selections he had made still stood. Apart from the surprise selection of Macartney, and the omission of Shane Warne and Victor Trumper, several points distinguished the team:

* Bradman played with or against eight of the selections.

* Bradman saw every player chosen perform in Test cricket.

* Charlie Macartney was the only selection who ended his Test career before Bradman began his.

* Charlie Macartney was the only selection who played Tests before the First World War.

* Six players – Morris, Bradman, Harvey, Miller, Tallon and Lindwall – played in Bradman's all-conquering 1948 side – the Invincibles.

* Two players – Macartney and Grimmett – were born before 1900.

* Five players – Bradman, Morris, Harvey, Lindwall and Benaud – captained Australia.

* Only Bradman and O'Reilly played Test cricket before and after the Second World War (O'Reilly played just one Test after the Second World War, against New Zealand early in 1946).

* Four of Bradman's selections played in Test cricket in the 1920s – Macartney, Ponsford, Grimmett and Bradman.

* Four of Bradman's selections played in Test cricket in the 1930s – Ponsford, Grimmett, Bradman and O'Reilly.

* Seven of Bradman's selections played in Test cricket in

the 1940s – Bradman, O'Reilly, Morris, Harvey, Tallon, Lindwall and Miller.

* Six of Bradman's selections played in Test cricket in the 1950s – Harvey, Morris, Tallon, Lindwall, Miller and Benaud.

* Three of Bradman's selections played in Test cricket in the 1960s – Harvey, Benaud and Lindwall.

* Only Dennis Lillee played in the 1970s and 1980s.

* No player who played in Tests in the 1990s was selected.

* All players chosen played at Test level between 1907 (the year before Bradman was born) and 1984 – a 77-year span.

* Seven members of the selected team played for New South Wales, four for Victoria, two for South Australia, two for Queensland and one for Western Australia and Tasmania.

* Eight players scored centuries in Test cricket (Morris, Ponsford, Bradman, Harvey, Macartney, Miller, Lindwall and Benaud); four hit double hundreds (Morris, Ponsford, Bradman and Harvey) and one (Bradman) scored triple hundreds.

Bradman's choice of Bill Ponsford as the right-hand opening bat was predictable. Bradman and Ponsford had forged some of the biggest, most important partnerships in cricket history. Bradman had seen his choice's exceptional skills and big-occasion capacities at first-hand. He considered Victor Trumper for the spot but, as he did not ever see him bat, Bradman opted for the devil he knew. He read everything published about Trumper, listened to experts who witnessed his playing performance and studied his Test and first-class record.

'There is no doubt Trumper was a great player,' Bradman said, 'and one of the finest stylists of all time. By all accounts he would have been great in any era.'

We discussed Trumper's averages as we did with all Bradman's choices for the team. In 48 Tests and 89 innings, he scored 3163 runs at 39.04 with a highest score of 214 not out. He hit eight centuries and 13 fifties. Against England in Ashes contests, which was the only real yard-stick of the era a century ago, he had 74 innings and scored 2263 runs at 32.79.

Ponsford played 29 Tests and scored 2122 runs at 48.22. He hit seven centuries. In 20 Ashes matches he had 35 innings and scored 1558 runs at 47.21, with a highest score of 266.

Apart from the statistics, the record shows Trumper was the more dashing player, while Ponsford was a more reliable opener and a better performer when a series depended on him lifting his rating. His massive scores of 181 and 266 in the last two Tests of the 1934 series in England and his 110 at The Oval in 1930 were evidence of his temperament under pressure. Ponsford performed at his best to help secure the Ashes in England on both these occasions. He was no slouch when it came to making his runs either. In his big partnerships with Bradman and others he blended solid defence with attack. He had a mind to go for his shots when he had set up an innings. Ponsford still holds the record for the most runs made in a day in first-class cricket in Australia – 334 not out against New South Wales at the MCG during the Christmas match of 1926.

Trumper, as spectacular as he was, often tended to go missing in action in Ashes series when it really counted. In his first series of 1899 in England he made a magnificent 135 not out at Lord's in the Second Test, but put together just 145 in the other eight innings. He averaged 35.00 and tended to perform more consistently against the counties. In 1901–02, he had a poor series, scoring 219 runs at 21.90 when Australia under Joe Darling and Hugh Trumble romped in 4–1.

In 1902, Trumper delivered at the appropriate moment for the first time in his career with a fine 104 at Old Trafford in the Fourth Test. Australia won and took the Ashes 2–1 under Darling again. Trumper was sixth in the averages for the two teams, scoring 247 at 30.88. In 1903–04, he had his best series, amassing 574 at 63.78. But in the series crunch game – the Fourth Test at Sydney – when a match-winning knock was required, he scored 7 and 12. England won the series 3–2.

Trumper delivered another forgettable Ashes performance in England in 1905, scoring only 125 at 17.86. In 1907–08, he had a mid-series slump at the top of the order, scoring 4 followed by three successive ducks. The selectors thought about dumping him for the dead-rubber last Test (Australia had an unassailable lead of 3–1). Instead, they opened with Charlie Macartney and dropped Trumper down to number seven. He scored 10 and was put back to number three for the second innings and this time he walloped 166. His series aggregate was 338 at 33.80.

In 1909, selectors' confidence in him as an opener was

low. He batted down the order for another ordinary return for such an outstanding talent. His 211 total was made at 26.38. Trumper, still down the order in Ashes competition, began his final campaign in 1911–12 against England in fine style, scoring 113 at Sydney in the first innings. But it was downhill from there as he hit 14, 13, 2, 26, 1 not out, 17, 28, 5 and 50 for an aggregate of 269 at 29.89. Australia lost the series 1–4.

In 1912, a dispute by several players with the Australian Board of Control over selection stopped Trumper going to England, then the First World War prevented international competition. Trumper died in 1915 of Bright's disease, aged only 37. Had he lived he would probably have played against a young Ponsford, who first represented Victoria at age 18 in 1918.

First impressions were lasting for Bradman. He missed the thrill of seeing Trumper play, but at 19, over Christmas 1927, he travelled by train to Melbourne to play in his second first-class match for New South Wales, having scored a century in his first against South Australia in Adelaide. Bill Ponsford was the man of the moment. While Bradman had hit his initial century in a fine knock against the great Clarrie Grimmett, the effort hardly rated a mention in the papers. At the same time in that previous week, Ponsford had hit a world-record 437 against Queensland. Melbourne, naturally, was abuzz with the feats of one of its own, Bradman recalled. 'He followed up with 202 against us – the first time anyone had scored successive first-class double hundreds in Australia. I remember it well. I did a lot of chasing in the outfield, which I didn't mind so much in my youth. It made an impact on me. I was particularly impressed by his powers of concentration. He played each ball on its merit and never lost control . . . He handled [leg-spinner] Arthur Mailey with aplomb. Bill crouched at the wicket and shuffled his solid frame into position with ease. He always seemed to be at the pitch of the ball.'

Bradman recalled that in 1927–28, when he first played for New South Wales against Victoria, Ponsford was given 'top billing' in Sydney. Posters would urge fans to 'come and see Ponsford play'.

'He was the big drawcard,' Bradman said, 'because of his ability to build big scores at a rapid rate.'

It made Ponsford the number-one target for bowlers in Australia from 1923, when he scored 429 in 477 minutes against Tasmania, until 1929, after which it became clear that Bradman himself had an even bigger appetite for scoring runs.

Bradman remembered the strategies to get Ponsford out with speed.

'I was privy to it from my first season,' he noted. 'He wasn't seen as vulnerable, not at all. It was simply that something had to be tried to remove him. Our (New South Wales) bowlers feared what would happen if he got set. Not everyone fancied chasing around while he accumulated two, three or even 400, as he did twice. The only player ever to have done so, I believe.'

England, too, worried about Ponsford's mega-scoring capacities. While Bradman was their number-one target during the Bodyline series, Ponsford opened the innings and faced the early onslaught. Larwood had broken a bone in Ponsford's hand in the Second Test of the 1928–29 series and this put him out of the Ashes contest. Ponsford had mastered him in 1930. Larwood aimed his short stuff at him in 1932–33. Ponsford's answer was to turn his back and take the ball on the body rather than risk a catch to the closely packed leg-side field.

'I saw him black and blue in the dressing rooms (during

Bodyline),' Bradman recalled. 'He showed a lot of courage, but he naturally didn't enjoy being hit so often. Bill didn't believe the game should be one where the object of the bowlers was to get the batsman out by any means – physical injury included. That aside, there have been few cricketers in history that could play fast bowlers as well as Bill did.'

Ponsford had a short backlift, but his strong wrists and heavy bat allowed him to get real power from his shots.

'Bill had excellent timing,' Bradman added, 'and preferred to play shots in front of the wicket. He drove extremely well, mostly on the on-side. He had a very, very good square cut, which he would use when the mood struck.'

Bradman concluded that Trumper would have been a better player to watch, but that he could not go past Ponsford, when selecting his best all-time Australian Ashes team, for efficiency and results. It was this that swayed his selection. Bradman would always choose an attacking batsman who would give his side a better chance of winning over an attractive player who didn't always achieve results. Bradman wasn't selecting a side for its aesthetics. He was after the best winning combination.

Ponsford's partner was the left-handed Arthur Morris. Bradman, in 1950, considered him one of the two best Australian batsmen playing (the other being Neil Harvey) and judged him the finest left-hander since Clem Hill. A half-century later no better opener, left-handed or right, in Bradman's opinion, had emerged, so Morris was selected at the top of the order in the best-ever Australian side.

Bradman found him a 'flawed genius with the bat, but a genius nonetheless'. He found fault with the way he gripped the bat and how his grip affected his late-cut. He thought

Morris played his off-side shots with stiff forearms and with less wrist than the purists would like. Bradman also noted that Morris wasn't always straight in defence and that he often played the cover drive with his bat well away from his pads. Yet all this was acceptable. Morris was still outstanding. He got results at the beginning of an innings.

'I believe it would have been wrong to consider asking him to change anything, as some of his critics did,' Bradman remarked. 'He was simply a superior cricketer with an elegance of his own.'

All shots except the late-cut came easily to Morris and he even conquered any difficulty he had with this, late in his career. He brought his artistry to the hook, cut, all the drives and glances. Bradman even admired the ease he brought to the lofted drive, a shot Bradman rarely played himself because of its riskiness.

'Other factors blended to make him "great" that nothing could change,' Bradman said. 'He had outstanding courage and a fine temperament. He was relaxed and with humour on any big occasion. I recall well his cheeriness and confidence at Leeds in 1948 when we were faced with a huge task. We managed a triple-century partnership [which won the Ashes Test and series]. His calm determination during our partnership was a feature. There was a certain tension in him before batting, yet this was always preferable to out-and-out nerves or, the other extreme, being unemotional to the point of carelessness.'

Bradman came to most of his conclusions about Morris during his sensational 1948 Ashes tour. The tour started ordinarily for Morris. Match by match he improved until mid to late in the tour when he was playing as well as anyone Bradman had ever seen on tour. The figures support this. Only Bradman himself did better.

* * *

Bradman's selection of himself at number three was auto-matic. With anyone else in his place, for instance, any of the best and most worthy of the number-three place in Australian cricket history such as Greg Chappell, Clem Hill, Trumper or Mark Waugh, Australia would appear vulnerable against the England attack. You can just imagine that the bowlers in Bradman's all-time England team – Trueman, Barnes, Bedser, Verity, Grace and Hammond – would have fancied themselves against any Australian line-up without Bradman. Bradman's killer instinct often choked off the opposition on the first day with a fast hundred or a massive score. No matter what happened to the openers, when Bradman entered any arena over his 20 years in top cricket, the opposition braced itself. Their only chance of staying in the competition would hang on the early removal of this one player from the field of battle. No other individual in any team sport in history had Bradman's impact on a contest.

In statistical and actual terms Bradman was worth two of the best of the rest in Australian cricket history. In effect, with a batting line-up of Morris, Ponsford, Bradman, Harvey, Macartney and Miller, Australia had the equivalent of a seventh batsman. In most of the tight Ashes contests over 125 years, Bradman would make the difference between winning and losing a series.

Bradman's ideal team on paper consisted of:

- two recognised opening batsmen of whom one is a left-hander;

- three other batsmen of whom one is a left-hander;

- one all-rounder;

- one wicket-keeper who is also a good bat;
- one fast bowler to open with the wind;
- one fast- or medium-pace bowler to open into the wind;
- one right-hand off-spinner, or a right-hand leg-spinner;
- one left-hand orthodox first-finger spinner.

Bradman's 'blueprint' team, then, would place two left-handed batsmen in the top six, if the player was superior or equal to right-handers vying for a place. He only ranked four other left-handers with Neil Harvey, his choice for the number-four spot. They were Arthur Morris, Garry Sobers, David Gower and Brian Lara. Bradman ranked Harvey with the finest batsmen – left or right – Australia has produced down the ages. These factors were important in deciding who would fill the number-four vacancy.

Bradman noted that Harvey was: 'strongly built in a compact frame. He had no technical faults. He was blessed with supple wrists and was a strong driver and powerful cutter. He could hook extremely well and enjoyed the shot. He appeared to struggle against spin early in his career, but mid-career became one of the best players of spin I ever saw. Neil liked to dance to the ball, and apparently his mastering of spin on tours of Pakistan and India was something special to behold. He was also one of the best outfielders of all time. His work in the covers, even late in his career, was sensational'.

Harvey was a player very much in the Bradman mould. He liked to get on with the game. He was a naturally attacking cricketer as was Bradman's choice for number five, Charlie Macartney.

* * *

Bradman's first impression of Macartney was from the first Test he ever saw – at the Sydney Cricket Ground on 25 and 26 February 1921. It was the Fifth Test of the 1920–21 Ashes series. Macartney played one of his best innings, making 170. His timing for such a show was impeccable. The 12-year-old fan from Bowral would never forget the all-round display of stylish, powerful stroke-play. Five years later, during the 1926–27 season, Bradman was selected to play for a New South Wales Country XI against a City XI at the Sydney Cricket Ground. Macartney, at forty years of age, had just retired from Test cricket and was playing for City. City batted first. Macartney, coming in at three, turned on a Test standard performance with a dashing century featuring leg-glances and drives. Bradman rushed around in the covers and in the deep, living his dream. A few years ago such a first-hand encounter with Macartney would have been a backyard fantasy.

City scored eight for 301. Bradman was soon in for the New South Wales Country team, also at number three. He went for his shots from the first ball.

'Yes, I was inspired by Charlie,' Bradman told me. 'I wanted to perform well in such company.'

Bradman found a partner in Frank Cummins from the Hunter Valley and they put on 82, Bradman making 60 of them and Cummins 19. Bradman stepped up his rate as wickets fell and raced into the nineties. He was on 94 and the score was seven for 167 when the game was officially over. Macartney, impressed by the country kid's verve, thought he deserved a hundred. He called for and got a one-over extension of the game from the sympathetic umpires. Bradman sliced his ninth four past point to reach 98. He lunged at the next delivery and was caught in slip. Macartney shook his hand, told him he had batted well and wished him luck. Bradman was buoyed by the gesture and when he spoke to me recalled the game as if it were yesterday. It may well have had a minor influence on his attitude in his assessment that Macartney would be in his Ashes team wish list more than seven decades later.

Macartney scored seven Test hundreds in his 35-Test career, including a century before lunch on the first day of the 1926 Leeds Test. He was perhaps the hardest hitting top-drawer batsman to play for Australia, and he had all the strokes. The shortish, square-shouldered right-hander loved to improvise. He refused to let bowlers get on top and would always attempt to dominate early in an innings.

He averaged nearly 42 runs an innings, which was close to the average of Mark Waugh, though well short of Greg Chappell (nearly 54) and Steve Waugh and Allan Border (both 50 plus). Macartney's bowling (45 wickets at the excellent average of 27.55) put him in the genuine all-rounder class, which provided the Bradman Australian Ashes team with a third strong spin option of a different variety to support the O'Reilly/Grimmett combination.

At the beginning of his career, Macartney was selected more for his spinners than his batting. On his first tour of England in 1909 he took 64 first-class wickets at 17.85 runs apiece. He took a long run for a slow bowler, and had a deadly quicker ball.

Macartney was one of five new faces in the Australian Ashes team along with the seven players Bradman selected in his world team taken from all nations. The four others were Bill Ponsford, Neil Harvey, Keith Miller and 12th man Richie Benaud.

More flamboyant, yet just as aggressive when in the mood, was all-rounder Keith Miller at number six. Miller was selected in front of a fine group of all-rounders including

Richie Benaud, Alan Davidson, Monty Noble and Warwick Armstrong.

Bradman saw Miller as a 'dangerous' new-ball bowler who could swing it both ways, and who was nearly as fast as Ray Lindwall. Bradman also admired Miller's batting and his big-hitting ability, but was critical of his lack of application and concentration at times.

Miller, another member of Bradman's 1948 Invincibles, had remarkable Test figures with both bat and ball. Here are the comparisons with the four other champions in Australia's history, and Garry Sobers, whom Bradman chose ahead of Miller for his best-ever world team:

	Tests	runs	average	centuries	wkts	average
Sobers	93	8032	57.78	26	235	34.03
Miller	55	2958	36.97	7	170	22.97
Noble	42	1997	30.25	1	121	25.00
Armstrong	50	2863	38.68	6	87	33.59
Benaud	63	2201	24.45	3	248	27.03
Davidson	44	1328	24.59	–	186	20.53

The statistics, of course, do not tell the full story for any cricketer. Performances under pressure or, at key moments, the strength of the opposition, should carry weight. Yet, over time, statistics are strong indicators of a player's capacities. Bradman's choice of Sobers as the number-one all-rounder of all time, as discussed in *Bradman's Best*, is hardly disputed by any astute observer or anyone who ever saw him perform on the field. But Miller was not far behind him in his overall impact. His batting did not have the sustained brilliance that Sobers attained over thirty-eight more Tests. Miller was more mercurial and more likely to surrender his wicket attempting a big hit. In his prime, probably during the unofficial 'Victory Tests' in England just after the Second World War, he was a magnificent performer. In a game at Lord's in August 1945, playing for the 'Dominions' against England, he smote seven sixes in a blast of 185.

Miller's bowling returns are far more impressive than Sobers', and because of this some have argued that the Australian was the more valuable player. He could be quick and lethal if in the right frame of mind. He and Lindwall formed one of the best-ever opening bowling combinations. Yet as Sobers ranked among the great batsmen of all time, and was effectively three bowlers in one with his fast-medium, orthodox left-hand spinning and wrist-spinning, he was Bradman's number-one selection as the best all-rounder of all time.

Monty Noble wasn't far behind Miller's achievements with his right-hand attacking batting and off-spin. Benaud, a hard-hitting right-hand bat and one of the best leg-spinners of all time, could hardly be separated in effectiveness from Davidson, an attacking left-hand bat and brilliant left-arm pace bowler. His returns of 186 wickets at just 20.53 place him at the top of the twentieth century's best in statistical terms and Bradman bracketed him among the elite.

Bradman placed Don Tallon, the wicket-keeper, at number seven in his Australian team. The selection and placement of him at number six in Bradman's world team brought criticism, yet it came from those who had never seen him bat or keep. All those who witnessed Tallon's keeping were at one in saying he was the best keeper ever. Without exception, Test players who played for or against him marvelled at his acrobatic skills behind the stumps. His leg-side catching, his stumping off medium pace and spin were superlative.

Tallon's place as a batsman at number six or seven suggests he was in the all-rounder class, and was someone who could bat. His Test average of under 18 runs an innings would tend to contradict that, however. Yet, if ever the figures lied about batting skills, they did so with Don Tallon. In the 1930s, he was judged as one of the most talented attacking batsmen in first-class cricket. He made the Queensland State team at 17, in 1933–34, and two seasons later, in 1935–36, impressed Bradman with a dashing 88 in a State game. It was just one innings among many in that season and the next four before the Second World War stopped play, that stamped the young Tallon, then still a teenager, as a prodigious all-rounder. Another innings of 193 in 187 minutes against Victoria at the Gabba in 1935–36 ranked as one of the finest innings of the 1930s. Bradman didn't see it but did read about it and was informed of its outstanding class by witnesses. Having experienced at first-hand Tallon's ability (both with the bat and behind the stumps) early in the season, Bradman was prepared to consider fast-tracking him into the Test team. Indeed, in the next season 1936–37, the way was opened up for him by Bradman and the other Test selectors when Tallon was chosen to play in a trial game between a Bradman XI against Victor Richardson's team that experienced a brilliant tour of South Africa. Bradman thought so highly of Tallon's batting that he placed him not at six or seven, but at five in his team's order. Unfortunately, Tallon was dismissed for 3, when only Bradman (212), Leo O'Brien (85) and Alan McGilvray (42) made runs.

After the war, when he made the Test team, Tallon's chances were limited by the great batting in front of him. Morris, Barnes, Brown, Bradman, Harvey, Hassett, Miller and Lindwall would variously, and in different combinations, build huge scores that would limit the chances for the rest of the side led by Tallon. Yet there were flashes of his 1930s brilliance. In Melbourne, in the Third Test of the 1946–47 Ashes, he managed 35 and a brilliant 92. There were other sporadic reminders of Tallon's batting skills.

Bradman would have chosen Tallon as a keeper even if he had been a bunny with the bat. His selection at number seven summed Bradman's attitude to Tallon's batting skills, which he considered even ahead of the bowling all-rounder, Ray Lindwall, who stood at number eight. He and Lillee (at number nine), were chosen ahead of a long list of fine speedsters including Jeff Thomson, Ted McDonald, Alan Davidson, Glenn McGrath and Fred Spofforth. Lindwall, all things being equal with the other candidates, was always going to be chosen because of his ability with the bat. He hit two terrific Test hundreds and impressed Bradman with his technical skills. Lindwall had started his career as a batsman, and was disabused of carrying on with it as his prime focus by Bill O'Reilly at St George, his New South Wales club. O'Reilly ordered him to open the innings and bowl as fast as he could. Raymond Russell Lindwall – of the poetic, smooth run-up and action – never looked back. His batting technique always suggested he could have done more. But his importance in maintaining Australia's world dominance in Test cricket 1946–52 was as a great opening bowler of enormous skill.

Bradman regarded Ted McDonald as the best Australian fast bowler he had seen until Lindwall came along. 'McDonald was tall and had a perfect rhythm,' Bradman recalled, 'rather like Larwood after him, and Lindwall much later. McDonald had real stamina and pace. Yet he didn't rely entirely on speed. He could swing the ball, cut back to medium pace and even deliver spin. I first saw him in 1921 [in the Fifth Test of the 1920–21 Ashes] and later batted against him in 1930 when he was playing for Lancashire. He was still very quick when he wished to be. He knocked my middle stump out of the ground.'

Bradman made 9 in the first innings of that Lancashire match of mid-May 1930. In a devastating spell, McDonald, then 39 years old, removed Archie Jackson (lbw 19), Bradman and Vic Richardson (caught, 0) in the space of a few deliveries. Australian captain Bill Woodfull, who normally opened, sent Bradman and Jackson in to open in the second innings. They weathered the McDonald onslaught this time, Jackson making 40 and Bradman 48 not out.

After the 1948 tour, Bradman ranked Lindwall as almost being in McDonald's class, but thought McDonald, who was much taller, had a better bouncer because he didn't have to dig it in so short to get lift. However, as Lindwall's career progressed through the 1950s, Bradman acknowledged his ability with the short ball was as good as anyone he had seen.

Bradman admired Lindwall's courage, and was aware of his capacity, learned from his rugby league days – which culminated with a first-grade season in 1940 with St George – to carry injuries.

'Lindwall had wonderful stamina. He could swing the ball either way, and had a nice, deceptive change of pace. Ray also had great control over line and length.'

By the end of Lindwall's career, Bradman ranked him with McDonald as the best Australian fastman he had seen. Bradman had the advantage of having faced them both. Another factor in his choice of Lindwall was his combination with Miller. They formed one of the best fast-bowling partnerships of all time. Such bowling partnerships have always coincided with Australian Test superiority. Ted

McDonald and Jack Gregory before them were a fearsome coupling in the early 1920s under Warwick Armstrong. Dennis Lillee and Jeff Thomson in the sides led by Ian and Greg Chappell in the 1970s were awesome. From 1999 into the twenty-first century the various combinations of Glenn McGrath, Jason Gillespie and Brett Lee were formidable in Steve Waugh's teams.

Bradman's Australian best-ever Ashes team allowed the use of Lindwall and Miller, or Lindwall and Lillee to open the bowling.

Dennis Lillee emerged a decade after Lindwall. Well before the end of Lillee's career, Bradman rated him with McDonald and Lindwall. Position nine went to Lillee.

'Taking his entire career into account,' Bradman said, 'he was the best paceman I ever saw. He showed enormous courage in returning from his serious back injury. Lillee was a dangerous bowler, who could both intimidate and out-think batsmen. He swung the ball both ways and had a magnificent leg-cutter.'

Lillee was one of Bradman's last selectorial decisions in Ashes cricket. The raw and lanky young Western Australian tearaway didn't let him down. Lillee took five for 84 in an innings in his first Test in 1970–71, and a year later turned on a performance in Perth that ranked him in Bradman's mind, after just two seasons in Test cricket, as one of the greats in history. In a Test against the World XI, he took six wickets for no runs in 13 deliveries, and ended with twelve for 92 for the match.

When Lillee made a comeback after breaking his back in 1974, he was less the demon and more the determined intimidator, who out-thought batsmen with his guile, accuracy and brilliance. He continued on as the world's leading speedman for another decade.

Positions ten and eleven went to the leg-spin twins, Bill O'Reilly and Clarrie Grimmett.

Once more, as in Bradman's selection of what he considered to be the ideal world cricket team, Bradman preferred the spin combination of O'Reilly and Grimmett to Shane Warne, the best leg-spinner of the last half of the twentieth century.

Many observers implied that Warne was omitted from Bradman's world team because of off-field controversial, headline-making actions. This controversy stretched back to the reasons Warne left the Australian Institute of Sport cricket academy in Adelaide in 1990. His worst year was 1994 when he verbally abused South African batsman Andrew Hudson, and later in Sri Lanka took money from an Indian bookie. Also, in 2000, an encounter in an English nightclub with a nurse and subsequent phone calls Warne made to her led to allegations of sexual harassment being made by her against him in London's *Daily Mirror*.

None of this sat well with the creed to which Bradman adhered throughout his life. He wrote it down for Sam Loxton, one of his 1948 Invincibles:

When considering the stature of an athlete or, for that matter, any other person, I set great store in certain qualities which I believe are essential in addition to skill.

They are that a person conducts his or her life with dignity, with integrity and, most of all, with modesty. These are totally compatible with pride, ambition and competitiveness.

I love to see people with personality and character, but I

resent utterly the philosophy of those misguided people who think arrogance is a necessary virtue. It is only endured by the public, not enjoyed.

Yet despite these standards, which may well be construed by some as ruling out Shane Warne from any Bradman team, I don't believe this was the reason for Warne's omission. We spoke often about Warne and the comparisons in performance to O'Reilly and Grimmett. At the time Bradman provided me with the details of his ideal world and Australian teams, in October and November 1998, the details of Warne's 1994 dealings with the Indian bookie – 'John' – had not emerged in the public arena. Yet Bradman knew of them. He had a private intelligence network that would put ASIS and MI6 in the shade. Warne's self-confessed 'stupid and naïve' taking of money from 'John' for match-day intelligence finally made the news in December 1998. A month later, on 8 and 9 January 1999, I attended the Pakistan Judicial Commission hearing into bribery and match-fixing. It was held in Melbourne. Bradman was particularly interested in a first-hand account of the hearings. I had long phone chats with him recounting and discussing the performances of Warne, Mark Waugh and Tim May under aggressive interrogation from Pakistani barristers (reported in detail in the book *Bold Warnie*).

At no point did Bradman stand in judgment on Warne about this episode or any other non-cricket incidents. Bradman only had one encounter with Warne – on Bradman's ninetieth birthday. He didn't find Warne arrogant and he liked his 'character'. While Bradman was a man of high principles – as expressed in his creed – and solid family values, he was also very much a man of the world. Not once in six years did I hear him moralise about the private lives of others. He did not approve of some off-field activity but did not let it affect his attitudes, unless that off-field activity impacted on a cricketer's performances for his country or State.

Rather than negative excuses for leaving Warne out, Bradman had positive reasons for selecting O'Reilly and Grimmett as a spin combination. He thought them the best spin team in cricket history. He regarded O'Reilly as the best bowler he had ever seen or faced. O'Reilly delivered fast leg-breaks with bounce and bite.

In four Ashes series from 1932–33 to 1938 O'Reilly sent down 1228 overs with 439 maidens and took 102 wickets at 25.36. Bradman also pointed to O'Reilly's outstanding first-class record (see table below) and club performances. In the 45 years from 1895 to 1939–40, only seven players in Sydney first-grade district cricket had a bowling average of less than 10 runs per wicket, when taking 30 or more wickets in a season. O'Reilly did it seven times. No other player did it more than once.

'This reflected his outstanding ability as much as his Test and first-class record,' Bradman said to me. 'It must be set against the fact that in his era [1927–40] batting averages improved by sizeable margins.'

O'Reilly was complemented by Grimmett, who preferred to bowl into the wind with his variety of leg-breaks, wrong'uns, top-spinners and flippers.

Bradman ranked Shane Warne up with O'Reilly and Grimmett but thought the latter two players were both marginally more effective performers at Test, first-class and club level – a view supported by the statistics.

The table below compares the Test and first-class figures of the three cricketers:

	Tests	wickets	ave	wkts/ Test	1st class wkts		ave	wkts ave/ match
O'Reilly	27	144	22.59	5.33	136	774	16.60	5.69
Grimmett	37	216	24.21	5.84	248	1424	22.28	5.74
Warne	101	450	26.52	4.45	192	803	26.58	4.18

Twelfth man went to leg-spinning all-rounder, Richie Benaud. Bradman preferred an all-rounder as his first reserve. He narrowed the choice down to Richie Benaud and Alan Davidson. Both players could hardly be separated on the figures or performances over coincident careers. Bradman always looked for a 'breaking point' – an attribute such as a specialist fielding skill that gave one player the advantage over the other. In this case it was Benaud's leadership abilities. Bradman regarded him as the best post-war captain he had seen.

Yet Benaud was a champion all-rounder in his own right. He rated highly in the line of outstanding Australian leg-break bowlers. They began with H.V. Hordern and Arthur Mailey and continued through Clarrie Grimmett and Bill O'Reilly, who all played before the Second World War. Banaud played in the 1950s and early 1960s, and was followed in the 1990s by Shane Warne and Stuart MacGill. Benaud was often a match-winner with the ball, most notably in England in 1961, but his aggressive batting also had its moments. In 1957–58 in South Africa he was instrumental in winning a series with two dashing centuries.

'No Greg Chappell, Shane Warne or Victor Trumper?'

That was my first surprised reaction to Sir Donald Bradman's all-time best Australian cricket team chosen from the years 1877 to 2000. In Chappell's place at number five in the batting order is the lesser known Charlie Macartney, whose career spanned from 1909 to 1926. Few selectors of the ideal, all-time Ashes team would leave out Chappell, let alone choose Macartney. Also, few selectors would omit Shane Warne and opt instead for the combination of O'Reilly and Grimmett. But Bradman had his reasons for choosing to do this. Bill Ponsford was chosen instead of Trumper, a decision that will probably receive evenly divided support and disagreement.

I asked Bradman why Greg Chappell had not been selected.

'Several batsmen of more or less equal merit could have been chosen,' Bradman replied. 'Greg Chappell, Stan McCabe, either of the Waugh twins, Allan Border and others would have filled the position admirably. But Macartney was not only a great batsman, he was also a very good slow left-arm bowler. He added strength to the bowling.'

Bradman's significant advantages over any other selector in terms of accomplishment and experience are indisputable. He was the greatest batsman, if not cricketer, of all time. He was a shrewd, knowledgeable captain with incisive tactical and strategic skills. He understood the technical aspects of the game as well as anyone, which he demonstrated in what many people regard as the finest manual on the sport ever written – *The Art of Cricket*.

Bradman had seen both Macartney and Greg Chappell at their best, which few other critics could claim. His memory was strong, even in old age, right up until his death in February 2001. He did not live in the past. He admired Greg from his early days as a schoolboy cricketer, and did much to assist his rise to pre-eminence in Australian cricket in the mid-1970s. Bradman even advised him when he was 19 and a State player to change his batting grip so that he could play off-side shots. Bradman was also instrumental as a selector and Australian Cricket Board member in handing Greg the Test captaincy once his brother, Ian Chappell, resigned from the job. Bradman ranked Greg as one of the finest stylists Australia has produced, in the line of Victor Trumper, Charlie Macartney and Mark Waugh. Yet Bradman only found a place for one of them, Macartney, in his list of his preferred all-time Ashes team, at number five.

Bradman took the exercise of selection seriously. He would not slot in a player just because that player happened to be glamorous or popular. Nor would he leave out a cricketer who was forgotten by most fans because he played nearly a century ago. Bradman selected the best combination of players, applying the same principles and approach he used over four decades as a State and national selector. Players were chosen according to their skills and how they fitted the team balance.

Bradman's vision was unique. No one else could look down the tunnel of the twentieth century and expertly choose the right combination of players to form the best all-time Ashes team. But for a few champions such as Trumper, Monty Noble and Clem Hill, Bradman had personally witnessed the performances of the best-ever Australian players over the entire twentieth century.

Bradman said there was to be 'no argument' with him over his selections. Yet while debate with Bradman over selection was impossible because of his level of expertise as a selector, you could attempt to understand his reasons and logic. We discussed and analysed his reasoning for his selection at length.

Some observers will suggest that Bradman left out Greg Chappell for other reasons, such as his stand for Kerry Packer's World Series Cricket. Bradman did express his distaste for Chappell's signing with World Series Cricket in

1977 when Chappell was already contracted to the Australian Cricket Board. Bradman had always been a stickler for maintaining a contract and therefore honouring your word. Yet Bradman also acknowledged to me much later – in 1995 – that the 1970s were a time of change and upheaval in the cricketing sphere. Cricketers of the 1970s era were caught in a time warp. They were year-round sportsmen who were paid poorly for their work – certainly not enough to maintain a family. No Australian players were professional cricketers (in Australia) in the 1920s, 1930s, 1940s, 1950s and 1960s – the whole time Bradman was a player and administrator. Then during the 1970s era of the Chappell brothers, the demands of cricket grew and players had to travel much more frequently. Players such as Bob Cowper (who was an investment broker) and Paul Sheahan (who was a schoolteacher) who, by necessity, had to have careers outside of sport to make a livelihood, limited their stays in Test cricket and retired five to 10 years earlier than they would have if they had contracted as professional sportspeople in the manner players have been since the 1990s. Most of the other players of the late 1960s and 1970s did not have professional work to fall back on. In the end, Greg Chappell took the only option remaining if he wished to continue playing for Australia and support a family. He joined Packer's breakaway cricket competition. Bradman better appreciated Chappell's actions as top cricket became fully professional by the 1990s. Bradman had himself always been conscious of developing a career away from cricket.

It is true that Bradman was also unhappy about Chappell's instruction to his brother Trevor to bowl under-arm on the last ball of a one-day game against New Zealand in 1981. The action prevented New Zealand from the unlikely chance of tying with a six off the last ball. There was a howl of protest from Australian and New Zealand critics, including Kiwi Prime Minister Robert Muldoon, with which Bradman agreed. Greg's bowling instructions were seen as being against the spirit of the game. Yet Bradman did not hold a grudge against Chappell for it. He viewed it as an unfortunate lapse, a silly momentary mistake by Chappell.

Another indiscretion by Chappell annoyed Bradman more. When Greg signed with Packer and resigned from the Australian captaincy after the tour of England in 1977, he was voted off the Queensland selection panel and not selected for the State team. The Queensland administration paid out his contract and he was made unwelcome in official State cricket circles.

In an interview Chappell gave that appeared in the Sydney *Daily Telegraph* and the Adelaide *Advertiser* on 2 November 1977, he attacked the Queensland administration. He repeated critical comments that Bradman had made in private to him about the Queensland administration when Chappell had been considering changing teams from South Australia to Queensland in 1973. Bradman was incensed and sent a blistering letter to Chappell in which he accused him of a breach of trust and of distorting the context of their private discussions. Bradman concluded by reminding Chappell of the old Chinese proverb: 'He who throws mud, loses ground'.

Chappell apologised in writing. Bradman, still riled, accepted the apology because Chappell had been man enough to make it.

These incidents happened almost 25 years before Bradman died. Bradman and Chappell, as correspondence between them in the 1980s and 1990s verifies, had long since patched up their differences that occurred in their 40-year connection. Early in 2000 I asked Bradman if those old rifts had caused him to omit Chappell from his best-ever Australian Ashes side. He was adamant that they had not.

'Greg's all right,' he said in a conciliatory tone, 'he's all right.'

I sincerely believe, from Bradman's reaction, that his choice of Macartney over Chappell was based purely on cricketing grounds.

Bradman chose a strong, well-balanced Australian side with six talented batsmen, arguably the best wicket-keeper of all time, and a bowling line-up with plenty of options. The three pacemen – Lillee, Lindwall and Miller – are nicely complemented by a trio of spinners. Grimmett and O'Reilly provide two different kinds of leg-spinner, while Macartney delivers variety with orthodox left-arm finger spin.

The following 12 chapters are profiles of Bradman's choices for the best Australia team in Ashes cricket. This team would always be hard to beat, especially with Bradman in the line-up.

CHAPTER 1

THE FIRST
MEGA-SCORER

BILL
PONSFORD

(Australia)

19 October 1900–6 April 1991

*'Bill Ponsford burst into cricket and
instantly began to tear the record book to
shreds by making abnormal scores with
great rapidity and consistency.
He carried all before him.'*

DON BRADMAN

Bill Ponsford, Australia's big-scoring opening bat, walked out with partner Bill Brown under the gasometer at The Oval at Kennington, London. It was the finale of the 1934 Ashes series – the decider with the series square at 1–1 – and Ponsford's last Test. He was 33, and had been playing for his country with distinction for a decade. Ponsford, his cap tilted at an angle, was in the mood for a big finish and he was in the best form of his career, having scored 181 a month earlier in the drawn Fourth Test at Leeds. Everything was in his favour. Captain Bill Woodfull had won the toss, giving Australia the advantage in a timeless Test. It was Saturday 18 August. In theory the game could go on until Christmas. Ponsford was just the character to concentrate hard on the job at hand from the start of the innings for a day or two. He had proved to be one of the two biggest-scoring Australian batsmen ever, the other being Bradman. England's attack was strong. It had pace, swing and variety in its pace line-up with left-arm quick Nobby Clark, Gubby Allen and Bill Bowes. Its fourth bowler, left-arm spinner Hedley Verity, was the best of his kind in cricket. Ponsford began watchfully, his crouching style – developed in Melbourne, a city that produced more wet wickets than any other Australian city in the 1920s – seemed more pronounced. Yet he was in a positive frame of mind on the true, midsummer Oval pitch as he played forward, showing the full face of his beloved bat 'big Bertha', at that time one of the heaviest bats seen in big cricket. With the score at 21, Brown (10) was bowled.

Bradman, who had had a 388 record partnership with Ponsford in the Leeds Test, joined him. The new man at the wicket was in touch too. Bradman had scored 304 at Leeds and was hungry for more after what had been a lean series for him. Clark and Bowes tested both men with bouncers to a leg-side field that hinted at Bodyline, which both had enjoyed bowling in the past. The batsmen weathered this style of attack. Ponsford began placing the ball with his usual perfection while seeking out the odd bludgeoning cut. Bradman was content with pushes, glances, late-cuts and the occasional drive. Both men were lifted by the assurance of the other. As usual, Bradman's presence saw the scoring rate increase.

Ponsford liked batting with Bradman. Bradman was always the centre of the attention for the crowd and the opposition as he went about his precision field bisections, which were meant to disrupt the opposition. Bradman also upset the bowlers' line by his tactical aggression. All this benefited Ponsford, whose confidence grew with the 'little fella' at the wicket. Ponsford could see the concern that Bradman created in the opposition. Bradman too enjoyed batting with Ponsford. Ponsford was a dependable stayer, a good runner between the wickets and someone who would go the distance with him. It was vital on this occasion. They were Australia's biggest run plunderers. If it were to post a sizeable total each batsman had to score big hundreds.

Ponsford reached 50 out of 89 in 82 minutes. The team's 100 came up in 98 minutes. At lunch the score was one for 123: Ponsford on 66 not out, Bradman 43 not out.

After the break, during which Woodfull told them that nothing short of a score 'approaching 1000' would suffice, England skipper Bob Wyatt had Verity in the attack. Both batsmen were circumspect with him, picking the right ball off which to score, for there was nothing loose from the English bowler. A half-hour into the second session, Ponsford was making steady progress, while Bradman had stepped up a notch in his desire to take command. Ponsford's role, as outlined by Woodfull, was to stay at the wicket with Bradman as long as he could. The opener had the right temperament for this assignment. The genial Ponsford rarely lived at the wicket beyond his means. He was a powerful hitter and had torn apart strong attacks before. His country needed him to be there, no matter what happened at the other end. His scoring rate was good and he was nearly keeping pace with his partner. Ponsford's century came up after 177 minutes at 3.17 p.m. It was a great moment for the veteran. He had wanted to make his mark in his final Test. He had now done so. But he didn't want it to end there. He took block and settled in for his next century. Bradman reached his hundred 20 minutes after Ponsford and went into overdrive as their partnership overwhelmed the bowling. They moved from 200 to 250 in just 39 minutes. Ponsford lost concentration for the first time at 115 and was dropped twice off Verity and Allen. But he settled down again to be 137 not out at tea, with Bradman now past him and on 150 not out. Ponsford had moved steadily, scoring 71 in the second session. Bradman in that period added 107.

At tea, the score was one for 307.

The 300 partnership came up soon after tea, then Ponsford reached 150. The Oval crowd, now resigned to the fact that the Test was slipping away from England before their very eyes on Day One of a timeless contest, was politely clapping milestones. Bradman raced through 200, while Ponsford kept his own pace. Between them they were destroying England.

Ponsford shuffled crab-like down to Verity. He moved his solid frame quickly and his feet were always in the right position. He was one of the best-ever players of spin, a great asset for an opener whose usual sporting employment was based on facing a barrage of speed. Verity was aiming at Clark's footmarks outside the right-hand batsman's off-stump. Ponsford's answer was to stretch his left leg down over the footmarks. He matched the great Yorkshire bowler's patience and won the battle of wits.

Ponsford's tackling of the pacemen needed more courage than patience. Bowes and Clark, on occasions, employed a diluted variation of Bodyline, with two men close on the leg-side waiting for the fended catch, and two in the deep hovering for the hook of frustration or bravado. Ponsford met this by either forceful strokes or by turning his body to take the blow on the thigh, backside or back. He had been bruised by Bodyline in 1932–33, but would not wilt, then or now, especially when the Ashes were at stake. The knocks didn't seem to bother him and he toughed them out for his country. This was the most important game of his career and it just happened to be his last. He wanted to go out earning glory for his team and himself. Ponsford was doing his job with exceptional distinction.

While Bradman murdered the bowling after reaching his double century, Ponsford, his cap now at a more rakish tilt, stepped up his driving, his delightful cutting and his plundering of on-side scoring opportunities.

As Australia raced to 400 after 305 minutes, Bob Wyatt, with his medium-pace swing (that would take 901 first-class wickets at 32.84), had himself and Maurice Leyland with his Chinaman (466 first-class wickets at 29.31) on alternating at one end. Bradman and Ponsford refused to take the bait by trying to loft them. Bradman directed all shots earthbound except for one hook for six off Clark.

At 6.16 p.m. Ponsford reached 200, after five hours 36 minutes. The score was now one for 466. He doffed his cap in a humble response to solid applause. Yet there was no sense that he was about to throw his wicket away. He was loving the moment as Australia sailed to a total that would mean it could push on towards Woodfull's suggestion of 'approaching 1000'.

Seven minutes later, with the score at 472, there was a surprise. Bradman tried to hook a Bowes bumper and top-edged it to keeper Les Ames. He was on his way for 244 in 316 minutes. He hit 32 fours and one six. His last 44 took 33 minutes.

Ponsford and Bradman put on 451 in 316 minutes, a world record for any wicket in a Test. (It would not be equalled for nearly half a century. In 1983, Pakistan's Mudassar Nazar, 231, and Javed Miandad, 280 not out, put on 451 in 533 minutes at Hyderabad against India.)

Stan McCabe replaced Bradman and a few minutes later stumps were drawn. Australia was two for 475, with Ponsford on 205 not out.

There was a rest day on Sunday 19 August and Ponsford resumed with McCabe on Monday morning feeling fresh and with thoughts of 250, even 300. Allen bowled McCabe (10) at 488 and this brought Woodfull – also in his last Test – to the wicket. In the interests of the best batting line-up, Woodfull had dropped himself down to number five since the Third Test at Manchester to make way for the in-form Bill Brown at the top of the order.

With the score at nearly 500, Australia now had its best opening pair together at the wicket. If England's players were demoralised looking at the scoreboard, they would be shattered seeing this couple engaged at the wicket. It was as if Australia was starting its innings again. Ponsford, refreshed after the Sunday break, looked in the best touch of his career as he drove, cut and nudged his way forward, while Woodfull put his head down, in what seemed to be, in the circumstances, a touch grimly.

Ponsford reached 266 and was out 'hit wicket' for the second successive innings. The last time it had happened, on 181 at Leeds, Verity had been the bowler. This time it was Allen. Ponsford's score was then the fourth-highest ever by an Australian in a Test. Only Bradman with two triple centuries and 299 against South Africa in the 1931–32 series had beaten Ponsford's score. Ponsford's innings had lasted 460 minutes and had included a five and 27 fours. He walked off The Oval to a standing ovation from an appreciative English crowd with hardly a lift of acknowledgment from Big Bertha. Ponsford's humility would not allow him to concede to any chest beating. He and Woodfull had put on 86 for the fourth wicket. The score was four for 574. If ever an opener had done his job, it was Ponsford.

Woodfull (49) let the innings continue until its natural close at 701. England fought hard to reach 321 (Leyland 110). Woodfull, mindful that the Test had no limit, batted again. Australia, this time, made 327. This result set England 708 to win. It was destroyed by Clarrie Grimmett (five for 64) for 145. Australia won by 562.

Bill Ponsford, with his two big innings for the series, had the best 1934 Test average at 94.83 from an aggregate of 569 (just pipping Bradman, 758 at 94.75). Ponsford was a key contributor to Australia taking back the Ashes 2–1 after the Bodyline debacle of 1932–33.

First of the Run Plunderers

William Harold Ponsford always had notable powers of concentration, even as a schoolboy at Alfred Crescent State School in Melbourne's inner-city suburb of North Fitzroy. Whether in the classroom studying Maths and English, or in the yard playing cricket or baseball, the quiet, solidly built kid could focus well on his tasks. He captained the school cricket XI for two seasons. His skills didn't manifest as anything freakish, but his batting, based on a solid defence and the capacity to drive and cut hard, was outstanding. He was a Fitzroy schoolboy medallion winner in 1913–14, and 1914–15, which allowed him to practise with leading club players. His hitting and catching ability was also noticed in baseball. At 13, in the winter of 1914, he made the Victoria State Schools cricket team that played the New South Wales State team in Sydney. Ponsford left school at the end of 1914 and studied at Hassett's Business College for a year. Then, at the age of 16 he became a clerk with the State Savings Bank. His father, William Senior, a post office employee, was moved to Elsternwick in 1915. Because of zoning regulations in district cricket, young Bill was forced to play cricket for St Kilda from 1916–17 rather than for his previous club. At 18, during the 1918–19 season, he was selected to play for Victoria against Tasmania. But an influenza epidemic in Victoria caused the game to be cancelled. In 1920–21 Ponsford was reselected for the State team, this time playing against the visiting English tourists led by tough all-rounder Johnny Douglas. Ponsford, just 20 years of age, made only 6 and 19. Victoria was beaten by seven wickets. This was not enough to keep his place in a strong Victorian team led by Warwick Armstrong, and it took Ponsford a year to be selected again – for the 1921–22 season. In his one appearance, he scored

162 against Tasmania at Launceston. It was his first first-class century, made in just his second game. Selectors took note of Ponsford's capacity to go on for a big score, an unusual ability because in those days district cricket was limited to Saturdays and didn't generally allow batsmen to think about setting their minds for huge scores that were possible in four-day first-class matches.

Ponsford kept fit in the winter playing baseball. He stood 178 cm (5 ft 10 in) and weighed 82 kilograms. His strong frame allowed him to pack a serious wallop with a cricket or baseball bat. Ponsford was an excellent outfielder and was adept at hitting home runs in baseball, a sport he enjoyed because it allowed greater individual participation than cricket. Baseball also appealed to Ponsford because it was a game that was all over in an afternoon. But by 1922–23 he was getting more opportunities to play cricket. Ponsford had at last found a place in the powerful State side. It was now first-class cricket, not baseball that challenged him.

Early in February 1923, he made the sporting world stand up and take notice of his capabilities when he came to the wicket against Tasmania at Melbourne, with Victoria's score at three for 201. He didn't leave until it was 1001, after scoring 429 (42 fours) in 477 minutes. It was the highest first-class score ever made to that point and super-seded the 424 by Archie MacLaren for Lancashire against Somerset at Taunton in 1895. Ponsford's amazing score upset MacLaren and English commentators, who wanted to downplay the standard of the Victorian game against Tasmania, and Australian first-class cricket in general. The English commentators poured scorn on Victoria's score of 1059, also a new record. But the records stood. Later in February 1923, Ponsford followed up his record per-formance with a 108 (in 162 minutes) and 17 in his debut in Shield cricket (Tasmania was not a Shield team then) against South Australia. He shared a 133 fourth-wicket partnership with Bill Woodfull, the first such partnership of one of cricket's great batting combinations. Then, in March, Ponsford managed 62 against a touring MCC side. These last three knocks showed he could score runs against bowlers of class. But the English preferred to remain unconvinced. They reckoned his 429 against Tasmania was either a one-off or not repeatable against quality bowling.

They were not so sure that their propaganda about Ponsford's performance was correct in 1923–24 when Ponsford opened the season in December 1923 against Queensland at the MCG with 248. He figured in an Australian record opening stand of 456 in just 350 minutes with R.E. Mayne (209). Few now could doubt Ponsford's intent and capacity for the super-score. During the season, he went on to score 45, 24, 81, 159, 110, 110 not out and a duck. His two scores of 110 came in the January 1924 game versus New South Wales, the only time Ponsford would score a century in both innings of a first-class match. His aggregate for the season was 777 at an average of 111.00. These figures stamped Ponsford at 23 as the first of the mega-scorers in Australian cricket.

He took time out at the end of the season in March 1924 to marry Vera Neill. (They later had two sons, Bill in 1928 and Geoff in 1932.)

Into the Big-Time

England toured Australia in 1924–25 under Arthur Gilligan and Ponsford knew that if he kept up his big scoring he would have a strong chance of breaking into the Australian team. He began for Victoria against South Australia with 10 (at number 6) and 77 as an opener (the talented leg-spinner Clarrie Grimmett got him in both innings). A week later he had one chance against the MCC at the MCG, but another fine leg-spinner, Tich Freeman, had him stumped for just 6. Ponsford lifted his performance in the return match against South Australia and this time posted 166 before Grimmett bowled him. It qualified him for an Australian XI against the MCC at Brisbane in December in the lead-up to the First Test. Ponsford came through it well with 81. It was enough to get him selected for his first Test at Brisbane beginning 19 December 1924.

Ponsford came to the wicket for the first time in a Test at one for 46 after Tich Freeman had removed opener Warren Bardsley. Maurice Tate had Ponsford in trouble early with his medium-fast swingers, but Australian skipper Herbie Collins farmed the strike until Ponsford settled in. They built a fine partnership. After the torrid start, Ponsford put aside his nerves and began to play the strokes – the drive, the cuts and the on-side pushes – that had already brought him international attention en route to his massive scores. He reached his century in 210 minutes. At 110 he tried to push Gilligan on the off-side and was bowled. Ponsford was only the third Australian after Charles Bannerman and Harry Graham to make a hundred on debut in a first innings. It was a dream start for a worthy young sportsman.

Collins went on to 114 in Australia's first innings of 450. England replied with 298. Ponsford batting at number five made 27 in Australia's second innings of 452 (Johnny Taylor 108, Arthur Richardson 98). England, with a second successive century-stand from its new openers Jack Hobbs and Herbert Sutcliffe, fought gamely in scoring 411, but lost by 193 runs.

There was just a few days break before the Second Test at

the MCG, Ponsford's home ground, and he was in good
touch again when he came to the wicket in front of a big
crowd on New Year's Day 1925. The score was two for 47
with both Collins and A.J. Richardson dismissed, then
three for 47 when Bardsley was removed and Johnny Taylor
joined him. Ponsford looked as if he were born for Test
cricket as he moved easily to 50 in 89 minutes, and his
second century in successive Tests in 174 minutes. He was
the first player ever to score hundreds in his first two Tests.
England's sceptics now had to acknowledge that Ponsford
was something special. Perhaps his 429 against Tasmania in
early 1923 was not such a fluke after all. Here, he was 128
not out at stumps but was bowled by Tate next morning
without adding to his overnight score. Australia reached
600 (Vic Richardson 138 run out) and England's opening
pair Hobbs (154) and Sutcliffe (176) looked like overtaking
Australia on their own as they piled up an opening stand of
283. But the tourists were reduced to all out 479, and
Australia went on to win by 81 runs.

Ponsford had established himself at the highest level. He
went on to record scores of 4, 31, 43, 21, 19, 80 and 5 (run
out) to give him a healthy first, series aggregate of 468 at a
46.80 average in Australia's convincing 4–1 Ashes victory.

Ponsford followed this fine season with a mixed domestic
performance in 1925–26. He began with a big hundred
against Western Australia, which meant he had introduced
himself to four States, Tasmania, South Australia, Western
Australia and Queensland, with a century. Only New South
Wales stopped him, but Ponsford saved his best for later for
Victoria's biggest rival of the era. After failing in a Test trial
in December, he thrashed 138 in 195 minutes against New
South Wales in late January, which sealed his trip to
England in 1926. But this tour was marred for him by ill-
ness. He had tonsillitis and flu, illnesses which forced him

out of the first two drawn Tests after he seemed ready for a big Ashes having scored a magnificent 110 not out against the MCC on a wet wicket at Lord's in failing light. He was not selected for the Third Test but solid scores ensured he was selected for the Fourth Test at Old Trafford. He made 23, while Charlie Macartney scored his third successive century in another drawn game that was thwarted by rain. Two scores over 140 against Glamorgan and Warwickshire proved Ponsford's return to top form by early August.

At The Oval in the final Test, Larwood proved to be Ponsford's downfall, but not as a bowler. Larwood's quick return to the keeper in Australia's first innings saw Ponsford run out for 2. He was promoted from number four to opener in the second innings. Larwood took a good catch low to his right at second slip off Wilfred Rhodes and Ponsford was on his way for just 12. Australia lost the match and the Ashes 0–1.

Despite his setbacks, Ponsford still managed a good season in England scoring 901 in 26 innings at 40.95, but he knew he had played below his potential.

Hundreds & Thousands

Ponsford returned to Australia via North America and saw the 1926 World Series baseball final in New York between the New York Yankees and St Louis Cardinals. The manager of the New York Giants, John 'Mugsy' McGraw, wanted Ponsford to try out with the view to him being offered a contract. Ponsford declined the offer. He had more to prove in cricket. This began with a magnificent 1926–27 season at home when he broke through the 1000-run barrier for the first time, reaching 1229 at 122.90. Ponsford displayed the full range of his power, concentration and run-making ability with scores of 214, 54, 151, 352, 108, 84, 12, 116, 131 and 7. His opening knock of 214 against South Australia came in just 270 minutes. The rest of the Victorian team mustered only 101 runs.

His season highlight came in the 'Christmas' match of 1926 (December 24–29) against New South Wales at the MCG. New South Wales batted first and made 221. Ponsford was now teamed up permanently at the top of the Victorian order with Bill Woodfull. They rested on Christmas Day and Boxing Day before starting the innings on 27 December. Their opening partnership reached 375, a record (not beaten until 1982–83 when Robbie Kerr and Kepler Wessels put on 388 for Queensland against Victoria).

Ponsford was 334 not out at stumps out of one for 573 in 322 minutes of batting. His innings was the highest first-class score made in a day in Australia. Only Charlie Macartney, with 345 against Nottinghamshire at Trent Bridge in 1921, had scored more.

Ponsford and Stork Hendry put on 219 in 117 minutes for the second wicket. Ponsford was out for 352 41 minutes into Day Three, 28 December, just 13 runs short of Clem Hill's Australian record of 365 in 1900–01. Victoria went on to 1107, a world-record first-class score (with Jack Ryder smashing 295 in 245 minutes).

Ponsford's innings of 363 minutes demonstrated he could score at pace in the right conditions if he had the mind to do so. Yet few could match his powers of concentration. He could keep his wicket intact for long periods of time and score at a good rate, better than anyone in the game until that season.

Despite his fame, Ponsford suffered from the usual problem facing top Australian sportspeople of not being able to make a good living while performing their sporting role in competition. A new chief executive at the State Savings Bank would not allow Ponsford to take leave to play first-class cricket. Ponsford moved to a new, five-year contracted job as a public relations officer at the Melbourne *Herald*. He was turning 27 and this alleviated his income worries.

The continuity of employment allowed Ponsford to concentrate on his batting and run his mega-scoring into the 1927–28 season. In his first first-class innings of the season at the MCG, he belted 437 in a marathon 621 minutes against Queensland. He became the only player in first-class history to make two scores of more than 400 (a record that was still standing into the twenty-first century). He hit 42 fours and gave two tough chances, one at 162 when he smashed back a rough return catch to the bowler, and another a stumping on 239. The biggest partnership of the innings in which Victoria made 793 was with Hendry (129) where they put on 314 in 221 minutes. Ponsford's huge knock ended after tea on Day Two, when he was caught-and-bowled by Gordon Amos. The innings made headlines and overshadowed 19-year-old Don Bradman's first-class debut for New South Wales against South Australia at Adelaide. Bradman made 118 and 33.

The gruelling Sheffield Shield schedule allowed both Victoria and New South Wales just two days break before they competed at the MCG on 23 December. Victoria batted first and Ponsford and Woodfull (99), already sounding like a reliable business firm, put on 227 for the first wicket in 177 minutes. Young Bradman, regarded as the best fielder in Australia in his youth, did a lot of boundary running that day. He was impressed by the Victorian openers.

'They were both Test players and I learned much about how they paced themselves and accumulated runs,' Bradman said. 'They never missed an opportunity to turn over the strike, or take a quick single. It unsettled our bowlers and the field. I actually enjoyed the experience of fielding to them.'

Bradman caught Ponsford in the deep when he was 202. Ponsford had now made 639 in two innings close together. Yet Ponsford's dismissal showed his strength. He was not tired when dismissed. In fact, he was annoyed he couldn't go on. He had scored 133 in the opening innings of the season against South Australia at Adelaide, which gave him 772 runs in three innings. He made 38 in the second innings of the New South Wales game, which gave him an aggregate of 810 in just four innings.

Ponsford's hunger didn't end there. In a haze of first-class cricket at the MCG, he padded up in a third match inside two weeks, this time in the return game against South Australia. He combined again with Woodfull (106) for an opening stand of 227 in 178 minutes. This time Ponsford showed himself to be both indefatigable and aggressive with a score of 336 (33 fours) in just 386 minutes at the crease. He was out with the score at 382. Victoria, in a blaze of massive scoring never equalled again in the twentieth century, accumulated 637. Ponsford had hit a staggering 1146 runs in a month (December 1927), a feat unlikely to be ever matched in Australia. He had now made four triple centuries in first-class cricket, a record (which would be bettered only by Bradman with six triples, and equalled by England's Wally Hammond). The mid-1920s had suddenly spawned an extraordinary run plunderer. From December 1926 until January 1928, Ponsford clocked up 2375 runs in 15 innings at an average of 158.33.

He ended 1927–28 with 1217 runs at 152.12 and capped it off with a tour of New Zealand in which he scored a further 452 first-class runs (top score 148 versus Otago at Dunedin) in nine innings at a more down-to-earth 56.50.

Ponsford's tally on tour, however, was 915, and he averaged 65.35 in all games.

Larwood's Lash

England toured Australia in 1928–29 and Ponsford looked set for another bumper year when in only his third match – in November 1928 – he clobbered 275 not out against South Australia. The tourists' fastest bowler, Harold Larwood, dismissed Ponsford for just 2 and 6 in the First Test at Brisbane, and Australia capitulated to his speed, and that of slow left-armer Jack White.

Nine days later, in the Second Test at Sydney, Larwood shattered a bone on Ponsford's left hand and so he retired hurt on 5. The injury put Ponsford out for the season. It was bad luck for him, and Australia. Larwood's bowling became wayward and offered little threat for the rest of the series after he had taken eight wickets in the First Test. He took another 10 wickets in the next four Tests at 66.20 runs each while George Geary and White were England's most effective bowlers. England won the series 4–1.

Ponsford came back in 1929–30 with a moderate – at least for him – 729 runs at 45.56. Once more, 'Ponny' managed to turn on a good performance when it counted. He made 131 in a trial game early in December, a game meant to be a guide to selection of the Australian team to tour England in 1930. It got Ponsford on board the boat for his second tour.

The second tour began with games against Tasmania. In one of the games, at Hobart in mid-March 1930, the sporting world received a foretaste of the heights that would be reached in a Ponsford–Bradman combination. The pair put on 296 for the second wicket in 150 minutes. Ponsford made 166 not out and Bradman 139. Something about their batting chemistry was like no other partnership before or since. It was a case of Bradman's dash and precision carving up the opposition meshed with Ponsford power cutting and driving. Ponsford was a perfect foil for the young Don. He didn't try to outscore him. Others did, and it was their undoing. Ponsford was happy to roll along at his own pace and share the strike. He knew instinctively when to stand aside and let the pocket dynamo take control. Ponsford and Bradman were all concentration as they set about destroying the Tasmanian bowlers. The Tasmanians may not have been the strongest lot to play first-class cricket. But the Ponsford–Bradman approach to them was the same as it would be in the big games of seasons to come. First, they would keep the score ticking over. Then Bradman, once settled, would lead the way by targeting the opposition's best bowler, who would be forced out of the attack. Then Ponsford would join in the destruction as the run accumulation rate increased.

The 1930 tour saw Ponsford consolidate his links with Woodfull at the top of the order. Ponsford was usually the faster scorer, and the two Victorians continued their understanding that had been honed in State matches. They were to figure in three important stands in the four Tests together. (Ponsford was hit by gastritis and missed the famous Third Test at Headingley where Bradman hit 334.) Ponsford's and Woodfull's Test partnerships were 4, 12, 162, 16, 106 and 159.

Ponsford was bowled by Tate for 3 and 39 (this being part of an important 81-run link with Bradman) in a losing First Test for Australia at Trent Bridge. At Lord's he cracked a strong 81. At Old Trafford for the Fourth

Test, he played superbly on a wet wicket to make 83.

In the final Test at The Oval, Ponsford delivered a fine innings. *Wisden* noted:

> He batted extremely well . . . the manner in which he dealt at the start of the innings with Larwood clearly disproved the idea that he could not face the Notts fast bowler. Scoring at the start chiefly on the leg-side, he afterwards cut and drove beautifully.

This final Test at The Oval in 1930 was an important occasion for Ponsford after he had been injured by Larwood in Australia in the 1928–29 series. The batsman had overcome his bogeyman. But Larwood endured a miserable series. Bradman hammered him out of the attack at Leeds in the Third Test when the erratic speedster returned one for 139 off 33 overs. In the final, series-deciding encounter at The Oval, Bradman again, along with Ponsford, disposed of him. (This was the Test in which Bradman, en route to a magnificent 232, was said by Larwood to 'flinch' when struck by a rearing delivery from a wet pitch.) Larwood had taken one for 132. The one wicket was that of Bradman caught behind, after he had scored 232. But no one except the umpire thought it was out. Larwood ended the series with four wickets at 73.00 runs apiece. In two successive Ashes series now he had been easily dealt with in all but one encounter. Larwood, the 'Nottingham Express', had been shunted aside. Bradman and Ponsford destroyed him in 1930.

Ponsford had a good 1930 tour, scoring 1425 runs at 49.13, with four centuries, six fifties and a top score of 220 not out in a day against Oxford University. He ended the trip with a fine 76 versus an England XI at Folkestone in early September. He had only been back in Australia off the boat from England for a few weeks when he was back into a full 1930–31 season at home, starting with a game between the national side and the next best combination – 'Australia versus the Rest' – at the MCG. This, in part, was to celebrate the return of the Ashes after the victory in England. It was also former Australian skipper Jack Ryder's testimonial. Ponsford didn't have his land legs and failed to achieve in this match, making 14 and 0. Ten days later though, he was firmly on his toes, belting the touring West Indian attack at the MCG with 187 in 286 minutes. Ponsford liked to make a statement in his initial encounters with teams, whether they be State or international sides. This, plus his knack of making runs when his future selection depended on it, indicated he was a player of temperament. Underneath his much-admired humility and pleasant demeanour was a most determined sportsman.

Ponsford's 1930 season was limited mainly to the Tests. In the First Test at Adelaide he hit 24 and 92 not out. Between this and the next Test he notched up 109 not out in the very wet Christmas encounter in the big match of the year playing for Victoria against New South Wales at the MCG. He carried his bat in this innings and passed 10,000 runs in first-class cricket. There was just enough time at the end of that game to catch the train to Sydney on 30 December, have a day off on New Year's Eve and turn up at the SCG for the Second Test on the first day of 1931.

Ponsford opened with Archie Jackson (8) and played, according to *Wisden*, 'in his most resolute and skilful style'. It produced 183 runs, three less than half the Australian total of 369. It included a 183 fifth-wicket stand with Woodfull (58). The rain around the country's east coast struck Sydney on Day Two and the West Indies suffered. Australia won easily by an innings and 172. Ponsford tumbled on to Brisbane for the Third Test and held his form, making 109 in a 229-link with Bradman (223), who came to the wicket at 1, after Jackson failed again.

It was back down to Melbourne for the Fourth Test in mid-February, where Ponsford opened with Woodfull and made 24 in a partnership of 50. Australia had another win, its third in succession by an innings plus plenty. Ponsford failed twice, scoring 7 and 28, in the final Test at Sydney (lost by Australia by 30 runs) yet topped the averages for the series at 77.83 from 467, ahead of Bradman, 447 at 74.50. Ponsford's Test figures reflected his complete 1930–31 season in which he scored 816 at 74.18. But, like all outstanding batsmen except for Bradman in the history of cricket, Ponsford had to have one 'shocker' of a season. His was the next, 1931–32. He had 15 innings and scraped together 399 at 30.69. He managed just one century, 134 against South Australia, early in the season at Adelaide. The Tests against South Africa were failures for Ponsford too. He managed 97 from six innings at 19.40 and he was unavailable for the Fifth Test due to influenza.

At the end of this poor period he ended his five-year association with the Melbourne *Herald* as a public relations officer and joined the Melbourne Cricket Club staff as an office manager. This meant that he would play with Melbourne after what had been 15 happy years with the St Kilda team.

Body on the Line

After a useful break in the winter of 1932, Ponsford looked forward to the 1932–33 season and his fourth Ashes contest, this time against the England team led by Douglas Jardine, the stiff-backed lawyer, who was very much an Empire and MCC man. He had designed 'Bodyline' – the method of fast bowling on or outside leg-stump that was meant to hit a batsman or force him into popping a catch to the pack of waiting fieldsmen. The main target of this bowling method was the prolific Bradman who had humiliated England and its bowlers in 1930. But all Australian batsmen, particularly Ponsford in his capacity as an opener, would be under attack.

Chief purveyor of this tactic – a tactic which was within the rules, but which flouted the spirit of the game was Larwood. He was supported by his left-arm paceman mate, Bill Voce, also of Nottingham, who delivered Bodyline from around the wicket. They had been employing a form of Bodyline – or fast leg theory – for their county since 1929. It had been used intermittently over four seasons, occasionally with devastating effect. Some countries had protested against its use. Yet it had never had a focus like this.

This time, Larwood was a completely different proposition from his battling performance in 1928–29 and his poor efforts in 1930. He had tightened up his bowling line during the 1931 and 1932 seasons in England and was pinpoint accurate. He always had pace – around 160 km/h (100 mph) at his peak. Now it was well directed. In his 1932 home season warm-up for the Australian tour he had taken 162 wickets for Nottingham at just 12.86.

Bodyline, if used judiciously, made it tough for those facing it. The pressure was always on the batsmen with Voce working in partnership with Larwood.

Unaware of the secret strategy about to be unleashed on him, Ponsford, at the 1932–33 season's start, found his form was back to that of 1930–31. He hit a commanding 98 run out for Victoria against Queensland, and a fine 200 at Sydney early in November against New South Wales. Unfortunately, he twisted his ankle in this Sydney game and it put him out of action for four weeks. Ponsford returned to the game for the First Test at Sydney in early December 1932 and ran into the full force of Bodyline. He battled stubbornly through the first day's first session but was bowled by Larwood for 32 soon after the break. Voce bowled him for 2 in the second innings. Larwood, with two bags of five wickets, destroyed Australia, which lost by 10 wickets. Bradman was ill with flu and missed the game but the rest of the Australian side was shell-shocked by Larwood's blitz. He had managed to bruise everyone in the top order, including Stan McCabe who had made a brilliant century in the first innings but failed in the second.

Selectors, in a seemingly thoughtless act, considered Ponsford was still in the form he had displayed against South Africa. He was left out again and made 12th man for the subsequent Second Test in Melbourne. It was a blow for Ponsford. He was replaced by the less accomplished Leo O'Brien. Bradman, though, was selected for the team again. He scored an undefeated century and Australia won the Second Test. The selectors now decided to bring Ponsford back for the Third Test at Adelaide.

Woodfull, who had overdone the struggle to find the right batting order, this time put Ponsford at five. It was the only batting move that worked. Ponsford performed well and with courage, often turning his back to receive a bruise rather than taking the risk of giving a catch. He made 85 in the first innings before Voce pushed one past his broad blade and bowled him. Many of the team received dangerous blows, notably Woodfull who was hit above the heart, and Oldfield, whose skull was fractured. Ponsford displayed big multi-coloured bruises from shoulders to buttocks when he removed his shirt. When his team-mates expressed sympathy, Ponsford remarked: 'I wouldn't mind having a couple more if I could get a hundred.'

Perhaps skipper Woodfull only heard him say he wouldn't mind a couple more. When the team batting order for the second innings was pinned up in the dressing room, Ponsford was at the more demanding first wicket down.

Larwood, this time, snaffled him, caught Jardine, for 3. England won easily.

Ponsford failed twice, scoring 19 and 0, in the critical Fourth Test at Brisbane. Australia lost for the third time in the series, and the Ashes went to England. Ponsford was dropped again from the Fifth Test, thus ending his second successive disappointing season. But he was not alone in defeat against Bodyline. Every batsman found it a hellish experience, and no one came through it unscathed. Even Bradman, with an average of 56.57 from 396, was reduced to half his previous effectiveness.

End Games

These two seasons, and particularly the bitterness of the Bodyline encounters, caused Ponsford, aged 33, to consider retirement but not before one last tilt at England on their home territory. He had done enough in the 1933–34 Test trial games to gain selection for the 1934 tour. It was a trip into the unknown. Jardine was still likely to be England's captain and Larwood and Voce were expected to play. However, on arrival in England, the team learned that Jardine had stood down. After Australian complaints, the MCC decided to dump him, a most ungrateful act given that it had directed him to use every means possible to defeat Bradman and the Australians in 1932–33. Larwood was disillusioned after his skipper's sacking about the MCC's attitude to his success during the Bodyline series. He quite rightly refused to apologise for his bowling in

1932–33 and was left out of selection calculations, as was Voce. This took the pressure off Australia's openers, to a degree, during the tour. Yet England was still tough opposition. Ponsford began the tour with scores of 13 and 9 against Worcestershire and Leicestershire, but struck terrific form against Cambridge University at Fenner's in May with 229 not out. Days later, he followed this performance with a thumping 281 not out in 437 minutes, including 26 fours against the MCC at Lord's. He put on 389 for the third wicket with Stan McCabe (192), a first-class record for two Australian batsmen that would stand for nearly fifty years.

Other worthy scores, including 125 against Surrey, confirmed Ponsford's return to the touch of 1930–31. He scored 53 and 5 at Trent Bridge in the First Test, which Australia won by 238 runs. He missed the Second at Lord's because of flu, and scored 12 and 30 not out in the high-scoring Third Test at Old Trafford. In the Fourth Test at Headingley, he hung on at the end of Day One, 20 July, to be 22 not out at stumps with Australia on three for 39 after England had made 200. He went on the next day to a sterling knock of 181 in 367 minutes, and was unfortunate to be out hit wicket (he trod on his wicket after hitting Hedley Verity to the boundary) late in the last session. He shared a heroic 388-partnership with Bradman (304) in 340 minutes. Rain saved England from defeat, but this great combination restored Australia's confidence for the Fifth and deciding Test at The Oval in August. Australia won. Ponsford's determination and skill in making 266 in his second huge link in two Tests with Bradman (244) ensured victory. The Ashes returned to Australia, and Ponsford came home a conquering hero. He was 33 going on 34, and he decided to retire at the peak of his form, a rare event in big sport.

* * *

In terms of his career statistics, Ponsford made 13,819 runs at 65.18, with 47 centuries, in first-class cricket. In Shield cricket, his record was even more remarkable – 5413 runs at 83.27. Only Bradman has averaged more. In 29 Tests, Ponsford scored 2122 runs at 48.22 with seven centuries.

He went on working for the Melbourne Cricket Club where he became Assistant Secretary. He retired in 1969, after 37 years of service. Ponsford was awarded the MBE and, in 1985, was one of the first inductees into the Sport Australia Hall of Fame. He and Bradman were the only cricketers chosen for this honour from the 1926 to 1950 era. An MCG stand was named after Ponsford for his long and outstanding service as a player and administrator.

Ponsford was second only to Bradman in terms of averages and run-scoring in Australian cricket. But it was when he got the runs that counted the most. Bradman was at the other end batting with him when Bill Ponsford's outstanding skills under pressure were on display. Ponsford helped clinch two Ashes series – 1930 and 1934 – with great performances in the final deciding Tests. This, above all, persuaded Bradman to choose him as his right-hand opener in his Australian all-time best team.

CHAPTER 2

MAJOR PERFORMER

ARTHUR MORRIS

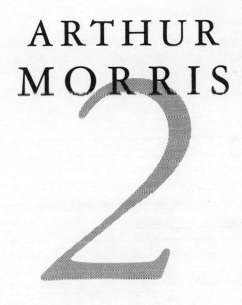

2

(Australia)

19 January 1922–

'Arthur was a wonderful player to watch
from the beginning of an innings.
He often set the tone for a game . . . Arthur
had an ideal temperament.'

Don Bradman

Arthur Morris, at 15 years, was a left-arm slow spinner, who batted down the order for St George's Second XI. The First XI captain, Bill O'Reilly, studied him in the nets and disabused him of a bowling career, suggesting there were plenty of bowlers at the club. O'Reilly calculated in the interests of St George. Morris might be well down the list behind O'Reilly waiting for a bowl, but the club was short of a left-hand opening bat. O'Reilly thought Morris had a sound technique and ordered him, at age 16, in 1938–39, to open the batting. The affable, easygoing Morris had the temperament to take on one of the toughest challenges cricket can offer. Openers are born, not made, and the curly-haired teenager of medium height and weight showed all the skills needed to make a strong start to his team's innings.

At 18, in the 1940–41 season, Morris made a huge impact in his first State game for New South Wales when he hit two attractive innings of 148 and 111 against Queensland. This was the first time a batsman had scored two hundreds in his debut first-class match. The cricket world sat up and took notice. Such a display revealed several things. First, the cricketer most likely had the right mental strength for big cricket. Second, his powers of concentration were clearly exceptional. Even the great and most experienced among batsmen in history rarely came up twice with such force and determination in one match. War stopped Morris from making a teenage entry into Test cricket in 1940–41 when England would have been due to visit. At 19, instead of opening for his country, he enlisted to fight for it in the Australian Imperial Forces. Morris was stationed in Australia and New Guinea. By the time hostilities ceased in 1945 he was 23. Morris found work with a motor parts distributor, a job that would allow him every chance to resume his rudely interrupted cricket career.

Morris began the 1946–47 season in good touch, scoring 27 run out and 98 for New South Wales against Queensland at Brisbane. It was enough to get him selected for his first big trial for an Australian XI against the England touring team at the MCG in early November 1946. Morris was in the team by default when Bill Brown fell injured. Brown, who had established himself as a Test opener in the 1930s, and Sid Barnes had been favoured to open for Australia. Now it was Morris's big chance. He opened with another prospect, Merv Harvey, from Victoria. Day One was washed out and, by agreement, the game was extended to a fifth day. England, led by Wally Hammond, batted first and made 314. Harvey fell first for 22. Morris, who began cautiously, was joined by Bradman, himself very much on trial. Bradman had batted for South Australia against the MCC at Adelaide, where he had looked frail and a shadow of his former great self. Should he fail in this match, it was probable that he would resign from cricket. The new partners – it was the first time Morris had met Bradman, who was one of his heroes – were both batting with their cricketing future at stake. Morris was calm and quiet, which was just Bradman's mood at the wicket. They developed their innings together. *Wisden* said that Bradman inspired Morris. Bradman saw it another way.

'I have no idea what Arthur was thinking,' he said, 'but he was having no trouble with the bowling when I arrived at the wicket. His defence was excellent, and when he did play shots they were executed with style, placement and power.'

The two built a solid partnership of 196 for the second wicket. Bradman injured a leg muscle, limped up to 106 and then threw his wicket away. Morris pushed on to 115 in 297 minutes. He looked sound — all middle and no edges. The link had wide implications for post-war cricket.

In my conversations with Bradman he told me he was 'very much impressed' with Morris first up.

Did it help his selection for the first Test at Brisbane?

'Yes. I brought that impression to the selection table.'

Bradman had one more match against Victoria before the forthcoming Tests, scoring 43 and 119, and declared he was ready to play Test cricket again. Morris faced the English again playing for New South Wales and scored 81 not out in a score of four for 165, declared in a rain-affected game. Notably, the New South Wales skipper, Sid Barnes, was out for just 1. Morris was doing everything right to gain selection.

Into the Test Arena

Morris made the Test side, and promptly ran into big Alec Bedser, the best medium pacer England had produced in decades, who beat him with an away-swinger and had him caught by Hammond in slips for just 2. In the Second Test at Sydney when on 5 Morris dragged an ordinary ball from Bill Edrich onto his stumps. These had been his only two chances in these games in which Australia amassed 645 and 659 and he didn't perform to expectation. Morris spent long periods in the pavilion watching his team-mates build big scores.

Matters looked even bleaker for Morris in the Third Test at Melbourne beginning on 1 January 1947, when he failed for the third successive time, this time lbw to Bedser who trapped him with an off-cutter. Yet this time Australia batted first, making 365, and when England made 351, Morris was assured of a second chance. He made the most of it, scoring 155 in a solid, 300-minute stay at the wicket. English critic Neville Cardus, ever England's fifth columnist, sowed doubts in readers' minds about Morris by writing that the Australian had a 'loose' technique. Cardus noted that his bat was not straight in defence. Bradman told Morris to ignore the criticism and 'keep doing what you are doing'.

Morris's confidence at the Test level was now apparent and he went one better in Adelaide, scoring 122 and 124 not out in the Fourth Test. He now had three successive Test centuries and this entrenched him as Australia's left-handed opener. His double feat at Adelaide put him in a special class. He hit another fine 57 in the Fifth Test and ended his first series with 503 runs at 71.86. He only had five starts against the Indians in 1947–48, but kept up a sound impression by making 209 at 52.25 with a score of 100 not out at the MCG in Australia's second innings exactly a year after he had made his breakthrough 155 against England.

Zenith in 1948

His performance in 1947 was enough to ensure Morris a boat trip to England for the historic 1948 tour, but he was one of three fine openers – Barnes and Brown being the others – who would be fighting for two places. Barnes was in good touch and had played in one Test in England in 1938, making 41 and 33. Brown had an excellent record in England. In 1934 he was recommended by Bradman ahead of Jack Fingleton and hit 300 at 33.33 with one century. In 1938, he starred, making 512 at 73.14 with a top score of 206 not out at Lord's, and 133 at Trent Bridge.

However, 1948 was a decade on, and Morris had a distinct advantage. All things being equal, he was a left-hander. Bradman, the team captain and a selector, liked the idea of having a left-hand–right-hand opening combination to break up the line of opposing opening bowlers.

Any tensions built up over the fight for places in the Test matches were submerged on the boat trip to England.

'We all had a chance to get to know each other,' Morris told me in 2001, during a conversation we had, 'especially those players from other States. It built real camaraderie. After all, we faced a very long tour and it was better that everyone was comfortable with everyone else.'

Morris said present-day players don't get that same chance. Planes take them to a destination in a day, and a few days later they are playing. By contrast, in 1948, the boat trip was followed by a useful build-up to the Tests in the form of matches against the counties, with plenty of nets to acclimatise in the cold days of April. Morris opened with Barnes at Worcester in the first game and hit the cricket ground running – between the wickets. He top-scored with 138, ahead of Bradman who broke a habit of making a double century (he did it three previous times – in 1930, 1934 and 1938) in the opening game versus Worcester, under the cathedral, by getting out at 107. Morris then had a slump. His feet weren't working. Vice-captain Lindsay Hassett watched him in the nets and announced that he wasn't using his feet enough. He was playing from the crease.

'Lindsay was most helpful,' Morris recalled. 'He advised me to go for my shots more, which meant moving my feet.'

Soon after this, against Sussex, at Hove in early June, Morris opened with Brown and they put on 153 before Brown fell for 44. Bradman, as captain, then joined Morris and saw first-hand that Morris had recovered as they put on 167 for the second wicket. Bradman made 109 in 118 minutes, while Morris went on to 184, hitting 26 fours in a most attractive knock. It was good timing for Morris and helped him get selected for the First Test. It was difficult for Bradman to separate the three openers based on their performances prior to the Tests. He decided to open with the left–right combination of Morris and Barnes and bring Brown in at number five. This selection move didn't quite pay off. Barnes succeeded, making 62 and 64 not out. Morris was bowled by Laker for 31 and fell to Bedser, bowled for 9. Brown made 17.

Morris was unhappy with both the county and England tactics of bowling down leg-side. He was once so annoyed that he took block from a foot (30 cm) outside leg-stump. Morris recalled that the bowler still delivered at the leg-stump. (He was later pleased when a rule was introduced to limit to two the number of fielders behind square leg.) In the Trent Bridge Test, the bowling tactic was aimed at restricting the Australians, especially Bradman. Fielders were kept in the outfield, forcing the batsmen to take singles. It slowed the scoring, but didn't change the expected result. In the first innings Bradman made 138 and Hassett 137, and these performances set up an eight-wicket Australian win.

Morris was in fine form in the Second Test, hitting 105 in the first innings in 200 minutes. His featured stroke in this knock was the cover drive. Australia was three for 166 when he left after giving a hard catch to gully. He made 62 in the second innings. His opening partner, Barnes, made 0 and 141, while Brown, batting at six, couldn't get going and was out for 24 and 32. Australia won by 409 runs.

Morris was now in an aggressive groove with his crease-bound early-season form well behind him. He launched into everything at Bristol against Gloucestershire, hit 42 fours and a six in a mighty innings of 290 out of 466 in 300 minutes of power cricket. Australia went on to seven for 774 declared and won the game. Morris carried much of this touch into the Third Test at Manchester early in July, hitting 51 and 54 not out. This was followed by 109 against Middlesex and then 6 and 182 in the Leeds Test. The latter knock gave him the most satisfaction. It helped turn a probable defeat into an unlikely victory when Australia was set 404 to make in less than a day. The innings began 20 minutes into the day and finished 15 minutes early. Bradman (173 not out) and Morris put on 301 for the second wicket in a partnership that won the match and the series for Australia. It was the greatest last innings to win a Test to that point in time. Once settled, Morris and Bradman batted superbly and at a rapid rate, which meant the target was achieved with ease – and seven wickets to spare.

Morris ranked his 196 at The Oval as his best innings for the Test series. The pitch was difficult and after Bradman made a duck, Morris had to concentrate and battle hard to consolidate Australia's position.

Morris told me that he rated the 1948 tour as the best for him personally and the most enjoyable of his career. Bradman ranked Morris's 196 at The Oval as the best innings of the 1948 Ashes. He also went further, telling me: 'I thought he was unlucky to be given run out. It was a close call. The decision robbed Arthur of a well-deserved double hundred. He had developed steadily through the tour into a young master of the game. That innings [196 at The Oval] placed him as the best left-hander in cricket at the time. I regarded him then as the best left-hander I'd ever seen.'

Bradman had not seen Clem Hill play, a cricketer who cricket author and broadcaster A.G. Moyes rated as good as Morris against slow- and medium-pace bowlers, and better at facing speed. Moyes, however, added the caveat that had Morris faced the pacemen that bowled to Hill, he would have handled them 'competently'. And while he appreciated Morris's capability in attacking the bowling, he thought Hill had more power in his shots.

Neville Cardus, now resigned to Australia's superiority in 1948, could afford to be more generous in his observations: 'Morris was once more beyond praise – masterful, stylish, imperturbable, sure in defence, quick and handsome in strokeplay. His batting is true to himself, charming and good mannered but reliant and thoughtful. Seldom does he spare a ball of suspicious character, yet he is never palpably acquisitive, never brutal. He plunders bowlers tastefully, and changes rubbish into cultured art.'

Post-1948

There was a lot of impressive Morris treasure about in 1948. He hit 696 at 87 with three hundreds and three fifties to dominate the Ashes. He returned home in 1948–49 and continued on his artful way. One innings among many fine knocks in that season stood out. It was when Morris was playing for New South Wales against Queensland, a team which always seemed to be on the receiving end of Morris adventurism. New South Wales needed 143 to win. Morris smashed 108 not out off 80 balls before lunch, in order to eat with a friend so the story goes. Bradman was the only other player to have been in such an apparent hurry before lunch. He achieved the same feat four times in State games. Morris kept up the standard that had so impressed his now retired skipper, scoring 1069 runs at 66.81. This gave him an amazing year of cricket. In the 12 months from April 1948 to March 1949, he had 46 first-class innings (3 not outs) and accumulated 2991 runs at 69.56. He got his team off to a good start every second time he batted. No opener in history could claim such a consistent and brilliant record.

Morris was 27 turning 28 during the 1949–50 tour of South Africa and there seemed nowhere to go but down from the astonishing heights he'd achieved. He was still in form, though not quite as spectacular, as he scored 422 at 52.75 in the Tests. He had trouble with Bedser again in 1950–51. After early failures, the big Surrey man presented Morris with a Lindsay Hassett book on how to play the game. Morris, who always had a determined streak under his gentle exterior, replied to the friendly jibe by hitting 206 out of an Australian innings of 371. It was his seventh Ashes century and a sign that he could still rise to the occasion. But Morris didn't seem to have the will or the inclination to do it quite as much. This was reflected in his returns of 321 runs at 35.67, and again the next season against the West Indies when he managed just 186 at 23.25. Those wily spinners Sonny Ramadhin and Alf Valentine caused him more trouble than Bedser. Morris lifted his rating against the touring South Africans in a more challenging series for Australia, which was drawn 2–2. He hit 370 at 41.1, with a top score of 99 run out at the MCG in the Fifth Test.

Morris began the 1953 Ashes campaign with four good innings of 67, 60, 30 and 89, but his form fell away after that as Australia lost its first Ashes series since the Bodyline series of 1932–33. Morris's 337 at 33.7 confirmed a permanent fall from the heady days of 1948. He was out of the blocks with 153 in the First Test of the 1954–55 Ashes but only accumulated 223 at 31.86 for the entire series. With increasing competition from new young blood like Colin McDonald from Victoria and Jim Burke from New South Wales, Morris was still chosen for a tour of the West Indies in 1955. He began with 157 against Jamaica, which gave him the record of having scored a century on debut in four countries – England, South Africa, the West Indies and Australia. This effort said much about Morris's will. He could often perform when he was determined. He managed 266 at 44.33, which was close to his career Test average of 46.48 from 3533 runs in 46 Tests. He hit 12 centuries.

He captained New South Wales at 25, and proved such a capable leader that he was vice-captain of the Test team for several series, and filled in twice as leader in 1951–52 against the West Indies and against England in 1954–55.

Morris played in 162 first-class games, in which he accumulated 12,614 runs at 53.67 with 46 hundreds. As a Trustee of the SCG for 21 years he put back into the game that had brought him joy, fame and an exceptional life. He was awarded an MBE for his services to cricket and had a successful career as a public relations man for security group Wormald.

Bradman summed up Morris thus: 'His most outstanding quality was plenty of time to play his shots. He could drive, glance, hook and cut. All were executed with the same facility. Arthur was a wonderful player to watch from the beginning of an innings. He often set the tone for a game. He wasn't always straight in defence. But this was merely a sign of genius. He rarely, if ever, got out from this. Arthur had an ideal temperament.'

With such sentiment, it was not surprising that Morris

was Don Bradman's first choice to open the batting for his country.

Perhaps Morris's most important sign of genius was his capacity to impose his will on a big or important occasion. This applied to scoring a century when first playing a foreign country and to performing at his best in a series-deciding Test. Bradman appreciated this quality immensely.

CHAPTER 3

THE SYMBOL OF TWENTIETH-CENTURY AUSTRALIA

DON
BRADMAN

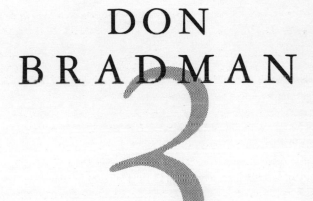

(Australia)

27 August 1908–25 February 2001

'If you were looking for one image, one face, one performer, one communicator that most represented Australia in the twentieth century, it had to be Donald George Bradman.'

Freedom fighter Nelson Mandela said on his visit to Australia in 2000 that Sir Donald Bradman was 'one of the divinities'. The Don himself was uncomfortable with such epithets, as was his son John, who said after Don passed away in 2001 that his dad should not be seen as 'a religious figure'. But why would Mandela, a sports lover all his life, make such an observation, endorsed by the bulk of Australia and the entire cricketing world — particularly India?

The complete answer could not be Bradman's ranking as second only to Muhammad Ali by many international expert analysts as the greatest sportsperson of the last one hundred years. It certainly is a factor, but not *the* factor in bestowing a kind of sainthood on Bradman. But just because his two-decade record at the top of his chosen sport placed Bradman statistically at least 40 per cent better than the rest of the best, does not explain the way he was deified and hero-worshipped by fans throughout the world. Nor is the fact that he was around for most of the century. Legends are more often than not created from those who die young. Consider Jesus Christ, Julius Caesar, or even Diana, Princess of Wales. Bradman lived three times longer than legends such as these and proved an amazingly durable, positive and awe-inspiring identity. Instead of dropping off as a hero after he retired from cricket at 40, his status grew and grew and never stopped. It wasn't for want of trying *not* to be hero-worshipped. Since Bradman's retirement there have been plenty of media people who experienced the wrath of Bradman for an indiscretion they might have made or from invading his precious privacy. Instead of ingratiating himself with members of the Fourth Estate, he eschewed them. It was the media that mostly pandered to him. For more than seventy years, the Bradman mystique developed around his inaccessibility. Yet his name was always associated with excellence and the best in sport.

So is there a clue to his 'divinity' or everlasting fame here? Become famous at something – anything – and then shut yourself off from the world for the rest of your life so that the mystery about you grows? Bradman didn't enjoy fame. It took him forty years to finally appear on commercial television in 1996. He only did it then because Kerry Packer donated $1.2 million to complete the building of the Bradman Museum at Bowral. Bradman did not receive a cent of that donation. And he hated the whole ordeal of exposure, an ordeal made worse for him by a stroke he suffered at the age of 87. Unlike others who moved into the media to maintain their profile and reputation, Bradman avoided media work apart from some journalism in the 1950s. However he did put an enormous amount back into the game. He was a key administrator (as a State and national selector and member of State and national cricket boards) until he was 78. But he still preferred the back room to the media room. It wasn't that he couldn't handle the media. Nobody could do better when it came to a succinct thought, direct statement, or good photo opportunity if it had to be had. It was just that Bradman thought the media limelight was mostly superfluous, and that the media should be used as a vehicle for a message, not for vanity or ego boosting.

Bradman chose stockbroking as his profession. At 26, he disappeared (when he wasn't playing cricket) into the confidential world of stocks and shares, essentially a world of discreet people in suits. If one wished to avoid media attention it was almost as good as the morgue, and nearly as completely shielded from the public as the upper echelons of banking are.

No Press Prince Charming

Bradman's attempt to become anonymous failed to give him privacy but instead enhanced his aura and made him seem, to many commentators, akin to royalty. Bradman's charm was that apart from exhibiting all the normal niceties at public events, he was always transparently *him*. He seemed incapable of small talk – another reason for avoiding, if he could, functions, where small-talking champions aired their skills.

Bradman avoided politics. Both major Australian political parties wanted him. Labor Party officials listened to his nasal accent, took into account his roots and considered him ideal for them. The conservatives looked at his job, noticed how all 'classes' of Australian society admired him, and claimed him as one of them. Bradman by the end of the twentieth century was far more universally popular – polls suggest at least twice as popular – as any politician from Billy Hughes to Bob Hawke. Yet Bradman decidedly resisted the notion of becoming a politician, although he did flirt with the idea of becoming a diplomat – as Australia's High Commissioner to the United Kingdom. By not becoming a political partisan Bradman enhanced, or at least maintained, his image as the 'greatest Australian ever born'.

DON BRADMAN

Bradman's Economic Inverse Rule of Success

The substance beneath the Bradman mythology was created by the perfect coincidence between his incredible feats with the bat and Australia's decline into a miserable economic depression that lasted from the late 1920s to the mid-1930s.

In 1927, Prime Minister Bruce opened the new Federal Parliament in Canberra, moved his office there and announced that Australia 'was on the threshold of achievement'. When these words were uttered the future looked fairly bright to the average Australian, who was unaware of the impact of over-borrowing in London by Australia, and especially by New South Wales. Bradman, at this moment of false national optimism, was unknown, except by those following grade cricket in Sydney. At 18, he had made his debut at the St George club with a run-a-minute innings of 110 before being run out. Yet his first season (an aggregate of 289 runs at 48.16 in six completed innings) was not world shattering. The fact that he made 320 not out for his country team Bowral in April 1927 was simply not newsworthy, even in Sydney.

In late October 1928, the price of wheat and wool – both then essential to Australia's prosperity – fell through the floor. Bruce's 'threshold of achievement' was suddenly, shockingly, the edge of an abyss. Right on cue, young Don, now 20, crashed a compelling double century for New South Wales versus Queensland at Brisbane's Exhibition Ground, scoring 131 and 133 not out. In a flash the unknown was being discussed as a prospect to make the Test team to play against Percy Chapman's English tourists. He was selected and scored a century in his second Test.

A few months later in January 1929, a loan issue for the

Commonwealth of Australia collapsed with 84 per cent of it under-subscribed and left in the hands of underwriters. Precisely at the same moment, Bradman cracked a formidable 340 not out for New South Wales versus Victoria at Sydney, a feat that was reported on the front page of every Australian newspaper, right up against items about the ramifications of the loan collapse.

In the Test arena, England, mainly due to Hammond with the bat (a massive 905 runs in the 1928-29 series at an average of 113.13 from nine innings) was giving a weak Australian attack a walloping. The only consistent hope in the wake of this onslaught was the form of Bradman. Spectators jammed all the grounds to see him and to will him on against the English. He and Australia were at once the underdog. Yet there was another dimension to the feeling among fans. English financiers were dictating to Australia how to manage its economy. This amounted to deflationary measures and an increase in the cost of borrowing – a squeeze that was putting, and would put, enormous numbers of Australians out of work. For the Australian spectators, the England players, then, were symbolic of the pressure being put on the 'colonials' by the British. The England team was heckled. Douglas Jardine, then a most accomplished bat, was a target. To the fans his harlequin cap and neck choker seemed to represent the image of the British establishment that was seen to be creating tough times for Australians.

At the time of Bradman's 340 – a score signalling that this gifted newcomer would challenge Hammond as world-champion run plunderer – the economic crisis became personal for Bradman. He lost his job at Deer Westbrook's Sydney real-estate office. The operation had been set up to sell housing estates, but the business went flat in the sudden 'recession' (it was yet to be labelled a 'depression').

Bradman, who had left school at 14 and had no qualification apart from his real-estate work, felt the humiliating experience of being just another statistic in the growing number of those out of work. Unemployment in the first quarter of 1929 rose from 9.3 per cent to an alarming 12.1 per cent. Wherever Bradman went around Sydney he saw men out of work and food lines. It worried him. But he didn't need to join the dole queues. Mick Simmons sports store employed him. He hated the job but was grateful for work. It took the pressure of financial worry off him and he celebrated by being the match-winner against England with 123 and 37 not out in the Fifth Test at Melbourne. The crowd was near hysterical at this result. For a few precious days the nation could submerge its mental anguish over the bleak immediate future and celebrate. England had been defeated. Bradman was proving the champion the fans had predicted and prayed he would be. By the end of the series only Hammond had performed better.

Through 1929, the recession deteriorated into the Great Depression, triggered by the crash on Wall Street. Wool and wheat prices fell to rock-bottom. Overseas loans from England, the monetary lifeblood of an over-extended Australian nation, evaporated. A countrywide drought added a heartbreaking physical element beyond anyone's control to the already deplorable conditions in the country.

At the beginning of the 1929–30 season, Australia's export revenues were plummeting. Half of it (heading for under 100 million pounds) would be used to service foreign debt, which meant that much less was available for loans. The banks restricted the amount of money on offer and interest rates climbed. Taxes went on non-essential items like cricket bats and tennis rackets. The squeeze threatened the Mick Simmons sports store. Bradman wondered if he would be out of work again.

Instead of panicking he went out and made runs. Fans flocked even to second-grade games in the bush to see him. Saturday afternoons at St George were a lockout. So were Shield games. Bradman lifted his performance rating for first-class matches, including 157 against a touring MCC side. Then he smashed a breathtaking double hundred *and* a century in the trial game that was deciding the team for the 1930 Ashes tour of England. It was an exhilarating feat. The fans – the masses of people from every walk of life who filled the arenas around the country – felt somehow symbiotically linked to this unassuming youthful new champion. They had cheered for him before he had been proven at the highest level, screamed when he was dropped from the Test side for one game, applauded as he fulfilled their dreams. Everyone from battlers to bankers felt a part of his indomitable rise and rise. They looked in the mirror and saw a bit of hope, a reflection of Bradman in all of them. They had willed him on and talked up what he would do in England in the upcoming 1930 Ashes. Figures and averages began to spill onto the sports pages in the country, in Sydney and across the nation. In five categories of the game in 1929–30 from second grade to first class, Bradman was averaging more than a hundred every time he batted. No one had ever done anything like this, not even the great Bill Ponsford and Victor Trumper, and certainly not the English champion W.G. Grace. In a desperate, dispiriting summer, here was someone to take the collective Australian mind off the continual bad news as businesses crashed, farmers committed suicide and dole lines stretched around the blocks in every city.

And finally, in early January 1930, just as everyone dreaded entering another fearful year of economic malaise, Bradman performed in such a way for New South Wales that he was in a dimension of his own. The location was

Sydney; the opponents Queensland. Bradman smashed and accumulated 452 not out in 415 minutes. It was an act of sporting obliteration, at once both brutal and poetic. It was the highest score by anyone anywhere in first-class cricket. This innings was beyond anyone's dream, except the performer himself. More importantly, it was a display that inspired and made everyone who saw it, read about it or heard about it, proud that one of their own, a humble country kid at that, could reach such sporting perfection. He didn't give a chance, not one in just under seven hours of precision carving-up of the opposition. What's more, he wanted to go on to 600. He was more than a little miffed that his skipper, Alan Kippax, declared when he was setting himself to achieve the 600 mark. Bradman's hunger was mindboggling, his powers of concentration as high as a human could achieve and his stamina formidable.

Hope of a Nation

Australians began to speculate seriously now that he might just challenge the might of England in their own backyard. And while this was being discussed in innumerable pubs, churches, businesses, homes and schools, the economic disaster subsuming the country was momentarily forgotten. Bradman, at the lowest point in a fledgling nation's short history, was one ray of hope. There was nothing else, certainly not on a national, unifying level, that could deliver.

When Bradman reached England for the first time those moments of distraction fused into a long running drama for Australia as millions followed the fortunes of Bill Woodfull's team. They read with anger that despite Bradman opening the tour under the cathedral at Worcester with a big double hundred, English critics were applying psychological warfare tactics by suggesting their hero was flawed. Australian indignation was reserved more for this than the squalor of the now entrenched Depression. Bradman, aware, but unaffected by praise or attacks, launched on and on. At The Oval against Surrey, he silenced one of his biggest critics, the county's captain, Percy Fender, by making 252 not out in a dazzling 290 minutes. Only the rain stopped Bradman going on to 400. It was a portent of the torrent of run-making that may never be bettered in Test cricket. He scored 974 runs from seven innings at an average of 139.14. It was a performance that more or less matched, for instance, the combined Test averages of Ian Chappell, Neil Harvey and Stan McCabe, or in another instance, Arthur Morris, Lindsay Hassett and Bill Ponsford. Instead of his career superiority of being nearly twice as good statistically as the rest of the greats of the game, he was, in that one glorious English summer, worth *three* top batsmen from any era.

As part of that huge aggregate, he hit four different kinds of innings that could truly be called unsurpassable exhibitions of each batting 'genre'. In the First Test at Trent Bridge he hit a fighting 131 in 260 minutes, which was hailed as one of the finest-ever rearguard performances in the final, uphill innings of a Test (lost by Australia). In the Second Test, he hit 254 in 320 minutes. Bradman himself claimed it as technically the best innings he ever played. In the Fourth Test at Leeds, he scored 334 – 309 of them in a day, a feat yet to be equalled in Test history. Its supremacy was, in the speed of accumulation – the fastest first-day pre-lunch century ever, and 220 was scored by tea. At The Oval he hit a series-winning 232 – a pressure knock of varying shades on a difficult wicket against a strong attack that included a hostile Harold Larwood. Early in this innings he defended. Late in the innings on a dangerous, wet track he smashed 98 in a pre-lunch session.

In July 1930 at the precise moment that Bradman was reaching the heights of cricketing glory with that mighty triple hundred, Sir Otto Niemeyer, a director of the Bank of England, was in Australia advising its leaders to 'balance its budgets', stop raising loans and cut back on expenditure on public works. This was accepted in a supine way by the Australian establishment, including James Scullin's ruling Labor Government. It led to a further spiral into the Depression's void.

Bradman came home the conquering hero and gave the local collective psyche an immeasurable boost, especially as Otto Niemeyer and his English bankers and financiers were being increasingly blamed for the nation's plight.

Right at the depth of the Depression, Bradman had dispensed hope, pride and inspiration to the Australian people. He had also humiliated the rulers of the British Empire, something that no other foreigner, in peace or wartime, had been able to do in several hundred years. The Empire reacted. It felt compelled to attempt to put 'that little bastard' – as England's new captain, Douglas Jardine, called Bradman – in his place.

Jardine, one of the Empire's establishment sons (a lawyer of Scottish background, brought up in India, educated at Westminster and Oxford), was just the disciplinarian to do it. His haughty manner, dress, and the attitude towards Australians, engendered since Warwick Armstrong had denied him a century for Oxford against his all-conquering tourists in 1921, was familiar to crowds. The corresponding attitude towards him in Australia was poor as well when Jardine's pacemen – Larwood, Bill Voce and Bill Bowes – hurled down 'Bodyline'. Jardine hated the spectator abuse he received in 1928–29 with a passion and his resentment fuelled his desire to bring Bradman down in front of his adoring fans. Jardine didn't quite succeed. Bradman was too clever to be brutalised as he set about devising a daring method to counteract Bodyline. But Jardine did reduce Bradman to half his effectiveness (an average of 56 resulted, which was still better than anyone else on either side) in previous Test series encounters against England, the West Indies and South Africa. It was enough to send the Ashes back to England.

The Martyr and His Enemies

The whole Bodyline affair served to elevate Bradman to martyrdom. He was now not just the great sporting hero. He was the target for foul play by Australia's former colonial masters, who had been seen by all of Australia to show their true colours. There were serious mutterings about Australia withdrawing from the Commonwealth and becoming a republic. Then, in 1934, Bradman returned to England to conquer with further masterful innings at critical times (304 at Leeds and 244 at The Oval) These performances were made while suffering from peritonitis (caused by a burst appendix) to which he all but succumbed after making a supreme effort for his country. Perceptions of heroism and martyrdom magnified him into legend, and even myth. And Bradman was still only 26 years old.

Phenomenal developments on the cricket field go some way to explaining why his image was so outstanding over the last seven decades of the twentieth century. But there were other traits and issues at play that would sustain it.

Bradman was diplomatic in public to the point where there probably is not a public record of his criticism of any other person. Even in private he rarely directly expressed ill feeling towards anyone, although he had his dislikes. You don't become the tallest of tall poppies in Australia without creating enemies. He was aware which members of the media or the cricket fraternity were against him. When Bill O'Reilly and Jack Fingleton tried to get rid of him as captain of Australia in 1936–37 claiming he was not a leader, Bradman went public and called for unity in the fight against the common foe – England. This diffused the captaincy issue and Australia united to defeat England 3–2 (thanks mainly to Bradman's great batting again, this time with scores of 270, 212 and 169) after losing the first two Tests. Yet undercurrents of ill will from O'Reilly and Fingleton flowed for decades afterwards.

Fingleton blamed Bradman for his non-selection on the 1934 Ashes tour of England (Bradman, when asked, advised selectors that Bill Brown was a better bat on English soil) and was viewed as the ring-leader of a minority cabal against the captain in 1936–37.

Fingleton seemed ambivalent about the Don. He wrote a book that suggested Victor Trumper was a better batsman than Bradman. Yet he also produced a compelling tome, *Brightly Fades the Don*, on Bradman's triumphant all-conquering tour of England in 1948. Although O'Reilly was open about his dislike for Bradman, he was always quick to say Bradman was the greatest bat who ever lived. As the decades rolled on the bad blood surfaced and O'Reilly carried it to the grave and beyond.

In the mid-1990s audiotapes made by O'Reilly that were critical of Bradman and held in the National Archive were released posthumously in a spurious journalistic beat-up. The tapes were long on hyperbole and devoid of specifics but received wide publicity. Justifying his bizarre act, O'Reilly said he didn't criticise Bradman in public while he (O'Reilly) was alive because he 'didn't want to piss on a national monument'.

When I asked Bradman for a reaction, he replied: 'In principle, I agree with Bill that you shouldn't desecrate a national monument.' He paused and a characteristic half-grin formed before he added: 'And if there were a national monument to Bill, and even if it was on fire, I would never desecrate it.'

He appeared the statesman, while his detractors were reduced to seeming like miserable hatchet-men. When I questioned him (over six years) about certain individuals he rarely replied with open criticism of a cricketer. Only once, in reply to one of my questions came the comment:

'Oh, him ... he's hopeless, always has been.'

The rest of the time he made his point by a subtle remark, a look or by lack of comment, or he rationalised why someone was against him.

What did he think of Douglas Jardine?

'He was a very good bat,' he replied, deadpan.

Bradman let his guard down once on Clarrie Grimmett, the great leg-spinner, who wasn't selected for the 1938 Ashes tour of England.

'He was difficult to captain,' he remarked, intimating that he wanted loyalty on the tour and that Grimmett would give him trouble.

Bradman saw his former New South Wales skipper Alan Kippax as 'jealous', which may well have been true. Bradman, the Bowral Boy, came along in the late 1920s and overshadowed Kippax's record (and everyone else's) to such an extent that Kippax, who had a fair Test record (34 innings at an average of 36.12), felt he didn't receive the accolades he thought were due to him. His sports store in Sydney also struggled against that of Mick Simmons, who employed Bradman as a front-of-store glad-hander.

You couldn't say Bradman loved to hate – for instance like writer Patrick White or New South Wales premier of the late 1920s and 1930s Jack Lang, men who bore grudges and continually honed them. But he certainly privately wished to find ways to take on attackers, and seemed to relish such challenges. Before he stopped playing he said nothing and let his blade and leadership do the talking, which made fools of critics for two decades. Upon retirement, and after his death, he received criticism – some of it malicious, most of it empty. But as he said, he had to 'take it on the chin'. If he judged it fair and factual, he didn't let it bother him.

The Bradman legend, begun in the Depression, remained untouched by the behind-the-scenes battles over his style and early captaincy. His ruthless application of cricketing genius allowed him and Australia to rule world cricket from 1930–48 except for the 1932–33 blip of Bodyline. It strengthened his image ever further until he retired in 1949 and was knighted. That accounts for his unshakeable hold on the title first coined by former Prime Minister Billy Hughes in 1930 of 'greatest Australian ever born' for most of the last century. But what of the other half?

An Image Maintained

Bradman's faults centred on a tendency at times to be unpalatably direct, especially for the pompous and for those who wasted his precious time. Yet over-riding this was a person of exceptional integrity and character: humble, vanity-free and quick to make a generous comment about another, if merited. In private he was humorous with a sharp wit and always interested in others' views. These features came through over the decades, coupled with other important factors that extended, maintained and built the Bradman legend from 1950 to 2000 and beyond.

First, no one, came remotely near Bradman's batting record. His average and his big innings grew in proportion as the decades since his playing career rolled on. Second, he became the most prolific and expert letter-writer of the era, sending out an estimated 1.3 million letters in response to the five or six million he received over his lifetime. It was the only way Bradman could reach out personally to his correspondents. Written responses became a habit – a self-imposed obligation to his countless fans worldwide. This developed into an obsession, even an addiction. Most recipients of any reply from him placed it among their most prized possessions. The result was a huge constituency of supporters, from the world's movers and shakers to the most humble fans. Bradman's clear, concise prose, often with a witty or penetrating line, reflected his outstanding mind, and made you comprehend in a small way what bowlers, or opponents in any competitive environment, faced. Third, he did endless work for charity, mostly in private and without help, which he couldn't really afford. Apart from sitting down at his battered portable in his modest upstairs study every day for at least four hours, most days of every week would see him signing or writing something for worthy causes, or for fans. If that seems unimpressive at first glance, think of anyone devoting everything to others half a day of every day for five decades, even well into their nineties. How Bradman stayed sane and on top of this output is remarkable, especially when there was fan-mail overload on his birthday and at Christmas. At these times a truck was needed to deliver all the mail addressed to him. At times he wrote to me that the mail was 'driving him insane' as he tried to keep on top of it. On his ninetieth birthday he told me: 'I've a pile of mail you couldn't jump over.'

After he turned 90, the mail really began to overwhelm him, and he needed secretarial help – provided to him by the Bradman Museum. In the week after his death on 25 February 2001, the outpouring in the media of memories and references to the letters he sent children, ordinary people and others, reflected the inspiration he gave to millions over the last 72 years of his life.

Another factor that bolstered public appeal for Bradman was that he put an enormous amount back into the game after he finished playing. Apart from some journalism on Ashes tours to England in 1953 and 1956, he did not seek media work to maintain his popular image and profile but instead became a key administrator at State and national level. This work kept him mostly behind the scenes. Far from the term 'recluse' that was often used to describe him, Bradman was prominent in all the decision-making involving critical issues in the game for several decades.

In 1960–61, Bradman, as Chairman of the Australian Cricket Board, was the individual who did most to foster a terrific series against the West Indies. Before the series he suggested to the Australian team that selectors would look kindly on those who played entertaining cricket. He created a mood behind the scenes by mixing with the West Indians throughout the tour, inviting them to dine at his home, and by encouraging their best on-field performances. The brilliant, tight series, which was played in a fine spirit thanks to the West Indies captain Frank Worrell, the first black captain to lead a West Indies team abroad, and to Australian captain Richie Benaud, captured the imagination of the Australian people.

At the end of the series, Bradman commissioned his old team-mate, jeweller Ernie McCormick, to create the Frank Worrell Trophy, for which the two teams have fought ever since. Half a million people turned up at

Melbourne to farewell the West Indians in February 1961.

At that time, the White Australia policy meant that it was extremely difficult for people with coloured skin to emigrate and settle in Australia. Entry was restricted to those working or studying for up to five years. The universal support from the Australian public for the mainly black West Indian cricketers was a factor in ending that racist policy. Bradman's dynamic approach as a cricket administrator helped create goodwill and an environment for a change of public attitude and eventually a change in government policy.

In the mid-1960s, Bradman, working for the South Australian Cricket Association, organised Garry Sobers to play for the State. In 1970 and 1971, it was Bradman who investigated the apartheid issue with his characteristic thoroughness in order to decide if South Africa should tour Australia in 1971–72. He shuttled between South Africa and England meeting with the prime ministers of the two countries. In Pretoria, South African Prime Minister John Vorster was uncomfortable with Bradman's direct questioning about the 'black problem'. In London, he met successive British Prime Ministers Harold Wilson and Edward Heath, who were impressed by the depth of Bradman's probe into the apartheid issue. In Australia, he was in dialogue with the apartheid protesters. He wrote to Dr Meredith Burgmann (later President of the New South Wales Legislative Council) who was then a protester organiser colluding with Peter Hain, the English 'rebel' (later a minister in Tony Blair's Labour Government). With his trademark directness, Bradman asked Burgmann to explain why she was protesting and what she perceived as the objectives of the protest. They began dialogue through letters.

'I could see his mind changing away from being in favour

of the South Africans' tour as he got his head around the issues involved,' Burgmann said, amazed to be communicating with a man she had understood to have been a conservative 'establishment' figure.

Bradman attended a rugby international at Sydney between South Africa and Australia with the then South African ambassador. Bradman didn't like what he saw. Barbed wire barricades, violent protest and police action. He told the ambassador he didn't think cricket could be played under such conditions.

After getting abreast of the issue, Bradman stopped the cricket tour of Australia by an all-white South African team planned for 1971–72. Instead of using the excuse of the disturbance he witnessed at the rugby match, Bradman said: 'We will not play them [South Africa] until they choose a team on a non-racial basis.'

True to this directive, it was more than two decades before these countries faced each other in an official Test, at about the time the South African apartheid regime had been dismantled.

In 1971–72, the ACB invited Bradman back to help select a multi-racial international team to tour in place of the banned South Africans and play against Ian Chappell's Australian team.

It was five years after this that Bradman became embroiled in the battle to stop Kerry Packer's World Series Cricket taking over the game. The ACB used him to lure back Bob Simpson to captain the 'legitimate' national side after a decade out of Test cricket. In the end, Bradman was a key negotiator on the ACB's behalf in the compromise with Packer that gave Channel Nine the TV rights to Australian cricket that Packer had been after in the first place.

In 1985, aged 77, Bradman was called upon by the ACB

to solve the problems caused by Australian players defying bans and playing international cricket in South Africa.

But Bradman wasn't just there as a troubleshooter for these and many other big issues, such as the problems caused by players throwing the ball instead of bowling it, which caused great concern in the cricket world in the late 1950s and early 1960s. He was very much the diligent administrator at State and national level involved in the tedious 'nuts and bolts' of administration. He attended a record 1713 meetings of the South Australian Cricket Association. Bradman was a member of the ACB (formerly the Board of Control – he changed the name to soften its image) from 1945 until 1972. He was board chairman from 1960 to 1963, and from 1969 to 1972, again attending hundreds of meetings.

Hero in Our Eyes

Bradman was named by *Time* magazine in 2000 among the top 100 most influential figures of the twentieth century, alongside Gandhi, Churchill and Mandela. Gandhi had expressed a fervent hope to meet him, but was assassinated before he could. Bradman did meet Britain's mighty wartime leader. He was leaving Victoria Station in London in 1938 when Churchill used some journalist connections to arrange a meeting and a photo opportunity. Mandela regarded him as a hero and was keen to meet him on two visits to Australia. Bradman, an admirer of the freedom fighter, was unfortunately too ill each time.

Bradman lit the imaginations of people worldwide, from the humblest human being to the high and mighty, because he reached perfection within his chosen sport and everything else to which he put his mind. In 80 Test innings over a two-decade period from 1928 to 1948 – with a seven-year break caused by war and illness – he scored 6996 runs at 99.94. Bradman hit 29 Test centuries including 10 double hundreds and two triples. Another measure of his legendary status was his first-class cricket career from 1927 to 1949, in which he scored 28,067 runs at 95.14. In 338 innings, he hit 117 centuries, including 30 double hundreds, five triple hundreds and one quadruple. Over 20 first-class seasons, he maintained a rate of 42 runs an hour (84 runs a session, or 252 in a day), and at a strike rate of 75 runs per 100 balls, which would be respectable even in modern one-day cricket.

The next best group of batsmen in history have Test averages ranging from 46 to 60, indicating that Bradman was effectively worth two top Test batsmen in any era. In no other sport from golf to boxing, or athletics to billiards has one performer so dominated a competitive field of endeavour.

When we first discussed his selection of an all-time world team, I suggested that he had to select himself. To omit D.G. Bradman would render such an exercise meaningless. I have no doubt that he never intended to leave himself out. He was a realist. Even in choosing a 'dream team', he would always construct the most talented and competitive combination possible. It was his nature, and there was no room for sentiment or false humility in anything Bradman did.

The same applied to the selection of his best-ever Australian team. His name at number three, which traditionally is the place for the best bat, gives the Australian line-up an authority, a steadiness, and a brilliance that no other choice could approximate.

Chapter 4

THE DANCING DASHER

NEIL
HARVEY

(Australia)

8 October 1928–

'He was technically perfect in his shot production ... He had no discernible faults ...'

DON BRADMAN

The choice of Neil Harvey at number four in Bradman's all-time best Australian team is perhaps as predictable as it is apt. The attacking, quick-footed batsman was selected on merit by Bradman. Yet it did help that he was a left-hander. In ideal circumstances, Bradman liked the concept of a left-handed opener and one more in his top six. In his best world team, Arthur Morris and Garry Sobers were the left-handed selections. Morris and Harvey were the choices in the Australian line-up, while no leftie was considered strong enough to join the ranks of Bradman's best-ever England team.

The dark-haired Harvey was a cricketing prodigy from a family that produced four brothers who played for Victoria. One other, opener Mervyn, got one cap for Australia against England. No other Australian family except for the Gregorys (Dave, Ned and Jack, Sydney and Jack – between 1877 and 1937) produced so many capable cricketers.

A competitive home environment of long summers of backyard and street cricket equipped the young Harvey with the nous and spirit to move well beyond the streets of Fitzroy, an inner Melbourne suburb. His left-handed sparkle and skill surfaced rapidly for the Fitzroy club at just 15 years and for Victoria at 18 during the 1946–47 season. Harvey was the first of the post-Second World War players not to have his career interrupted by war. In fact, his career was enhanced by the war. Selectors in 1945 and 1946 scoured the country searching for young talent to replace the ageing players from the 1930s, a period already being called another era. In the early post-war years, Bradman saw in Harvey a mirror image of himself: short at 171 cm (5 ft 7 in), compact (66.5 kg) and ultra-talented with an aggressive, youthful outlook. Like Bradman, Harvey was nimble-footed between the wickets and a brilliant field. When Bradman was first seen in the 1927–28 season playing for New South Wales, commentators dubbed him the best in the country. Likewise, in the 1940s and 1950s, there was no one swifter or surer than Harvey in the covers. Opposing batsmen, even with the driving capacity of Garry Sobers, Rohan Kanhai, Frank Worrell, Peter May, Tom Graveney and Colin Cowdrey, had to be at their best to penetrate an off-side field patrolled by Harvey and the other brilliant Australian cover, Norm O'Neill.

In the Line of Darling and Hill

Harvey was the third in the line of great Australian left-handers after Clem Hill and Joe Darling. He hit the ball hard like them and inherited their attitude of batting aggressively. This is why Bradman smiled upon Harvey and was one selector that wanted him in the Test team as soon as possible. Harvey was just 19 when chosen to play for Australia against India in the Adelaide Fourth Test in 1947–48. He made 13 and feared he would be dumped. But the series against India was already wrapped up by Australia. Bradman was using the Tests as a trial for selecting the Australian side for the 1948 tour of England. Harvey was chosen again for the Fifth Test at Melbourne. In that game Bradman, on 57, retired hurt with an attack of fibrositis. Harvey came in at the MCG in front of a partisan home crowd and batted beautifully, compiling a stylish, forthright 153. To many observers, this was a seminal moment in Australian cricket. The young Harvey was expected to assume the baton held since 1928 by Bradman, when, as a 20-year-old, he became the mainstay of Australian batting. A little prematurely, Harvey was being dubbed the left-handed Bradman. His Melbourne performance assured him a boat trip to England for the 1948 tour.

When assessing his charges for that crusade, Bradman said of Harvey: 'He has the brilliance and daring of youth, and the likelihood of rapid improvement.'

Rapid advancement looked unlikely in 1948 in England. Harvey struggled early on the lower, slower pitches. He began with a run of low scores: 12, 7, 18 not out, 7, 16 run out, and 23, and his progress worried him. Harvey, the junior member of the squad, was too much in awe of the busy Bradman to ask him what he was doing wrong. Instead, Harvey asked Sam Loxton, the Victorian all-rounder to ask 'the boss' – Bradman – what he should do. Loxton, who had a good rapport with Bradman and called him 'George' which was his middle name, came back with the directive: 'Just keep the ball along the ground and you'll be all right.'

'Is that all?' a disappointed Harvey responded.

'That's what the boss said,' Loxton replied.

When I asked Bradman about this later, he said that there was nothing to tell Harvey.

'He was technically perfect in his shot production,' Bradman remarked. 'He was batting well enough and simply getting out early. It happens to all cricketers. If anything he seemed a little anxious when bogged down (early on the 1948 tour) and there was a tendency occasionally to play a rash shot, but that was about it.'

The instruction to 'keep the ball along the ground' was meant to focus his mind and to remind him to avoid the desperate lofted shot. It seemed to do the trick. In the next game against Lancashire, he made 36 in the first innings, and again was batting, according to Bradman, 'well enough'. But he was out-bowled playing over a faster ball. However, his confidence was buoyed by form that took him beyond 25 for the first time on tour. In the second innings Harvey attacked from the start knowing that the game was petering out to a draw. He hit 76 not out and took part in an unfinished fifth-wicket stand of 122 with Ron Hamence (49 not out). His confidence was now up. He had a setback against Hampshire but found form again against Sussex, making a sparkling 100 not out in 115 minutes with 16 fours. Harvey continued to be consistently good, scoring 14, 49, 56, 43, 73 not out, 95 and 10 before he replaced the injured Sid Barnes in the Fourth Test at Headingley, beginning on 22 July.

England batted first and made 496 (Cyril Washbrook 143, Bill Edrich 111), and on Day Two Australia was three for 68 when Harvey, still 19 years old, came in for his first Ashes Test. He joined Keith Miller. Harvey began nervously, playing and missing. Miller wandered down the pitch to have a brief chat that calmed him down. Harvey proceeded to play a wonderful Ashes debut innings. His driving was powerful on both sides of the wicket and his timing was precise. His on-side shots were varied, but it was noticeable that this left-hander used his front foot to drive through covers with the aplomb of any right-hander. He and Miller delivered a fearful onslaught, slamming 121 in 91 minutes. Miller was dismissed for 58 at 189 and then Harvey was joined by his mate and 1948 'minder' Loxton. They carried on the blistering attack. Harvey reached 112, his second successive Test century, in a 105 partnership in

95 minutes. He hit 17 fours and faced 183 balls. It was a mighty start in Ashes cricket and the innings helped swing the game back for Australia. Loxton went on to a towering 93 with five huge sixes and nine fours.

Australia's tail wagged (particularly Lindwall 77) and the team managed to wriggle up to 458. England batted again and declared at eight for 365, leaving Australia 404 to make in less than a day's cricket. Bradman (173 not out) and Morris (182) did the job and young Harvey hit the winning runs to be 4 not out in one of the great Tests of all time. His confidence rocketed. He hit two more centuries on tour and ended it with a 22-innings aggregate of 1129, with an average of 53.76.

Harvey often said that with mentors such as Loxton and Miller the 1948 experience developed him as a man and a cricketer. He always defended that team as the best ever and said, late in 2000, that he thought only leg-spinner Shane Warne of the Australian team in 2000 would have been worthy enough to make the 1948 side.

Post-1948

Harvey came down to earth in the 1948–49 domestic summer scoring 539 runs in first-class cricket at just 33.68. He didn't manage a century and had a top score of 87. Bradman now was a non-playing selector and was one of three who voted for him to tour South Africa in 1949–50. Harvey reclaimed the faith that everyone who counted had in him by having a magnificent tour. While he fulfilled the development that Bradman expected of him on the English tour, on this second tour he demonstrated full maturity at 21 as he plundered bowlers across the veldt, scoring 1526 runs at 76.30. He hit eight centuries from 25 innings – at an impressive one every three innings. In the Tests he lifted a notch, scoring 660 at 132. His scores were 34, 178, 23 not out, 2, 151 not out, 56 not out, 100 and 116. Without the benefit of hindsight, commentators licked their lips at the prospect of another Bradman-like performer in the Australian line-up. He had batted down the list, often at six, but was expected soon to be number three, the spot secured for 18 years by Bradman.

But any comparisons with Bradman were pushed aside for a time after the more sobering results of the 1950–51 Ashes series in Australia. Harvey was 'serviceable', scoring 362 at 40.22, and without a century. During the series he batted at three for the first two Tests and then was switched to number four for team balance. Lindsay Hassett, a right-hander, was at three. Alec Bedser gave Harvey some trouble with his off-cutter (leg-cutter to the right-hander), which swung in hard on Harvey's pads and stumps, and his stock away-swinger outside off-stump. Bedser was the only bowler to remove him – five times – until Freddie Brown bowled him in the second innings of the Fourth Test. (Bedser was the bête noir of Australia's two great left-handers, Morris and Harvey. The English medium pacer – the best in the world at the time – also gave Bradman trouble in 1946–47 and 1948.)

The following season, 1951–52, Harvey experienced more difficulty still in countering the West Indies' spin twins, Alf Valentine and Sonny Ramadhin. Harvey was terrific at using his feet to the spinners, but these two particular spinners made him feel less confident than usual. They too dismissed him five times between them, and Harvey rarely got into stride for the second successive series. This time he managed 261 at 26.1 at number four. His top score was 74. He relished the next season 1952–53 against South Africa as an opportunity to rebuild his career.

Against a similar attack to the one he demolished away in 1949–50, Harvey, now 24, hit a mammoth 834 at 92.67 in nine innings, batting mainly at number three. His scores were 109, 52 run out, 11, 60, 190, 84, 116, 205 and 7. This performance was so very Bradmanesque that Harvey took an aggregate record from the great Bradman. (Bradman had scored 806 at 201.5 from five innings against South Africa in 1931–32.) Harvey kept up this compelling form on the tour of England in 1953 but more so in the first-class games than in the Tests. Over all first-class matches, he scored 2040 at 65.8 with 10 centuries, which put him up with Victor Trumper and Bradman. Yet in the Tests he was yeoman-like, scoring 346 at 34.6. His top score was 122 at Manchester.

Australia lost the series. Harvey, who had been in the side in the all-conquering tour of 1948 and the team that had held supremacy over England in 1950–51, now had to swallow the bitter pill of defeat in an Ashes series. This defeat was repeated in 1954–55 although Harvey came out of the blocks determined to be part of the team that restored the urn of burnt bails, at least symbolically, to Australia. He smashed 162 at Brisbane and 92 not out at Sydney. After that, he fell victim to the speed of Frank Tyson and the fast off-spin of Bob Appleyard. His aggregate was 354 and he averaged 44.25. Australia lost again. Harvey had experienced the absolute historical highs under Bradman's captaincy. Now he was feeling what it was like to be in a team battling and well below the best, the best being England.

Harvey returned to his best form in the West Indies from March to May 1955 when in just seven innings in five Tests he accumulated 650 runs at an average of 108.33. His scores were 133, 133, 38, 41 not out, 74, 27 and a classic 204 at Sabina Park, Kingston, in the final Test of a series that

Australia won 3–0. In this series he conquered spinners Ramadhin and Valentine. Only Ramadhin got him out – once.

He was in fair touch in the domestic season of 1955–56, scoring 772 at 55.14, with three centuries. This consolidated his position in the squad for the 1956 tour of England, which, in retrospect, he and most of his teammates would prefer to forget. Rotten weather and poor pitches conspired to see him accumulate just 197 runs in the Tests at 19.7. His best effort was a fighting 69 in four hours at Headingley. Harvey (and indeed Australia) was destroyed by Surrey spin twins Jim Laker and Tony Lock. He had now gone through three straight Ashes defeats. The 1956 England team led by Peter May was formidable in both batting and bowling. It looked set for a long reign at the top.

Harvey recovered form in 1956 on the way home against India, hitting 253 runs at 63.25. He had a top score of 140 at Bombay. His confidence against spin was high. He was a natural dancer and loved going to the pitch of the ball, which he could do on true wickets.

The Dutiful Deputy

Harvey, 29, was overlooked as captain in 1957–58 in favour of Ian Craig, 22, and for the first time struggled against South Africa, hitting just 131 at 21.83. Nevertheless, Australia won 3–0 against a strong home team. While Craig also failed with the bat, Richie Benaud, the all-rounder, had a fine series, averaging 54.83 with the bat and taking 30 wickets with his leg-spin at 21.93 runs apiece. When Craig was too ill with hepatitis to play in 1958–59 it was Benaud with his recent record that took over as skipper against May's all-conquering England team. Harvey, who had further lessened his chances by moving to Sydney to take up a job offer, was disappointed but pledged his support to Benaud. They both knew that the Australian team had to be at its best and harmonious to overcome the tourists. Personal accolades and positions were nothing compared to the prospect of beating England, which Benaud's team did, 4–0. Harvey played his part, scoring 291 at 48.5, which was close to his career average. His 167 in the Second Test at Melbourne was the dominant batting performance of the entire series.

On a tour of India and Pakistan in 1959–60, Harvey once more showed his masterful, attacking technique against spin, returning 273 at 54.6 against Pakistan in three Tests, and 356 at 50.83 against India in five Tests. He hit two centuries, but his finest knock was a brilliant 96 on matting at Dacca against Pakistan.

Harvey was less successful in 1960–61 against the talented West Indian line-up featuring Wes Hall, Frank Worrell, Garry Sobers, Alf Valentine and Lance Gibbs. He struggled in three Tests to score 143 at 17.88 in eight innings and was injured in the last two Tests. Australia scraped in for a 2–1 victory. So far, as deputy to first Craig then Benaud, Harvey had been in five successive series victories. The next victory against England in 1961, was most vital to Harvey and Benaud, who had hated the experience of losing the 1953 and 1956 Ashes. Their combined skills and leadership talent ensured a mighty tour for the Australians, who won the Ashes 2–1. Harvey led Australia to victory at Lord's in his one and only chance as skipper when Benaud was out with an injured shoulder. Harvey began the Test series with a beautifully compiled 114 at Edgbaston and scored a commendable series aggregate 338 at 42.25. Only Bill Lawry, the best bat of either side for the series, had a higher aggregate. On tour, Harvey hit five centuries in an aggregate of 1452 at an average of 44.

The Ashes success meant that Harvey had now competed in seven series for four wins and three defeats. He fronted for one more Ashes – in Australia in 1962–63 – and in a dull series drawn 1–1, Harvey was consistent, accumulating 395 at 39.5, including his specialty – one big innings. He hit 154 at Adelaide in a drawn game.

Harvey, 34, retired after 15 years at the top. He was never dropped from the Australian team and only missed selection through injury. His affable manner endeared him to all who played with and against him. In 79 Tests, Harvey scored 6149 runs at 48.42, with 21 centuries, and 64 catches. He played in 306 first-class games, amassing 21,699 runs at 50.93 with 67 centuries.

Harvey pulled no punches during his time as a player. In retirement, he gave his opinion when asked and was always direct and quotable. He left the game playing strongly and was most scathing about players who hung on too long, past their use-by date. He was not a fan of sledgers. Harvey disliked players who in any way, off or on the field, lowered the game's standards or who did not play according to the spirit of cricket. It could easily be said that Harvey was one player who left the game in a better condition than he found it. He expected everyone else to do the same.

In 1998, he toured Australia celebrating the 50-year anniversary of the Invincibles' amazing tour of England. In 1999–2000 he was named by an ACB panel as a cricketer in their best Australian team of the twentieth century.

It is surely the crowning accolade for Neil Harvey to be selected by Bradman, the ultimate peer in the cricket fraternity, to bat next to him in a star-studded Australian team chosen from all players since Tests began.

Bill and Bertha. Bill Ponsford faces up with his heavy bat, known as 'Big Bertha'. Ponsford favoured weightier blades for his mega-scoring.

The Man and Stan. Ponsford going out to bat with Stan McCabe. These two cricketers, along with Bradman and Woodfull, formed the nucleus of a powerful Australian Test line-up in the early 1930s.

Morris's Major Combatant. Here, Arthur Morris is caught in slips off Alec Bedser. The English swing bowler often ended a Morris innings but not before the Australian opener had made more than 60 runs on average.

Head-Steady Hooker. Arthur Morris executes the hook behind square. He was always looking to start the innings well for his country, and usually succeeded in this mission.

Mates and Masters. Bradman goes out to bat with Stan McCabe in England in 1938. Bradman ranked McCabe's 232 at Trent Bridge, Nottingham, in the First Test of the 1938 Ashes as the best innings he ever saw in an Ashes Test.

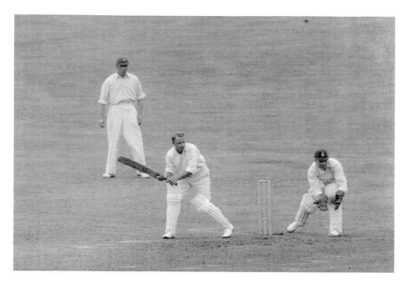

Bradman the Unorthodox. Here, Bradman seems out of position playing a spinner down leg-side. Yet he was not afraid to play the unorthodox shot to break up a bowler's line or the field.

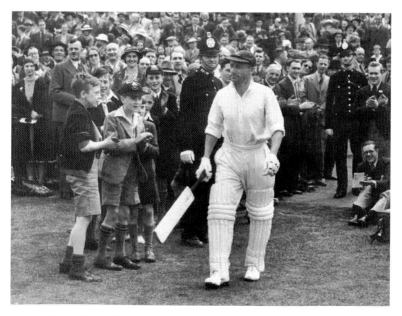

Boys' Own Hero. Bradman walks out to bat in the Leeds Test of 1938. He had scored triple centuries in the corresponding Ashes Tests of 1930 and 1934, but this time settled for 103.

Forearm Force. The strength of Neil Harvey's wrists and forearms are seen here at the finish of a cut shot.

Driving Demonstration. Neil Harvey is all balance and grace as he drives a ball in the nets.

On the Run at Leeds. Charlie Macartney on his way to 115 in the Leeds Ashes Test of July 1921. It was a happy hunting ground for him. In 1926 he scored a century before lunch at the same ground.

Stand and Deliver.
Macartney cuts a four
with his usual
commanding flourish in
the Leeds Ashes Test of
July 1921.

Miller Time. Keith
Miller delivers in the
nets. One of the world's
top all-rounders, he
could deliver pace and
spin with variations.

On Bended Knee.
Keith Miller on one
knee plays an
attacking sweep shot.

A Keeper of Prey.
Tallon shows his
technique as he waits
for a delivery. He had
tremendous spring
behind the stumps
from any position.

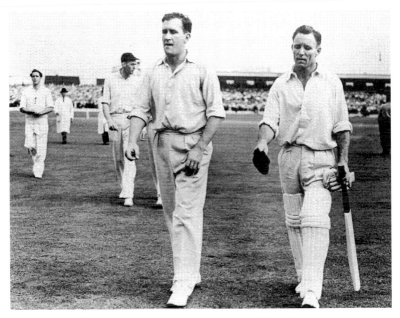

Atomic Ray. Ray Lindwall (right) coming off the field after combat with one of England's finest spinners, Jim Laker. Lindwall was an attacking bat who hit two quickfire Test hundreds.

Ashes Heroes. Richie Benaud (left) and Ray Lindwall. Both were match-winners with the ball.

Lindwall, Windmill. Ray Lindwall gallops in. He had one of the most graceful and rhythmic run-up and delivery styles of all time.

Side On Power. Dennis Lillee, perfectly balanced, delivers with force.

What the Batsman Saw. Dennis Lillee charges at the batsman.

A Swarm of Bees. Long-limbed Bill O'Reilly delivers his leg-break. Don Bradman likened him coming at the batsman to 'a swarm of bees'.

O'Reilly, the Leftie. Bill O'Reilly bowled right-handed, but batted left. He liked to play aggressively and could be a useful bat when he put his mind to it.

'Scarl'. Clarrie Grimmett was known as 'Scarl' after the Scarlet Pimpernel, who batsmen sought here and there but never found easy to fathom as a spinner.

Round-Arm Groucho. Clarrie Grimmett walked in like Groucho Marx, his derrière stuck out, and he bowled round-arm, which, at first brought mirth to spectators. But no batsman who ever faced him thought it an amusing experience.

Well Done Skipper. Australian captain Richie Benaud shakes hands with the captain of England, Peter May, after the Australian victory in the Adelaide Fourth Test in the Ashes of 1958-59.

Spinner With Attitude. Richie Benaud, characteristically with shirt unbuttoned, delivers his leg-break. He was one of Australia's best all-rounders and finest captains.

Read All About It. Australian opener Arthur Morris (left) and England's opener Len Hutton batting together at a match between Authors and England's National Book League at the Westminster School ground, Vincent Square, London in 1956.

CHAPTER 5

THE GOVERNOR-GENERAL

CHARLIE
MACARTNEY

5

(Australia)

27 June 1886–9 September 1958

'Macartney's batsmanship was always personal art, as much so as if he had composed allegros or had woven the Bayeux Tapestry; there was always chivalry in his cricket, a prancing sort of heroism. He lifted cricket far above the narrow circumstances of partisan interest . . .'

NEVILLE CARDUS

I t was a shocking start for Australia. First ball of the 1926 Headingley Ashes Test, stand-in skipper Warren Bardsley was well caught low down at slip by Herbert Sutcliffe off Maurice Tate. England's skipper, Arthur Carr had listened to the locals, who had said that the terrific thunderstorm of the previous day, 9 July, which had flooded the wicket, meant he just had to bowl if he won the toss. Carr and the England selectors examined a dark, damp adjacent strip. It looked every centimetre a typical sticky. He decided to leave out paceman Harold Larwood for spin. Trouble was they examined the wrong strip. The one adjacent to it was used for the Test. Nevertheless, as the much-feared Bardsley trudged his way back to the pavilion, this blunder seemed to have provided a touch of serendipity for England. He was replaced by square-jawed, shortish (5ft 6in/167 cm) Charlie Macartney. The 40-year-old, broad-shouldered all-rounder from New South Wales took block with the touch of arrogance that had earned him the sobriquet 'The Governor-General'. No Australian batsman

149

had seemed more imperious as he strode to the wicket, gloveless but ready to attack. Despite his nickname, the jut-jawed, strong-armed cricketer oozed determination and confidence more in keeping with an all-conquering military commander inspecting the ranks than a desk-bound representative of His Imperial Majesty. Only England's ('Lord') Ted Dexter in the 1960s or the West Indies' Viv Richards in the 1980s appeared to have as much authority.

After he had surveyed the field searching for holes to punch shots through, Macartney faced up in his most erect manner and called down the wicket, 'Let's have it!'.

On the fifth ball of the over, Macartney, on 2, edged one low to Carr at third slip. It was a tough chance. Carr grassed it. Yet nearly two wickets in the first over appeared to vindicate sending the Australians in. Within a few overs, the perspective on the pitch and the decision to bowl changed dramatically.

Macartney, with a mix of his copybook style and something very much more adventurous, began in a rush of cuts, hooks, pulls, drives, and deflections that made fielders look flat-footed. This great batsman left all onlookers on and off the field slack-jawed in wonder. He drove the half-volleys, and interspersed them with eye-popping flicks through slips or down to fine leg. All these audacious shots were intended. Some strokes, such as his late and back cuts, were so cheeky they could be described as insulting to the bowlers. Cricket writer Raymond Robertson-Glasgow saw these strokes as 'so late they are almost posthumous'.

After his one chance on 2, Macartney gave nothing else away while taking risks to score brilliantly. His partner Bill Woodfull began to open out too as he was swept along with Macartney's magic. It was as if Macartney had a bet he would make a hundred before lunch on the first day of a Test. Perhaps he had. Herbie Collins, the skipper, out with tendonitis, was a heavy gambler, as were others in the squad. Had someone offered him good odds? It could have been so. Or maybe Macartney was thinking of the late, legendary Victor Trumper, the only other batsman to achieve such a feat. Trumper had stroked 103 not out in 108 minutes before lunch during the Old Trafford Fourth Test in the 1902 Ashes series. Macartney and Trumper had played in the same teams for five years, 20 years earlier and had been friends. It was one record Macartney would like to have taken, or at least matched.

Whatever the inspiration, he punished George Macaulay's medium-pace swing and off-spin, and the slow left-arm spin from Roy Kilner, and, for a few overs, more left-arm spin from Frank Woolley. Macaulay had, in fact, been the main target. Macartney judged him the most dangerous bowler for the Australians in England in 1926. Macartney asked his captain, Herbie Collins, for permission to attempt to obliterate Macaulay. He succeeded. Macaulay took one for 123 and was never chosen for England again. Only Maurice Tate's medium-pace, naggingly accurate, short-of-a-length deliveries checked him here and there, early in his innings.

Former England captain Pelham Warner watched this innings and observed: 'I have seen all the great batsmen of the last 35 years [1891–1926], and I say without hesitation that I have never seen a greater innings . . . Not even the immortal Victor Trumper could have played more finely than Macartney, and what higher praise could I give to any batsman, Australian or English?'

A half-hour short of lunch, Macartney was full throttle at every delivery. Dancing to even the medium-pace bowlers, his timing was perfect. Macartney reached 40 in as many minutes. Australia was 50. The 100 was reached in 79 minutes. Macartney had 83. He made his century in 103 minutes out of 131 scored. He was the second cricketer to do it. (Bradman would later become the third to reach a century before lunch in a Test. He did it at Leeds in 1930 on his way to 309 not out in a day.) He went to lunch on 112 not out in 116 minutes. After the break the mayhem continued until the score was 235. After 170 minutes Macaulay had Macartney caught by Patsy Hendren for 151. He hit 21 fours. The packed 30,000 crowd rose and applauded him all the way to the pavilion.

Neville Cardus noted: 'For nearly three hours every man, woman, and child had been sitting there, willing prisoners to the spell woven by Macartney.'

Woodfull went on to 141 and Australia 494 (Arthur Richardson 100 run out). England replied with 294 and three for 254. Although the game fizzled to a draw, that innings ensured the Headingley 1926 Ashes Test would forever belong to the dashing Charlie Macartney. His 151 was in the middle of three centuries in succession. He enchanted a Lord's crowd with 133 and then after Leeds walloped 109 at Old Trafford. He was also a prominent bowler in these three Tests, delivering 86 overs. It was an amazing all-round effort, especially for a 40-year-old.

Moore in his Heritage

Charles George Macartney's early penchant for cricket can be traced back to his West Maitland, New South Wales birthplace and home. When he was about five, in 1891, his maternal grandfather, George Moore, an intercolonial cricketer for New South Wales, used to bowl apples to him in his orchard. The family moved to Sydney in 1898, when Charlie was 11. He attended the Fort Street Model School (later to become Fort Street High School), but claimed to have got more cricket development out of long summer days on the Chatswood Oval where he played cricket with his brother. Their dog, Towser, was the fielder. He saved Macartney and his brother much chasing in the heat.

Macartney began by playing in a copybook fashion and was more a defensive player in his teenage years. At 16, he made the North Sydney Club Firsts. At 19, at the beginning of the 1905–06 season, he transferred to the newly formed Gordon Club. His form – more in bowling his left-arm spinners than in batting – was so good in his first year at his new club that he was selected to play for New South Wales against Queensland. He took three for 80. Batting down the order he scored a solid 56. There were no fireworks. His playing style hadn't developed to this point yet. He was consistent with bat and ball through his first season and the next. In mid-December 1907 he was selected to play for Australia against England at Sydney. He was 21 and regarded as a spare-parts all-rounder who could bat anywhere and bowl his slow left-armers, as either a stock or strike bowler.

Macartney showed promise in his first Test. Batting at number seven, he scored 35 in Australia's first innings of 300 following England's 273. He then had England opener Wilfred Rhodes caught for 29 in England's second innings of 300. Australia's captain Monty Noble was impressed with Macartney's first-innings batting form and he asked him to open with Trumper in Australia's second innings. He made just 9. Australia scraped in by two wickets.

Macartney's form was strong enough to allow him to be picked for the Second Test at Melbourne early in January 1908 where he made 37 in an 84-run opening stand with Trumper (49). Batting at six in the second innings, he made 54. England won a thriller by one wicket. He had a good Third Test at Adelaide, scoring 75 (now batting at number three) and 9, and taking two for 49 in England's first innings. Australia won this and the last two Tests when Macartney scored 12 and 29 batting at eight, and 1 and 12 opening again. His best performance for the series with the ball came in the final Test at Sydney when a turning deck helped him to three for 44 and two for 24.

Macartney's figures – 273 runs at 27.30 and 10 wickets at 26.60 – were good by all-rounder standards, and set him up for his first trip to England in 1909. At Leeds in the Third Test in early July, Macartney made an international name for himself – as a bowler. After Australia struggled to make 188 in the first innings, England was dismissed for 182. In conditions conducive to spin, Monty Noble used himself at one end bowling off-spin and Macartney at the other delivering orthodox left-arm. This gave Australia bowling variety with the ball spinning into and away from the batsmen. Macartney projected his deliveries high, inviting batsmen to come to him. He had a rhythmic, slow run-up of six metres and his mighty wrists allowed him to put a great deal of spin on the ball. He had a faster ball that he delivered from the tips of his strong fingers. He could flight the ball beautifully and could vary his pace deceptively. Batsmen, like the great Jack Hobbs, who played the spinners by watching the bowler's hand, reported later that Macartney disguised or hid his intentions with his quicker delivery until it was too late for the batsman to react appropriately. Macartney bowled Hobbs with a faster delivery. Others who played him off the pitch found themselves too late to combat it.

Macartney, in this match, also demonstrated his outstanding control and capacity to land the ball where he wished. He lured the more aggressive John Sharp further and further from his crease and then slipped a faster one past him. Keeper Sammy Carter effected a swift stumping.

While Noble kept the batsmen tied up at one end taking none for 22 off 13, Macartney's mix earned him a fine bag of seven for 58 off 25.3 overs with six maidens. It included Hobbs, Johnny Tyldesley, Sharp and Archie MacLaren. In the second innings he took four for 27 (including Tyldesley and MacLaren again, and Wilfred Rhodes), off 16.5 overs with five maidens, giving him eleven for 85 for the match, his best-ever Test figures. Australia won by 126 runs. It was the first of several games that would go down as 'Macartney's match', but the one and only time in a Test as a bowler.

He made a timely 51 in the second innings of the drawn Old Trafford Test and an accomplished 50 in the final drawn Test at The Oval, but otherwise failed down the order, batting at seven, eight, nine, and then at ten. The era demanded players to be flexible about where they batted, but the chopping and changing didn't help Macartney to sort out his batting strengths. He only averaged 18.50 with the bat but returned the best figures with the ball thanks to his Headingley success, taking sixteen at 16.13.

Hard Home Truths

In Australia's 4–1 victory over South Africa in 1910–11, Macartney was ineffective on harder home pitches, taking just one wicket for 164. He had a shocking time with the bat making 15 runs in five knocks and was dumped after the Third Test.

He took the time out to find form and hammered 119 and 126 for New South Wales against the tourists at Sydney. This was enough for selectors who were looking for an opener. Macartney was reinstated for the final Test of the series at Sydney. He made the most of the chance as an opener, scoring 137 – his first Test century – and 56.

The rest of his pre-war Test performances were modest, with highlights at Lord's during the Triangular Tournament of 1912. First, in June 1912, he played a fine innings against England, when he scored 99 in a drawn game at Lord's against S.F. Barnes, Frank Foster, Harry Dean, Wilfred Rhodes and John William Hearne. In July he took three for 29 against South Africa in its second innings of a game that Australia won by 10 wickets. He also stroked a century in each innings of a match – this time against Sussex – for the second time in his career, and scored 2187 runs at 45.56 in first-class matches for the tour.

In 1913, Macartney went on a cricket tour of North America with Arthur Mailey, Warren Bardsley, Herbie Collins, Jack Crawford, Edgar Mayne and others. Macartney was the star, topping both batting (2390 at 45.92) and bowling averages (189 wickets at 3.81). He also scored most centuries – seven – and the highest score, 186 against a combined Canada and US team.

During the 1913–14 domestic season, Macartney captained New South Wales for the first time, against Tasmania, in an innings of brilliance. It was the precursor to wonderful performances to come. But his maturation as one of the greatest batsmen of all time had to wait.

Macartney had been working on the Sydney wharves until, in 1914, he joined the staff of the New South Wales Railways & Tramways in the Chief Mechanical Engineer's Office at Redfern.

The First World War intervened and Macartney enlisted as a private in the army for four years, attached to the Artillery. He rose to Warrant Officer's rank while serving in France and was awarded the Meritorious Service Medal for his work at the front. Many Test and first-class cricketers were killed during the war.

Test cricket revived in 1920–21 in a five-Test Ashes series in Australia. Macartney was 34. He had missed six years of official top-line cricket at the peak of his powers, but was selected for the First Test at Sydney in December 1920. He returned to the game with a more aggressive attitude to batting.

He opened in the first innings and made 19. New skipper Warwick Armstrong thought Macartney might be better at first wicket down in the second innings. Macartney obliged with a dashing 69 in a 111 second-wicket stand with opener Herbie Collins (104). Australia won by 377 runs as it hit the ground running against its old sporting enemy, which had been hit hard by losses and retirements during the long lay-off from international competition.

Macartney became ill and missed the next three Tests. He was fit enough for selection in the Fifth Test at Sydney beginning Friday 25 February 1921. Among the crowd that day was George Bradman, a carpenter from Bowral, New South Wales and his 12-year-old son, Don, who was witnessing his first-ever Test.

England batted first and made 204. At stumps, Australia was two for 70, with Macartney 32 not out. The next day in front of the Bradmans and 30,000 other spectators, Macartney performed magnificently in making his highest Test score of 170. Watching this, young Don Bradman knew at which level to pitch his dreams of playing for Australia.

Nearly eight decades later, Bradman recalled the innings 'as if it were yesterday'. He remembered it was full of 'delicate leg-glances, powerful pulls, cuts and glorious cover drives'. Bradman would watch cricket for another eighty years and see few innings as fine and comprehensively brilliant as the first innings he ever saw. He returned to Bowral with the next 28 years of his life roughly mapped out for him in his own mind. He was determined to be a Test cricketer and bat just like Charlie Macartney did that hot February Saturday of revelation and inspiration.

Macartney's Massacres

Gone was any caution Macartney had ever shown in his approach to batting. He would be attacking for as long as his Test career would hold out. His remaining years as a cricketer were too short not to be bold. He thrilled English crowds on the Warwick Armstrong-led tour of England in 1921 midsummer when he crashed four centuries in succession. The third century was against Nottingham at Trent Bridge, when he crunched 345 in 232 minutes – the equivalent of just two sessions. It was the highlight of the tour and the 1921 season. Macartney came to the wicket at one for 1 after Bardsley had been dismissed. He began in a blaze of shots and was dropped in slips at 9. It didn't slow him down. Rather, such breaks at this stage of his career were green lights to proceed. Macartney worked on the principle that he would give one chance under 30 in about half his innings. Usually that was it. He felt that if he were spared in those moments, he would bat on as if nothing had happened.

'I hardly ever gave more than one chance before a century,' he said, enforcing his post-war cavalier attitude. That day at Nottingham he slashed, drove, cut, upper-cut, flicked, pulled, hooked and deflected his way to an innings of controlled obliteration. He seemed in charge of every shot.

'This was the most destructive innings I ever saw in England or Australia,' wrote cricket writer Sumner Reed. 'Not Trumper at his brilliant best, not even Bradman in his calculated genius, ever performed with more unadulterated, murderous power and masterful technique – an amazing, combustible mix that exploded over Nottingham.'

After reaching 200 in 150 minutes, Macartney signalled to the pavilion. Nottingham's skipper Arthur Carr asked him if he wanted a drink.

'No,' Macartney replied, 'I want a heavier bat.' Then he added without blinking an eye: 'I'm going to have a dip.'

True to his word, he used the heavier blade to cruel effect, belting the next 100 in 48 minutes.

He reached 300 in 198 minutes – the fastest-ever triple century in first-class cricket. The complete innings included 47 fours and four sixes. Australia made 675 and won by an innings and 517 runs, the biggest Australian win ever recorded in first-class cricket.

Macartney took his century-making mood into the following game, the Third Test at Headingley, making a fine 115. It was the only Australian century of the entire wet 1921 Ashes and his fourth first-class hundred or more in succession. Australia won by 219 runs, giving it a 3–0 series lead. The last two Tests were marred by rain and were drawn. Macartney scored 300 at 42.86 in the Tests, but didn't take a wicket in 13 overs. He scored 2317 runs at 59.41 in first-class matches for the tour and headed the Australian averages.

His left-arm tweaking days were not over. He toured South Africa with Armstrong's team on the return to Australia and played in two Tests. In the opener at Durban he turned it on in both Australia's innings, making 59 and 116 in a drawn Test. In the Third Test at Cape Town, he made 44 and took five for 44 off 24.3 overs with 10 maidens in South Africa's second innings. This effort wrapped up the match. Australia won by 10 wickets.

Macartney's Test figures were the most flattering of his

career to that point: 219 runs at 73.00 and seven wickets at 14.86. But it was to be his last international contest for five years.

Macartney married Nan Bruce, a schoolteacher, in 1922. At the time the *NSW Railway & Tramway Magazine* noted that Charlie was a 'strict teetotaller and non-gambler' who loved his pipe, tennis and music.

Illness kept him out of the 1924–25 Ashes against England in Australia. Yet fair form in the 1925–26 season saw him selected for his fourth tour of England in 17 years in 1926. He was 39 and would turn 40 mid-season. It proved to be his most prodigious and brilliant Test series with the bat. He scored three consecutive Test hundreds. His aggregate for the series (which Australia lost 0–1) was 473 at an average of 94.60, his most lucrative return, especially noteworthy because it was in his last series. Macartney's tour average was 53.82.

His 35-Test career aggregate was 2131 at 41.78 with seven centuries. He took 45 wickets at 27.55.

Macartney continued to play club cricket. At the beginning of the 1926–27 season, he captained a Sydney 'City' team against a Combined New South Wales country team, which included Bradman, then 18 years of age, who made 98. Macartney made 126. This was a significant match of transition – a passing of the golden bat from the most gifted player (along with Trumper) since 1900 to another younger cricketer, who would prove to be the finest of all time until he retired just short of midway through the twentieth century.

Macartney published an autobiography, *My Cricketing Days*, in 1930. He retired from cricket aged just short of 50 years of age, after a tour of India and Ceylon (Sri Lanka) in 1935–36. In first-class cricket he scored 15,019 runs at 45.78, including 49 centuries. He took 419 wickets at 20.96 and took 102 catches.

After retiring he wrote for the *Sydney Morning Herald* from 1936 to 1942. In the 1950s, he worked part time as an amenities officer at Prince Henry Hospital where he would entertain patients with tales of his distinguished cricket career. He died of a heart attack at work in 1958.

Bradman's choice of Charlie Macartney to bat at five in his all-time best Australian XI brings further brilliance to the order. It gives the skipper of this 'team' a genuine option of a left-arm orthodox slow bowler of quality.

CHAPTER 6

THE GOLDEN NUGGET

KEITH MILLER

(Australia)

28 November 1919–

> *'Miller was Australia's greatest all-rounder and with regard to the statistics or ignoring them, he ranks with the best of all time.'*
>
> DON BRADMAN

Keith Ross Miller was a hero and role model to a generation of cricketers and spectators after the Second World War. He matched his film-star looks and athlete's physique with skills fine enough to win Tests with bat or ball, or even simply as an extraordinary fielder. Miller was also admired by the opposition on the field. Batsmen feared him, especially when he decided to bounce them. And bowlers were worried if he was in the mood with the bat to bounce them – balls, that is – over the fence. But there was more to Miller than cricketing heroics. He was a flamboyant individual; a one off, who played the game in a spirit that mixed up the ages. He never bent the rules to his advantage and he played cricket with a brilliance that caused observers like Neville Cardus, who saw the un-folding of cricket's Golden Age early in the twentieth century, to compare him with Victor Trumper. Yet Miller had the devil in him more in keeping with the most in-timidating bowlers of the late twentieth century, such as Dennis Lillee and Malcolm Marshall. With a theatrical flick of his ample black hair, he could move in from any length, run up and deliver ferocious bouncers. They reminded observers of Bodyline – deliveries aimed at the batsmen that could bruise or intimidate. Once, at Nottingham in 1948, he was booed from the ground for his aggression with the ball. Another time, in 1951–52 against the West Indies, he was attacked even by friendly commentators for his overuse of the bouncer in tandem with his speed partner Ray Lindwall. Yet Miller took it all with a nonchalance that had also brought him legendary status in the skies over Germany as a night fighter pilot during the war. He had walked away from a crashed fighter so he was hardly going to be upset by a mindless mob or an offended commentator.

Flying Start

Keith Ross Miller was named after two famous Australian aviators, Sir Ross and Sir Keith Smith, and this 'branding' seemed to destine him. He was always adventurous. Brought up in Sunshine, then Elsternwick in Melbourne, Miller, the son of a factory worker, was an outstanding sportsman at his school, Melbourne High. As a young teenager he was known as a talented, aggressive performer on cricket and Australian Rules football fields. At sixteen he was just over 5 ft (153 cm). He made up for his lack of height with vigour, courage and skill. His ambition was to be a jockey and win the Melbourne Cup. A year later, that dream was in tatters as he shot up to more than 6 ft (183 cm). The nearest he got to racing horses after that was as a punter and a mate of the great Australian jockey Scobie Breasley.

Miller joined South Melbourne Cricket Club at 16. At 18, in February 1938, he made his first-class debut for Victoria against Tasmania (not yet in the Sheffield Shield competition) and scored 181. In the following season of 1938–39, he was on tour for Victoria against Tasmania and Western Australia, the other State not yet with Sheffield Shield status. He scored 125 at an average of 25 with a top score of 55 against Western Australia. Remarkably, the bowling columns under Miller's name remained blank. Selectors saw him as a batsman only, and he felt the same way. In the following season, 1939–40, Miller had his initial taste of first-class Sheffield Shield cricket against Bradman's South Australian side. Miller was caught in slips for 4, and was bowled playing back to Clarrie Grimmett in the second innings for 7. Miller's big moment in a lean start came when he ran out Bradman for 76.

In the return match against South Australia at the MCG a month later, he played easily his best innings for the season, scoring 108 from Victoria's 475 (Percy Beames 104, Lindsay Hassett 92). It, and everything else, was overshadowed by a thumping innings of 267 from Bradman, but Miller now knew he could mix it with the best.

'He did a good job in countering Clarrie [Grimmett] by playing forward,' Bradman noted, 'but still showed fine style off the back foot in shots through the covers.'

The rest of his season was ordinary for Miller. He had trouble with Bill O'Reilly's spin while batting against New South Wales and scored 298 runs at 29.80 for the season. At that point Miller was a player with potential, but the 20 year-old's aspirations to go further were thwarted by war. First-class cricket was shut down after the 1940–41 season. The VFL Australian Rules competition continued and Miller played for the St Kilda club for the 1940, 1941 and 1942 seasons. He was a versatile key-position player, who was equally adept at full forward and full back. The fierceness of the physical contact toughened him and he performed with passion. Miller was a strong mark and a terrific kick. He could send his raking drop kicks and punts more than 60 metres.

Miller's War

Miller applied to join the Royal Australian Air Force and, while waiting for the call-up, he took on several jobs, including one with the Vacuum Oil Company. Early in 1942 he was enlisted as a trainee pilot and just short of his 23rd birthday in November, he was awarded his pilot's flying badge. Early in 1943 he was shipped to New England in the United States. While waiting in Boston for the boat to England for active service he met American Peggy Wagner who he married after the war (they ended up having four sons together). After two months in Boston he sailed to England and was stationed on the South Coast at Bournemouth. One weekend, he travelled to Dulwich, London, for an RAAF cricket match. While he was there, a bar he frequented in Bournemouth was hit by a German fighter-bomber at lunchtime. Seven of his drinking companions were killed. He had little time to dwell on the loss of his friends and his own good fortune, fortune which blessed him throughout the war. He was soon in the air flying combat aircraft and established himself as a Mosquito pilot with the RAF's 169 Squadron. Miller had some narrow escapes, and once walked away from a plane he crash-landed, quipping to those who rushed to his aid: 'Nearly stumps drawn that time, gents.'

Although he survived the crash, Miller paid the price of a back problem that would interfere with his cricket at various times and plague him throughout his life.

He kept his hand in with cricket during 1943 for the RAAF, and turned his attention to bowling. There was no one around quite as good as him, so he kept delivering. Opposition players such as England's star batsman Denis Compton found him particularly quick. In July 1944, still performing for the RAAF on the ground when not on flying missions, he collared a century at Lord's. He fell in love with the high style and beauty of the place.

In early August 1944, he made a dashing 85 at Lord's playing for 'Australia' against 'England'. In 1945, after Germany had surrendered on 8 May, Miller played in five Victory matches between the English and Australian servicemen in the country.

England chose a near Test-strength team with seven who had played Test cricket (including Len Hutton, Cyril Washbrook, Les Ames, Wally Hammond, Bill Edrich, Walter Robins and Doug Wright) and another three in the side who would play after the war. Australia only had one Test player, Lindsay Hassett. Australia began as underdog, but Miller's stylish, responsible 105 in the first Victory match at Lord's went a long way towards Australia's six-wicket win. Miller played everything along the ground except the shot that got him caught behind by Les Ames.

At Bramall Lane, Sheffield, Miller was the fifth bowler used. His speed from different-length run-ups impressed the England players. He riled the Yorkshire crowd by hitting their favourite son Hutton on the forearm. A bumper hit Washbrook in the forehead. The crowd screamed abuse and booed. Cries of 'get off Larwood!' – in reference to Harold Larwood's roughing up of Yorkshire cricketers with his aggressive bowling in the 1920s and 1930s – touched Miller, but not in a negative way. He had played Australian Rules in Melbourne where verbal reaction from crowds was far more emotional. He had long ago learned to shut out the crowd, unless he was inclined to have fun with the spectators. Miller could play them like a harp. It depended on his mood. If he felt like upsetting opposition football fans further he would do this with a hard bump to an opponent. If he wanted them on-side, he might give the crowd a gesture – a bow or a wave. It was different in cricket. He had a new-found aggression and impact with the cricket ball which really pleased him. He delivered a few more gratuitous bouncers. The batsmen were ill at ease. The crowd was restless. Miller, the show-man, who liked to assert his physical presence with the bat, could now do it with the ball.

It was a moment that changed Miller's career and prospects. From the time of that Bramall Lane game, he was a potent weapon as a bowler. The moment was not lost on his skipper Hassett.

At the third Victory match at Lord's, Miller was still used as the fifth bowler in England's first innings. He had use of the old ball, which didn't allow him to extract bounce on a docile pitch. He took the wickets of Donald Carr and John Dewes, two young students in their first representative international matches. Australia's reply was 60 short of England's total. Hassett decided to take a gamble. He tossed the new ball to Miller, who marked out a 15-pace run-up. He now looked more like a serious opening bowler. A flick of his hair indicated he meant business as he charged in to opening bats Hutton and Dewes. He bowled the left-handed Dewes with a very quick out-swinger that pitched middle and took the off-stump. Miller enjoyed himself. In his second spell he removed Edrich before he and Hutton could create a meaningful partnership. Later he dismissed tail-ender Dick Pollard. His figures of three for 42 off 16 overs were not startling. But the reaction to Miller's bowl-ing was. The members in the pavilion at Lord's saw the 25-year-old's pace, and heard of the reaction of the batsmen. They also whispered 'Larwood'. Those with memories stretching back two decades spoke of Ted McDonald, who played for Australia and Lancashire. The Tasmanian-born McDonald, like Miller, was mercurial. Give him an ordinary batsman and he would go through the motions of fast bowling. Put the young Wally Hammond, Jack Hobbs or Bradman in front of him and he, like Miller, would rev up to amazing pace from a medium-length run-up.

England's second innings reached 164, leaving Australia 225 runs to get in 300 minutes. Miller made 71 not out (top Australian score for the match). Australia got the runs in 117 minutes and won by four wickets.

Miller was the best player of the match, excelling with bat, ball and in the field. But his sudden success with the ball proved to be a dual-edged sword. In the fourth Victory match he pulled up with a back muscle strain while fielding his own bowling. Whenever he put pressure on his back there was the danger of a problem first created when he walked away from that plane crash.

Nevertheless, he scored a classy 118 in 177 minutes. The game was drawn. In the fifth Victory match at Old Trafford, Manchester, he batted beautifully again, coming in at four for 66 and smashing 77 not out from the 107 added. A low score 173 never allowed Australia into the game, despite Miller's shining effort. England won by six wickets and squared the series 2–2. Miller headed the batting with 443 runs at 63.29. He took 10 wickets at 27.00.

He celebrated Allied victory in other matches for the RAAF and had one more chance to demonstrate his glittering skills when England played 'the Dominions', also at Lord's, in August. This composite side was made up of mainly Australian and New Zealand cricketers and led by the outstanding, volatile West Indian all-rounder Learie Constantine. Miller played the most dynamic innings of the entire summer. He was 61 not out at the end of Day Two. Those who turned up for the morning of Day Three witnessed an exceptional exhibition of graceful strokes and controlled power-hitting that was unprecedented at Lord's. Miller smote seven sixes en route to 185. One landed on the top tier of the pavilion. Another crashed into Block Q to the right of the pavilion. A third landed in a shrapnel dent in the roof of the broadcasting box above the England players' dressing room. A fourth mighty blow to the Nursery End nearly saw the ball lost.

None of his shots in the evening before or on that explosive morning seemed unplanned. English commentators were at once agog and in love with Miller's display of aristocratic destruction. They reached for superlatives and compared him with Trumper for his dash, and Hammond for his class and strength. It was widely reckoned that his technique, based on front-foot play, especially his cover drive, had something more English about it than Australian. English experts and contemporary players viewed him as a brilliant all-rounder who would be a force in post-war cricket.

Post-War Realities

There was more international cricket for the still enlisted Flight Lieutenant Keith Miller on a six-month Australian Services Team tour from October 1945 of India, Ceylon (Sri Lanka) and finally Australia. At home the servicemen played against the States. Only vice-captain Miller, with an average of 57 in five games, maintained his Victory matches form. He made Australian cricket sit up and take notice with a superb batting performance against a New South Wales team that included the other new 'find' – speedster Ray Lindwall, and wily Bill O'Reilly, who was still a great spinner despite knee problems. Miller thumped 105.

It was an important occasion for Australian cricket. Miller made the acquaintance of Lindwall for the first time. They became close mates and would form one of the greatest opening bowling combinations ever.

The next step was a tour of New Zealand in March and April 1946 by the best Australian team available. Only Hassett and Miller from the Services team made the side, which was led by Bill Brown. (Bradman was still months away from attempting a comeback after illness.)

Miller played his first Test – the only one on tour – at Wellington and acquitted himself well in the damp conditions. New Zealand won the toss and was bundled out for 42 (O'Reilly five for 14; Toshack four for 12). Miller didn't get a bowl but made 30 in Australia's response of eight for 199. Miller took two for 6 off six overs before his back played up again and stopped him from bowling further. New Zealand made 54 in its second innings. Australia's post-war cricket was off to a fine start with a big innings win on tour. In the Australian winter of 1946, Miller, 26, demonstrated his athleticism and versatility by making a comeback for St Kilda football club. He was selected to play for Victoria.

It was in September 1946 that Miller took a boat to the United States to marry Peggy Wagner, the girl he'd met in Boston before his active service in the war. They returned to Australia in October. Miller, as expected, was picked to play for Australia. He made an immediate impact in the First Test of the 1946–47 Ashes series with a driving 79 before falling lbw to fast leg-break bowler Doug Wright. Australia reached 645. Rain produced a sticky and Miller, bowling off-breaks, took seven for 60. Unlucky England made 141 and 172 in its second innings. Miller took two for 17 in support of Ernie Toshack (six for 82) and his left-arm medium pacers. Australia won by an innings and 332 runs. Miller's all-round performance made him the star of the match. He had joined with Lindwall in bumping Australia's main target, Len Hutton. Miller had removed him twice, cheaply, and established an early psychological hold on the

England champion. All the tourists' bats had been un-comfortable against the sustained attack from the two ruthless, yet fair competitors. English commentators murmured the word 'Bodyline'. While technically – in field placing and the bowler's line – it was not the same as the method used by Douglas Jardine in 1932–33 to attack Bradman, the tactic of using the short ball frequently did intimidate the batsmen. In that way the result was the same. Lindwall was usually quicker than Miller and had what batsmen described as a 'throat ball'. His round-arm action slung the short ball so that it reared at the batsman's chest and head. Miller used the bouncer much more. He pounded the ball in from his shortish run and had the bats-man hopping and hurting. Bill Edrich was hit about 40 times in a courageous 105-minute stay at the wicket while making just 16 before Miller had him caught.

This, in addition to the rivalry between the captains of the two teams – Bradman and Hammond – created a tense atmosphere between England and Australia. It was exacer-bated by the incident in which Bradman was 'caught' in slips. Bradman, the two umpires and Lindsay Hassett, who was batting at the other end, thought it was a bump ball. Bradman was given not out. He was 28 and went on to a match-winning 187.

Miller bowled steadily for the rest of the series and ended with 16 wickets at 20.88. His batting was consistent with scores of 79, 40, 33 and 34, 141 not out, 23 and 34 not out. His 141 at Adelaide was one of his finest-ever innings. Bradman spoke of the 'sheer artistry, the classical style and power' of the innings. Only Norman Yardley delivering boring leg theory – balls on or about leg-stump with a defensive on-side field – with his medium-pace trundlers was able to quell him. Miller hit hard and often, but with the polish that had so excited cricket's elite at Lord's.

Miller's series batting average was 76.80 from an aggregate of 384. This put him second in both bowling and batting averages (to Lindwall and Bradman respectively) for the series. He had established himself as a world-class all-rounder in his first Test series, which Australia won 3–0.

He was even more outstanding in the Sheffield Shield season, scoring 667 runs at 133.40. Scores of 188 at Adelaide against South Australia (judged by many as one of the best innings ever seen at Adelaide), 153 against New South Wales at the MCG and 206 not out against New South Wales at Sydney, further set him up as a new batting powerhouse to succeed Bradman when he retired.

Yet it seemed for a while that Miller might be lost to Australian cricket. Now married and with plans for a family, he needed the security of a regular income, a problem common to Australian cricketers until the 1990s. He was offered a contract to play with Rawtenstall in the Lancashire League, but ended taking a job with a Sydney soft-drink manufacturer. This meant he would be playing cricket for New South Wales, but he first represented its Australian Rules team as vice-captain at a football carnival in Hobart during the 1947 winter. He then saddled up for his new State in 1947–48 and played for Australia against India in a five-Test series. He had a less effective second series – scoring 185 at 37.00 with a top score of 67, and taking nine wickets at 24.78. Yet these figures were still more than respectable for a Test all-rounder. He was also a regular partner for the lethal Lindwall.

They were both on the boat to England in 1948, a trip which Miller looked forward to. He had so many wonderful, exciting experiences in his jam-packed three years 1943, 1944 and 1945 that it was more than a nostalgic return for him. He loved England, and had plenty of friends there – many in high places – and innumerable admirers. His reputation as a wartime fighter pilot, brilliant cricketer and convivial 'player' off the field made him second only to team captain Bradman as the man of the summer of 1948.

Miller's mien was always going to be uneasy here and there with the dynamics of Don Bradman's style of leadership. There were differences of temperament and ambition. Miller complained much (in private and later in his writing) about Bradman's fervent desire for victory at everything from billiards to festival matches during the 1948 tour. Bradman thought Miller could have been a better batsman if he had kept the ball along the ground rather than hit sixes. This analysis came in reviewing the 1948 tour. Miller didn't like Australia crushing poor Essex when the tourists scored 721 in a day's batting. He faced one ball and got himself out. Miller also thought Bradman could have given more of a 'go' to the fringe players in the county games on tour. The captain wanted to get through the tour undefeated in all 34 games. Miller thought the final festival game at Scarborough at the end of the season should have been just that, a fun occasion. Bradman looked at Leveson-Gower's XI, noted it was Test quality, and treated the game as almost a Sixth Test by selecting his best team. The game was rained into a draw with Australia in total domination, the way Bradman liked it.

There was a much-discussed incident at Lord's in the Test when Bradman threw the ball to Miller, giving him the opportunity to bowl. Miller, whose back was hurt, tossed it back. The press made a meal of it. Some Lord's members saw it as insubordination.

'Nothing of the sort,' Bradman told me. 'Keith said before the game he didn't think he could bowl. I waited until we were playing just to see if he had changed his mind. It was Lord's after all. He wasn't up to it . . . There was nothing in it [the alleged incident].'

Both Miller and Bradman were terrific fighters. Adverse conditions brought the best out in them. The difference was that in favourable conditions – that is, with Australia on top – Bradman still played in top, or near top, gear. Miller would lose interest. Bradman also had an eye for cricket history and in 1948 was much more a part of it than Miller. Bradman was in his twentieth year as a Test player; Miller, his third.

Critics said Bradman carried 'baggage' from the 1930s – particularly after Australia's crushing defeat by England at The Oval in 1938. Len Hutton then took Bradman's Ashes-record score of 334 and made 364. It was all vividly implanted in Bradman's mind. He injured an ankle in that game and couldn't reply on a ground at which he had already posted massive scores on three tours. Bradman did not want any repeats of that 1938 experience when England piled up seven for 903. He was also conscious that before 1948 no touring team had ever gone through an entire season without a defeat.

By contrast, Miller had been in the Victory Tests in England that had been competitive but were played in an atmosphere of celebration and relief. Nothing was at stake. Miller had come from a cricket wilderness – a short time in first-class cricket in Australia – to perform brilliantly with the bat. Nothing could diminish or hinder his fluent big-hitting. Yet there was not the focus that an Ashes competition provided.

Attitudes and conditions were different on Miller's return in 1948. Commentator John Arlott noted that Bradman ran his 1948 campaign better than any commander had ever run a military operation, although it wasn't with an iron fist. Bradman's one simple dictate was that everyone turn up fit, whenever they were chosen to play. Bradman let the big drinkers party. He was aware he was dealing with ex-servicemen such as Miller and Lindwall who liked to hit the nightspots and enjoy themselves. But when they entered the dressing room and put on the baggy green, he expected them, and the rest of the squad, to be disciplined. He even overlooked some obvious hangovers in the interest of team harmony.

Miller, the dashing war hero, showman, crowd-pleaser, six-hitter, party-lover, did not always sit comfortably in the ranks in the Bradman regime. Yet Miller the fighter, attacking bowler, outstanding batsman, did. He was an integral part of Bradman's grand plan to win big and not see defeat – ever. One key strategy was once more to knock out England's top bat, the stubborn, talented Hutton. Lindwall and Miller were to gang tackle him with bouncers, although Bradman never instructed this. He didn't need to. He had the instinctive measure of both his pacemen. They did not want to be beaten in a Test, or any big county encounter such as a match against Yorkshire, Hutton's home. Miller and Lindwall came out firing and shot down Hutton. He was rendered ineffectual in the eyes of the England selectors, and dropped. This was precipitate and wrong-headed. When that happened, the 1948 Ashes were as good as in the hands of Australia. That key tactic in the campaign had worked. Lindwall and Miller had seen to it.

Miller did not have an outstanding Test series, scoring 184 (top score 74 at his favourite ground Lord's in front of some of his most ardent fans among the members) at an average of 26.29, and taking 13 wickets at 23.15. But his part in nullifying Hutton, and his strong first-class match record (1088 runs at 47.30 and 56 wickets at 17.58) made him an important factor in the all-conquering tour by Bradman's Invincibles. He did have one memorable innings at Leeds in the Fourth Test when he compiled a fine 58 in a 105-run partnership with 19-year-old Neil Harvey (112).

In 1948–49 back in Australia, Miller put in the least impressive all-round season of his career to that point, scoring just 400 runs at 33.33 from 13 innings. Back problems allowed him to take only 11 wickets, but still at the very good rate of 24.09. Despite the figures, there were two top performances with the bat – 109 in the opening game against Queensland and 99 in a hard-fought match against Victoria.

Late in the season, Miller bowled in a testimonial match at Sydney for Alan Kippax and Bert Oldfield, which was Bradman's second-last first-class match. Bradman, now 40, had not played cricket for nearly three months, but still delivered a superb innings, scoring 53 in 65 minutes. He dispatched all bowlers, including Miller who tried to bump him. Bradman responded with what Miller's biographer and close friend, Richard Whitington, called the 'highlight of the whole Bradman knock … a perfectly executed hook stroke'. The ball was hit off his nose to the square-leg fence for four. Miller responded angrily with another bumper, which Bradman let fly over his head. Miller then let go of a third successive short one. It was a poor delivery. Bradman attempted to pull it for four more, but mis-timed it and hit a catch to Ken Meuleman at mid-on. The Sydney crowd booed Miller for his petulance. They felt robbed of a final century from the Don. But Bradman was unperturbed. If anything, he was disappointed that he had been dismissed by a bad delivery that should have been another hit to the boundary.

Through the season, Miller declared he wanted to be considered as a batsman, rather than an all-rounder. The selectors – Bradman, 'Chappie' Dwyer and Jack Ryder – perhaps taking him at his word, dumped him from the squad to tour South Africa in the 1949–50 season. This, in addition to his poor season, may have seen Miller as a fringe selection tipped out by the usual trade-offs between the States. Yet it was an ill-considered non-selection. While Miller's returns had not been great in 1948–49, he was still the best all-rounder in Australia, if not the world at that time, however he viewed himself then or later. The omission stunned the cricket world. Critics attacked the selectors. They searched for a reason for the dumping. It was even rumoured that Bradman had not wanted Miller because he had bowled bumpers at him in the Kippax–Oldfield Testimonial.

When the tour of South Africa began in November 1949, it wasn't long before a thin excuse – a minor car accident involving fast bowler Bill Johnston – was used to invite Miller to join the Australians.

His batting in South Africa was strong and consistent. He made 246 at 41.00 in the Tests, which ranked him sixth behind Harvey, Hassett, Morris, Jack Moroney and Sam Loxton. But he was placed second behind Johnston with the ball, taking 17 wickets at 22.94, which was an important score for the tourists. His partner Lindwall lost form during the series and was dropped after four Tests. Whether Miller liked it or not, he was being forced to perform as an all-rounder. His country needed him.

Burning for the Ashes

England provided the best opposition in that era and when it returned to fight for the Ashes in 1950–51, Miller lifted his rating perceptibly around the country in preparation for the Tests. In the opener against Queensland he smashed 201 with five sixes. Another double hundred – 214 against the tourists – followed this soon after. He was in superb touch with the bat and in six innings ran up 616 runs at 154. It was nigh impossible to keep up such a rate and there were predictable lapses, which carried into the Tests. But by the time he reached Sydney for the Third Test he found that pre-series touch and made a two-stage innings to reach 145. In stage one, he made a slow 96 not out before stumps one day and then clipped another 49 the next morning. He was also in form in the field, taking a brilliant one-hand catch at second slip to get rid of Cyril Washbrook (34) off Johnston in England's first innings. Then, in a devastating spell with the old ball, he mopped up Hutton, Compton and Reg Simpson for five runs inside four overs. Miller finished with four for 37 off 15.7 overs.

Spinner Jack Iverson upstaged him with the ball but his overall effort at catching, bowling and batting would have ranked him as player of the match. The story was similar in the Fourth Test at Adelaide. There were other fine individual performances. Morris got 206, Hutton managed to carry his bat with 156 not out, and Bill Johnston took four for 73 in England's second innings. But Miller chimed in with 44 and 99, and took three for 27, also in England's second innings. Those three wickets came for just three runs to close out the match in Australia's favour. It had four wins to nil, but England won the last.

Miller's series figures were 350 runs at 43.75 and 17 wickets at 17.71. He was the most decisive player in the series. The Ashes, and a wish to do well against England, drew out the best in him.

Miller was similarly dominant during the 1951–52 season's five-Test series against the West Indies. He was hardly out of any game, making an impact with either bat or ball or both. Miller and Lindwall were at different times in the series again accused of delivering a variation of Bodyline. Yet once more the field placings and the line of delivery were not the 'fast leg theory' sent down by

Larwood and Voce in 1932–33. Nor was the bowling necessarily aimed at the body. But there was a surfeit of bouncers and again they were intimidatory. The West Indies, led by its three champion bats – Clyde Walcott, Frank Worrell and Everton Weekes – was never comfortable against them. Miller took 20 wickets at 19.90, Lindwall 21 at 23.05. Bill Johnston's medium pace left-armers (23 at 22.09) completed a trio of speed that left the West Indies with little relief.

Miller was once more consistent with the bat, collecting 362 at 40.22, with a best effort of 129 at Sydney in the Second Test.

Captain Material

Miller, 32 going on 33, was surprised to be named as New South Wales captain from the beginning of the 1952–53 season, replacing Arthur Morris. He was also named vice-captain of the Australian team, and most observers thought he would be the natural successor to Lindsay Hassett. Miller led New South Wales to three Shield wins in four years. He had a poor series with the bat against South Africa in a 2–2 contest, scoring just 153 runs at 25.50. He had problems with off-spinner Hugh Tayfield, who removed him five times in six knocks. Yet his impact with the ball (13 wickets at 18.54) was up to the standard of previous seasons. He injured his back in the Fourth Test and this put him out of action for the Fifth Test. Lindwall was also out injured and the loss of these two key Australian players saw South Africa win by six wickets and draw the series.

Miller was replaced by Morris as vice-captain on the tour of England in 1953, which created the unusual situation of the New South Wales State captain being subordinate to the national vice-captain. Miller's maverick streak off the field seemed to have not pleased the authorities. But he was proving a strong leader of his State. Players such as Richie Benaud, Alan Davidson, Bob Simpson and Ian Craig looked up to 'Nugget', as he was nicknamed. He could deliver telling performances – with runs or an important wicket – at critical moments. Yet Miller was overlooked by the selectors. He didn't help his cause by the ill-timed comments in a book, *Bumper*, released in April 1953 and coincident with the beginning of the 1953 Ashes tour. Miller criticised Hassett's captaincy, saying he was too cautious and 'no lover of criticism'. On the way, he had a more careful swipe at Bradman. These comments were all made public at a time when the Australian team would have wished to appear united. Excuses were made that the comments were more the words of his writer/collaborator Richard Whitington. Yet the book itself carried Miller's name as author. It was not considered an intelligent move by Miller, especially when England sniffed a chance to beat Australia for the first time in England since 1926.

Hassett would pay back Miller later by not supporting him for the captaincy. For now, the skipper was pleased that the star all-rounder seemed to have assumed the role of an unofficial leader of a young, inexperienced side with a responsible, attacking 220 not out at Worcester in the opening match. This set a pattern for the first-class season and Miller produced excellent all-round figures. In 31 innings he accumulated 1433 with a dazzling 262-not-out highest score against the Combined Services (made up of mainly Australian and New Zealand servicemen from the Second World War who had stayed in England) that included a fiery young Freddie Trueman, who was clobbered. Miller's tour average was 51.7. He took 45 wickets at 22.51. Yet in the tighter, more competitive war of attrition in the Tests, he appeared limited. He did manage 55 in the first innings of the First Test at Trent Bridge. He lifted for 109 in the second innings at his spiritual home, Lord's, in the Second Test. But apart from those innings, Miller's efforts were negligible and he was left with 223 runs at 24.78. It was much the same with the ball. Miller took just 10 wickets at 30.30, and turned in only one top display in England's second innings of the Fourth Test at Headingley (four for 63). Overall, it wasn't enough to force victory for Australia, which went down 0–1 in the 1953 Ashes.

After the Ashes loss – the first in 20 years – the critics hoed into the Australians. Jack Fingleton remarked that 'Miller should be allowed to die an honourable death as a bowler' – in other words, not bowl at all.

Hassett retired and that left the Australian captaincy vacant. There were three candidates: Morris, Ian Johnson, who had been left out of the 1953 tour, and Miller, who was popular with the press and the public. Miller would have been a surprise selection given that he had been demoted for the 1953 Ashes tour. The 13 members of the ruling cricket body, the Australian Board of Control – each with a vote – decided on Ian Johnson, which meant that, as ever, a certain amount of horse-trading between the States had gone on.

Another factor that worked against Miller was the fact that the three New South Wales representatives on the ACB may well have been split on who they recommended – Miller or Morris. On top of that, the other 10 members were probably set against any choice of the New South Wales three because of a division caused in a libel case involving Sid Barnes. In effect, the three New South Wales representatives had testified on Barnes's behalf in the case, in contradiction to the rest of the board members. Under those circumstances, the non-New South Wales members were never going to support a New South Wales player for the leadership, especially one who was viewed in a similar way to Barnes – someone they couldn't control and who would not be subordinate.

Hassett also seemed to favour Johnson. He had advised the Victorian off-spinner to improve his rating (which he did by topping the bowling averages in 1953–54), and probably recommended him. Johnson was a good first-class bowling all-rounder, but not in Miller's class. Yet he had the right credentials. His father was a former Australian selector and Ian was a born diplomat able to handle himself admirably in the fringe aspects of cricket, such as speech-making, duties that were always a burden for captains.

Miller was not surprised that he didn't get elected. It was later written in his biography, *Cricket Crossfire*, that he never seriously entertained election, saying he was 'impulsive' and that he hadn't ever been Bradman's 'pin-up'. The Don, he said, rated high when it came to policy matters.

Had Miller overstated Bradman's influence? The Don had just one vote out of 13 and was not chairman of the board when it came to the vote for captain. Furthermore, he was South Australia's representative on the board, and even if he were lobbying against Miller, for which there has never been any evidence, the inevitable trade-off between the States would have further diluted his influence. When there was not one outstanding candidate in the eyes of the electors, a compromise candidate who nobody disliked – Ian Johnson – got the collective nod.

Miller, who had not been one to bow to officialdom, had been ruled out for factors other than cricket reasons, which was not the best way to create team harmony and win Test matches. It meant that Australia lost the chance for exceptional leadership when the country's fortunes were on the wane.

Miller was disappointed, but held no grudges towards Johnson, a good friend, and a former team-mate at South Melbourne and Victoria. In 1953–54, he turned his mind towards New South Wales attempting to win another Shield. In 12 innings, he scored 710 at 71.10, but his bowling figures (16 wickets at 33.75) seemed to echo Fingleton's observation.

Yet Miller, who again grumbled about being seen as an all-rounder, could still perform brilliantly with the ball, although in shorter spells. He showed this in the First Test at Brisbane in the 1954–55 Ashes. He only took one wicket in each innings, but each was an opener – Reg Simpson and Hutton – back in the pavilion cheaply.

Miller was now 35, and with a knee injury to add to his chronic back problem. He missed the Second Test, but came back for the Third at the MCG. In that Test and the Fourth at Adelaide he produced short, penetrative spells that rocked England. He took three for 14 off 11 overs with eight maidens in England's first innings at Melbourne, which reduced the opponents to four for 41. In Adelaide, he cut them down to three for 18 and four for 49 when England was chasing just 97 for victory. His final figures were three for 40.

Miller ended the series with 10 wickets at 24.30, and indicated he was not quite ready for the post-bowling pastures recommended by Fingleton. His batting, however, disappointed. He made just 167 at 23.86. Hutton's team won the Ashes 3–1, thanks mainly to speedsters Tyson (28 wickets at 20.82) and Statham (18 wickets at 27.72). England went home ecstatic. It had unearthed bowlers to more than match Australia's ageing trio of Miller, Lindwall (14 wickets at 27.21) and Bill Johnston (19 wickets at 22.26).

Caribbean and Other Final Challenges

In March 1955, soon after the thrashing from England, Miller was vice-captain of the Australian team in the Caribbean and was faced with new challenges, particularly as a bowler. He and Lindwall would have to take on the strong West Indian batting line-up featuring Worrell, Weekes and Walcott, along with John Holt, Collie Smith and Denis Atkinson. It was to be a big-scoring series and Miller turned it on with the bat, hitting 147, 137 and 109 in an aggregate of 439 at 73.17.

Miller took charge as acting captain in Kingston's First Test on Day Two when Johnson's foot was injured. It was a relatively easy time to take over. Australia had notched nine for 515 (Miller 147, Harvey 133) and the West Indies could only manage 259 and 275. Australia won by nine wickets. Miller took two for 36 and three for 62. It was his one time as acting skipper and it turned out to be very much his match.

He did little in the drawn Second Test at Port of Spain but knocked over three openers at Georgetown in the Third, which was won by Australia. At Bridgetown in the Fourth Test, he made 137 as Australia compiled 668. The West Indies replied with 510, made notable by young Garry Sobers belting Miller for several fours in a bright opening of 43, and 219 by Denis Atkinson, who figured in a record 347 seventh-wicket partnership with Clairmonte Depeiza. Miller was in dispute with his captain on how he should bowl during this stand. Miller wanted to deliver his off-breaks. Johnson wanted speed. It got a little nasty in the dressing room with Johnson offering to settle it 'outside'. It was patched up by the time they returned to their hotel, but the tension highlighted Miller's frustration. He wasn't the leader, but he wanted to do things his way. He considered himself a better skipper than Johnson, and didn't always control the urge to express it.

After the drawn Fourth Test, the teams returned to Kingston where Miller dominated again. This time he made 109 and took six for 107 and two for 58. Australia won by an innings and 82 runs, giving it a great 3–0 victory. Miller took 20 wickets at 32.05 and Lindwall 20 at 31.85. On paper, these figures looked expensive, but considering the batting line-up, they were outstanding. Walcott, for instance, scored 827 at 82.7 with a record four centuries. Weekes notched 469 at 58.63.

It was the last combined effort by Lindwall and Miller that won a series for Australia. Lindwall, struggling against injury in England in 1956, could only take seven Test wickets. Miller, however, showed all the doubters on his last tour that at 36 years of age he could still turn it on with the ball. He saved his best performance for Lord's – something he had done for more than a decade – where he took five for 72 and five for 80. Australia won by 185 runs. It was Miller's best return in a Test, a most satisfying way for him to bow out at the historic arena.

Miller took 21 wickets at 22.24 for the series – the best figures by an Australian. His batting on poorly prepared wickets suffered at the hands of off-spinner Jim Laker (who got him six times in 10 innings), as did all the Australians.

Despite the gloom for the tourists, Miller accompanied Johnson to Buckingham Palace where they received their MBEs. He also mixed with the movers and shakers in British society who had invited him to join them whenever he was in England.

The press now attacked the Australian line-up and called for the sackings of the older players, including Miller. Miller jumped before he was pushed, after playing one more

Test against Pakistan in Karachi in October 1956. Despite his injuries, he was still athletic enough to carry on for a season or two more, but he'd had enough.

Miller played 55 Tests making 2958 runs at 36.98. He scored seven centuries and 13 fifties, and took 38 catches. He captured 170 wickets at 22.98 with seven five-wicket hauls and one 10-wicket match – at Lord's in his last match there in 1956. In first-class cricket he played in 226 matches in which he scored 14,183, including 41 hundreds and 63 fifties. His average was 48.90. Miller took 497 wickets at 22.30.

Miller wrote several cricket books with Whitington from 1950 to 1969, and continued writing about cricket for the *Daily Express* until 1974 when he took a job with Vernons Pools in Australia.

Miller has never lost his love of horse-racing and music. He will be remembered for his exceptional cricket ability, positive approach and fine sportsmanship, which went a long way towards him being one of the most popular men to play the game and Australia's greatest ever all-rounder. Bradman's placement of Miller at number six in his all-time Australian Ashes team is recognition of him as a top-drawer batsman. He formed one of the best-ever opening bowling combinations with Ray Lindwall.

CHAPTER 7

KEEPING AHEAD OF THE REST

DON
TALLON

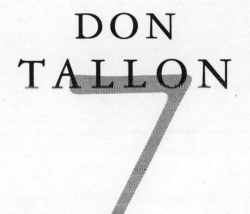

(Australia)

17 February 1916–7 September 1984

'The surname tells everything—
instinctively prehensile,
naturally predatory.'

JOHN ARLOTT

Don Bradman chose Don Tallon as the Australian team's wicket-keeper simply because he was the best keeper he ever saw. Tallon's batting, which had its glittering moments in the 1930s, did not figure in Bradman's thinking. The sole selector always thought it better to have someone of Tallon's brilliance behind the stumps. Tallon's amazing catching, especially down the leg side, and his lightning stumping presented an extra dimension for wicket-taking by a fielding side. Often the wicket taken was credited to the bowler. In truth, it should have gone to Tallon. He could create with a near-impossible catch or with a brilliant stumping. His anticipation, leap and agility made him outstanding, whether taking to pace or spin.

'Oldfield and Healy were both technically the equal of Tallon,' Bradman observed, 'but Tallon covered more territory on the leg-side than any other keeper to fast bowlers. He also made fewer mistakes than anyone else. Tallon had the gift of anticipation, or at least he made it seem like a gift. He could pull off the spectacular, near-impossible dismissal that would change the course of a game.'

Tallon perfected a leg-side movement copied by Wally Grout and Godfrey Evans whereby he positioned himself to take the fine leg-glance in his right glove, while still keeping the slim option of catching a thick glance with his left glove.

Australian Test bowler Alan Davidson judged Tallon to be as far ahead of all other keepers as Bradman was ahead of other batsmen. Even his keeper peers acknowledged it. England's Godfrey Evans, who entered the Test scene at about the same time as Tallon, saw him as an inspiration and the most accomplished gloveman of all time. Lindsay Hassett, who captained him near the end of Tallon's career, said he had the fastest reflexes of all keepers. 'No Wild West gun-man was quicker on the draw when it came to a stumping. But Don personified "quick". He was tall for a keeper and lithe and had the mobility to move into position with speed. I don't recall his feet in my mind's eye, but they must have been dainty. His movements were always swift. He used to skip to keep fit and I'm told he was good on the dance floor.'

The Prodigy

If there was a standout prodigy in cricket it was Donald Tallon. At 12 years of age he volunteered to keep wickets in a match for Bundaberg, his home town in country Queensland, so he could get into the game. He rarely had the gloves off over the next quarter-century. It helped that Don had three brothers (older brother Bill went on to play for Queensland) and had the benefit of many games in the backyard on rough pitches. These games continued summer after summer until he was playing grade cricket. His father Les, a boilermaker by trade, and a one-time cricket-ground curator, often joined in and offered coaching advice. He was authoritarian, but not too rigid in his observations to recognise Don's skills. Les stopped his son playing rugby league so that Don would concentrate on cricket. He captained a Queensland schoolboy team at 13 and, about this time, his batting began to attract attention. He was a forceful driver, who could play all the key attacking shots.

Tallon became Bundaberg's regular keeper after taking part in a match against a touring New South Wales State team in April 1931 that was led by Alan Kippax. Bradman, 23, was part of the New South Wales team but was out with a foot injury for the Bundaberg match.

'I was in hospital and did not see Don play,' Bradman recalled, 'but I heard very good reports about his ability from Kippax. He was clearly, at 15, a player of enormous potential.'

Later, during the 1931–32 season, Queensland selectors were so impressed with Tallon that they trialled him at the Gabba against State bowlers, including the Aboriginal speedster Eddie Gilbert, who was then regarded as the quickest bowler in Australia.

Tallon had just turned 17 in February 1933, when he played against the touring England team at Toowoomba and had the honour of being bowled for 2 by Harold Larwood, who had just won the Bodyline Ashes for his team. Tallon showed his skill with the gloves by stumping England's Herbert Sutcliffe off a leg-spinner. The batsman's back foot slid out of the crease for a fraction of a second. Tallon whipped off a bail.

In 1933–34, he made the Queensland State team while still aged 17 and a year later toured the southern States. At 19, in 1935–36, while playing against a touring Marylebone Cricket Club (MCC) side, Tallon took six wickets in an innings and demonstrated a facility for keeping to leg-spinners when he stumped five victims. His keeping was displaying increased confidence with every game, as was his batting.

More important for Tallon's career was his performance in a State game against South Australia at Adelaide, played over Christmas 1935. South Australia amassed eight for 642 declared. Bradman, back after his near-death experience in England when ill with peritonitis, showed the cricket world that he was back as a force by smashing the Queensland attack for 233 in 175 minutes. Tallon could not recall any delivery going through to him from Bradman who hit every ball he faced. Bradman praised Tallon's keeping effort, in which he conceded just seven byes. Queensland replied with 127 and 289 and, in its second innings, Tallon batted with style and force to post 88, thus displaying his all-round talent to the most influential person in Australian cricket.

Suddenly, at the end of the 1935–36 season, everything gelled for Tallon. He smashed a magnificent 193 in 187 minutes against Victoria at the Gabba. In a formidable, all-round effort, he also took five Victorian wickets in an innings.

His efforts against South Australia and Victoria played a big part in getting Tallon selected for a Test trial at the beginning of the next season, 1936–37, between the team captained by Victor Richardson that had been successful in South Africa, and a side led by Bradman. Significantly, Bradman chose Tallon to bat at number five and six in the two innings. It was an early indication of Bradman's opinion of Tallon's batting prowess. But the keeper missed a golden opportunity when bowled for 3 after batting for a short time with Bradman, who was alight in a glorious knock of 212. Bert Oldfield was still the keeper of choice for the national team but Tallon was clearly now in contention for Test selection. He hit 100 at the Gabba against New South Wales in the first State game of the season a few weeks later, in a game notable for the exceptional keeping of Oldfield, who did not concede a bye in either innings. Tallon was challenging with the bat but was never going to succeed Oldfield while he was keeping so proficiently. Yet, in

November 1936, Tallon was chosen to play under Bradman in an Australian XI against an MCC XI. Tallon kept efficiently and made a creditable 31 in an Australian score of eight for 544 declared. Again, it wasn't quite enough for him to force the issue with Oldfield, who was never going to bat as well as his young rival. Tallon missed selection and Oldfield kept throughout the Tests. Nevertheless, the youthful Tallon, still only 20, continued to impress around the country with his keeping and batting. He hit three centuries for the season and nearly made it four when he was removed for 96 against Victoria at the Gabba in mid-January 1937. A month later, the Queenslander had one more chance that season to impress Bradman, in a State game at Brisbane. Tallon made just one dismissal, but the right one – Bradman stumped for 123. Tallon batted well again in front of the Don in a cameo knock of 48 in an hour.

Unfortunately, in the following season 1937–38, he could not repeat his batting form and this told against him in the selection of the two keepers to go to England in 1938. Had he batted with the same force as in the 1936–37 season, there is little doubt he would have toured. Oldfield, at 43, was considered too old. That left Tallon, Ben Barnett of Victoria and Charlie Walker from South Australia. Not for the last time, Bradman was outvoted at the selection table. He opted for Tallon and Walker but horse-trading between the States saw a compromise selection of Barnett and Walker.

The omission brought greater determination into Tallon's play the following season, 1938–39, when he began it in November with impact by taking six wickets – three stumpings – in an innings against New South Wales. In December, in Sydney, he proved how great he could be by taking six wickets in each New South Wales innings, giving 12 for the match. This equalled a world record held by

Surrey keeper Edward Pooley since 1868. Tallon caught nine and stumped three.

In February 1939, he snared seven in an innings (four stumpings) against Victoria at the Gabba, equalling another world record. These mighty performances, along with the occasional explosive batting effort, placed him ahead of all other keepers in Australia. In six matches he made 34 dismissals – 21 catches and 13 stumpings – all, it was noted by cricket writer Ray Robinson, at 'camera-shutter speed'. Tallon's movement began before he took the ball, his gloves heading towards the stumps in one swift operation. His eye was so good that often just one bail would go flying. Yet he was too quick for scorers. On several occasions in 1938–39 they had to ask umpires the mode of dismissal – whether it was because of being stumped by Tallon or bowled by medium pacer Geoff Cook.

Tallon, 23, was a near certainty to play for Australia in the next scheduled Ashes series in Australia in 1940–41. War intervened and Tallon joined the army and so was robbed of his greatest years of cricket. He was rarely able to rise to quite the dizzying heights of the pre-war days with either bat or gloves. Yet he was still ahead of the rest of the world's keepers and was an attacking bat, as he demonstrated in Melbourne during the Third Ashes Test of 1946–47. It was there that he dashed off 92 in 105 minutes. He and Lindwall (100) thumped 154 in 87 minutes in a sustained burst of power-hitting rarely, if ever, repeated in Test cricket.

Stomach ulcers hampered Tallon. In 1943, he suffered from a life-threatening ruptured duodenal ulcer. He was discharged from the army and had to wait another two years before resuming big cricket. He toured New Zealand with Bill Brown's team in March/April 1946. Tallon made a stumping, took a catch and made 5. It wasn't sensational on paper, but newspapers reported his performance as admirable.

After a long wait he was on his way as a Test player. England toured Australia in 1946 and he had his first encounter with the Ashes opponents while captaining Queensland at the Gabba. He, and leg-break bowler Colin McCool, ambushed Hammond's men. McCool took nine wickets. Tallon helped in six of them – four stumpings and two catches. He was, from that moment, a psychological force in the Ashes. The England players had heard much about him. Now they had experienced his genius behind the stumps. It was daunting. They were not just facing the bowler but also a keeper with an aggressive demeanour, who appealed loudly and patrolled the stumps like a hungry panther at close quarters.

'It did feel like Don was literally breathing down my neck,' Denis Compton remarked, 'especially with McCool bowling. You had to block it out of your mind or it would affect your stroke-play.'

Tallon further demonstrated his freak skills in the Second Test at Sydney. During the lunch break on Day One, Tallon told Bradman he thought he could get Len Hutton – 39 not out – caught down leg-side. McCool's stock leg-break broke to the off so he was less likely to induce a nick. Bradman brought on off-spinner Ian Johnson, with the instruction to push for a catch down leg-side, which meant the precision placement of a ball on middle stump, breaking slightly to leg. Johnson obliged. Hutton played back and glanced, expecting to look round and see the ball on its way to the boundary. Instead he saw Tallon running towards the square-leg umpire, appealing to the other umpire. He had snaffled the catch.

'I was positioned to see the ball slide off the bat,' Tallon told a reporter after the game, making the toughest of dismissals sound routine, 'and I caught it.'

The second outstanding dismissal came when standing to McCool. Compton went to drive a leg-break outside off, but misjudged it and edged it to Ian Johnson at slip. The ball slapped him in the chest and headed towards the grass. Tallon threw himself backwards and just managed to slide a glove under the ball to take one of the great Test catches of all time. Witnesses doubted that anyone else but Tallon could have moved with such alacrity and precision.

Despite his ulcers, which upset him on some days, Tallon, at 30 years of age, was a success in his first Test series, making 20 dismissals, then an Australian record. It would never make up for the lost years, but Tallon was at least satisfied he had performed at the highest level with great credit. Yet he was hungry for more. There were few laurels to rest on. Although a man of few words – or more like 'mumbles', as room-mates recalled – Tallon made it clear that he wanted to be around at the top for as long as possible.

He was unassailable in 1947–48 in all five Tests against India but his batting fell away.

'He lost confidence in his ability to drive forward of the wicket,' Bradman recalled, 'and this diminished his opportunities to score. But it still remains that he was a very good bat indeed before the war.'

Tallon's great keeping in 1948 went a long way towards the Australian team's invincibility. On three occasions he took sensational catches that influenced the course of the Tests. The first came in the Second Test at Lord's. Ernie Toshack was bowling his medium pacers to Cyril Washbrook. Tallon was standing up at the stumps. Toshack bowled a full toss. Washbrook went onto the back foot, swung at it and got an inside edge. The ball headed towards Tallon's boots. He got both gloves under the ball at bootstrap height and held it. Bradman called it 'miraculous' and remarked at the time: 'Wicket-keepers are not expected to perform miracles.'

The second marvel was a low-down catch on the off-side off Lindwall to dismiss George Emmett for a duck in England's second innings of the Third Test at Old Trafford. Bradman said that this was one of the best of its type ever executed.

The most astonishing catch of the series came in the Fifth Test at The Oval, during a devastating spell by Lindwall. He had all but cleaned up England except for Hutton, who had played a brilliant, rearguard cameo of 30. He again tried a leg-glance, this time off Lindwall. All eyes looked to Neil Harvey, fielding on the boundary at fine leg, as Tallon jumped three metres to his left and scooped up a catch on the leg-side, a few centimetres off the grass.

He made some errors – a couple of dropped catches he should have taken – but these didn't amount to much. *Wisden* selected him as one of its five cricketers of 1948. It was a peak period in his career.

Tallon demonstrated his prowess with the bat in a Bradman Testimonial at the MCG in December 1948. Tallon played in Bradman's XI against Hassett's XI. On the fourth day, Bradman's XI was seven for 210, still 192 runs short of victory. Tallon let loose and smashed his way to 55 in no time. With one hour to go in the game and 101 needed for victory, Tallon proceeded to play what Bradman described as his best-ever innings. He crunched his way to 91 out of 100 and was left on 146 not out when play ceased. The match was a tie.

Tallon played Test cricket for another five years but by 1953 had trouble holding his place in the Test side. Apart from his ulcers, he had some trouble with deafness, and was branded with the harsh, stark nickname 'deafie'.

Still, there were flashes of genius with both gloves and bat. He hit a thrilling 77 at Sydney in the Third Test of the 1950–51 Ashes.

Tallon played 21 Tests. He kept in 41 innings and made 58 dismissals, taking 50 catches and making eight stumpings. He batted 26 times, scoring 394 runs at an average of 17.13. Bradman ranked him as the best keeper he had seen and, despite his low batting average, rated him as second only to England's Les Ames with the bat. Bradman thought more highly of Tallon as a batsman than he did of Rod Marsh or Ian Healy. Bradman watched on television Adam Gilchrist's magnificent 149 not out in the Second Test of the 1999–2000 season against Pakistan and remarked that if Gilchrist kept up that form, and an average of fifty or more, he would eventually take the number-one spot in terms of batsmen/keepers, in his opinion. But Bradman still preferred Don Tallon, above all these other players, to be in his all-time best Australian side in Ashes cricket.

CHAPTER 8

THE NATURAL

RAY
LINDWALL

(Australia)

3 October 1921–23 June 1996

'No one ever had better rhythm . . . Ray didn't rely on speed all the time, and varied his deliveries intelligently.'

DON BRADMAN

Australian bowler Ray Lindwall had summed up Denis Compton, England's star bat of 1948, as incapable of avoiding the hook. Compton was courageous and loved to get on top of speedmen who bowled bouncers by smashing them to the boundary. In the final Test of the season at The Oval, Lindwall delivered him a short one, soon after he arrived at the wicket at two for 10. Compton, who had been waiting for it, looked most uncomfortable, as he seemed to be trying to fend off the ball rather than play a positive stroke. The force of the delivery knocked the bat out of Compton's hands and deflected high beyond the slips, but short of a pouncing Lindsay Hassett at third man. Len Hutton, batting at the other end, called for the run. Compton fumbled for his bat while watching Hassett as he gathered in the ball. Then Hassett did an honourable thing by not hurling in the ball until Compton had retrieved his bat and was on his way. This noble act from Hassett, even unusual in cricket in 1948, saw Compton scamper safely to the other end. Lindwall stood, hands on hips, mid-pitch. What he thought of this stolen chance to get rid of the English champion was never recorded but, in the next over to Compton, he let him have another bouncer. This time the batsman swivelled perfectly into position and hit the ball sweetly and square, rolling his wrists enough to keep the ball low but close in. Arthur

Morris moved a few paces right and snaffled a terrific catch – one of the best of the entire season. Lindwall, Bradman's main strike weapon, had removed England's key batsman in the series by out-thinking him. England was three for 17. Keith Miller started the bowling collapse after the game had been rain-delayed half an hour by bowling new man John Dewes for 1. It was the toughest of starts for the Cambridge and Middlesex opener, who had to face one of the finest line-ups in history in the Lindwall, Miller and Bill Johnston, the swinging left-armer, combination. Bradman rang quick changes to find the right formula on a damp track. Johnston took Miller's lead by removing Bill Edrich who was well caught by Hassett when going for a hook. Now Lindwall had struck with the most important wicket. He was fired up. Bradman could claim to have played a part in Compton's fall by remembering a similar stroke on a previous occasion. Morris had been placed in the appropriate spot for the catch.

Miller then had Gloucestershire's Jack Crapp caught behind for a duck after 20 sorry minutes. England was four for 23, in a series already lost. Len Hutton was the home team's only hope. He was 17 not out and rock-solid at lunch. England was four for 29, with skipper Norman Yardley on 4. Not long after the break, Lindwall bowled Yardley with a sensational swinging yorker that Bradman branded 'unplayable'. England was a miserable five for 35. Lindwall's pace and accuracy impressed Bradman.

'Ray was particularly on song,' he recalled, 'although the wicket was giving him much help. I can't recall a loose delivery in his spells. He had the most beautiful rhythm in his delivery in which he turned side on, without any jerking break in the action. A key to his success was his ability to vary his speed of delivery without any discernible variation in his action. Everything worked perfectly for him as he built to a peak pace. He caused concern and forced players into errors.'

Johnston then removed Glamorgan all-rounder Allan Watkins, leaving England six for 42. Lindwall then went into overdrive, yorking Alec Bedser (0), Godfrey Evans (1) and Jack Young (0). England was nine for 47. Lindwall had five. He had not bothered with any short stuff at the tail. It was a waste of energy and time. Only Hutton had stood strong against the onslaught. He hit Lindwall high and straight for four, the only one for the innings. It took something special to remove him, not from the bowler but from the brilliant Don Tallon behind the stumps. Lindwall strayed a fraction to leg. Hutton (30) leg-glanced it fine. Tallon dived left and scooped it up with a fully extended left glove.

Former Australian opener Jack Fingleton, then covering the series as a journalist, regarded it as the best wicket-keeping catch ever. Bradman said he had never seen a better leg-side catch. Such support in the field allowed Lindwall to claim six for 20 off 16.1 overs. His post-lunch figures were 8.1 overs, four maidens and five for 8.

England was all out for just 52. Australia went on to win by an innings and 149 runs, Lindwall taking another three for 50 in England's second innings.

'It was the best I ever saw Ray bowl,' Bradman said of Lindwall's effort in England's first innings. 'His pace was tremendous. I had never seen a more sustained top-level performance by a fast bowler.'

Lindwall versus Larwood

Lindwall modelled himself on English cricketer Harold Larwood. He copied his delivery style, even to the point of noting how Larwood slid the inside of his trailing right foot smoothly at the point of delivery a moment before transferring weight to his left leg. Lindwall also mimicked the way the Notts star looked over his left shoulder at the batsman. Lindwall made it deliberate and distinctive, and was not aware when he first tried it at age 11 that this action further balanced him perfectly at the point of weight transference from right side to left, at the point of delivery. The harder he hurled his body into the movement, the more Lindwall looked like Larwood, in the revolution of his right hand that began close to his left buttock and ended near his left knee. It felt right to the young Lindwall, and the powerful propulsion got immediate results for him as a child. He worked on the Larwood style with variations from then on until it became his own. The most obvious variation was the murderous short ball. It hardly ever sailed over a batsman's skull. Most times it screamed in at high chest or throat level, making it often impossible to play properly with a defensive or attacking stroke.

Bradman considered Lindwall a better bowler than Larwood. The Australian could generate pace and accuracy more consistently than the Englishman. Lindwall had a grip on more variations than Larwood, demonstrating these with a prodigious late out-swinger early in his career, an inswinger mid-career, the capacity to change pace, a fearful bouncer and perhaps the best yorker of all. While statistics, if taken alone or out of context, may be misleading, the numbers here seem to suggest Lindwall's superiority. In 21 Tests, Larwood took 78 wickets at 28.35. Remove his Bodyline figures and his returns of 45 wickets at 37.26 for three-quarters of his Test career give a more realistic reflection of his effectiveness. In 61 Tests Lindwall took 228 wickets at 23.03.

Master Bowler

Lindwall, 180 cm (5 ft 10.5 in), developed his tactical skills to be a master bowler. He knocked over the stumps or gained lbw decisions in 60 per cent of his 794 first-class wickets (at 21.35). This demonstrated not only his accuracy, but his ability to deceive the batsmen with swing and deliver a slower ball, which came out as exactly the same action as his bumper. It was not all brute force with Lindwall. The threat of the short delivery kept a batsman on edge, rendering him unsure and likely to do something precipitate. Another strength was his ability to move the ball in the air – and very late.

Underlining all this was his superb fitness. Lindwall was a fine all-round athlete, excelling at rugby league, swimming, golf and athletics. His rugby experience taught him how to nurse and carry injuries, such as groin tears. Lindwall entered several Tests with a niggling groin injury, but only Bradman, when he was Lindwall's captain, realised he was in trouble. By sheer will, the bowler covered for it by adjusting his run and follow-through. Bradman never reprimanded him or left him out of the Australian Test side on the suspicion that he was not fit. He always took Lindwall at his word that he was fit enough to perform well for his country.

Lindwall learned never to mention injuries to anyone. Rumours spread and selectors heard them. Instead, he just worked harder at his recovery and general fitness. He regularly used a makeshift home gym in his garage and was a jogger in the 1940s and 1950s, long before it was fashionable. This dedication allowed him to stay longer in the game at the top than any genuinely quick bowler in history. Lindwall returned to the Test team in the 1958–59 Ashes at the age of 37 years and broke Clarrie Grimmett's Australian wicket-taking record. Lindwall was the first fast bowler to 100 wickets, then 200. His survival so late in his sporting life was all the more remarkable because he had contracted malaria and hepatitis during the Second World War. His first Test break came late at age 24, which was not late for a quick of any era, but the war had robbed him of five years of cricketing development. The malaria was debilitating. It came in waves that weakened him. Yet Lindwall fought on.

Raymond Russell Lindwall was brought up in Sydney's Hurstville and played cricket on a road with a garbage tin as wickets, just like countless Aussie kids in suburbia in the 1930s. The Marist Brothers at two Catholic colleges helped him refine his bowling. He was also a fine attacking batting prospect. Lindwall joined St George, which was captained by Bill O'Reilly. He was ordered to bowl fast and, by implication of his lowly place in the batting order, was directed to concentrate on his bowling. Lindwall fought for recognition with the blade, but was more or less ignored early at St George. O'Reilly wanted a paceman and that was that.

Lindwall, at 20, made his State debut against Brisbane in November 1941 and delivered nothing to suggest greatness to come. The Japanese bombed Pearl Harbor in December and the Second World War widened to the Pacific. Lindwall joined Army Signals and was part of the action in New Guinea. He came back to play his fourth game for New South Wales at the end of the war against Victoria at the Carlton ground. Encouraged by skipper O'Reilly, he let rip with several bouncers that shook the Victorians in their second innings. Observers said that they hadn't seen anyone quicker since Larwood, 12 years earlier. Lindwall, at 24, was suddenly a name whispered in cricket circles as something special. He was selected for his first Test against

New Zealand at Wellington and took a wicket in each innings. In 1946–47, he lived up to expectations in his first Ashes series, in combination with Miller, taking 18 wickets at 20.39, the best figures for either team. Lindwall was always a threat to England's batting line-up. He unsettled them all, including their key bats Len Hutton and Denis Compton. Lindwall took three wickets in four balls in the Fourth Test and secured seven for 63 on a perfect Sydney pitch in the Fifth. He also scored 160 runs at 32. This included a dashing century at the MCG in the Third Test. While O'Reilly's directive to concentrate on bowling proved the right one, Lindwall always displayed a fine technique with the bat.

He maintained his form in 1947–48 against India, taking 18 wickets at 16.89, which was once more the best of the series. In 1948, under Bradman's shrewd leadership, Lindwall reached his peak taking 27 wickets in the Ashes at 19.63, which were the best figures for the series for the third successive time. Lindwall's back-foot 'drag' looked like being a problem in England but Bradman made sure that his main striker complied with the law early in the tour. The issue of his cribbing down the pitch was dissolved by the time the Test series began. Bradman nursed Lindwall through the season and called upon Miller and Bill Johnston to support him. The captain had an intimidatory speed combination for the first time in England, in Lindwall and Miller. Bradman directed them well but left both men to their own devices, especially when it came to the contentious use of the bouncer. Only once, and not in a Test, did Bradman ask Lindwall to not deliver a bumper. The opening bowling combination proved both too skilled and lethal for England. Lindwall took 86 wickets at 15.69 on the 1948 tour, and Bradman argued that he was the key bowler of either side.

'After 1948 and his other series performances in the 1950s, I ranked him ahead of Ted McDonald,' Bradman told me. 'Ray didn't rely on speed all the time, and varied his deliveries intelligently.'

His outstanding attribute, Bradman noted in his autobiography, was his control of direction, which he ranked better than any other bowler he had seen. His length left little to be desired. Bradman admired his stamina and regarded him as a top-class fielder. He also thought much of his batting and suggested he could have made the Test cricket team for that alone had he concentrated on it.

Lindwall's reputation was so strong at the end of the 1940s that when he toured South Africa in 1949–50, the home team's batsmen prepared for him by practising against baseball pitchers. Lindwall, however, struggled with injury and hardly delivered in anger. Yet he still took 12 wickets at 20.67, which were figures only bettered by the underrated Bill Johnston, who took 23 wickets at 17.04.

Lindwall remained below peak fitness against Freddie Brown's touring England team in 1950–51, but still played in all five Tests and snared 15 wickets at 22.93, backing up Bill Johnston and spinner Jack Iverson. Lindwall was devastating at home against the West Indies in 1951–52, taking 21 wickets at 23.05, and South Africa in the following season, when he captured 19 at 20.16. There was no falling off of his form against England in the Ashes of 1953. He and Miller turned on the fastest opening combination in tandem seen for years at Lord's. Lindwall took 26 wickets at 18.85 despite being overshadowed by the brilliance of Alec Bedser, who took 39 at 17.49.

Lindwall was still very quick when he wished to be. But by the mid-1950s he was relying more on guile than ever before. He developed his skills and was still a menacing bowler in the Ashes of 1954–55 (when England retained them after their long-awaited series win in 1953). This time he took just 14 at 27.21 in four Tests after being hampered by hepatitis. He missed one Test through injury but he was still effective, dismissing Hutton twice and England's new star Peter May four times. Lindwall, 33, conserved his strength on a tour of the Caribbean in early 1955. The wickets were decidedly in the batsman's favour yet Lindwall lifted and took 20 at 31.85. His higher than usual run rate for each wicket reflected the condition of the wickets and the brilliant batting. Lindwall also batted outstandingly, scoring 187 at 37.40, including a dashing innings of 118 at Bridgetown, Barbados. Older, wiser and with leg injuries, he could still claim to be a top all-rounder.

His groin problem caught up with him on the Ashes tour of 1956 when he missed almost two complete Tests and only took seven wickets at 34. On the way home, the squad competed in Pakistan at Karachi in October 1956 when Lindwall turned 35 years old. The game was on matting and Lindwall felt there was not much reason to turn up. It was only fit for spinners. Australia lost by nine wickets and then moved on to India. Lindwall got the chance to captain Australia for the first and only time when Ian Johnson fell ill in Bombay. Lindwall led well, despite injuring his knee. He showed his fortitude by carrying the injury and taking two for 100 over the two Indian innings. He scored 48 not out in Australia's only innings. The game was drawn.

The critics attacked the failed Australian side that went down 2–1 in the Ashes. They called for sackings, Lindwall included. Miller saw the signs and retired. Ian Johnson, the skipper, also left big cricket and handed the leadership to young Ian Craig. But Lindwall, 35 at the commencement of the 1956–57 season, made no noises about bowing out. He recovered from injury and maintained his standard in domestic cricket, taking 27 wickets at 23.74 and making

243 runs at 27. He was shocked when omitted from the 1957–58 tour of South Africa, but made an impressive comeback late in the 1958–59 Ashes against England, breaking Clarrie Grimmett's record of 216 wickets. He took just seven wickets at 29.86 but his impressive season figures of 40 wickets at 20.55 were enough to get him a final Test tour of India and Pakistan at age 38. He lifted his wicket tally to 228 at 23.03. He hit 1502 runs at 21.15 and this made him the first player ever to score 1500 runs and take more than 200 wickets in Tests.

Lindwall played in 228 first-class matches, scoring 5042 runs at 21.82, including five centuries. He took 794 wickets at 21.35. Lindwall was a Test selector for a short time in the early 1980s. He also coached. He and his wife Peggy ran a florist business in Brisbane for many years.

Bradman ranked Ray Lindwall as one of the two best Australian pacemen of all time. He forms part of a formidable line-up of speedsters in Bradman's team alongside Lillee and Miller, and is supported by the spin of O'Reilly, Grimmett and Macartney.

CHAPTER 9

IMAGES OF A DIGGER HERO

DENNIS LILLEE

(Australia)

18 July 1949–

'Lillee was a superior paceman with command over all the skills of force and science.'

DON BRADMAN

Dennis Lillee was cast in the image of an Anzac digger throughout his illustrious career. There was more than a touch of the Aussie larrikin about him. He loved his mates, his beer and his country. He liked a bet and was disdainful of any type of authority, which is just the sort of picture portrayed of heroic Aussies since they fought together for the first time at Gallipoli during the First World War. Lillee was a fighter on the field. He showed this in his many great performances, beginning with his eight for 29 crash-through of a World XI led by Garry Sobers in Perth in December 1971, and ending with eight for 153 in his last Test, against Pakistan at Sydney in 1984. The depth of his courage and dedication was even more graphically demonstrated in overcoming a broken back, an injury sustained early in 1973. It took him 21 months, including many weeks in a plaster corset and then a back brace, before he could return to Test cricket. Most pundits wrote him off. Who had ever returned to the top of any sport after breaking his back in three places? No one except D.K. Lillee. He returned with a changed action and more science to his bowling. There was naturally a greater sense of self-preservation about him. Yet, as English batsmen of the 1974–75 Ashes series in Australia will confirm, he was still a force. While Jeff Thomson with his lethal slingshot action pummelled them from one end, Lillee picked them off from the other. Thomson, in fact, was the perfect partner at that moment. His speed and innate aggression took the pressure off Lillee having to live up to the fire and brimstone reputation of his pre-back-injury years. Lillee was the foil, the jackal who could pick off the softened-up batsmen desperate to get up the other end and away from the torture of 'Thommo'. Thomson had better figures in seven out of nine innings in which they bowled together. Yet Lillee improved gradually through the series until a peak match performance in the Fifth Test at Adelaide in January 1975 when he took four for 49 and four for 69. By the six-Test series' end, Lillee had collected 25 wickets at 23.84 – not far off his best before the break. Most importantly, his back held up.

Lillee may well have been a more canny and thoughtful bowler than before, yet he was still a fierce competitor hellbent on making life uncomfortable on the pitch for the bravest of batsmen. There was still a lot of anger in Lillee. If this was not directed at opposition cricketers on the field, then it was aimed at authority off it. He resented the pressures of continual representation of his country for pathetic pay and conditions. Lillee had suffered a crippling injury for Australia and had been pushed by administrators, schedules, the media and captains. He wanted reward for his considerable labour. His disgruntlement manifested in his efforts against the cricket establishment to support Kerry Packer's World Series Cricket (WSC), the breakaway competition that threatened traditional cricket from 1977.

He helped sign up other stars at home and abroad, and then followed through in the ensuing breakaway competition with indefatigable efforts against the great bats of the era. They included his two biggest on-field challengers, South Africa's Barry Richards, and the West Indies' Viv Richards.

Lillee was in his element. In 15 'Supertests' in 1977–78

and 1978–79 he took 79 wickets at 23.91. He dismissed Viv Richards seven times and his figures were superior to his rivals in the fast-bowling fraternity, Andy Roberts and Michael Holding. This was Lillee's second stanza performing against World XIs, and once more he lifted his performance in exalted company.

WSC ended in 1979 after Packer was sold television rights to official Tests in Australia, a deal he had wanted in the first place. Lillee made a second comeback to Test cricket. This time he was an even more rounded performer after lifting his rating to take on the world's best bats for two seasons of WSC.

Rebel with a Cause

Lillee never lost his larrikin streak. During the 1972 Ashes tour of England he was inebriated when he met the Queen and the Duke of Edinburgh, and was only able to utter the great Australian salutation of 'g'day!' when he shook their hands. Undeterred, he gave 100 per cent on the field as ever, taking 31 wickets at 17.67, which followed his 24 at 20.09 versus a World XI in 1971–72.

The March 1977 Centenary Test between England and Australia at the MCG was vintage Lillee. When play stopped and the Queen met the teams Lillee asked for her autograph. It was hardly the act of a rebel, but it didn't endear Lillee to those in the media who thought he should be more reverential. But Her Majesty and Australian fans enjoyed his cheek. She sent him a signed photograph. The punters loved his sense of fun. They also appreciated his enormous endeavour on the field. A quarter of a million Melburnians turned up during the game to celebrate 100 years since the first-ever Test had been played at the same ground in the same month. In 1877 Australia won by 45 runs. By a fluke, and an unusual symmetry, there was the same winner in 1977 with the same margin of victory.

Lillee was the key force in generating this historic victory for his country. An outstanding all-round effort by England bowlers Lever, Willis, Old and Underwood put Australia back in the pavilion for a miserable 138. Lillee responded in front of the adoring MCG crowd, if not with blood, then wickets – six of them for 26. He sent down 13.3 overs of sheer brilliance. Australia responded with nine declared for 419, his mate – keeper Rodney Marsh – thrashing a fine 110 not out. England fought back gallantly in its chase to make 463 for victory. The knockabout, cheerful Derek Randall showed exceptional backbone and skill in compiling a superb 174. Lillee toiled and sweated through 34.4 overs to return another match-winning haul of five for 139. He dismissed everyone except Dennis Amiss, Tony Greig, and Bob Willis (who was 'not out' twice) in at least one of the two innings. Lillee's back held up once more. His spirit and determination to see victory for Australia were evident in his every move on the field. He even put in with the bat, with which he was no mug, scoring 10 not out and 25, and was easily the player of the match. Lillee was a big-occasion performer, whether at this grand celebration of the game's highest level or against the best batsmen in the world. He was always competitive. When challenged, he lifted to a stratum reserved for few.

After WSC (1977–79) Lillee returned to the official Test team for a demanding three Tests each against West Indies and England in 1979–80. Lillee used an aluminium bat that he was involved in attempting to market. England captain Mike Brearley objected to the bat, which he claimed was putting the ball out of shape faster than any willow would. The umpires stepped in and asked Lillee to replace it. He threw the implement away petulantly, but then replaced it with a conventional willow. Yet around this minor incident in the series he managed to collect 23 English wickets at 16.87.

On the 1981 flight to England for the Ashes series, he 'paced' Marsh in his bid to create a beer-consuming record for the three-leg 30-hour flight to London. On the first nine-hour leg, he stayed can for can with Marsh. However, he couldn't quite find room inside his taut, lean and fit frame on legs two and three of the flight. Another competent drinker, fellow Western Australian Graeme Wood, took over. Marsh, wearing a tracksuit, reached the target of 41 cans and collapsed. Lillee helped change his comatose mate into more suitable attire for landing. Lillee likened it to dressing a whale. It was not easy. He and Wood managed to commandeer a luggage cart to hide Marsh from the media. But the reporters caught the trio of Sandgropers. It was not an auspicious start to the Aussie tour. Yet once more it did not hinder Lillee's endeavours in the Tests. In the six Tests he snared 39 wickets at 22.30 and was just pipped by Terry Alderman who removed 42 English wickets.

There were other incidents on a topsy-turvy tour. Before the Second Test at Lord's Lillee had a run-in with MCC Secretary Jack Bailey when he and Allan Border tried to get in some unscheduled practice. Bailey told them they could not use the practice wickets. Lillee thought Bailey high-handed, while the Englishman had little time for insubordinate colonials. Lillee and Border got their way, but it left them with ill feeling towards the English establishment. Lillee had been incensed a year earlier at The Oval in 1980 in the one-Test celebration of 100 years of Test cricket in England. Lillee's mate English umpire Dickie Bird had been booed and jostled by MCC members when play was delayed because of the weather. Lillee was furious at this, and would have gone to Bird's aid had the situation developed. Bailey's apparent lofty intransigence over such an issue as an unscheduled net practice consolidated Lillee's view of the British establishment running cricket. He thought some in Australia's cricket authority – those against fair remuneration of players – were tarred with the same brush. It reinforced his digger attitude to those who gave orders.

And like all self-respecting diggers, he enjoyed a bet on anything from two flies climbing a wall to the outcome of a Test, even while he was playing in it. Lillee used a bookie at the ground to put a 10-pound bet on England to win the Third Test at Headingley on the fourth day. The odds were 500 to one against it. The home team's score was seven for 135, leaving them 92 runs behind, with Australia able to bat again if they needed to. Marsh put down a five-pound bet at the same odds. Lillee and Marsh collected 5000 pounds and 2500 pounds respectively, thanks to their good pal Ian Botham scoring 149 not out and Bob Willis (eight for 43) rolling Australia for just 111 in the second innings, leaving the tourists 18 runs short. These crass but innocent bets hardly caused a ripple in the fawning media at the time and were seen in the context of those simpler times as typical Aussie fun. In the early twenty-first century both players would have been banned for life or worse and forever experience the opprobrium of former adoring fans. More than a decade of minor and major betting scandals changed attitudes.

Yet in 1981 the worst aspect of such behaviour was the damage to Aussie morale caused by the gambling. Lillee and Marsh were not seeing eye to eye with the skipper Kim Hughes. Lillee and Marsh had been part of the breakaway WSC group, whereas Hughes had come to prominence in the vacuum left by their defections. They thought they could lead better than Hughes. It didn't create team unity when solidarity was needed against a forceful England team, which sensed rare rifts and the chance to widen them. Nevertheless, Lillee took 39 wickets at 22.30 – five more scalps than Ian Botham. Lillee was just pipped for the series best figures by Terry Alderman (42 at 21.26). Lillee could not be blamed for Australia going down ignominiously by three Tests to one after leading 1–0.

Lillee, the hothead, emerged later that year during the 1981–82 season after Pakistan's Javed Miandad appeared to clip Lillee in the ribcage while making a run. Lillee responded by appearing to try to kick Miandad in the back of the leg. Miandad lifted his bat to retaliate before an umpire stepped between them. It was an unseemly act, which only reinforced the opportunity for Lillee's critics, especially in the English media, to attack him. He was too brash for some commentators.

'Lillee,' wrote English cricketer Christopher Martin-Jenkins in his book *World Cricketers*, 'was a great showman, but one who too often appeared to show a vicious streak.' Martin-Jenkins likened him to England's Fred Trueman for his ostentatious fire-and-brimstone personality, which was part bluff, part playing to the gallery. Garry Sobers on the field made a similar observation, yet with more generosity. He saw Lillee and Fred Trueman as very similar – great battlers, cursers and big-hearted men who would applaud a batsman who got the better of them. Needless to say, there weren't too many that received hand-clapping from either of these greats who were rarely knocked out of an attack by batsmen. Sobers was a rare performer. He had at different times conquered both Lillee and Trueman.

Close Encounters

Yet no batsman got on top of D.K. Lillee for long. There had never been a more driven or competitive cricketer. He was very much in the Bradman mould in this respect. Lillee has recalled a couple of memorable incidents he had with Bradman. In his last season as Test selector, Bradman was responsible for choosing Lillee for his first Test at Adelaide, early in 1971. The media pushed for Lillee to retaliate with bumpers against English bats after John Snow had roughed up Australia's bladesmen in the previous five Tests of the series. Bradman advised Lillee not to bother about a bumper war, and told him to concentrate on bowling the way he had all season. A relieved Lillee took the advice and made a more than promising debut, taking one for 41 and five for 84.

Again, early in his career, Lillee was invited to dinner at Bradman's Kensington Park home. Bradman wanted to know which bowlers Lillee had idolised as a child. The West Indies' Wes Hall was one. He had inspired Lillee to bowl fast, just as Harold Larwood had inspired Ray Lindwall. Lillee also looked up to three Australians – Lindwall, Miller and fellow West Australian Graham McKenzie. Hearing this, Bradman set up a film projector and showed him the action of 15 bowlers, including his three Aussie favourites. Bradman had collected film of many bowlers, particularly in the time of the throwing crisis a decade earlier. He liked to demonstrate how hard it was for umpires to deem a delivery fair or not.

Lillee took 355 wickets at 23.92 in 70 Tests, giving him an outstanding rate of more than five wickets a Test. He scored 905 runs at 13.71. At times, he performed well with the bat and showed a technique that allowed him to average more than 40 in club cricket in the 1973–74 season when he was recovering from his back injury and could not bowl.

In first-class cricket from 1969 to 1988 he captured 882 wickets at 23.46 and scored 2,377 runs at 13.90. Lillee snared five wickets in a Test innings 23 times, and 10 wickets in a match seven times. He led Western Australia to a Sheffield Shield in his last first-class match for them. Since his retirement, Lillee has been recognised as one of the finest bowling coaches.

Bradman became a fan and supporter of Lillee's. He was particularly struck by his performance against the World XI in 1971–72 and his struggle to return to Test cricket after breaking his back.

Until the emergence of Lillee in the 1970s, Bradman had ranked Ted McDonald and Lindwall as the two best pace bowlers he had seen. Bradman had faced both of them, and it was an enormous compliment to Lillee that although Bradman never batted against the master bowler of the 1970s and 1980s, he still ranked him with Lindwall and ahead of McDonald for his best-ever Australian Ashes team of all time.

CHAPTER 10

SPINNER WITH A PACEMAN'S TEMPERAMENT

BILL
O'REILLY

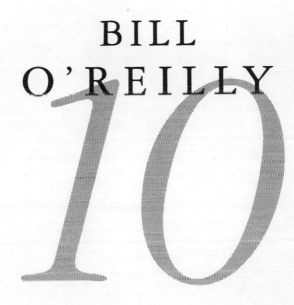

(Australia)

20 December 1905–6 October 1992

'He was a continual menace to all our batsmen . . . he could make the ball jump more than any other bowler . . .'

WALLY HAMMOND

If William Joseph O'Reilly had disappeared into the bush as a schoolteacher and never returned to Sydney, the cricket world would have waited another six decades before a spinner with a paceman's demeanour – Shane Warne – appeared at Test level.

Fortunately for Australia and the game, O'Reilly, banished to the country by the New South Wales Education Department for being a 'nuisance' (because of his requests for time off work to play first-class cricket), contrived his way back to the city in 1931. He soon broke into the Test team in the 1931–32 series against South Africa. His first game was at Adelaide in the Fourth Test. He took two for 74 and two for 81. It was just enough to gain a second chance in the Fifth Test. He bowled creditably on a wicket that helped him and he took three for 19 off nine overs with five maidens in South Africa's second innings.

A season later, he was a star in the Bodyline series of 1932–33 against England. Despite being pushed out of the limelight by the obsessional, yet successful efforts of England skipper Douglas Jardine to bring Bradman back to the ranks of the next best batsman in history, the leg-spinner made his mark. His match-winning effort at Melbourne in the Second Test – the only one won by Australia – in taking ten for 129, propelled him to stardom.

O'Reilly took 27 wickets during the Bodyline series at

26.81 apiece. Only Harold Larwood, the man who curtailed Bradman, did better with 33 wickets at 19.51. But while Larwood's effort marked an abrupt end to a Test career, O'Reilly was to rank as the best bowler in the world from then until he retired in 1946.

The Wayward Windmill

O'Reilly's action was akin to a windmill – all long arms and legs. His height, 6 ft 1 in (186 cm), and long stride gave bemused batsmen the impression that he was halfway down the pitch on delivery. He was fast for a spinner and regularly sent down balls at speeds of around 70 mph (more than 120 km/h). Despite his gangling approach, O'Reilly was well co-ordinated, athletic (he had been an accomplished hop, step and jump performer) and strong, with big hands. He could extract alarming bounce with his three main deliveries: the leg-break, the wrong'un and top-spinner. He had a surprise faster ball that was said to be even above medium pace. O'Reilly wasn't known to have bowled a flipper and said dismissively that he didn't need it. The three main deliveries, and variations within them, were enough for him to be an enormous challenge to all the great bats of the 1930s.

Bradman, who skippered him in two Ashes series and played alongside him in three other series (two more Ashes), remarked that O'Reilly was equally adept as a strike bowler, or someone who could be used defensively. His outstanding control and accuracy worked handsomely in these extreme tactical modes. For the adventurous bats who liked to use their feet, he was a worry. O'Reilly invariably saw the batsman coming, or calculated his intent and varied his pace and length accordingly. Only the most nimble could reach the ball for any sort of drive.

Hammond recalled him being a continual 'menace', who could make the ball jump more than any other slow bowler. Hammond ranked him with Grimmett, who was especially tough for the English bat in 1930. O'Reilly's nickname – Tiger – was apt. He was aggressive and had plenty to say on the field. His pathological hatred for all batsmen on the pitch translated into a fierceness that unsettled batsmen in the manner of Fred Trueman or Dennis Lillee. Very few batsmen conquered him. Lindsay Hassett for Victoria relished batting against him and won most encounters. O'Reilly himself rated Mosman's Stan McCabe as someone difficult to conquer, as was Gordon's Ray Robinson. They both played for New South Wales and Australia but met O'Reilly in club encounters. O'Reilly said, without qualification, that Bradman was the greatest batsman of all time. They had terrific battles and Bradman occasionally gave him stick. Their competitions began at Bowral in December 1925 and went on for another 15 years. In their first meeting, Bradman slammed 234 and was to maintain an ascendancy over the man he ranked as the best bowler he ever faced. They didn't face each other at first-class level until October 1936, eight months after O'Reilly returned triumphant from a tour of South Africa, in which he took 27 wickets at 17.03 in Australia's 4–0 Test series victory. (Grimmett took 44 wickets at 14.59.) The occasion was a trial game, which would have a significant bearing on the future of Australian cricket. O'Reilly and Grimmett were chosen in the team skippered by Victor Richardson, who had led Australia in the 1935–36 series in South Africa. Bradman led the opposing team. Performances were expected to influence selectors in their choices for the forthcoming Ashes series. Bradman, in murderous form, belted 212 and drove both spinners out of the attack. For one of the very few times in his career, O'Reilly refused to bowl after three spells. He was content to watch others being slaughtered. It brought back memories of their first encounter at Bowral late in 1925 when Bradman gave O'Reilly the biggest shellacking of his career.

Even when at his peak on a wicket conducive to spin, O'Reilly usually found Bradman uncontrollable. Unlike the English batsmen, he was prepared to use his feet to get out to the spinner, or the crease in exaggerated movements back or forward. In a first-class State game at Adelaide in December 1937, O'Reilly produced superlative spells, taking 14 wickets in the two innings – including nine for 41 in the first on a big-turning wicket. South Australia notched 217 and 191. Bradman top-scored in the first innings with 91 and was second-top score in the second innings with 62 (Badcock 77) but O'Reilly, after titanic struggles, removed him twice, caught both times, first by O'Brien and in the second innings by Arthur Chipperfield. The latter catch caused O'Reilly to clasp his hands triumphantly over his head like a boxer who had just been given a favourable judges' decision.

Commentator A.G. 'Johnny' Moyes wrote that when Bradman came to the wicket, O'Reilly could be seen to galvanise all his remarkable energy. There seemed more pep in the step and wind in the windmill's spokes.

O'Reilly had never forgotten that day of humiliation at Bowral in 1925. Fresh in his mind too was the hammering from Bradman in the trial game of October 1936.

The spinner knew he had his big chance to dismiss Bradman cheaply, but he was the one batsman equipped to counter him. This Bradman did, despite, as Moyes reported, 'every ball being charged with hostility, filled with venom and calculated to destroy'. Sometimes Bradman got on top; sometimes O'Reilly nearly broke through or just missed shaving the batsman's probing willow.

'It was a battle of mastery, one champion against another,' Moyes noted.

Snaring Bradman twice in the one game after such monumental encounters gave the spinner, according to O'Reilly, 'the greatest sense of achievement' in his entire career. When asked why he replied: 'Because Bradman was Bradman. He was the greatest batsman who ever lived. Did any other Australian get him twice in a match?'

Encounters like these led Bradman to rank O'Reilly as the best bowler he ever saw or faced. He made this judgment after a considered opinion of the great S.F. Barnes, whom he never saw play. Bradman ranked the Australian higher for two reasons. First, O'Reilly had a superb wrong'un or googly. Second, Bradman's first-hand experience of his leg-spin convinced him that no one could bowl it better. Being an adequate leggie at club level himself, he had a feel for this from more than one perspective.

Bradman and O'Reilly played against each other in 10 first-class matches and in 18 innings. Bradman scored 1207 runs at an average of 86.21, nearly 10 runs short of his first-class average. Bradman hit four centuries, including two doubles, with a highest score of 251 not out.

Double Act with Grimmett

Another enormous asset of O'Reilly's was his spin twin Clarrie Grimmett. They formed, arguably, the most lethal spin combination on all types of wickets. Their nearest rivals in Ashes cricket were Jim Laker and left-armer Tony Lock, the Surrey duet that played Test cricket together in the 1950s. Yet their only penetrative efforts as a combination against Australia were on wickets that were of the greatest help to the bowler, such as the dustbowl at Manchester in 1956.

Bradman ranked Shane Warne with O'Reilly and Grimmett, but Warne was left out and they were chosen primarily because, at their peak, the other two were an outstanding strike combination. Maurice Leyland and Lindsay Hassett said that in any eight-ball over from O'Reilly he might serve up eight different types of delivery. Grimmett often complemented this with a tactically different approach. He might bottle up a batsman serving eight consecutive leg-breaks when the batsman was expecting a wrong'un or a flipper. O'Reilly preferred bowling with the wind. It accentuated his strengths by gaining him extra pace and bounce. Grimmett loved performing into the wind. This way he could use the anti-forces of nature to conjure his magic. O'Reilly was the aggressor. Grimmett was cunning. O'Reilly would intimidate if he could. Grimmett cogitated solely on how to outthink his opponent. One was a showman who liked centre stage. The other preferred to be unseen and unheard, the more to surprise a batsman. Even their names had distinctive connotations. The name O'Reilly played up to the expectations of his Irish temperament and nature. His nickname of Tiger was that of a predator. Grimmett's name implied something more mystical from the land of warlocks. So did his nicknames – The Fox, Old Scarl and Grum.

Each would deliver an eight-ball over in under two-and-a-half minutes. Five minutes would see 16 deliveries from the world's best-ever leg-spinners, next to Warne. How many batsmen in history could have won through against them? Bradman has been mentioned, but after that, one imagines Jack Hobbs at his best being able to win through against the duo; Denis Compton now and again; Victor Trumper on a very good day; Sachin Tendulkar on song;

Neil Harvey at his peak against spin in the 1950s; Viv Richards if he put his mind to it; and Charlie Macartney intent on assassination. Hammond used defence to wear them down, but never could take total command in his few opportunities against them in tandem. Very few batsmen could claim to have conquered them individually. None, except Bradman, had dominated them together.

Grimmett empowered O'Reilly and vice versa. Little wonder O'Reilly grumbled when Grimmett missed out on the 1938 tour of England. He muttered little when Grimmett was dropped for poor form in the Bodyline series. He was not heard to complain about the omission during the 1936–37 Ashes in Australia. But when the pairing was abandoned in 1938, O'Reilly was steaming. He felt that Grimmett was at his best in England and that they combined well there. He blamed Bradman for Grimmett's non-selection and never let the cricket world forget it.

Yet when it came to Bradman's selection of his best-ever teams, he recognised the full weight of the Grimmett–O'Reilly twosome.

Talent Delayed

O'Reilly was as ambitious as the next man when it came to sporting aims, but he was also sensible with a feel for the real world. He did not abandon his teaching career, despite pressures to do so. His father, also a teacher, had urged him to maintain his working career. O'Reilly made his Shield debut in 1927–28 but was sent by the Department of Education to teach in the bush for three years. For a moment in 1928 he contemplated giving up his profession, knowing in his heart that he was Test material. But this moment of doubt about his teaching career passed quickly.

He loved teaching and was good at it. O'Reilly was not qualified for anything else. In those days, cricket was played as a sport. It was not a job. He did not fancy any of the fringe work in sports stores that many cricketers resorted to, especially when he found teaching rewarding. He looked around him in 1929, 1930 and 1931 and saw dole queues everywhere. He knew plenty of people who suicided in the bush in the tough times of the Depression and was thankful that he would always have work via the State-run teaching system. It rankled with O'Reilly that he had to be content with bush cricket for three years. But when he returned to Sydney in 1931, he pushed his way into the State side by sheer weight of wickets in Sydney club games. Near the end of season 1931–32 he made the Test side and cemented his place in the team during the 1932–33 Bodyline Ashes series. A rib injury in 1933–34 threatened him. Yet when he took nine for 50 in one innings against Victoria the selectors inked him in for the 1934 tour of England.

Grimmett's name was already established in England after his magnificent tour in 1930, in which he was the dominant bowling force of the entire summer. In tandem, he and O'Reilly seemed lethal in the build-up to the Tests. In the First Test at Trent Bridge, they brought all their talents to bear on a batsman's pitch. O'Reilly took seven for 54 in England's second innings to bring victory for Australia with just 10 minutes to spare. His match figures were eleven for 129. No finer performance had ever been delivered by a leg-spinner against class opposition on a good track. The spin twins took 19 of the wickets to fall. In one game, O'Reilly had established himself as one of the game's greats.

'O'Reilly's performance was magnificent,' Bradman recalled. 'The sheer force of his skilful deployment of the art of spin had to be seen to be appreciated. He was the match-winner, ably backed up by Grimmett, who never let up the pressure at the other end.'

The Lord's Test belonged to the talented left-arm Yorkshireman Hedley Verity (fifteen for 104) and England. O'Reilly demonstrated his tenacity and gifts once more by taking three wickets in four balls in the Third Test at Old Trafford. He took the first six England wickets to fall and finished with the figures of seven for 189 off 59 overs – a remarkable effort in England's nine for 627 declared. This was capped by his best performance so far with the bat in scoring 30 not out in the first innings. It saved the follow-on and the match for Australia. The game was drawn. O'Reilly's all-round effort would have made him favourite to take man-of-the-match. He played an important part in the final two Tests, and finished with the top return of 28 wickets at 24.93.

Despite threats of retirement because of work commitments as a teacher during 1934–35, in which he played only one Shield game, O'Reilly toured South Africa in 1935–36 where he took another 27 wickets, but this time at just 17.03. Remarkably, Grimmett took 44 wickets at just 14.59. Allowing for South Africa's weak opposition, these returns were still splendid. England, however, proved more testing in the next Ashes – 1936–37. O'Reilly, this time without Grimmett who had been dropped, took 25 wickets at 22.20.

O'Reilly didn't enjoy his 1938 tour of England as much as 1934, mainly because he felt English curators had 'cooked' the Test wickets in favour of batsmen. He scorned the Trent Bridge First Test pitch as being prepared to last forever. It certainly seemed that way to the spinner as England amassed eight for 658. At The Oval in the final Test England reached seven for 903. The series provided nightmares for bowlers, particularly O'Reilly, who was

Australia's number one. Yet he remarked dryly that the weather had intervened in the Third Test at Manchester, where not a ball was bowled, and in the Fourth at Leeds, where he took ten for 122 and won the match for Australia. In the four Tests played, O'Reilly took 22 wickets at 27.7. Despite pitches not being conducive to spin, he was Australia's dominant bowler for the fourth time in five series.

In 19 first-class matches spread over four seasons after the 1938 Ashes tour and before the cessation of interstate cricket due to the Second World War, O'Reilly took 138 wickets at 15.07. His rate was a remarkable 7.26 wickets per match. He came back after the war, played one more Test in Wellington, New Zealand, early in 1946, taking eight for 33 in two innings. In a gesture of recognition that his knees wouldn't take any more, he threw his boots out of the dressing-room window. If a young Kiwi spinner had been struck by that flying footwear, apart from being injured, he would have found them too big to use. Very few spinners in history could claim to fill them figuratively or in actuality.

In all, O'Reilly took 144 wickets at 22.59 in 27 Tests. He scored 410 runs at 12.81. He won most of the big encounters with the world's best bats in a cricketing career spanning two decades. Hammond, the scourge of Australia in 1928–29 when the New South Wales Department of Education sent O'Reilly bush, was his biggest international success. The greatest English batsman of O'Reilly's era fell to the Tiger seven times for 26 runs or less.

O'Reilly took 774 wickets at 16.60 in first-class cricket, and scored 1655 runs at 13.13.

He moved from teaching at Sydney Grammar in 1939 to become Secretary at the Lion Tile Company. It meant a substantial increase in salary and he remained in the job for 35 years until 1974. After that, O'Reilly concentrated more on his most readable, pithy journalism, with its heavy bias towards spinners and fair play.

Bradman's judgment of O'Reilly as the best bowler who ever lived will be disputed by some but, invariably, they never saw or faced him. Certainly, it is safe to say that there could be few or perhaps no better performer with the ball in the history of Ashes cricket.

CHAPTER 11

PIMPERNEL OF SPIN

CLARRIE
GRIMMETT

(Australia)

25 December 1891–2 May 1980

Clarrie Grimmett is the odd man out in Don Bradman's selection of his all-time best Australian Ashes team. Unlike all the other members of this team, Grimmett was not a cricketing assassin. He used his subtle and cunning skills in the art of spin bowling to outfox batsmen. Bill O'Reilly, his spin partner, said he was the deepest thinker on the game that he had ever met. Yet in his own way, Grimmett was every inch the competitor, albeit in a different way to O'Reilly, Ray Lindwall or Dennis Lillee. He proved this in his spectacular effort during the 1930 Ashes in England when bowling against the great Wally Hammond. The England champion admitted later that Grimmett demoralised him more than any other bowler he ever faced. It was Grimmett's relentless pursuit of the batsman, ball after ball, over after over, that wore down the receiver until he was forced into error. His outstanding overall strength was his amazing control, which was similar to that of Shane Warne and Stuart MacGill 70 years later. From the first ball of a spell Grimmett could put the ball on any spot he wished. He was also the master of disguise. A batsman had little idea of what was coming. Grimmett could dish up to eight different varieties of spin in one over. Or he could completely perplex a batsman by heaving down eight balls of the same style but with varying degrees of spin that would gradually trap an opponent lbw or slip through to bowl him. Grimmett used his round-arm action to spear the ball in low. The batsman would be driven back. The bowler would be trying to then slip through a top-spinner or flipper which would be aimed at pads or stumps. He varied pace, flight, spin and length with such panache that no batsman ever felt 'in' against him.

Clarence Victor Grimmett, a New Zealander until he was 22 years of age, was the only selection in Bradman's all-time best-ever Australian team not born in Australia and one of two players (the other being Macartney) born before 1900. Above all, compared to the other players Bradman chose, he had by far the toughest route to success in Test cricket.

Grimmett, Eminent Emigrant

In 1914, Grimmett, an unathletic-looking 5 ft 4 in (162 cm), who had a walk like Groucho Marx, took a risk by moving to Australia. In his mind it was not a gamble. New Zealand cricket in the early 1900s was decades behind Australia in development, and decades from being allowed in to competition to play official Tests. If Grimmett wished to test his ability then it had to be in the big brown island across the Tasman Sea. Grimmett had played against a touring Australian team earlier in the year. He even bowled an over at the great bat Victor Trumper. The leg-spinner knew that Australia presented the highest standard of the game in the world. He wanted to be part of it. He wished to succeed against the best.

Yet life wasn't meant to be easy for Clarrie Grimmett. He arrived in Australia just as the First World War began. Cricket competition was curtailed yet he managed three seasons of somewhat interrupted grade cricket for Sydney. When the State contests resumed, the flamboyant Arthur Mailey, a big-spinning, profligate leggie, who was always prepared to buy a wicket, blocked Grimmett's way into the New South Wales side. Mailey was one of the finest purveyors of the fine art of spinning the game had seen. He was not about to step aside for a foreign challenger, no matter how capable. Grimmett's record in and around the club and State scene easily matched Mailey's. But with the belief that Mailey would be chosen before him for New South Wales, Grimmett packed his bags again in 1917 and left rustic, brash young Sydney for the more conservative suburbs of Melbourne – namely South Melbourne and Prahran, for which he played.

Perhaps his unprepossessing appearance with the cap he always wore to hide his thinning hairline, and the fact that he bowled a near round-arm delivery, both conspired against him. There was no decent explanation for his non-selection in Victoria, despite it being a strong State in the post-war years and dominated by Warwick Armstrong, also a leg-spinner. Perhaps the Big Ship (Armstrong was about 155 kg in weight) thought he was a rival. If so, this was an even bigger block to first-class and then Test selection.

Clarrie toiled on, collecting vast harvests of wickets in club games but only gained State selection five times in as many years. He was never conquered in these matches. Spectators and players alike reckoned he was the best bowler ever seen in Victoria. He had a brilliant, deceptive wrong'un that very few batsmen could pick, and a marvellous flipper that was accurate and a tad faster than his leg-break. It was only State selectors who seemed to refuse to appreciate him, despite his bags of qualifying wickets at club level.

Clarrie worked as a sign-writer and had married and settled in Melbourne. Wherever he went he constructed a backyard pitch so that he could practise for hours with his faithful fox terrier Joe. Grimmett would bowl into a net. Joe would fetch the balls for him. The obsessive spinner kept practising, despite his setbacks. If he were ever to receive a promotion, he would be an especially well-prepared performer.

S A C A ' s   M a s t e r s t r o k e

After having given Victoria every chance to watch him playing cricket and select him for their State team he took up an
offer from the South Australian Cricket Association in
1924. Its committee had witnessed him taking eight for 86
in one innings for Victoria in Adelaide against South
Australia. He was offered a job for 10 quid a week as a sign-
writer, in addition to seven pounds a week as a retainer for
playing State cricket. He had a three-year contract at age
32. These were just the conditions he needed to prosper.

He continued on at the State level as if he were still at
Prahran Club, seven times taking hauls of between four and
seven wickets. This launched him into Test cricket in the
Fifth Test of the 1924–25 season. Herbie Collins, the astute
Australian skipper, gave him his big chance on the second
day of the Test, 28 February 1925. Grimmett was 33. He
had landed in Sydney more than 10 years earlier in the
grand hope of reaching this moment quickly. After all, he
had played first-class cricket in New Zealand's Plunket
Shield and had been successful. However, he was forced to
take many steps backwards and sideways before he could
savour this occasion of his first Test cricket match in front
of a big Sydney crowd. His chest-on, round-arm delivery
brought mirth from those in the crowd who had never seen
it. But no batsman, before or since, ever laughed at Clarence
Victor Grimmett. That day he targeted one of the world's
finest left-handers, England's Frank Woolley. Left-handers
usually could handle leg-spinners with more ease, and
traditionally leg-spinners prefer to have their standard
delivery turning away from the right-hander. Grimmett,
who had a mental file on every player he ever bowled to,
recalled tackling Woolley four-and-a-half years earlier in a
game for Victoria against the MCC. In that game the

batsman had slightly mishit a wrong'un, although it seemed he had picked it. The ball had fallen harmlessly between two fieldsmen who had hesitated to let the other catch it. Woolley, who had made nearly 60,000 runs in first-class cricket at 40.77, with 145 centuries, was well aware of Grimmett's underrated skills. Woolley knew much about spin deception himself and would go on to take 2000 wickets at under 20 runs apiece with his slow left-hand orthodox spinners. This day in Sydney he watched, poker-faced with concentration, for Grimmett's wrong'un. Woolley aimed to cover drive it properly this time if it was delivered. But Grimmett, the poker player, held back the ball that spun, contrary to the norm. Instead he delivered orthodox leg-breaks – off-breaks to the left-hander – that turned in towards him. Grimmett was able to extract a fair amount of spin. He worked the ball closer and closer to the line of Woolley's off-stump, while imperceptibly, to the naked eye, gradually slowing down the delivery. Woolley got fairly to the pitch of each delivery, hitting it gracefully into the covers, against the spin. Then Grimmett hurled down the killer ball – one imparted with hardly any spin and delivered faster than the average ball. Woolley shaped for the cover drive, but the ball swerved, dipped in the air and beat him. He was bowled for 47. It was a classic set-up by a master bowler of a master all-rounder. There would be few more satisfying wickets in Grimmett's illustrious career. He loved snaring such a champion, but showed little elation. He was lower than low key. He kept his wits about him, determined to capitalise on this wicket and his first big chance at the highest level of the game. He ended with five for 45. A champion had arrived at the scene where he should have been admitted years earlier. He took another six for 37 in the second innings, giving him the magnificent first Test figures of eleven wickets for 82. There would be

few better figures for a first-timer, and no better performance by an Australian on home soil. Grimmett took the
honours for the match, and outshone his former rival Arthur
Mailey, who took just 0 for 13.

Former Australian captain Monty Noble believed
Grimmett gave one of the finest exhibitions of slow bowling ever seen in Australia. English critics likened
Grimmett's impact to that of William Clarke, who nearly a
century earlier in England had dominated the game with
his prodigious underarm spinners.

In 1924–25 Grimmett took 59 wickets at 22.03 in first-
class cricket and he was thrilled to be on his way. Joe, the
foxy, was fetching more balls in the backyard as Grimmett
pushed himself further. In 1925–26 batsmen around
Australia went after him and landed a few blows, breaking
down his economy rate. His wickets were at a relatively
expensive 30.41 each. Yet he took more than anyone – 59 –
for the season and dominated first-class cricket. He took six
hauls of five wickets and three of 10.

He ran neck and neck with Mailey in England in 1926,
but it was clear that the new man was on the way up and
the older man at 38 years of age was on the way out.

A failure with investment in a fashion business late in
1926 curtailed Grimmett's 1926–27 season, in which he
took 30 wickets at 34.33, which proved to be his worst
season for some time. Once his off-field business problem
had settled he performed better in 1927–28, taking 42
wickets at 27.40. He took two 10-wicket hauls and four
five-wicket bags. During the season he had his first
encounter with 19-year-old Don Bradman. As he would
prove for the better part of the next 20-odd years of cricket
he played, Bradman rose to the big occasion to assert his
authority over a bowling opponent. Anxious to make a
point, Bradman went after Grimmett from the first over he

faced from the nearly 36-year-old veteran and smashed him for two fours. It was Bradman's first first-class match. He made 118 and won the encounter with the then world's greatest spinner. They played 15 matches against each other (27 innings) and it would be fair to say that Bradman came out squarely on top. Grimmett only dismissed him five times under 50 – for 33, 14, 35, 13 and 17.

Home in Glory

Early in 1928 Grimmett toured New Zealand – the first time he had been home since 1914 – and was feted as a national champion. He took 47 wickets at 16.91 including good performances in the unofficial Tests. Grimmett's 1928–29 figures – 71 wickets at 34.25 – reflected the success he had in general, and particularly in the tough contest with Percy Chapman's powerful touring England team. In the Tests, he took on the burden of being both the only 'striker', and the stock bowler against England's batsmen, who included Hobbs, Sutcliffe, Hammond, Jardine, Hendren and Leyland. There had never been a stronger batting line up to come to Australian shores. Grimmett took 23 wickets at 44.52. Only England's slow left-armer, Jack White, was better with 25 wickets at 30.40.

The 1930 tour of England made Grimmett a sporting legend. Grimmett with the ball, along with Bradman with the bat, won a series for Australia against all odds. Given the opposition, both players performed better than any bat or spinner, arguably in the history of the game. Grimmett took on world-beater Wally Hammond, who had crushed Australia in 1928–29 with 905 runs, and beat him. The greatest English bat of the era dubbed Grimmett 'the most formidable bowler in the world'. Hammond further articulated his problem by saying that while Grimmett was bowling, he had 'the nightmarish feeling that somebody was after you'. Every English bat, he added, found him a 'real horror'.

He took 38 wickets at 31.90. Grimmett dismissed Hammond for 30 or less in his first four innings of the series. Given the Englishman's dominance in 1928–29, this paved the way for Australia's unlikely 2–1 victory. With Hammond reduced to an uncertain prodder for most of the Ashes, England could rarely build a winning score. This allowed Bradman time and energy enough to obliterate England's powerful attack. He made 974 runs at an average of 139.14.

Grimmett took 144 wickets on the 1930 tour at 16.85, including 15 five-wicket hauls and five 10-wicket bags. On one occasion he took all ten Yorkshire wickets in an innings for just 37 runs. He returned to Australia a hero, and lived up to his effort in England by taking 74 wickets at 19.14 in 1930–31, and another 77 wickets at 19.93 in 1931–32. Grimmett had reached a peak and was acknowledged by all commentators as the best leg-spinner of all time. The West Indians toured Australia and were all at sea in the Tests as Grimmett ran through them, taking 33 wickets at just 17.96 – his best Test figures to that point. The Caribbean cricketers had never experienced such a bowler. Nor had the South Africans in 1931–32. They were similarly completely bamboozled and 33 more victims fell prey to him at just 16.87. After Hammond and company, who knew how to play spin of this kind, the West Indians and South Africans were easy-beats. They had rarely seen a wrong'un bowled. None had ever seen a flipper.

Both the touring teams thought it was best to smash their way out of trouble. Their admirable bravado proved their undoing against Grimmett and his spin partner Bill O'Reilly.

In the 1932–33 Bodyline series, Grimmett had a setback and was dropped for the final two Tests. He had taken just five wickets in three Tests and they had cost 65.2 runs each. The spin combination of two leggies, who complemented each other so well, had to be broken up. Yet he still had a good first-class season, taking 55 wickets at 28.67. Grimmett fought on. In 1933–34 he took 66 wickets at 21.83. The selectors had to reselect him for the 1934 England tour and did, especially after his 1926 tour (105 wickets at 17.68) and his dominance of all English batsmen in 1930. It was the right move. He again starred, taking 25 wickets at 26.72 in the Tests and 109 at 19.80 for the tour.

Fox, Scarl and Old Grum

Grimmett's nickname from about 1918 was 'The Fox' because of the resemblance to this creature in his features, demeanour and shrewdness in outwitting his opponents. When he made State and Test sides he was also known as 'Scarl' after the Scarlet Pimpernel, whose enemies sought him here and there, without success. From the 1934 season he picked up the sobriquet 'Old Grum'. Grimmett was nearly 43 years old. He was slow and had to be hidden in the field. Yet his magic with the ball was still there. He was a consistently big wicket-taker again in the Australian season of 1934–35, and dominated the tour of South Africa in 1935–36 where he snared 92 at 14.80. In the Tests he captured 44 wickets at 14.59. Yet this was his last effort at the top of the game. When England came to Australia in 1936–37 under Gubby Allen, Grimmett was ineffectual in a game against the tourists and was out-bowled by his rivals in the Test trial. Selectors had kept in mind his struggle on harder Australian wickets in the previous Ashes competition four years earlier. His 1936–37 season figures of 48 wickets at 30.06 appeared to mark the beginning of his decline as a formidable force in big cricket. Grimmett turned 46 during the 1937–38 season. Bradman, his State captain from 1936, felt that at this time his leg-break did not have the turning power of former years. The leggie was not chosen to tour England in 1938 and his non-selection remains a controversial topic to this day. Many, including his former spin partner, Bill O'Reilly, thought he should have been given a fourth tour.

Yet Grimmett was hardly a spent force in first-class cricket. In the full season of 1939–40, he snared 73 victims at 22.65. His leg-break may have declined but the master bowler was compensating by thinking of new ways to beat his opponents. During the curtailed 1940–41 season, Grimmett played in five matches and took 25 wickets at 26.72. He worked on a new delivery, a delivery that seemed to be a wrong'un, but which broke the other way – a sort of wrong'un wrong'un. Grimmett expressed his disappointment at war breaking out in the Pacific. It meant he was not able to use his new style of delivery in first-class cricket.

In 37 Tests he took 216 wickets (an Australian record until Ray Lindwall broke it in 1959) at 24.21. In 248 first-class matches he captured 1424 wickets at 22.28.

Grimmett was, in the modern parlance, a cricket tragic. He lived and breathed it, hardly relaxing during off-seasons. Long after his retirement he would bowl into the empty net in his Adelaide backyard. He continued on as a coach well into his seventies. When South Africa toured Australia in 1963–64, Grimmett, a sprightly 72-year-old going on 73, bowled impressively in the nets to the tourists, who numbered among them some of the best batsmen in the world, including Graeme Pollock, Trevor Goddard and Eddie Barlow. He could still give the ball a tweak. His wrong'un worked and he could even hurl down a flipper, although he admitted it took a fraction more effort.

Bradman's logic in choosing for his all-time best Australian Ashes team two leg-spinners, who were so devastating in combination, made good sense. But had Bill O'Reilly never existed, Bradman would still have chosen Clarrie Grimmett ahead of all the other spinners in his ideal Australian team. He regarded him as the best pure leg-spinner he ever saw or faced.

CHAPTER 12

THE ALL-ROUNDER WITH ATTITUDE

RICHIE BENAUD

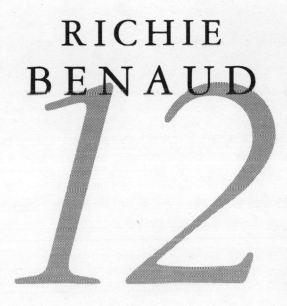

12

(Australia)

6 October 1930–

> *'He was one of Australia's top all-rounders, a tough competitor and a fine leader.'*
>
> DON BRADMAN

A despondent Richie Benaud handed a prescription to a Timaru pharmacist early on an Australian tour of New Zealand in 1957. The pharmacist noticed the split and swollen fingers on his right hand, and asked what was wrong. The cricketer explained how they had been torn by the ball's seam slicing into the skin. It was a burden that he had to live with and he worried that his career would be cut short by this painful, debilitating skin condition, which was beginning to affect his normally genial demeanour.

The pharmacist, Ivan James, suggested he try rubbing oily calamine lotion into the wounds and rubbing boracic acid powder on them to make a waxy filling. It had worked on ex-New Zealand servicemen from the Second World War and the Korean War who had leg ulcers. Benaud, who had tried 'everything', was sceptical. But as James had gone to the trouble to advise him and make up the remedy, he was willing to experiment with this seemingly simple answer to his problem. It worked.

This providential meeting with the Kiwi chemist came at a critical time in Benaud's career. He had a fair Test record with bat (887 runs at an average of 22.73) and ball (72 wickets at 29.11 runs a wicket) until that point. The remedy gave Benaud a new bowling career, free of raw, bleeding fingers and incessant pain. He never played without using the remedy and applied it diligently every time

271

he had to perform with the ball. His new-found injury-free condition coincided with him becoming the Australian team's number-one spinner. He set out to remain that way during the side's tour of South Africa in 1957–58 under Ian Craig. In the Tests he took 30 wickets at 21.93, an outstanding return. He also made 329 runs at 54.83. This haul included two fine centuries – 122 in the drawn First Test at the New Wanderers Stadium, Johannesburg, and 100 batting at number four in the Fourth Test – again at New Wanderers, which Australia won.

It is commonly held that leg-spinners mature and peak late – around 30 years of age – and Benaud, at 27, was well on target. Without being clouded by injury worries, his exceptional thinking approach to the game was allowed free rein. He fell between the styles of two great leggies, Arthur Mailey and Clarrie Grimmett. Benaud was never going to be the profligate billionaire with the ball like Mailey, yet at times he was prepared to toss the ball up and tempt a batsman into having a heave-ho and he took plenty of wickets by catches in the deep. Also like Mailey, Benaud (taller at 185 cm) could get bounce. Yet, on the whole, he was more like the economical Grimmett, who used the top-spinner and wrong'un as surprises rather than stock deliveries, and who applied relentless pressure to batsmen. Benaud worked on tying a batsman down and forcing error through adventurism or frustration. He could be as pinpoint accurate as the other great spinners, but was not afraid to vary his length to unsettle a batsman and keep him guessing. It was rare in Benaud's career, particularly from the time of the 1956–57 tour of Pakistan and India (24 wickets at 17.66) and for the next seven years, for him to be smashed out of the attack. Not even the great Garry Sobers took control of him more than a couple of times in their many encounters.

The healing of Benaud's spinning finger in South Africa prepared him perfectly for the coming season 1958–59 as captain against England in Australia. When it began Benaud had no idea that events, fate and timing would conspire to see him elected skipper. He was ranked number three behind Ian Craig (the 22-year-old leader) and vice-captain Neil Harvey. Craig contracted hepatitis and not long into the season decided to pull out to help a full recovery. Neil Harvey, who had moved to Sydney to take up a job, found himself vice-captain to Benaud in a State game against Queensland. Matters of leadership were complicated further by Harvey skippering an Australian XI to a disastrous loss against England at Sydney just before the First Test. It was not Harvey's fault that Tony Lock used Fred Trueman-generated footholes to bundle the Australians out cheaply in their second innings and forge a win for the tourists. But the selectors (one of whom was Bradman), in what must have been an agonising and hairpin decision based on hunches, hopes and thin 'winning' leadership form, chose Benaud as captain for the First Test at Brisbane.

He had much to prove after thrashings by England in three series – in 1953, 1954–55 and 1956 – and never experiencing an Ashes win against the near-ancient enemy. Benaud had been written off by English critics as a second-rate bowler. Revenge and an I'll-show-you approach were on his mind when he marched out at Brisbane to take on Peter May's all-conquering team that was stacked with batting and bowling talent.

Benaud was a natural leader with charisma. It enabled him to impose his personality rather than his will on the Australian squad. Discipline came from dedication rather than dictatorship. His intensity and enthusiasm were contagious and players seemed to lift and unify around him.

He was the archetypical successful Aussie leader who could be both one of the boys and still followed by others into battle. Benaud's manner also managed to cajole more out of his finest performers, notably Alan Davidson, who was bowling at his peak. When 'the claw', as Davidson was known because of his ability to pull in amazing catches close to the wicket, was spent after a big spell, Benaud could be seen imploring him for one more over. The broad-shouldered champion speedman invariably took another breath and delivered – for captain and country.

The First Test introduced a Benaud-ism that would change cricket: *the embrace*. At the fall of an important wicket, he would run to the bowler or fielder and hug them. Soon the entire team was running towards each other for affectionate bodily contact each time a wicket fell. The old-timers winced but, for the under-30s, it was something refreshing in a country unused to demonstrative displays on the sporting field, even in Australian Rules football and rugby, where bodily contact was frequent but anything but affectionate. Benaud was doing nothing more or less than embodying the enthusiasm the fans felt, especially in this series where the Australian public and media were nervous about another thrashing by England. It feared spiflication by the tourists' powerful batting line-up that included Peter May (captain), Colin Cowdrey, Tom Graveney, Peter Richardson and Trevor Bailey. England's bowling line-up too seemed intimidating with fine speedsters Trueman and Brian Statham, and Frank Tyson, who had destroyed Australia in 1954–55. They were backed up by the fabulous 'spin twins' from Surrey, Jim Laker and Tony Lock. The spinners had so comprehensively accounted for Australian bats in the 1956 Ashes in England.

Some observers put Benaud's non-Anglo-Saxon shows of emotion down to his French background, as if he had just stepped off a boat in a beret and smoking a Gauloise. In reality, his great-grandfather Jean, from Bordeaux, had arrived in 1840 as a free settler on the vessel *Ville de Bordeaux*. While proud of his adventurous French heritage (and his English heritage on his mother's side), Richie, a fourth-generation Australian, was as Aussie as they come. Whatever the reason for the on-field exuberance, the mediocre, frustrated crowds at Brisbane in early December 1958 were most appreciative of *the embrace*. It was the most exciting thing happening in the painfully slow Test. For some reason beyond the good, tight bowling by Benaud, Davidson, Meckiff, and Ken Mackay, the English captain and his men seemed hell-bent on defending the Ashes. Perhaps the huge hype about their talent upon their arrival in Australia had affected them. They were defending the oldest trophy in international sport, won and held by England for three successive series. Maybe the pressures of the hype had got to May's team, which was the best in the world before that 1958–59 series. Trevor Bailey hit (if that is the appropriate word) the slowest first-class half-century ever. England's stodgy performance played into Benaud's hands, as both a leader and bowler. He dictated play, out thought May, and rattled the opposition in general. His seven for 112 for the match were by far the best returns. There were real nerves in the Australian camp, the media and the fans over whether or not the home team would make the 147 runs needed to win – in a day. None of the three previous innings had reached 200, and there were fears that Laker and Lock would spin Australia to oblivion. There was more than relief in the home camp when Norm O'Neill made a scintillating 71 not out in 113 minutes. After the sludge and boredom of the previous days this was ecstasy for Australian supporters. O'Neill attacked. The home team won. That one innings had a significant psychological impact on everyone involved in the series. Until then, the England players had looked like winners. Australia's team contained the battlers, destined to lose. After that first Test win, tall Benaud walked taller, with reason. He was leading a team of supermen.

And, as is often the case with people of enterprise, the luck went with him. The Second Test in abstemious Melbourne began on New Year's Eve and was played over the New Year without a break for revelry. Day One was dull and overcast. Peter May looked at the firm pitch and had no second thoughts about batting when he won the toss. He had never played in Melbourne in such conditions, for if he had, he would have let his fastmen loose. Benaud seized the chance offered by May's mistake. Davidson took advantage of the low weather and provided prodigious swing, with the essential other ingredient – accuracy. Within a few overs England was three for 7. May, realising the predicament in which he had placed his team, batted beautifully and as if driven by guilt, notching 113. England made 259. Neil Harvey replied with 167 out of 308. He had supported Benaud after the disappointment of not being appointed skipper. Harvey was a player of strong character, but more important to him than leading was beating England. He had been brought up under Bradman's leadership where no quarter was ever given. You played it hard but fair. And you went for victory at every opportunity.

Harvey's innings set Australia up for a win. Then Meckiff (six for 38) and Davidson (three for 41) rolled the tourists for just 87. Benaud had a poor game, making a duck and taking just one for 65. But his leadership was now brim-full of confidence. He came off the MCG beaming, clapping and walking on air, behind his two speedmen. It was 5 January 1959. Five weeks earlier he didn't even think he would be leading his country. Now he was skipper and he had his team 2–0 against their Ashes foes.

Benaud and Harvey, who had suffered in the last three Ashes hidings, were feeling better than anyone else. They could sniff an Ashes victory and they were loving it. The touring camp, by contrast, was in disarray and looking for excuses for their shocking fall from grace. The media in Australia and England found one in the form of lanky, double-jointed Ian Meckiff. There were doubts in a small section of the press about his actions and rumblings were heard in the tourists' dressing room. Other Australians around the country came under scrutiny, including Jim Burke, Keith Slater and Gordon Rorke. Tony Lock was also accused of 'chucking' his faster off-break. In this controversial climate, the shrewdness and intelligence of Bradman, and the smooth diplomatic skills of Benaud, an experienced journalist, came to the fore. Bradman suggested that there were just two points to consider when judging if a player was bowling or throwing: first, whether the umpires were interpreting the law correctly; and second, whether the law should be altered. Bradman said it had 'to be one or the other'. (Two years later the law was altered with Bradman, as Chairman of the Australian Cricket Board, a key figure in the revision.) For his part, Benaud held firm in support of his players in media briefings, telling journalists that Meckiff's bowling was 'fair and legitimate'.

The Third Test at Sydney was drawn, with Benaud starring again (five for 83 and four for 94), and his team having the better of the contest. Now it was crunch time. If England won the next two Tests it would retain the Ashes. A draw or win at Adelaide in the Fourth Test would see Australia take them back after six years of being locked safely in England's keeping.

Peter May again made a strategic error in winning the toss and sending Australia in. Colin McDonald (170) and all the other key bats were among the runs. Benaud returned to form with the blade, scoring a useful 46 and Australia reached 476 – enough to demoralise England. Benaud was thrilled to be able to welcome the great speedster Ray Lindwall back into the Test team, and this helped the home team's dominance in the psychological stakes. The focus and even the sentimentality of the media were directed to the popular Lindwall. He only took three wickets, but nicely augmented Benaud's bag of tricks, while the spinner himself secured another haul of nine wickets (five for 91 and four for 82), and the Ashes with a 10-wicket victory.

It could not get much sweeter than this for Benaud. Perhaps only an Ashes victory or defence in England would be even more satisfying. The Australians wrapped up the series 4–0. Benaud collected 31 wickets at 18.84 and was the dominant bowler with Davidson (24 wickets at 19.00). Only England's Laker (15 wickets at 21.20) had any real penetration for the visitors.

Benaud had now dominated three series in succession, beginning with the tour of Pakistan and India in 1956–57. In 1959–60, in a five-Test tour of India (won 2–1 by Australia), he again proved too much for opposing bats taking 29 wickets at 19.59 and was just pipped as the most effective bowler of either side by Davidson (29 wickets at 14.86). Benaud, at 29 years of age, lay claim to being the best leg-spinner in the world; a batsman who could still deliver when required, and an astute, inspiring captain.

The next big international challenge came a year later in 1960–61 when a mighty West Indian team, led by Frank Worrell, toured Australia. If England was reputed to be one of the best-ever teams before the 1958–59 drubbing, the Caribbean squad ranked with it and included an extra dimension of aggression with bat and ball that held frightening promise for the Australians. If its speedmen

(Charlie Griffith, Garry Sobers) and spinners (Alf Valentine, Sonny Ramadhin, Lance Gibbs) got on top they would run over any batting line-up. If the dashing, flamboyant and formidable batting line-up of Conrad Hunte, Cammie Smith, Rohan Kanhai, Sobers, Worrell and Gerry Alexander gained control, Australia's bowlers would face obliteration.

Before the confrontation in the First Test at Brisbane, Bradman, chairman of selectors, created an historic Test precedent by asking Benaud if he could address the players. As ever, Bradman didn't waste a syllable, telling them that it could be a wonderful, attractive season of cricket, but that it was totally up to the players. Then came a fascinating caveat.

'The selectors will choose players they believe are playing good cricket,' Bradman told them, 'and they will look in kindly fashion on players who play aggressively and are clearly thinking about those who pay their money at the turnstiles. The selectors want you to be winners but not at the cost of making the game unattractive for the cricket follower.'

This was typical Bradmanese. He put everything in a positive – even cheerful – light, but with a clear, underlying warning that the drudgery of the last Test series in Australia against England two years earlier would not be tolerated. Bradman had been as pleased as anyone with Australia's regaining the Ashes. But crowds and revenues were down. The prosperity of the game was at stake. With increasing post-Second World War wealth and disposable income, and the rise of alternative summer sports, Australia had to attract spectators. Television rights then were not going to be the saviour of the game and one-day cricket was yet to be contested at the international level.

With this speech ringing in their ears, the Australians began the toughest assignment yet under Benaud. He would lead from the front especially in combating the greatest cricketer of all (according to Bradman), Garry Sobers.

The Bradman influence, subtle but with force, was evident at a critical moment in the First Test. Australia was six for 92 at tea chasing 233 to win. Benaud and Davidson were in. Bradman came to the dressing room, poured himself a cup of tea and told them how much he was enjoying the match. Then he asked Benaud if he were going for a win or a draw.

'We're going for a win of course.'

Bradman's dry reply of 'I'm very pleased to hear it' reinforced what he had said to the team before the game. Benaud's resolve to chase victory was increased. He and Davidson were involved in a fine, fighting partnership of 134 that all but pulled off one of the great wins in cricket history. Instead there was a tie, the first ever in a Test.

Benaud told Bradman after the game that he was unhappy with what he saw as a big chance for a win thrown away by panic batting at the finish in which there were three run-outs. Bradman disagreed saying it was the 'best thing which could possibly have happened to cricket' because of the exciting finish and the media attention it brought to the game. Benaud wouldn't accept this verdict and said that as captain he would have preferred if Australia had played better and won. Bradman insisted that Benaud would change his mind in the future.

Sobers had belted the Australian attack, making a brilliant 132 in the first innings at Brisbane. The left-handed West Indian had murdered anything a fraction loose or off-line during a titanic duel with Benaud, yet the bowler did not shirk the confrontation. Before the Tests he discovered a small chink in Sobers' mighty armour. It revolved around an apparent uncertainty over the top-spinner and the wrong'un — that deadly ball to a left-hander that heads towards slips rather than into him like the conventional leg-break. Despite the shellacking at Brisbane, Benaud worked on these deliveries with all the attention and diligence of an Antwerp watchmaker, bringing fellow wrist-spinners Bob Simpson and Johnnie Martin into the picture to turn the screws further. The three spinners removed Sobers five times in nine innings (the tenth being a run-out), while Alan Davidson, with his left-arm swing, got him three times and left-arm paceman Ian Meckiff got him once. Their combined force kept the world's most devastating batsman of the era down to 430 runs at 43.00. Given that only a few years earlier he had broken the world Test batting record with a score of 365 not out, this was a sizeable success for Benaud and his cohorts. It went a long way towards Australia's narrow 2–1 series win.

Benaud's figures – 23 wickets at 33.87 – reflected two factors. He was expensive in terms of runs per wicket but could be forgiven in the face of mighty batting. But he also took a big swag of wickets and had a steady influence on the series. Only Davidson, of all the Australian bowlers, had the measure of the West Indians with 33 wickets at 18.55.

The series could lay claim to being the greatest of all time. It had everything and, in the end, only two wickets separated the two sides. Benaud and Frank Worrell took the credit for leading aggressively most of the time. The tie, as Bradman predicted, was great for cricket. It was just the right prescription for its dull image after the 1958–59 series. The game's sudden recovery was evident at the end of the series when 90,800 people – a world record for a cricket match – turned up for the Saturday of the MCG Fifth Test.

That enormous challenge of the Australian summer over, Benaud prepared for the goal he wanted above all else: an Ashes victory in England. He nearly lost in the first game of the 1961 season at Worcestershire when he injured his

shoulder. Early in his career he had received a shattering
blow to the skull when he mis-timed a bouncer. Surgery
saved him. He recovered and showed courage in becoming
an aggressive hooker again. But the shoulder breakdown
was a bigger threat. He carried the injury in the drawn First
Test at Edgbaston, taking three for 15 in England's
first innings, but the longer the game went on the more he
suffered. The measure of the problem, kept quiet by
the tourists, was realised when Benaud stood down for the
Second Test at Lord's. Fortunately, Australia, under Harvey,
won by five wickets, thanks to great batting by Lawry (130
in the first innings on the difficult wicket) and outstanding
bowling by Davidson (five for 42 in England's first innings)
and McKenzie (five for 37 in the second). Benaud came back
at Headingley but struggled in Australia's loss by eight
wickets, the loss generated by Trueman's devastating form
(eleven for 88). Then, with everything on the line on the last
day of the Fourth Test at Old Trafford, Benaud bowled an
amazing spell, taking five for 12 in 25 balls in England's
second innings and Australia won by 54 runs. *The embrace*
had more affection than ever in front of a stunned
Manchester crowd. Benaud, who was steady but unable to
penetrate England's strong batting line-up in the first
innings, took six for 70 in the second. His bowling around
the wicket and into the rough was a rare step for a leggie in
that era. (Such bowling lessened the chance of an lbw
decision and allowed batsmen to hit more freely – or
perhaps this is what Benaud hoped. A less cautious batsman
would often be an easier target for a spinner.) The move won
the game and swung the Ashes. The final Test was drawn
with Australia on top.

Benaud's series figures of 15 wickets at 32.53 masked his
true impact, but not the shoulder problem, which would
plague his final years. He led New South Wales to a Shield

win in 1961–62, when no Tests were played, and then played host to the visiting England team under Ted Dexter in 1962–63. The unprepossessing series, marked by three boring draws, ended 1–1, thus allowing Australia to retain the Ashes. Benaud took 17 wickets at 40.47, unflattering figures that demonstrated his injury was retarding him. He resigned as captain during the 1963–64 series, but played four Tests. He left the playing scene without losing a Test series as captain. Benaud played 63 Tests, took 248 wickets at 27.03 and made 2201 runs at 24.46, with three centuries. He was the first player ever to achieve the double of 2000 runs and 200 wickets in Tests.

He moved seamlessly into a cricket afterlife as a commentator and journalist both in England, where he had an association with BBC TV for 35 years, and Australia. He began a long link with Channel Nine in 1977, and was a consultant to Kerry Packer when he formed World Series Cricket. In the late 1990s, Channel Four took over broadcasting cricket in England and Benaud, by popular demand, was contracted to them.

Benaud and his wife and business partner, Daphne, divide their time between homes in Sydney and Beaulieu-sur-Mer, a village outside Nice on the French Riviera. When in France during the Northern summer, he is never more than a 90-minute flight from any of England's major cricket grounds where he commentates. Benaud enjoys writing and, apart from his several magazine and paper outlets, has found time to produce eight books.

Bradman's choice of Benaud as 12th man in his best-ever Australian team was based on his great ability and the leadership, experience and intelligence he brought to all facets of the game. Bradman ranked only Keith Miller ahead of Richie Benaud in choosing an all-rounder for his all-time best-ever Australian Ashes team.

PART 2

THE ALL-TIME ASHES TEAM: ENGLAND

In batting order, Bradman's ideal England Ashes team is:

JACK HOBBS (Surrey)

LEN HUTTON (Yorkshire)

DENIS COMPTON (Middlesex)

PETER MAY (Surrey)

WALLY HAMMOND (Gloucestershire)

W.G. GRACE (Gloucestershire, London County)

GODFREY EVANS (Kent)

FRED TRUEMAN (Yorkshire)

ALEC BEDSER (Surrey)

S.F. BARNES (Warwickshire, Staffordshire, Lancashire)

HEDLEY VERITY (Yorkshire)

IAN BOTHAM (Somerset, Worcestershire, Durham) (12th Man)

Bradman sent me his selections for the best-ever England team in February 1999 and late in 2000 he confirmed he had not changed his mind about his selection.

Some features that distinguished the team were:

* Surrey and Yorkshire each produced three selections. Hobbs, May and Bedser were from Surrey. Yorkshire's three were Hutton, Trueman and Verity. Two players – Hammond and Grace – played their county cricket at Gloucestershire.

* Bradman had played against seven of the players chosen: Hobbs, Hutton, Compton, Hammond, Evans, Bedser and Verity.

* He had not played against the remaining five: May, Grace, Trueman, Barnes and Botham. Two of them, Grace and Barnes, finished playing before Bradman was a Test player. The other three, May, Trueman and Botham, played after he had retired.

* Bradman never saw Grace or Barnes play. These were the only two selections he made in his three ideal teams (world, Australia and England) that he never saw.

* Hobbs, Grace and Barnes played before World War I.

* Three players – Grace, Barnes and Hobbs – were all born before 1900.

* Only Botham played Test cricket in the last quarter of the twentieth century. He played his 102 Tests from 1977 to 1992.

* Grace began playing Tests in 1880 and Botham finished playing in 1992, so the Test careers of Bradman's best-ever England side span 112 years.

* Five players captained England: Hutton, May, Hammond, Grace and Botham.

* Three players – Hutton, Compton and Hammond – played in Tests before and after World War II.

* One player played in the 1880s – Grace.

* One player played in the 1890s – Grace.

* Two players played from 1900 until 1914 – Barnes and Hobbs.

• Two players played in the 1920s – Hobbs and Hammond.

* Five players played in the 1930s – Hobbs, Hutton, Compton, Hammond and Verity.

* Five players played in the 1940s – Hutton, Bedser, Compton, Hammond and Evans.

* Six players played in the 1950s – Hutton, Compton, May, Evans, Trueman and Bedser.

* Two players played in the 1960s – May and Trueman.

* Only one player played after 1970 –Botham.

* No player who has played in the twenty-first century was chosen by Bradman.

* Eight players hit Test centuries (Hobbs, Hutton, Compton, May, Hammond, Grace, Evans and Botham); six players hit doubles (Hobbs, Hutton, May, Compton, Hammond and Botham); and two players hit triples (Hammond and Hutton)

Jack Hobbs was one of the many fine early twentieth-century England players Bradman did see play, but late in his career. Hobbs didn't have the force or stroke range of earlier seasons when Bradman played against him in 1928–29. Yet what Bradman saw was enough to convince him that Hobbs was one of the game's greats. He had emerged as a Test player early in 1908, the year Bradman was born, and nearly a decade after Grace had bowed out at the top. It was a suitable time for a contender to challenge Grace's past dominance of the game in England. Hobbs, a taciturn, low-key character, was a contrast to the forceful Grace, yet he was to develop as a batsman of greater quality. Bradman, ever the detective looking for clues concerning a player's technical faults, observed Hobbs, for the period he was aged 46 to 48, at close quarters in 14 matches, including 10 Tests, in 1928–29 and 1930. Bradman branded Hobbs to be without any deficiencies at all. He ranked him technically the best batsman he ever saw.

Bradman found his choice of the other opener for the best-ever England Ashes team, Len Hutton, similarly faultless with footwork, stroke-play and shot production, yet believed he could have been more aggressive in his approach to batting. Bradman thought less of batsmen who were intent on keeping the ball out of their stumps and not giving a catch than of those who had a forceful way whenever they were at the wicket. He always believed it was necessary for batsmen to take the initiative from bowlers, set a mood and pave the way for team-mates to follow.

The Don scorned what he referred to as 'stodgy' play. It left the bowlers in charge and 'fellow batsmen in the dressing room with an air of gloom'.

Bradman noted that Hutton eschewed the hook if

bowlers tried to tease it out of him, but found him a good hooker when he wanted to use that shot. Hutton's dour character, lightened by a whimsical sense of humour, was too much in evidence at the crease for Bradman's liking, yet he recognised him as an outstanding cricketer. Hutton achieved much in his career. In 1938 he made 364 at The Oval against Australia, and surpassed Bradman's record of 334 made in 1930 – two records that still stand in Ashes cricket. Hutton was the first professional to regularly captain England, and the man who won back the Ashes in 1953, and successfully defended them in Australia in 1954–55. He was also the first professional to be elected to the Marylebone Cricket Club before his career finished and the second (after Jack Hobbs) to be knighted for his services to cricket.

The main contender for Hutton's position was an equally dour fellow Yorkshireman, Herbert Sutcliffe, the one-time partner for Hobbs in the actual England team.

'He performed far better than he looked,' Bradman remarked. 'He was more at home against pace than spin, but he managed to work his way through against spin with courage. He played one of the finest ever innings on a sticky at Melbourne in 1929.'

Bradman played in that game, which England won by three wickets. The opening stand by Hobbs (49) and Sutcliffe (a chanceless 135) of 105 was arguably the best-ever partnership in Test cricket on a rain-affected pitch. It set up an unlikely victory when England was set 332 to win.

Sutcliffe was a good hooker and scored more from the on-side, which was perhaps a consequence of being brought up playing on wet wickets in England's north. He wasn't keen on the drive and preferred pushes and edges through slips and gully. It irritated spectators at times, but he could refer to his big scores as evidence of his value to his county or England.

In 27 Ashes Tests, Sutcliffe scored 2741 runs at the excellent average of 66.85, the second-best average in Ashes history (Bradman averaged 89.78 from 5028 runs in 37 matches) for anyone playing in at least 20 games. Hutton, also in 27 Tests, scored 2428 runs at 56.46, while Hobbs averaged 54.26 from 3636 in 41 encounters against Australia.

Bradman described his choice for the number-three spot in the England side – Denis Compton – as a 'glorious natural cricketer' and regarded the Middlesex champion as a master batsman, despite his occasional unorthodoxy.

'His left elbow does not always please the purists,' Bradman wrote in *Farewell to Cricket* (Hodder & Stoughton, London, third edition, 1952), 'and in some respects his stroke production is not up to the standard of other masters.' Bradman thought Compton had a good cover drive, although he didn't rank it with that stroked by Wally Hammond. He admired Compton's daring in playing the sweep and his other improvisations, which some incorrectly saw as imperfections. Bradman thought Compton had a weakness against the short ball after the 1948 series and put it down to indecision over how to play it – either by getting his back foot across in the technical prescribed position to hit it, or by a more 'stand-and-deliver' pull shot. However, that assessment was made when he had to face Lindwall and Miller, who peppered him with head-high bouncers. Then he won some or lost some, mainly because of inexperience in facing such a lethal delivery, at least as sent down by these two intimidators. Bradman considered that later in Compton's career he was more circumspect in playing the shot and more selective in his counterattacking.

'He had another characteristic capacity common to all the

masters,' Bradman added. 'He played the ball late and had time to do it.'

Compton was a poor runner between the wickets. England all-rounder of the 1950s, Trevor Bailey, noted that 'a call from Denis was merely the basis for negotiation'.

Compton, barring injury, was an automatic pick for England from 1938 to 1956, and in the late 1940s was the most attractive of all the country's batsmen. At times, Hutton, an almost exact contemporary, and later Peter May, were regarded as more effective batsmen, but Compton's aggressive yet cheerful and carefree demeanour at the crease made him one of the most attractive crowd-pleasers of all time. Compton, who was also capped for England in soccer, was the superstar drawcard of his day.

His only rival for the coveted number-three spot in England's team was left-hander David Gower, who Bradman also regarded as one of the great natural talents in the history of the game. Bradman enjoyed watching Gower and ranked several of his innings highly, particularly his 123 at Sydney in 1990–91 and his 157 at The Oval in 1985. Gower scored 8231 runs in Test cricket at an average of 44.25 and made 18 centuries.

Peter May, Bradman's choice at number four in the batting order of the best-ever all-time England Ashes team, superseded Compton as England's leading batsman by the mid-1950s. His polish and style were accompanied by a temperament that pulled England, Surrey and Cambridge University out of many a predicament. Perhaps his best hour, in this respect, came at Melbourne in the Second Test of the 1958–59 Ashes when he arrived at the crease with the score at three wickets for 7. Alan Davidson, swinging the ball prodigiously with his long left arm, had England on the ropes under low cloud. May weathered the conditions and the brilliant bowling and went on to a century.

'May was the finest batsman in arguably the best and most balanced line-up England ever put in the field,' Bradman said, referring to England's 1956 team. Its batting order through the Ashes series, which Bradman covered as a journalist, included Peter Richardson, Colin Cowdrey, David Sheppard, May, Tom Graveney, Cyril Washbrook and Denis Compton.

May at 183 cm (6 ft), was broad-shouldered and had strong forearms. Blessed with excellent timing, he was a superb driver, especially through mid-on.

Behind May at number five in the batting order Bradman chose Wally Hammond, who he regarded as the best England bat produced from 1928 until the Second World War. Hammond, according to Bradman, had the most majestic and graceful cover drive of all, whether on the back or front foot. His athletic build allowed him to deliver shots with precision timing and power. Hammond was balletic in his movements. He used his dainty feet to advantage, learning all the steps from the great Charlie Macartney on Australia's tour of England in 1926.

'There probably was never a more balanced player than Wally,' Bradman said.

Hammond was Bradman's biggest rival over the decade 1928–38. Hammond, aged 25, on the tour of Australia in 1928–29, outgunned the Test tyro Bradman, aged 20, in their first Ashes encounter but Bradman was never 'beaten' again over the next six series contests. Honours were even during the Bodyline series of 1932–33, although considering England captain Douglas Jardine's tactics, Bradman, with a marginally superior average (56.57 to 55.00), could claim to have done better, especially when his team was soundly beaten 4–1.

Bradman noted two areas in which Hammond could be restricted. One was his reluctance to hook or pull when 'bounced' or attacked with short deliveries. The other was his lack of an attacking on-drive. But these were mild deficiencies in an otherwise near-perfect technique. Bowlers could only concentrate on Hammond's deficiencies hoping to force an error. The only factor that could beat such a champion was brilliant bowling. Leg-spinner Clarrie Grimmett delivered this in 1930, and gained a psychological hold on Hammond. Bill O'Reilly, on occasions, also challenged him with his exceptional skills, but that was it. No paceman ever really had his measure.

Bradman also noted that Hammond was, at times, a talented medium-pace bowler.

'He was most dangerous when he failed with the bat,' Bradman said. 'He liked to have some success, one way or another, in every game he played. If he had concentrated on his bowling I believe he would have been bracketed with the best medium pacers in history.'

Hammond took 83 wickets in Tests at 37.80. In first-class cricket he took 732 wickets at 30.58.

Number six in Bradman's all-time England line-up was W.G. Grace – an attacking bat, who would have stood up as a 'great' in any era. The selection of W.G. Grace ahead of Ian Botham, named as 12th man, is arguably one of the most controversial decisions in Sir Donald Bradman's all-time best-ever England team, 1877 to 2000.

Bradman, once more, was looking for the best team balance. When I asked why he chose Grace as the all-rounder over Botham, he said that he wanted a batting all-rounder at number six. If he had been looking for a bowling all-rounder, he would have chosen Botham over Grace.

'The first five – Hobbs, Hutton, Compton, May and Hammond – are all top-line batsmen,' Bradman said, 'and Grace made up the complement of six.'

Bradman judged Grace a more effective batsman and leader than Botham.

'Many observers in England rate Grace the greatest cricketer of all time,' he said. 'He was certainly the most outstanding cricketer, character and leader of the nineteenth century.'

Bradman judged him the best captain ever in the England team, ahead of Hutton and May.

The comparative figures for the Test careers of Grace and Botham are:

	Tests	runs	average	100s	wickets	average	catches
Grace	22	1098	32.29	2	9	26.22	39
Botham	102	5200	33.54	14	383	28.40	120

These statistics don't reflect the fact that Grace was 32 years of age when he first played Test cricket. Furthermore, batting averages were much lower in the nineteenth century because of poorer pitches. Grace's average of 32 would be equivalent to at least 50 in the twentieth century.

The career figures of Grace and Botham in first-class cricket present more instructive comparative analyses:

	Matches	runs	average	100s	wickets	ave.	catches
Grace	878	54,896	39.55	126	2876	17.92	875 and 5 stumpings
Botham	402	19,399	33.97	38	1172	27.22	354

Once more, Grace's batting average is deflated by comparison because of the conditions of the pitches and his bowling figures seem flattering for the same reason.

'The other bowlers chosen [Trueman, Bedser, Barnes and Verity] would be selected ahead of Botham, and Grace for that matter, taking into account their specialty and importance to team balance,' Bradman noted. He also pointed out that Hammond at times was a 'superb' medium pacer, which gave England a sixth bowling option. This further offset the need for Botham in the balance of Bradman's particular line-up.

The best-known images of Grace were of a portly man, but his physique was not done any justice by the camera. When he was 20, in 1868, there was no more athletic cricketer, yet there were few photographers around to show future fans his lean, fit figure. He was a sprinter and could throw a cricket ball 120 yards (110 metres), which was further than anyone else in England.

When I received Bradman's handwritten letter containing his all-time England team, at first I had a little trouble deciphering who he had picked at number seven. I rang him, congratulated him on a 'work of art', and told him I wished to check who he had at number seven.

'Is it Godfrey Evans at number seven?' I asked.

Bradman retorted sharply:

'He'll bat where his captain tells him to!'

'I'm not questioning his position in the order. It's just that I'm not sure of your handwriting.'

'Yes,' Bradman said, 'it's Evans.'

Godfrey Evans, the wicket-keeper, was a stocky extrovert. This man from Kent was a character with flair, who took advantage of his showmanship. He stumped with a flourish and caught with movements that reminded onlookers of a Catherine Wheel. Bradman, as ever, chose the keeper for his

ability behind the stumps rather than his capacity to keep
and bat.

'Evans was both spectacular and safe,' Bradman said. 'On
occasions when Australia amassed huge scores, he hardly let
a bye go through, which demonstrated his skill and concentration. [Alan] Knott and [Les] Ames were better batsmen,
but Evans was the superior keeper. I also rank George
Duckworth highly as a keeper, despite his raucous
appealing!'

Bradman recalled that Duckworth was so deft down the
leg-side that Australian batsmen refused to glance in case he
caught them. Bradman also spoke highly of Bert Strudwick,
a Surrey and England keeper from 1902 to 1927, but never
saw him play. Some English experts ranked him above all
others.

A comparison of their figures reads:

	Tests	runs	average	100s	dismissals	catches	stumpings
Evans	91	2439	20.49	2	219	173	46
Knott	95	4389	32.75	5	269	250	19
Ames	47	2434	40.56	8	97	74	23
Duckworth	24	234	14.62	–	60	45	15
Strudwick	28	230	7.93	–	72	60	12

Bradman regarded Yorkshire's Fred Trueman, at number
eight, as the best England fast bowler ever.

'Fred Trueman was England's pace bowler with the lot,'
he remarked. 'Fire, courage, guile, pace, line, length, swing
and cut. I don't think any batsman I saw was comfortable
against him in his prime.'

Trueman began as a blustering tearaway but, when his
career settled, he emerged as a master bowler who could lift
for the big occasion, especially in Ashes contests. In 10 consecutive seasons he took 100 or more first-class wickets,

including 175 at 13.98 in 1960. Again, at this level, Trueman took four hat tricks, 10 or more wickets in a match 25 times and five wickets or more in an innings 126 times. His 307 Test wickets at an outstanding 21.57 took just 67 matches. Trueman was a hard-hitting tail-ender, who usually had a dip at the bowling. His swashbuckling leg-side affronts with the blade got him three centuries, but none of them were in Tests. He was a brilliant, natural fielder, specialising at short-leg.

His biggest challenger as England's best paceman came from Frank Tyson, who in 17 Tests had the remarkable figures of 76 wickets at 18.56. He was the fastest bowler England has produced. During the second innings of the Third Ashes Test at Melbourne in 1954–55, Tyson delivered what Bradman regarded as the quickest spell he ever saw in a Test. Tyson skittled Australia, taking seven for 27. He took most wickets in the series, won by England – 28 at 20.82. Leg injuries cut him down in his prime.

Another bowler with an impressive record was Bob Willis, who in 90 Tests in a career that spanned 1970–84 took 325 wickets at 25.20.

Bradman was not as impressed with Harold Larwood, the speed demon of the Bodyline series. He was well aware of the statistics that show that Larwood took just 31 wickets in Tests against Australia at 41.29, apart from the 1932–33 series. Larwood's only other Ashes series in Australia yielded 18 wickets at 40.22, when Bradman had no trouble with him in his debut Tests for Australia. In 1930 in England, Bradman particularly, and other Australian bats, put him to the sword. Larwood then took four wickets at 73.00. In the 1932–33 Ashes, when Larwood came to prominence armed with Bodyline tactics, he managed 33 wickets at 19.52. Larwood in all bowled in 21 Tests and took 78 wickets at 28.35.

In *Farewell to Cricket*, Bradman spoke of Larwood's 'notoriety' during the Bodyline series and thought almost any of the leading fast bowlers could have achieved his dominance with the ball using similar methods.

In their tussles, Larwood dismissed Bradman four times during Bodyline, and unsettled his normally dominant rhythms against the English attack. Larwood's effort won the Ashes for England. Bradman ranked medium-fast Ken Farnes as a superior bowler because he moved the ball off the wicket better. Farnes took 60 Test wickets at 28.65.

Alec Bedser was Bradman's choice at number nine. He also chose him in his world team and placed him ahead of all other medium pacers, even Maurice Tate. Bradman personally found Bedser a more difficult opponent than Tate in England but qualified that he was at his prime as a batsman when he faced Tate, but in his declining years when he faced Bedser.

'Alec had a dangerous leg-cutter, which was really a fast leg-break,' Bradman observed. 'He also had a brilliant in-swinger that dipped late. I always had problems with it.'

Bradman was dismissed six times by Bedser. The Surrey star removed the world's greatest batsman ever five times in succession in the final Test in Sydney of the 1946–47 season and the first two Tests of the 1948 season in England. Bedser squeezed four catches from him close on the leg-side when his late-dipping in-swinger was employed.

Bradman admired Bedser's never-say-die attitude and his physical toughness. Bedser never left the field from injury in all his 51 Tests.

Bradman placed S.F. Barnes in the England team at number ten. Bradman had been intrigued with the career of the dark, brooding Barnes ever since he could remember. The great English medium pacer was very much in the psyche of Australian cricketers and fans in the early part of the twentieth century from dominating Ashes series in Australia. Bradman was only three years of age in 1911–12 in Australia when Barnes had a sensational Test series, taking 34 wickets at 22.88, and would have been too young to appreciate the bowler's effort in the Triangular Test Series in England in 1912. It was there that Barnes took 39 Australian and South African wickets at just 10.35 followed by 49 wickets at 10.93 in four Tests in South Africa in 1913–14. But at the age of seven or eight, Bradman became aware of Sydney Francis Barnes.

'When we played scratch "Test" matches in the schoolyard or the street, all the boys wanted to be Trumper when batting and the bowlers all wanted to be S.F. Barnes, even though he was English,' Bradman recalled with amusement. 'He was very much the talk among cricketers. His performances in Australia had given him legendary status here. He was the most respected English cricketer of the so-called Golden Era before World War One.'

When Bradman began playing first-class cricket in 1927–28, the conversations he had with bowlers who had seen Barnes in action and batsmen who had faced him confirmed for him Barnes' genius. Bradman also read widely about Barnes' style, ability and record.

Barnes could deliver swing and cut, and then spin, with such cunning that few batsmen knew what was coming from ball to ball. Like O'Reilly, he was tall, long-limbed and straight-backed, and with a short, springing run-up.

Bradman concluded in 1950 that Barnes and O'Reilly were the two greatest bowlers of all time, and maintained that view for the rest of his life. Yet he could not find a place for Barnes in his best-ever world team. When asked about this Bradman replied:

'My understanding was that they (Barnes and O'Reilly) were similar in style, aggression, intelligence and abilities. Barnes was probably quicker but did not have a wrong'un [googly], which gave O'Reilly the most marginal advantage. There was not much point in having two such similar players in the one team. I could only choose one. Another point for O'Reilly [in the world team] was his pairing with Grimmett.'

In 1938, when discussing with cricket writer Neville Cardus the comparison between these two giants of the game, Bradman made another point, which was also in O'Reilly's favour:

'I never saw Barnes, so I could not speak of how he bowled the leg-spinner. I only know that O'Reilly bowls it as well as I can imagine anyone bowling it. It couldn't possibly be nastier.'

In Ashes Tests, Barnes had a slightly better record, taking 106 wickets at 21.58, but in an era where the pitch conditions were better for bowlers.

Barnes was one of just two players in the three ideal teams (world, Australia and England) chosen by Bradman who he never saw play – a great compliment to Barnes' reputation and record. However, Bradman and Barnes were playing in the same English seasons in 1930, 1934 and 1938. In 1930, when Barnes was 57 and Bradman 21 years old, the press tried to arrange a match where they played against each other. Bradman would have loved the experience but the long, tight schedule for the Australians on tour, and Barnes' commitments to the Lancashire League, didn't allow the confrontation.

* * *

Bradman was not inclined to leave out any of his three pacemen choices – Trueman, Bedser and Barnes – which meant he could only select one spinner. He narrowed down his choices to either Verity or Laker.

Bradman had batted against both left-arm orthodox spinner Verity and right-arm off-spinner Laker, but took into account that Laker was not at his prime during the 1948 Ashes when Bradman faced him. Laker played in three 1948 Tests and his series figures of nine wickets at 52.44 reflect the pasting he received.

'He was inexperienced then,' Bradman recalled, 'but developed into the best off-spinner of the post-war period along with [the West Indies'] Lance Gibbs. Laker managed outstanding accuracy and control. He had a nice high arm action and could spin the ball hard.'

Laker is best known for taking a world record nineteen wickets for 90 runs at Manchester in the Fourth Test of the 1956 Ashes. Bradman reported on that match where the wicket was described as 'a dustbowl, a substandard Test wicket, conducive to prodigious spin'. He recognised the performance as one of sustained brilliance, but ranked Hedley Verity's fifteen for 104 at Lord's during the 1934 Ashes as an even more impressive effort, 'given the comparative conditions and batting strengths of the opposition'.

In 1956, Laker bowled to McDonald, Burke, Harvey, Craig, Miller, Mackay, Archer, Benaud, Lindwall, Maddocks and Johnson. This line-up on paper was deep in batting ability – everyone down to number ten, keeper Les Maddocks, and number eleven, off-spinner Ian Johnson, could bat. That was on paper. They were a demoralised bunch a week after England had thrashed them by an innings and 42 runs at Headingley. Laker had then taken eleven for 113. Australia lacked top-quality batsmen compared to its 1934 line-up to which Verity had delivered.

The line-up was: Woodfull, Brown, Bradman, McCabe, Darling, Chipperfield, Bromley, Oldfield, Grimmett, O'Reilly and Wall.

Verity took seven for 61 and eight for 43 on a rain-affected pitch, but Bradman concluded that 'while it was testing for a period after lunch on the final day, I played on worse pitches. Hedley bowled superbly, taking advantage of the conditions. He kept a remarkable length and, encouraged by some indifferent batting, made the ball spin and jump awkwardly'.

Bradman's decision to include Verity in his best all-time Ashes England team may well have been influenced by the fact that this particular Yorkshireman had dismissed him eight times in Tests – more often than any other bowler.

Verity took 144 Test wickets at 24.37 in 40 Tests. Laker took 193 at 21.24 in 46 Tests.

Ian Botham, selected by Bradman as 12th man, was an outstanding slipper. He was England's 'warrior' all-rounder, who took on the Australians at their own aggressive game. His medium-fast bowling record ranked him with the best in England's history. Botham also could be formidable with the bat. He would invariably attempt to dominate bowlers from the first deliveries he faced in an innings, and was a key factor in winning big games, with adventurous batting that thrilled spectators.

When comparing the Australian and England batting averages, an average score for England (in all Tests, not just Ashes matches) would be 376.59 and for Australia 400.53. England's batting seemed superior with four of the top five batsmen averaging more than 50 compared to Australia's

one batsman who averaged more than 50. But this one batsman was Don Bradman with an average of 99.94 in all
Tests. He was the difference between the Australian and
England teams. If an artificial intelligence expert designed
a five-Test contest between these two teams with each
player batting or bowling in his prime, Australia would win
each contest, as long as Bradman was in the side and other
things were more or less equal.

In actuality, Australia did not lose a contest from 1930 to
1948 when Bradman dominated, except for the Bodyline
series.

The following 12 chapters are profiles on Bradman's choices
for the best England team in Ashes cricket. Apart from the
obvious outstanding ability of the players chosen, they had
other common traits. All were team players. All could turn
a game with a flash of brilliance, and every one of them
recovered from setbacks to go on to be a champion.

CHAPTER 13

ONE MAN SHORT

JACK
HOBBS

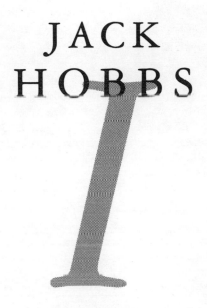

(England)

16 December 1882–21 December 1963

'I first saw Jack Hobbs in the year he turned 46 {1928} when he was past his prime but he was still the best-equipped batsman technically I ever saw. Hobbs was a master batsman in all conditions.'

DON BRADMAN

A thunderstorm broke over London early on the morning of 18 August 1926 as Jack Hobbs slept on 28 not out at his Clapham Park home. The day before he and Herbert Sutcliffe had taken England to none for 49 in its second innings of the Fifth and deciding Test – without a time limit – of the 1926 Ashes series, giving it a 27-run lead with all second-innings wickets intact. Prospects looked bright for England until that 3 a.m. storm lit up The Oval and torrential rains swept over it, flooding the uncovered pitch.

Hobbs was gloomy as he had breakfast with his wife and four children and read his morning paper. The rain had stopped but the evidence of the night's upheaval was dripping from roof guttering. Hobbs assumed that the game would not start on time at 11 a.m. But at 10 a.m., as ever during the Test, he walked the short distance to Clapham High Street for the one-mile (2 km), three-penny tram ride to The Oval. He had been appearing there for 21 years since he first began as a novice for Surrey, yet even now as the world's greatest batsman, he retained a trademark humility that endeared him to all cricket fans at home and abroad, but most of all to Surrey fans. There was no chauffeured limousine for this superstar. He couldn't afford it and, in any case, he didn't want any special attention. Hobbs stuck to tried and trusted simple routines and wished to be as unobtrusive as possible. He would have preferred to have been magically beamed from his living room to The Oval locker room.

The overnight weather had dampened the ground and his spirits. He feared in his heart that the sticky wicket that was sure to result from the torrent would diminish his chances of making a Test century for the first time against Australia at The Oval in front of his adoring fans. He had scored 10 hundreds against the traditional enemy and 136 first-class centuries in all. But this was the one he had wanted above all others. Time was running out. He didn't know whether he would still be playing at age 47 in 1930 – the next visit by the Australians. In his mind it was now or never. More important still was the need for him to make a big score to help England to a win in the Ashes, something that had not been achieved since before the First World War.

The atmosphere was humid and heavy as Hobbs moved briskly to the members' entrance beside The Oval's main gates. As ever, autograph hunters swamped him. He scribbled a few signatures, then hurried past the countless other pleas and pieces of paper thrust in his face to the players' rooms to the left of the pavilion. Hobbs joined team-mates near the players' entrance gate to the arena and was surprised to find the ground had dried. The pitch had changed from brown with a green tinge to black, the tell-tale colour of turf clogged with moisture and the precursor to the dreaded sticky.

The team captains became animated after inspecting the wicket at 10.40 a.m. England's big Percy Chapman called for the heavy roller. Australia's lean, craggy-faced Herbie Collins asked for sawdust. He would be using an all-spin attack and could call on four such bowlers: Arthur Mailey, left-armer Charlie Macartney, Clarrie Grimmett and the tall, lean, bespectacled Arthur Richardson, the hunched figure who was to gain centre stage for the wrong reasons. Collins' hope was that the sun would come out and create a glue-top. Australia, most observers reckoned, could run through England for another 60 runs at most.

When Hobbs and Sutcliffe resumed their innings on time at 11 a.m. the cloud cover was still heavy. The sun couldn't shine through to make the wicket unplayable. A packed crowd was undeterred by the weather and the signs outside the ground reading 'Play Not Guaranteed'. Settling into a seat in the members' enclosure was the Prince of Wales, the future King Edward VIII, who had come like everyone else to see, as he was reported as saying, 'a great contest and Hobbs get a hundred'.

Collins began with Grimmett, his most accurate spinner, from the pavilion end and Macartney, whose job it was to keep the batsmen quiet while the wicket dried. This he did, sending down nine overs for just two runs. Both openers did more farming than batting – patting, wiping and filling with their willows between balls and overs. Hobbs was doing most of the scoring, and off Grimmett. It was an alarming time for Australia because there was no wicket in the first 40 minutes, which saw 26 scored. In theory the wickets were there to be had once the sun came out. But in reality, England was none for 75 and with 10 wickets still intact, full of hope.

Collins then pulled one of the strangest moves in a series-deciding Test in Ashes history. When the sun appeared not long before high noon, Macartney was replaced, not by leg-spinner Mailey, who was always prepared to toss the ball up in the interests of more turn and more wickets, but by Richardson with his off-spin. Richardson could expect more turn on this potent wicket, but he was not in Mailey's class as a slow bowler and wicket-taker. What perplexed observers more was Collins' directive to the bowler to go around the wicket so that his deliveries spun from leg-stump towards the on-side. There was less concern about securing an lbw or bowling the batsmen. The intent was to get a catch to fieldsmen in a ring around the short-leg area from leg slip to silly mid-on.

Hobbs took most of the bowling and shielded the less gifted Sutcliffe. He faced up well outside leg-stump. As soon as Richardson let go of the ball, Hobbs made his instant calculation about line and length. More often than not he shuffled *across* in front of his stumps to meet the popping, jigging ball. Usually Hobbs employed 'soft hands' and dropped the ball at his feet with no effort to play through the shot; a move that would have given the five fielders a few paces from him something to catch.

During this period it was even suggested by some observers that Hobbs feigned problems with Richardson in order to fool Collins into keeping him on. Hobbs later denied it but there would always be suspicions that England's superstar outwitted the Australian captain.

The sun grew hotter and the need for sawdust on the wicket diminished as the game stretched into the immediate afternoon. The glue-pot began to form. But Hobbs and Sutcliffe had survived. They had devised a pattern of play to counter the uneven bounce and vicious turn, and were comfortable, if ever a pair could be on such a wicket. Richardson sent down eight successive maidens. Runs trickled from the other end. The score reached none for 100 – a dream score-line under the conditions.

Collins replaced Grimmett with Mailey but left Richardson on. Hobbs immediately survived an lbw verdict after a ball that turned in from the off and caught him dead

in front. Even Sutcliffe at the other end, and the umpire,
Frank Chester, adjudged it out. But, oddly, Mailey and his
keeper, Bertie Oldfield, did not appeal. They thought the
ball pitched outside off, situation in lbw law in 1926 that
meant 'not out'. Chester put his hand back in his pocket,
thankful that no Australian fielder had seen him taking it
out of his pocket to give a decision against Hobbs. Such is
the idiosyncrasy of cricket. The Australians in that era, as in
any other, were not averse to giving voice but, at that precise
moment, the two players in a position to give credence to a
shout did not utter the expected cry. The Australians had
appealed often in the first two hours of play, but the yelps
had subsided as the pre-lunch session slipped England's
way. By the time Hobbs misjudged one dead in front,
Australian heads were down and their voices muffled.

Just before lunch – taken after 150 minutes at 1.30 p.m.
– Richardson delivered his thirteenth over and Hobbs
spanked him through mid-on for four, signalling a big
victory in the first session. England had added 112 runs and
was none for 161. It had a lead of 139, with all wickets
standing. Sutcliffe was 53 not out. Hobbs was 97, and
tantalisingly close to his last great professional Test dream
and aim – a century against Australia at The Oval. At
lunch, instead of walking off with the Australians and the
umpires, the two conscientious batsmen did further farming, in a more concerted effort than they had made all
morning. The pitch was a mess, but their attending to the
divots on a good length made it less of one.

They were hardly inside the dressing room when they
were summoned to meet the Prince of Wales. One of the
few among the Royals to appreciate cricket, Prince Edward
had some encouraging things to say to the two heroes before
he put on his neutral face at lunch when he joined the two
teams. According to Bill Woodfull, the Prince had 'quite a

few laughs' with Arthur Mailey, who was in a jovial mood despite the scoreboard.

Hobbs, as ever, remained his reticent self as he contemplated those three little runs he needed for his century. When play resumed, the glue-pot had dried. The run-ups were no longer slippery and Collins opened with paceman Jack Gregory for the first time since the previous evening. Hobbs seemed untroubled with speed. Within a few minutes of the resumption he picked off two singles. On 99 he hit one just forward of square leg. Sutcliffe responded to the 'yes!' from his partner and Hobbs achieved an even 100. The roar from the expectant crowd, it was claimed later, could be heard across London.

The Oval rose to John Berry Hobbs for if not his finest moment, then definitely his most satisfying one. He had the coveted century at home. England, at none for 172 and 150 ahead, was in the box seat. The Prince of Wales, having seen what he wished, began to make his way out of the members' stand. Prince Edward was almost away when Gregory too had seen enough. He bowled Hobbs with one that nipped back and brushed the off-bail. The Prince turned to clap Hobbs all the way to the pavilion before departing for other royal duties.

England went on to 436, with Sutcliffe scoring 161. Australia collapsed to all out 125, with Harold Larwood (three for 34) and Wilfred Rhodes (four for 44) doing the damage. England won by 289 runs, its first Ashes victory (1–0) since 1912. Hobbs, already a legend, was now a cricket immortal.

A postscript to this Test was the opprobrium heaped on Collins for the inept handling of his attack, especially in relying on Richardson and in the instructions Collins gave him. According to some English and Australian critics, this allowed Hobbs, Sutcliffe and England to make a 'great escape'. Hunter 'Stork' Hendry, part of the touring Australian squad, even went as far as to suggest that Collins, a chronic gambler, had thrown the match by betting against Australia. Former Australian captain Monty Noble attacked Collins in print, and in private said much the same as Hendry in terms of accusations against the Australian skipper. There was no hard evidence against Collins. The suggestions of a 'fix' could have resulted from the Australians' disgust at losing the seemingly unlosable. Given Australia's long-term dominance, it was a shock to its supporters, especially as Collins, before The Oval debacle, had been generally regarded as an astute leader. He had only ever lost one other game to England – in Australia in 1924–25 when England was beaten 4–1 – in seven previous starts as skipper.

Nevertheless, Hobbs' performance was masterful. Many hailed his hundred as one of the best innings ever played. Both Arthur Mailey and Charlie Macartney (Australia's best bat at the time) – who were on the field bowling and fielding to Hobbs, as opposed to Hendry and Noble in the crowd – said it was Hobbs' best-ever innings. They argued that the Englishman outplayed all the bowlers with the dominance you would expect under perfect playing conditions, rather than the worst.

The Rise without Trace

At the very least, Jack Hobbs was destined to be involved in cricket. His father was the groundsman first at Fenner's, Cambridge, where he bowled at the nets and umpired, and later at Jesus College, Cambridge. Young Jack grew up with the sound of willow on leather, the smell of linseed oil and the vision of green playing fields impinging on his senses for half the year. At home, especially in the summer, the conversation in the family of 14 – Jack was the eldest of 12 children – would often turn to the game that was not just a love for Hobbs senior but his way of life. Cricket became a way of life for Jack too. He had his father's reserve and quiet dignity, which he never lost. This characteristic masked a drive and ambition that were to take him as far as any person could go in cricket.

The environment was right for Hobbs' development. And he just happened to be right for the environment – so apt, in fact, that Archie MacLaren, a former England skipper, even wrote a book about him called *The Perfect Batsman*. Hobbs was self-taught. No coach was mentioned as a mentor from Parker's Piece, the municipal park area where as a boy and teenager in the summer months he practised and played morning, noon and evening until it was dark. His father gave advice here and there, and so did Tom Hayward, the local boy who made good for England and Surrey before Hobbs, and was his first top opening partner. But neither Hobbs senior nor Hayward was a coach.

Hobbs learned much by simply watching the game. He was a natural. Too much instruction would have been detrimental. There was more innate skill in the tips of his toes and fingers than in the bodies of a whole raft of teachers. Yet a sensational triple century or a hat trick did not mark his early days. With young Jack there was, instead, a steady sense of someone skilled and outstanding developing without fanfare. Yet, around England at the time of the Golden Age of cricket at the end of the 1890s there were any number of talented hopefuls who may or may not have gone on to success at county level.

The Unobtrusive Centurion

At age 18, in 1901, Hobbs made his first century in an annual match between the Ainsworth Club – a club established by and developed from a local Bible class – and the Cambridge Liberals, who tossed for his services. His effort for the Liberals went unremarked in any journal, although when he retired it was noted as the first of 244 such scores by him spanning more than three decades. Hobbs, the centurion, was on his way. He followed this with an unspectacular 36 not out in an annual charity match organised by Tom Hayward between county and local Cambridge players. It led to him being invited to play for Cambridgeshire as an amateur. A modest entry in *Wisden* for 1901 marked his average as 8.75 – the second-bottom average for the county. There were no fireworks here. No special report noting him as even a 'prospect'. Yet Hobbs moved on in 1902, beginning his life as a professional cricketer, after a fashion, by coaching at Bedford Grammar School. He continued with professional cricket but found his humility and reticence were not suited to teaching others. He stuck to developing himself. Underneath that taciturn exterior was a fellow who knew what he wanted.

The death of his father squeezed urgency into Hobbs' desire to make it as a working cricketer. In 1903 at 21 he applied to play for Essex and also Surrey. Essex rejected him without even bothering to give him a trial in the nets. Surrey, with a nod from Tom Hayward, invited him to London to The Oval for a try-out. The tried and trusted 'net' more often than not sorted out the haves from the have-nots. Practice wickets are meant to be worse than those in the middle. If a young cricketer demonstrated skills there – especially against the ball lifting around the ears, then it was an indicator that he had some prospects. And so it was with Hobbs after 20 minutes of net time. It gained him a practice game that day in which he made 37 before another novice who would subsequently make it, Philip Mead, bowled him. Mead did it again in a second trial the next day, this time after Hobbs had notched just 13. This modest 50 in two games – again nothing sensational – led to him being offered a chance to qualify for Surrey. This meant living in the county for two years and working as part of the ground-staff. He was paid a meagre wage, but he didn't care. To be paid for playing the game he loved was a dream come true.

Hobbs moved to London and fell in love with the mighty metropolis. In 1903 he did nothing with bat or ball to indicate genius. It was as if the genial, respectful young man was determined to rise without being noticed. He averaged fewer than 30 and, with his effective medium-pace swingers delivered with an ungainly action, took no big hauls of wickets. The careers of all the greats down the decades were credited with buckets of runs and bags of wickets by the time they were in their twenty-second year. Not Jack Hobbs. He was just thereabouts in 1904, the final qualifying year, with two scores in the nineties. Again, there was never a thought to discard him. He was promising, efficient and born not to offend anyone; just the right calibration for a professional career in county cricket.

In July 1904 he was invited to pad up for Cambridgeshire. Now, for the first time in his career, with two days of play he became offensive to opposition bowlers. He belted 92 against Norfolk. A century would have brought him more attention, even given him a mention in the London papers. Ten days later he did rate a small item for a spanking 195 against Herts. The magic of a double hundred would have gained him some decent review column space rather than a few paragraphs. But, once more, this was perhaps Hobbs' unconscious way of slipping into prominence without the accompanying trumpets. Still, *Wisden* devoted a line to him remarking on his 'remarkable average' of 58 in the final months of 1904. There was no mention of 'promise'. It was not the great yellow tome's style to say 'mark this chap down as a fine prospect'. But he was one. Keen judges already knew it.

Hobbs batted for Cambridgeshire for the first time at Lord's in the last game of the season because one of the teams was one man short. He made an attacking 55.

Travelling First Class

Hobbs was pleasantly shocked to learn that he had been picked to play for Surrey's Firsts in the opening game of the 1905 season against the Gentlemen of England, a team of top amateurs led, as ever, by W.G. Grace. Hayward ordered Hobbs to open with him, and so began one of the finest opening firms in English cricket. Hobbs made equal top score (18) in the first innings and top (88) in the second. Thus, belatedly, at 22 years, his mighty career began without ever playing for Surrey's Seconds. In just his second game he crafted a brilliant 155 against Essex and was awarded a county cap. No one had ever been more quickly rewarded in English county cricket. There may have been no heralding of Hobbs' emergence, yet there was already certainty about his ability to sustain a long career beyond the batters in the county's second team.

His first big test came in early May at The Oval when Surrey played the Australians who were led by Joe Darling. Hobbs came through it well, making 94 (run out), which included four dropped catches. It wasn't enough to bring him into contention for the 1905 Ashes series (won by

F. S. Jackson's team 2–0) and his season fell away with him
only recording six scores over fifty. His first season's figures
were 1317 runs at 25 from 51 completed innings. *Wisden*
thought him 'easy and finished in style', but criticised him
for 'playing too much with his legs' and for being tardy in
the field. It was hardly an endorsement, yet Hobbs was
satisfied with his initial season. His unexpected elevation to
the Firsts made him think that every game was a bonus,
especially batting with his hero, Tom Hayward, then
England's opener, who had an exceptional 1906. Hobbs,
again, was very much second fiddle. Yet he made gains. His
aggregate was 1913 at 40. *Wisden* was less patronising that
year. It patted him on the back for lifting his fielding
standards and reckoned he may even do better with the
bat.

1907 was a wet season that reduced all county averages
and created bowling bonanzas. But Hobbs maintained his
form, especially with 166 not out against Worcester on the
day his wife gave birth to their first son. During the season
four top professional players, including Hayward, refused
the terms offered by the MCC for the 1907–08 tour of
Australia as they were not lucrative enough. But Hobbs, as
a novice, was happy with any offer. Again, his career
advanced because selectors were short of a quality man or
two. Yet, it was deserved.

Severe sickness on the long boat voyage to Australia
debilitated him and he struggled in the run-up to the Tests.
He didn't make the First Test at Sydney in mid-December,
but was chosen for his debut game at Melbourne, which
began on 1 January 1908. Hobbs acquitted himself well
with 83 (in 195 minutes) and 28 in a thriller won by
England by one wicket. He went on to hit two other fifties
– 57 and 72 – for an aggregate of 302 at 43.14. Only
Nottingham's George Gunn (462 at 51.33) did better in the

Tests for England, which lost the series 4–1 to Monty Noble's team.

Hobbs' technical perfection was almost complete after the demanding tour. His advance was evident, not in a consolidating 1908 home season, but in 1909, when he hit his first double hundred (205 versus Hampshire, which included Philip Mead among its bowlers), and scored a century in each innings of a match for the first time (against Warwickshire: 160 and 100). His aggregate of 2114 at 40 was again commendable, but his Test performances against the visiting Australians led by Monty Noble were disappointing. Hobbs scored 132 at 26.40 in three Tests. But early in 1910 in South Africa, at 27, he blossomed as an outstanding Test batsman with scores of 89, 35, 53, 70, 11, 93 not out, 0, 1, and finally 187 (in just 225 minutes) at Newlands, Cape Town, in the Fifth Test. It was his first Test hundred. His aggregate of 536 at 67.37 was exceptional, especially since England lost the series 3–2.

Now Hobbs' batting had reached full maturity with off-side shots, developed on Australia's harder wickets. By mid-season they were flourishing just as well as his strong on-side strokes.

He seemed to mark time in 1910 at home, with just under 2000 runs at an average of 33, perhaps in reaction to his South African success. However, with six seasons under his belt at the top level in cricket, another factor concerning his batting emerged. He was remarkably consistent. At no point did he have a horror stretch. A few low scores would invariably be followed by some good ones. It was a feature of only a few cricketers in history. Bradman was another, of course, who enjoyed such consistency.

Hobbs had a far better boat trip to Australia for the 1911–12 season and Ashes tour, and this set him up for better performances. England lost the First Test at Sydney, but in Melbourne Hobbs steered his team to an eight-wicket victory with his first of 12 centuries against Australia – 126 not out. His form held over to the next Test innings at Adelaide, a game he dominated with 187. England won by seven wickets and took the lead in the series. By employing lightning footwork to get to the pitch of the ball, Hobbs had beaten the googly or wrong'un bowler, H.V. Hordern, just the way he had conquered South Africa's spinners two years earlier. His partnerships with Wilfred Rhodes (463 at 57.88) were key factors in England's series win of 4–1. S.F. Barnes (34 wickets at 22.88 runs per wicket) and F.R. Foster (32 wickets at 21.63) were the destroyers with the ball.

Hobbs' scores of 63, 22, 6, 126 not out, 187, 3, 178, 32 and 45 gave him an aggregate of 662 at 82.75. He was the best player for the series and, at 29 years, had reached his career peak. He maintained it during the less than success-ful Triangular Tournament in which England, Australia and South Africa played Tests against each other in England in 1912, scoring 224 at 56 (107 at Lord's in the First Test) against Australia, and 163 at 40.75 versus South Africa. The weather and the participation of an Australian team that was almost a Second XI due to withdrawals of its star players because of a dispute with the Australian Board of Control, conspired to weaken the contest.

In 1913, Hobbs had fewer distractions without Tests and a visiting team, and was able to play more games for Surrey and so notched nine centuries in his 2605 aggregate at 50.09 – second to Phil Mead who averaged 50.51 – the nearest he had come to topping the averages. But while that honour eluded him, there was no doubting his position as the world's premier bat as he collected 443 at 61.86 with a run of even scores – 82, 23, 92, 41, 64, 97, 33 and 11 not out – in South Africa in 1913–14. These efforts underlined his importance to England. They meant that even if his opening partner Rhodes didn't get going, Hobbs never failed to give England at least a sound start, and often an excellent one. The performance of this solid opening partnership was again a determining factor in England's 4–0 victory.

It was to be the nation's last cricketing hurrah before the beginning of the First World War. Early in August 1914, on a Bank Holiday Monday, Hobbs went about fashioning a brilliant 226 out of Surrey's five for 472 against Notts, unconcerned about Germany declaring war on Russia, a declaration which would lead to England entering the war. A crowd of 15,000 were entranced by this artist with a willow as he created something special, as if he knew that many young men in the crowd that day would never again be so entertained.

Hobbs, perhaps aware that his career might be curtailed, went on belting big scores – 11 centuries – until cricket ceased at the end of the 1914 season, the season in which *Wisden* named him batsman of the year. It was, in fact, the end of the first half of his career at exactly 10 seasons, including four overseas tours – two each to Australia and South Africa. Hobbs had made 25,517 runs and hit 65 first-class hundreds, enough to secure him an elevated position in the pantheon of England greats.

The Second Half

The war did not weary Hobbs of the desire for runs. He returned to the game in 1919 at age 36, robbed of four peak years – maybe what could have been even his finest cricketing years. Yet it could be argued that the break did him no harm and that it refreshed him. He was eager for the contest and revitalised with a new opening partner at Surrey in Andrew Sandham, the first partner who was junior to him.

Hobbs distinguished his return to at least his prowess in 1914 with a dashing 205 not out against the Australian Imperial Forces attack that was spearheaded by Jack Gregory. The season saw Hobbs score more than 2500 runs and accumulate eight centuries, including one each in the three traditional Gentlemen (Amateurs) versus Players (Professionals) matches. He had lost none of his former skills and seemed to peak again in 1920 with 2827 runs, including another eight County Championship centuries. At 38 years of age, he was still the country's number-one bat and prepared to tour down-under for a third time.

The 1920–21 Ashes in Australia, however, was not a happy one for England, which suffered at the hands of the strongest Australian combination since Joe Darling's era, thirty years earlier. The home team was led by the experienced and indomitable 155-kg Warwick Armstrong. England went down 5–0. Yet Hobbs, with 505 runs at 50.50, only enhanced his reputation by being the only bat to handle the pace attack of Jack Gregory and Ted McDonald, and the spin of Mailey, who took 36 wickets at 26.28.

He was looking forward to doing even better in 1921 when Armstrong's team came to England, but a torn thigh muscle and a troublesome appendix prevented him from playing one Test innings. Approaching the age of 40, Hobbs realised his days of all-out attack were not an option. The spirit was willing but the body was prone to tissue injury if he didn't look after it. Nevertheless, his longish legs carried him up and down the wicket for 10 centuries in 1922. If his powers had diminished, it was not noticed on the scoreboard. However, Hobbs was now thinking ahead. Instead of automatically touring, he deferred to business interests and did not go to South Africa. From now on, only the Australian visit, the toughest and longest of all, was on the agenda.

Hobbs turned 40 while his erstwhile team-mates slogged it out on the veldt, and he was now very much the mature gentleman. The shy youth, who avoided rushes of autograph hunters, was gone. In his stead was a still retiring but happy character, secure in his fame without being overwhelmed. If time was running out, he didn't seem anxious. Injuries apart, Hobbs could see no reason for not carrying on with his cricketing career until he was 50 or until his form fell away. His rationale received confirmation when he seized a slice of immortality in 1923 at age 40 by scoring his hundredth hundred against Somerset at Bath. Finishing his cricketing days then would have given him a legendary status. Yet he was just a little over halfway through his career output of 197 centuries.

In 1924, he even enhanced his reputation against a weak South African team with his only double century in Tests – 211 at Lord's – while England scored two for 503 in a day. The opening stand with his fourth top-drawer partner – Herbert Sutcliffe – was a record 268.

Confirmation of Number One

Hobbs had learned from his previous tours of Australia and prepared for the 1924–25 campaign meticulously. The result was a substantial run of scores in the Tests that maintained him as the world's best bat. He hit the pitch running at Sydney over Christmas 1924 in the First Test with 115 and 57, then a few days later early in the New Year rode his form into Melbourne in the Second Test with 154 and 22. He kept rolling at Adelaide with 119 and 27. England had lost every Test, but Hobbs was not responsible. Nor was Sutcliffe. When Hobbs notched 66 in the Fourth Test at Melbourne in mid-February it was their fourth century link of the series – 157, 110, 283 and 126. Hobbs' series aggregate was 573 at 63.67, in a team under Arthur Gilligan that went down 4–1 to Herbie Collins' Australians. Only the home team's Johnny Taylor (541 at 54.10) and Jack Ryder (363 at 72.60) challenged Hobbs and Sutcliffe (734 at 81.56). These four were the standout batsmen of the high-scoring series. Too often the strong innings bedrock laid by the English openers was not capitalised upon by the rest of the team.

Hobbs was buoyed by his continuing success in the post-war era. Once off the ship from Australia and back on English soil, he went straight into the 1925 season in late April in terrific form, managing a century in five consecutive games in May. Bowlers could hardly lay a glove on him, but he laid plenty of willow on leather. Everything was done with grace, timing and consummate skill as the master batsman of the era plundered on – a century in each innings against Cambridge, a double against Warwickshire, and a respectable score against all opposition. By the end of June there were 1700 runs in the bank. Hobbs, the elder, was holding back the clock, defying the laws of physical decline and daring to bat on and on in his perfection. He cultivated, rather than clobbered, 16 centuries and more than 3000 runs at an average of just over 70 in that mighty post-Australian tour summer. He admitted that conquering county bowlers was a breeze after subduing Jack Gregory, Clarrie Grimmett, Charlie Kelleway and Arthur Mailey on foreign soil. Yet there should be no underestimation of that phenomenal season. Hobbs had reached a pinnacle in a prolific run of 10 months in two countries. He may have had the capacity to top this, but there would be little point.

He would continue on in the knowledge that there could
not be higher peaks than in 1925. Hobbs was human after
all. Even Bradman never quite scaled a higher mountain
than that of 1930 in England when he hit 974 runs at
139.14. But although Hobbs may not have ever come close
to those halcyon days of 1925 in terms of run production,
his average leapt to 77 in 1926 – the year England took
back the Ashes after the 12-year break. In the Tests, his
returns per innings were even higher – at 81   from the best
aggregate, 486, of the two teams. Only Australia's best bat
of the period – Charlie Macartney – challenged him with
473 at 94.60. In 1928, Hobbs' season first-class average
jumped again – to 82.

In the mid-1920s Hobbs was a national hero, the most
famous man in England, made all the more authentic by his
congenial humility, which endeared him to all across
England's class divides and rendered him always approach-
able, if he could be found at least. He lived a quiet life with
his family when away from the game.

Hobbs made his fifth tour to Australia in 1928–29 and
performed admirably yet again at 46 years of age in the
season that Bradman first played against him. His Test
returns were up to standard   451 at 50.11. But, for the
first time in his Test career, he was eclipsed by another
player – Walter Hammond, who notched an incredible 905
runs at 113.13 – with two doubles and two other hundreds
for the series.

Despite Hammond's dominance, Hobbs had his
moments with 49 on a glue-pot in the Third Test at
Melbourne – an innings that demonstrated to Bradman,
at close quarters, what a great all-round batsman Hobbs
was. There was also a fine 142 in the Fifth Test at
Melbourne. The Australian crowds had mixed feelings
about Douglas Jardine with his harlequin cap and neck

choker, and Hammond, who seemed at times stony and aloof. But their hearts, as with the English fans, were with Hobbs. In his last Test appearance at Sydney in mid-December 1928 he scored 40 in England's eight-wicket win, and showed his relaxed nature by approaching the 'professional' barracker who was always in attendance at Test and first-class games, 'Yabba', on the Sydney hill. Hobbs told him he appreciated his humour, and would miss him. (Not so Jardine, who did not like being told to keep his 'hands off our flies'.)

During the 1930 Ashes series, when Bradman eclipsed Hammond and everyone else, Hobbs decided that he would end his fine Test career at the final game at The Oval. His performance for the series was mediocre by his standards – just 301 runs at 33.44, with a top score of 78. This inevitably had to be compared with Bradman's triple century, two doubles and a single hundred in just seven innings, and it helped Hobbs conclude that he was too old in his forty-eighth year to compete the way he would have liked. Australian skipper Bill Woodfull called for three cheers for him when he appeared at the crease for the last time in a Test at The Oval. He made an unsatisfactory 9, but it didn't matter. His mighty career had scaled the heights. Hobbs accumulated 5410 runs at 56.94 and hit 15 centuries in 61 Tests. This record placed him tenth in the top averages of all countries in the history of Tests.

But there was still much more waiting for him in first-class cricket in England. He plundered on, undaunted by age or the new breed of speedsters, although he objected vehemently to over-use of short-pitch bowling as practised against him by Yorkshire paceman Bill Bowes. Despite the less than Hobbs-like Test performances in 1930, he still hit more than 2000 runs for an over-fifty average. In 1931, he hit his ninth-best aggregate – 2418 runs – and this included 10 centuries, indicating that at 48 years of age he could still deliver at the standard of the younger Hobbs. With such a confidence-engendering year, he went on to 1932, in his fiftieth year, with a remarkable performance of 161 not out for the Players against the Gents. A year later he batted 387 minutes for a brilliant 221 for Surrey against the West Indies. No one in the history of the game, W.G. Grace included, performed so well with the blade when they were past their own half-century in years. Preserving his strength, he turned out less for the county, making just 1100 quality runs at the excellent average of 61.

As a journalist, Hobbs covered the Bodyline series of 1932–33 in Australia and the England (MCC) 1933–34 tour of India under Jardine for the *Star* newspaper. In 1934, a new set of gates dedicated to Hobbs was constructed at The Oval, a gesture that touched him as he prepared for a final assault on 200 centuries. He had racked up 196 hundreds during his career, as at the beginning of the 1934 season. Hobbs notched number 197 – against Lancashire in late May at Old Trafford. But it took him four laborious hours to do so. The struggle bothered him. For the first time since he first played 40 years earlier, he worried that he had lost 'it'. His timing – as precise as the best Swiss clock – was not there. Later, he ran himself out for 79 in another slow knock, brought on through the necessity of the ball not coming off the bat with any pace. That precious precision tool, which had served him at the top of the game longer than any other cricketer, was not returning.

Hobbs mulled over his future during the 1934–35 winter and then wrote to Surrey in February 1935 announcing his retirement at age 53. He had scored 61,237 runs at 50.65. Apart from those 197 centuries, he had taken 113 wickets at the more than respectable 23.97 runs per wicket, and had snaffled 317 catches, not to mention plenty of run-outs – including 15 on a tour of Australia.

His remarkable figures warrant deeper analysis. He scored more runs than anyone else in first-class cricket. Hobbs hit 316 not out for Surrey against Middlesex at Lord's in 1926 and his 266 not out at Scarborough in 1925 was the highest score in a Gentleman versus Player fixture. His aggregate of 4052 runs is the highest ever for those traditional matches. Hobbs has the highest number of centuries – 12 – of any player against Australia. He and Andrew Sandham shared 61 opening century-stands, the highest being 428 against Oxford University at The Oval in 1926. Hobbs made eight century-stands in Tests with Rhodes and 15 with Sutcliffe.

On retirement, he concentrated more on his sports outfitters business, which he had developed over more than a decade, and was elected an honorary life member of Surrey. Jack Hobbs was knighted in 1953.

Bradman didn't have to linger long over his choice of player to open the batting for England for his all-time best-ever English Ashes team. He admired Jack Hobbs for his faultless technique, skill in all conditions, and a desire to attack. No better batsman has ever opened an innings in the history of the game.

CHAPTER 14

HERO OF THE CLOCKLESS KNOCK

LEN
HUTTON

(England)

23 June 1916–6 September 1990

Len Hutton strode out to open the batting for England at The Oval in the last Test of the 1938 Ashes series knowing that if ever he was going to make a big score the conditions were tailor-made for it. The weather was fine; the pitch perfect for batting thanks to groundsman 'Bosser' Martin; the game was timeless, and therefore dictating big scores; and Australia had a weak bowling attack. Yes, there was the great Bill O'Reilly delivering his fast leg-breaks but after him there was only left-handed 'Chinaman' bowler Chuck Fleetwood-Smith. The team's sole fast bowler, Ernie McCormick, was out injured. Captain Don Bradman could then only turn to his part-timers, Mervyn Waite, the medium pacer, and Stan McCabe, also a medium trundler at the best of times. Bradman's fourth successive loss of the toss, calling 'heads', meant he was faced with England's strong batting line-up aiming for 600 runs at least – under directions from the stern captain Wally Hammond.

Hutton, 22 years old, had batted just three times in the series for 100, 4 and 5. His main problem would be the wily O'Reilly, to whom he would not attempt to dictate terms. The idea was to keep him out and turn over the strike. If he could be patient and do that, a huge score beckoned. This would give England every chance of a win and of levelling the series 1–1. The big bogeyman for England was Bradman. He had scored a century in each of the 1938 Tests played and had a formidable record at The Oval, including two Test double hundreds in 1930 and 1934. The thought of him batting on this perfect strip was enough to keep England out there as long as possible.

Bradman opened with the innocuous Waite and McCabe, but soon called O'Reilly to the bowling crease, and then Fleetwood-Smith. Australia had to have them bowling early in the hope of a breakthrough.

Hutton lost his partner Bill Edrich for 12 lbw to O'Reilly at 29 and was joined by the strong Yorkshire left-hander Maurice Leyland. They presented different styles in playing the spinners. Hutton stretched forward or back from the crease. Leyland skipped out to meet them at every chance. The result was much the same, with both batsmen driving well, especially on the off. These two were there at lunch, the score one for 89 with Hutton on 39 not out. It was now a matter of concentration, especially starting a new session. Hutton had added one run and had forgotten himself by leaping at Fleetwood-Smith. He was stranded against a high bouncing ball. Fortunately for him, it troubled the keeper, Ben Barnett, who fumbled the ball and missed the stumping. Hutton didn't need another warning. He would stay at home no matter what was lobbed at him from the tempting, profligate left-armer. He didn't have to remind himself to concentrate against O'Reilly. Hutton preferred to play as much off the back foot as possible, watching the ball onto the bat. Once set, they built a partnership against the mediocre attack, which Bradman presented in various combinations, none of them penetrating.

Hutton brought up his century and the team's 200. Bradman took the new ball. McCabe and Waite were easy pickings for the two Yorkshiremen who had faced many faster and better new-ball bowlers in county cricket. They plundered on to be one for 347 at stumps, with Hutton on 160 not out and Leyland 156 not out. On the way they had broken all records for the second wicket and were just five short of the record for any wicket against Australia – 323 – by Hobbs and Rhodes at Melbourne in 1912. The runs had been scored in 355 minutes, an excellent rate for Test cricket, and helped along by the use of three spinners, including nets trundler Sid Barnes if he could be so categorised. They worked through their overs in quick time. Hutton's cutting and off-driving, with the occasional lofted on-drive, accelerated the scoring late in the day. He was playing an innings that was neither thrilling nor dull. His technique was perfect. Because he played all the strokes, the spectators and the critics forgave him for not punishing everything loose. Hutton had put away his desire to go after the bowling in the interests of a huge score.

A Drink at the Brink

A teetotaller, Hutton declined the invitation to celebrate on Saturday night and instead spent the evening back in the team hotel – the Grand Central above Marylebone Station – with spinner, and another fellow 'Yorkie', Hedley Verity. They talked cricket. Hutton enjoyed a long sleep. Knowing Sunday was a rest day, O'Reilly did not trouble him in his dreams. He travelled to Bognor with Verity and other friends and ended up playing a game of beach cricket. Hutton did more bowling than batting, yet was pleased to sense his 'eye' was still in. He dearly wanted a double hundred and to go beyond it, and could not wait until Monday. He slept well again on Sunday night and was eagerly into the nets in the morning. Hammond reminded him that his 160 on Saturday was another innings and that he had to start again.

Rain tweaked his nerve a fraction and delayed play for 35 minutes. Yet the wait focused the young Hutton, as did Bradman's field placings. He crowded the young opener with Fingleton in his pocket at forward short-leg. The Australians' fielding kept a high standard and maintained a pressure of sorts, although the wicket was still batsman-friendly. Hutton and Leyland overcame a few early jitters and began to pick up the scoring rate. A score of 400 came and receded quickly. On 411, Hassett fielded a shot into the covers by Leyland and threw the ball to Bradman at the bowler's end to run out Leyland for 187. The partnership had reached 382. England, with a mighty order to follow against the wafer-thin attack, was in an impregnable position. Or so it seemed. Next man in, Hammond, still thought of what his career rival Bradman would probably do on such a track. The England captain was rumoured to want his team to make 1000.

England was two for 434 at lunch with Hutton on 191 not out, Hammond 20 not out. Bradman took the third new ball and Waite was able to beat Hutton twice. It seemed to subdue the two batsmen. Just 43 came up in the hour with Hutton crawling through 200. But he was still there and the whole of England was with him now on a journey into high-scoring country, ventured into by very few in Test cricket. Among the few were Hammond and Bradman, for whom this territory was common enough.

The next milestone was the team's 500. The fielding was alert, the Australians realising that a run-out was just as likely as any other form of dismissal. Hutton and Hammond countered with short singles. Apart from these features, the game had become grim. At 546, Hammond fell lbw to Fleetwood-Smith for 59 in a partnership of 135. Hutton was past Hammond's 240 at Lord's in the Second Test of the series two months earlier. The timing of the dismissal marked the changing of the guard at the top of English cricket. Hutton, who would take over as England's number-one batsman, was replacing Hammond, who would never score a Test fifty against Australia again.

The Oval became gloomy. Lightning flashed and O'Reilly struck, removing Lancastrian Eddie Paynter lbw for a duck. Tea on Day Two came with Hutton having reached his 250. A rainstorm turned tea into something more like a lunch break but the players resumed at 5 p.m. after 50 minutes. Waite got one through the unfortunate Denis Compton for a duck and England was five for 555. Hutton was exhausted and almost out on his feet after more than 11 hours at the crease – already the longest innings in Test cricket. He was lifted by Nottingham's Joe Hardstaff, who hoed into Fleetwood-Smith with cuts, drives and pulls. At 280 Hutton pushed uncertainly at O'Reilly and edged a ball centimetres from the outstretched hand of slip. Hutton admonished himself for the error and practised the shot, elbow up. He took a single to forward square leg to reach 288 and take R.E. Foster's record of the highest score by an Englishman against Australia – made 34 years earlier in Sydney. The clapping turned to wild cheering 30 minutes later when he took a similar single to reach 300 – his not-out score at stumps. Reaching that mighty target left him with one more aim in this innings: Bradman's 334 at Leeds in 1930. Hutton had witnessed that knock as a 14-year-old and regarded it as the greatest performance he had ever seen. Bradman hit 309 in a day. Hutton was scoring at half Bradman's rate against an attack half as strong. Bradman faced Larwood, Tate, Geary, Tyldesley and a more robust Hammond. Yet Hutton's was a formidable performance in terms of concentration, determination and stamina, with every stroke possible on display and executed in fluent text-book style. Only brilliance and aggression were lacking.

Then again, if Hutton had attacked it would not have been the same innings. It may not have lasted to ultimately prove to be the important performance it was.

England was five for 634 with Hardstaff 40 not out. The interest across the cricket world was whether or not Hutton could get that extra 35 runs to outdo Bradman's 1930 score. There was no question about Hammond's intention to bat on. He had fielded to Bradman (232) in 1930 when Australia racked up 695, and again in 1934 when it was all out for 701 (Bradman 244, Ponsford 266). The thought of 1000 was now not a rumour or a joke in the English camp but a goal. Hammond would go for it if he could. This meant Hutton had another day to bat. Yet when he slumped in the hotel lounge two hours after running the gauntlet of the media and well-wishers, he didn't think he had the energy for a slowly run single, let alone 35. Verity ordered the teetotaller a drink of stout and port and demanded that he drink it to revive himself. Hutton obeyed and relaxed. It did him good but later in bed he could not sleep for the first time in the Test. Hutton's mind would not rest, thinking about O'Reilly's bowling (which was 'like a swarm of bees', as Bradman once described) and partly too because of exhaustion. He was stiff the next morning and running on adrenaline as he joined Hardstaff in front of a packed crowd of 30,000. They had come to see Hutton beat Bradman's record. The Australian captain was not keen to relinquish it without making the Englishman earn it. He opened with O'Reilly and Fleetwood-Smith, holding back the fourth new ball.

Hutton showed enormous application by talking himself into beginning the innings on Day Three as if he was 0. This approach worked as he set about calibrating a new innings, playing himself in slowly and cautiously. His mind was on defence and advancement by singles. There were gaps enough to reach those precious 35 by them alone. He was nearly bowled by O'Reilly but managed to withstand the pressure, especially from an elaborate leg-trap. Hutton and Hardstaff saw off the spinners. Bradman called for the new ball at five for 670 with Hutton on 315. The crowd cheered but then went strangely quiet, except when responding to a run. They couldn't believe Bradman would leave the world's greatest bowler out of the attack, even on this unresponsive wicket, for long. Sure enough, O'Reilly was on again after a short rest. But Hutton's confidence was building. His nerve had held. He was not inclined to indulge in a reckless lash, even at loose deliveries from Fleetwood-Smith or McCabe. He was going to get that record. After an hour he was 321. England was five for 694 with Hardstaff on 77 not out.

Hutton cut Waite for four to reach 326 and England sailed through 700. Two more singles pushed him up to 328. Bradman brought on Fleetwood-Smith once more, knowing he was capable of the unplayable delivery, even more than O'Reilly. He then brought the field in to cut off the singles and to force Hutton to play his strokes. Fleetwood-Smith got a delivery past Hutton's bat. He appeared trapped in front, back on his stumps. All the Australians appealed. Umpire Chester adjudged it not out, suggesting the ball would have bounced over the stumps. A few moments later Hutton survived another lbw appeal, dead in front. This time Chester thought he may have got the faintest of edges. He didn't have the reputation as the world's number-one umpire for nothing.

Hutton scratched around for three singles in the next three overs, reaching 331. His 31 had been compiled under extreme pressure. Gone was any sparkle of the previous two days. This was a hell of a struggle. But he was now within a boundary of the record. Fleetwood-Smith delivered a wrong'un that came out as a long-hop. Hutton cut it for four.

The spectators rose to rapturous applause and hurled hats and anything else they were holding into the air in celebration. Bradman, fielding close to the wicket, was first to shake Hutton's hand. The famous photo of Bradman grinning and Hutton smiling is one of the most memorable images in sport. The record for the highest score in an Ashes Test had been broken. It was Hutton's. He had deserved it after a marathon performance. Unburdened, he continued more freely to 364 until O'Reilly had him caught by Hassett, close to the wicket. Hutton had batted 13 hours and 20 minutes – 800 minutes in all – in the longest Test innings ever.

England was six for 770. There was no signal from the dressing room. Hammond was pushing his team on. At 798, Bradman himself came on to bowl. He was a capable leggie, who from the time he was 18 never worked on his skills, but could keep any batsman concentrating in the nets. Hardstaff and new man, Yorkshire keeper Arthur Wood, paid him overdue respect and only took six off his first 13 deliveries. Bradman went a fraction wider on the crease for his fourteenth delivery and literally fell in the hole dug up by O'Reilly's boots over 75 overs. He fractured an ankle and was carried off the ground. Hammond did not know how bad the injury was, and he let his team meander on towards 1000. When the score was seven for 903, it was confirmed by Bradman himself that he would not bat in the game. Only then did Hammond declare, with Hardstaff on 169 not out.

Australia, without the injured Bradman and without Fingleton, who had pulled a thigh muscle, crumbled for 201 and 123, with only Bill Brown with 69 in the first innings managing to reach 50. England won by an innings and 579 runs, the biggest win in Test history due to Hutton's magnificent effort. Inspired by Bradman's capacities and his own self-belief, he did his best to ensure a colossal score and an England victory. Australia still held the Ashes but England was satisfied to have achieved parity with the old enemy in such a comprehensive way. The innings bestowed on Hutton cricket immortality. Just one other feat in his career would rank alongside it: his captaincy of the 1953 England team that won back the Ashes for the first time in 20 years.

Building a Future

Leonard Hutton, the son of a builder and the youngest of five children, was raised in Fulneck, midway between Bradford and Leeds. He first came to notice as a promising cricketer while playing for Pudsey St Lawrence's First XI in 1933, when he turned 17 mid-season. The quiet, modest, yet determined young Hutton did well enough to gain the attention of the county club and was placed in the Second XI. His elegant, correct, left-elbow-up style attracted those who recognised technical skills. His score of 86 not out against a weak Derbyshire team was also noted. There was early criticism for his slow run rate and lack of aggression. But the footwork and range of strokes caused most critics to forgive him, or at least rate him worth a second and third look. Attacking strokes could come at any time, it was felt. The display of such class in one so young would carry him forward. The critics, for once, were uniformly correct as they watched him develop.

A highlight of that year, for Hutton, was a confrontation with the great Sydney Francis Barnes, then 60, who was playing for Staffordshire. Bradman had selected this medium-fast purveyor of swing, cut and spin in his best England XI. The combat between one of England's finest bowlers, whose skills peaked in the nineteenth century, with a young man who would turn out to be one of the country's finest batsmen of the twentieth century, was a special moment in time. According to the *Leeds Mercury*, who covered the match in the media, Barnes' bowling, despite his years, was 'a little short of miraculous in conception'. Hutton stood up to it 'with a confidence and correctness which could hardly have been surpassed by Sutcliffe himself'. He was 69 not out in two hours at the crease before rain ended the match.

In all, for the Yorkshire Second XI in 1933, he notched 699 at 69.90. It was an outstanding beginning. The club cultivated his performance in 1934, and he made the Firsts permanently in 1935, scoring a century as an opener with Sutcliffe.

The *Yorkshire Post*'s sports correspondent in 1935 showed a remarkable prescience with the comment:

> In this 18-year-old batsman Yorkshire have surely found a future Colossus of the game. He may be safely entrusted with the task of regaining for England records which Bradman has made his own.

At an end-of-the-1935-season dance he met Dorothy Dennis, the sister of a stalwart of the Yorkshire club, Frank, and they married four years later. In 1936, not long after his twentieth birthday, Hutton was capped as a professional by the county. It was a reward for his record so far and his promise with the bat. He was also bowling leg-spin, but experts were predicting it was his batting that would carry him into the England XI. Being capped meant he would earn 11 pounds a match, a fair start for a youth who aimed at making a living as a cricketer rather than following in the family tradition of the building trade. Yet being capped as a professional cricketer symbolised more than money. It placed him among the elite of his own working class, and would allow him a certain upward mobility in England's economically and socially layered society.

In the same year, he played in a Yorkshire versus Nottingham benefit match for Harold Larwood, who showed some of his old fire to dismiss Hutton for 4 (and Sutcliffe for 9). In the last game of the season against the MCC Hutton took eight for 77 and made 58, but it was too little and too late for him to be considered for the 1936–37 Ashes tour to Australia in the team led by Gubby Allen.

Test Advancement

England's loss in the 1936–37 series (2–3) after winning the first two Tests, and the failure of its opening batsmen to have much impact, caused selectors to choose Hutton to play his first Test at Lord's against New Zealand, three days after his twenty-first birthday. He took half an hour making 0 and 1 in a drawn game. The selectors went with the concept that class is permanent – Hutton had been seen at county level for four seasons now – and picked him again for the Second Test at Old Trafford. Hutton cracked a well-honed century in 210 minutes in the first innings and 14 in the second. England won by 130 runs. The critics were not altogether heavy in their praise. Hutton's inevitable advance to such a performance had been foretold, but it was designated a 'more than yeoman-like, thoroughly accomplished' innings by the *Observer*, and 'good enough' by the *Times*.

In the third game he scored 12 in another drawn game. It was a mixed start, but he was on his way at the highest level. *Wisden* named him as one of its five cricketers of the year.

1938 heralded the arrival of Bradman's Australians and the beginning of rumblings in Europe that threatened war. Hutton hit the ground running with three superb centuries against counties in innings that confirmed his sure-footed maturity against all types of bowlers, a maturity displayed on every variety of wicket. He carried this form into the First Test at Trent Bridge and proved to be a solid counterpoint to the aggressive Charlie Barnett, who hammered 98 not out by lunch on Day One, and went on to 126. Hutton hit another even 100, but was also overshadowed by the debut of Denis Compton (102) who was nearly two years younger, and Eddie Paynter, who notched 216 not out. But Stan McCabe, who made a masterful 232, outshone them all. Australia's 411 left it 247 behind and forced to follow on. Bill Brown (133) and Bradman (144 not out) put Australia beyond defeat in a drawn game. Hutton's century was ranked as the least impressive of seven in the match by observers, but it was his second hundred in four Test innings.

Hutton's 4 and 5 at Lord's was further disappointment in a Test at the home of cricket. A broken finger kept him from the crease until the final Ashes game at The Oval where he guaranteed his name in cricket history with 364.

This innings pushed Hitler off the front pages, but could not overshadow the general expectation of conflict. Nevertheless, England took the boat to South Africa for five Tests in 1938–39, and Hutton hit form immediately with two early hundreds and big opening stands with Bill Edrich. But his advance towards the Tests was cut short by a bouncer from Transvaal's express bowler, Eric Davies. It knocked Hutton unconscious and out of the First Test. His confidence was dented when he came back for 17 and 31 in the next two Tests, but he mastered tough bowling on a damp wicket in the Fourth Test at Johannesburg, scoring 92 in 210 minutes. The Fifth Test at Durban was set up as a decider with England leading 1–0 in the series. The wicket provided a run feast but Hutton missed the chance for another huge score when run out for 38 in the first innings. In the second innings he reached 55 and was bowled playing over a looping delivery from spinner Bruce Mitchell. The Test went on for 10 days – the longest in history – but was declared a draw when the England team had to make a two-day dash for Cape Town to catch the boat home. With war clouds gathering over Europe, no one wanted to be far from home, a Test without end notwithstanding.

In the Wars

There was little respite before the beginning of the 1939 home season as Hutton prepared for a three-Test series against the West Indies. It took him a month to warm up with a century for Yorkshire against the students at Cambridge. The weak attack allowed Hutton time to regain some touch. A few days later he hit peak form against Warwickshire with another century. His opening stands with Herbert Sutcliffe were giving Yorkshire starts that set up wins in two days thus allowing the team to recuperate for the next onslaught. The pair belted their best-ever effort – 315 – against Hampshire. Hutton went on to 280 not out. He loved the terrain of the huge score and his fit body and strong mind thrived on the challenge. Such beginnings gave Yorkshire's great bowling trio of Bill Bowes, Ellis Robinson and Hedley Verity a psychological advantage and the county cut a swathe through England.

Hutton's staggering form was maintained through June

and this time he gave himself a twenty-third birthday present at Lord's against the West Indies with 196, but again paled a little in comparison with the dashing Compton (120), who outscored him in a blistering fourth-wicket stand of 248 in 122 minutes. They were both upstaged by the fight and brilliance of George Headley, who scored a century in each Test innings – the second time it had been done by him and the first time by anyone at cricket headquarters. England's superior all-round skills gave it the game by eight wickets.

Hutton, this time, failed at Old Trafford but came back at The Oval, the scene of his triumph over the Australians a year earlier, with scores of 73 and 165 not out. He and Hammond (138) flayed the bowling for a then world-record third-wicket stand of 264 in just 181 minutes. Even though he was not as aggressive as his partners, Hutton was pre-pared to step up a notch in Tests if the occasion was right.

A week or so after the final Test, German troops were marching through Poland. German planes were bombing Cracow and Warsaw. Hutton, coming off a century at Hove, drove back to London and was met by carloads of people escaping the capital. It marked the end of cricket for the season and the beginning of the Second World War. There would be no more Tests, but cricket in England would continue, unlike its cessation in the First World War. The nation realised the value of the game as a form of relaxation and distraction from the horrors of the war and as a propa-ganda machine. Matches at Lord's and The Oval particularly would continue to show the Germans that the seat of the Empire was not cowering and giving up all its everyday pursuits, despite the bombing and the threat of invasion.

County cricket ceased in 1940 but the lower levels of the game such as the professional leagues continued and thrived. Hutton played for Pudsey St Lawrence again in the

Bradford League and topped the averages. Hutton had joined the Army Physical Training Corps and was made a sergeant-instructor. He trained to be a commando. This would have led him to combat on the Continent but he had a gymnasium accident, which damaged his left forearm and wrist. Three operations later his left arm was a few centimetres shorter than his right and it was thought that his career was in jeopardy.

He could not play cricket at all in 1942 – the year his son, Richard, was born. After rehabilitation, he played again in 1943. In 1944 and 1945 he maintained form with games for Pudsey and in international matches against Australian services teams that included big names such as Lindsay Hassett and also Keith Miller, whom he found a formidable foe on the field. The five 'Victory Tests' (to celebrate winning the war) versus the Australians were at times played with the intensity of real Tests and Hutton was the better for them. In the third – at Lord's – he made 104 and 69. Hutton had just turned 29 and he looked like the young star who had blitzed Australia in 1938.

As You Were

Hutton lived up to expectations in 1946 as crowds flocked to see the three Tests England played against the visiting Indians. He made 183 not out against them for Yorkshire, a score that made it seem as if the year was 1940 again. It was a typically correct big Hutton knock, in which he eschewed the desire to take the attack apart, but still compiled his runs at a comfortable rate and with a wide range of shots. Only one, the hook, was made difficult by his injured arm. It was a shot he would use less and less, not because – as his critics would say – he lacked an element of adventure with this most aggressive and courageous stroke of all. It was simply because he could not roll his injured left wrist.

In the Tests he had only one reasonable score – 67 – at Old Trafford, and averaged just 30.75, but his form in other first-class cricket demonstrated he was still in a class shared by few cricketers in the world. Compton had captured the public imagination and was ranked alongside him in terms of skill. The end of the 1946 season was soon followed by the boat trip to Australia, which Hutton regarded as a main achievement. The Ashes tour of Australia was the most challenging of all assignments abroad for an English cricketer. The Australians took to him with ease. Not only was he a batsman of elegance and enormous skill, his laconic, naturally friendly manner and humility engaged cricketers and fans alike. Like Bradman, he was vanity-free, a quality Australians appreciated in their heroes above all else. Hutton responded to this approval with fine perform-ances in the build-up to the Tests, including centuries at Adelaide and Melbourne. Before the international contests most cricket fans down-under now had a feel for Hutton's superiority and they looked forward to the contests against Australia's untested new bowling line-up led by Ray Lindwall and Keith Miller. The latter's capacities as a tough opponent were known to Hutton and to most of the other tourists.

Miller took first honours in Brisbane, sending him back bowled for 7 and caught for a duck. Both the Australian speedmen did not spare Hutton short-pitched deliveries. Miller's bouncer was fast and accurate. Lindwall's was nothing short of lethal. He could skid a ball faster and lower so that it lasered at the throat. And there was no doubt Hutton was the main target. The last time he had played the Australians at this level – at The Oval in 1938 – he had humiliated them. There was a determination, stemming from captain Bradman himself, that this would not happen again. Australia won the game by an innings and 332 runs – a crushing victory in the vicinity of the thrashing England had given them in that Oval match. In the Brisbane game, England suffered from the weather. It was twice forced to bat after violent storms.

The England caravan moved down to Sydney in mid-December for the Second Test where Hutton, defending stoutly, got past the pacemen on a friendlier, slower wicket but then fell to Ian Johnson's off-spinning. Hutton nicked Johnson's third-ever ball in Test cricket to keeper Don Tallon. His 39 took 122 minutes. In the second innings, England faced an impossible situation after Australia had amassed eight for 659, with Bradman and Sid Barnes each scoring 234. The tourists, it seemed, were still paying for that Oval experience. Hutton responded with one of the finest of cameos. Playing every shot, he slammed 37 in 24 minutes.

'Then he hit his wicket (bowled Miller),' cricket writer A.G. Moyes recorded in his *Century of Cricketers*, 'and the sun was hidden by clouds. It was a glorious piece of batting, a choice miniature that I will carry with me always. The Hutton who scintillated that day was one of the masters, a man who removed the dungarees he wore at The Oval (in making 364) and had arrayed himself again in flannels.'

Moyes, who had seen all of the masters of the first half of the twentieth century, had been often critical of Hutton's lack of aggression. Yet Hutton's justification of his defensive nature was to note that his short innings cameo didn't help England. Australia had another innings victory.

In the Third Test at Melbourne, Lindwall dismissed Hutton for 2, and when he struggled past the menacing speedsters in the second innings, the more docile medium pace of Ernie Toshack saw him caught by Bradman for 40. The match was drawn.

By the Fourth Test, Hutton was looking like the Hutton England knew and Australia had seen in the games against the States. He fell to the spinners, McCool for 90, and Johnson for 76. The second dig was brilliant as he counter-attacked the speedsters. Yet Denis Compton and Arthur Morris, who both scored centuries in each innings, out-performed him. The game was a draw once more and the Ashes and the series were lost. With the pressure off, Hutton hit his first century in Australia – 122 retired ill in the Fifth Test at Sydney – but it was not a knock to remember, being laborious and taking a day to compile. A day later Hutton had a sore throat and fell ill with tonsillitis. He missed the only Test in New Zealand but was well enough to fly home – a novelty in 1947. (It wasn't until 20 years later that flights were the norm and seafaring a thing of the past.)

His illness didn't seem to impact on his form in the 1947 England season as he lapped out early centuries against the universities, then against counties Glamorgan and Sussex. But he failed to carry this form into the Tests against South Africa with scores of 17, 9, 18, 13 not out, 12 and 24. Then he hit his straps at Headingley in the Fourth Test with 100 run out and 32 not out, followed by 83 and 36 at The Oval. Those last four innings silenced his critics who were suggesting other openers for England. Yet with England winning (3–0) there was little excuse or reason for him to be dumped. Besides this, there was simply no one to match him and his experience at the top of the order. Hutton seemed stronger by the end of the season. He ended it with even more running than he began the season with – scoring 270 not out against Hampshire in the final game.

Hutton, Edrich, Compton and Bedser (England's four best performers) were stood down for a tour of the Caribbean in an early version of the current rotation system in modern one-day cricket. England's selectors wanted this group to be fit and ready for Bradman's Australians who were set to tour England in 1948. However, Hutton received an SOS from the tourists after injuries in the first two Tests in January and February 1948. The West Indies proved a much stronger opposition than in previous decades, with players such as the brilliant batsmen Everton Weekes and Frank Worrell. Hutton had little impact on the 2–0 result in favour of the West Indies from four Tests. His scores were 31, 24, 56 and 60. It was a warning to the cricket world that the Calypso cricketers were no longer easy-beats.

Bradman's Target

Hutton carried Yorkshire in 1948, scoring eight centuries and averaging 92.05 in less than half the games he would normally play when a Test team wasn't touring. There was no doubt that he was the main target again for the Australians who still regarded him then as England's most important batsman. The fact that he opened made their attempts to dismiss him even more dramatic. Hutton wouldn't be shielded down the order. Instead, he took the full brunt of the most aggressive Australian bowling combination – Lindwall and Miller – the tourists had produced to that point, Jack Gregory and Ted McDonald included. If he were to make it past their barrage, Hutton would still have to overcome more subtle problems in dealing with Ian Johnson's off-spin.

In lead-up games against the tourists for Yorkshire and the MCC he managed 5, 11, 52 and 64. Then apart from an excellent second-innings 74 at Trent Bridge he struggled in the Tests after being bombarded with bouncers by Miller, who bowled him (and also in the first innings for 3). Ian Johnson bowled him for 20 and Lindwall had him caught for 13 in the Second Test at Lord's in late June. The English selectors, perhaps mortified at having seen their star's wicket disturbed so much and for little return, blundered by dropping him for the Third Test. Hutton came back to prove a point in front of his home crowd at Headingley in the Fourth Test with good performances of 81 and 57. He went further with brilliant displays in the Fifth Test at The Oval, scoring 30 (last man out) from 52, when Lindwall (six for 20) delivered one of the fastest-ever bowling spells in England, and 64 out of 188. The Australians won the series 4–0. Bradman had succeeded in curtailing Hutton by the use of speed from two outstanding pacemen in their prime. It was the fastest combination Hutton had encountered, and he had come through it showing courage and skill, but not with enough big scores to make England competitive against the strongest Australian unit ever assembled.

Hutton was more comfortable against South Africa away, where he played a dominant part in England's narrow 2–0 win from five Tests. The home team was always competitive. Hutton notched three centuries before the First Test at Durban where he scored 83 and 5 in a tight game, which the tourists won by just two wickets. He handled the express pace of Cuan McCarthy well, and commented at the end of the series: 'It's never easy, but after the summer [in England] against Lindwall and Miller, I was well prepared.'

Hutton and Washbrook set a world-record opening stand of 359 in 310 minutes (Washbrook 195, Hutton 158) in the Second Test at Johannesburg, but in compiling 608 didn't leave enough time to dismiss South Africa twice. The game was drawn.

Hutton followed with 41 (run out) and what the *Times* called a 'masterful cameo' of 87 in the Cape Town Test. In the Fourth Test at Johannesburg, his second-innings 123 held England together and warded off defeat. He contributed 46 and 32 in the final Test at Port Elizabeth, which England won by three wickets.

Amateur Dramatics

England ignored experienced professionals by appointing amateur skippers – trying Gubby Allen again after more than a decade – and bringing back the gallant, jolly Freddie Brown after a similar period. Their main claim to the post was their amateur status, although Brown was a fair all-rounder in his prime (he scored 734 Test runs at 25.31 and took 45 wickets with his leg-breaks and later leg-cutters at 31.06). If Hutton had been an Australian he would have been appointed skipper long before he turned 34. But the tradition of bypassing professional cricketers to lead England, regardless of their skill or suitability, had left it without the hard-headed, tactical and strategic capacities to win back the Ashes. The selectors turned first to George Mann of Cambridge University and Middlesex for the first two Tests against New Zealand. Then Brown came back to skipper the team for the last two games of the four-Test series. Through this dithering over the leadership, Hutton consolidated by leading from the front in the Tests with scores of 101, 0, 23, 66, 73, and 206. In this double hundred, his third fifty took just 35 minutes, showing his frustrated critics like A.G. Moyes and Neville Cardus that he could deliver if he wished. His methodical approach to scoring fuelled the arguments of the ditherers who said fellows such as amateurs Mann and Brown were more adventurous in their approach to leadership, presumably because they were not being paid for their efforts. They took a less dour attitude to winning, and losing, it was claimed. But the key here was the winning and losing. If England was ever to win back the Ashes it would have to break tradition, pick the best XI and the best leader from within the team. If the selection process was faced pragmatically, this would leave selectors with just one choice, Len Hutton. It has long been said that Yorkshire played the game more like the Australians than any other county. Hard, uncompromising but fair cricket was the rough common denominator. Whenever Bradman played in Yorkshire, he was, as one scribe noted, treated 'like an emperor with pads'. It wasn't just because he was the finest batsman of all time. The response had a lot to do with his attitude to winning. It resonated with a certain Yorkshire tenet in the England team that they were *the best*. The description 'cavalier' was hardly ever applied to Bradman. He and Hutton were rarely regarded as gallant or free and easy, and certainly never regarded as supercilious in their cricket. But they were winners. They wanted like-minded players around them.

After nearly two decades, the cricket establishment was getting fed up with being flogged by the Australians. But still procrastination won over progress. The English continued to delay appointing a suitable professional cricketer as captain. Norman Yardley, again of Cambridge University and Yorkshire, was appointed to lead England at home against the touring West Indies and the team was thrashed 3–1. It wasn't just the Australians who were tough to beat at the beginning of the second half of the twentieth century. Hutton struggled to combat the spin twins Valentine and Ramadhin, notching 39, 45, 35, 10, and a magnificent 202 not out at The Oval – surely his favourite ground outside Yorkshire – in carrying his bat in the final Test. Freddie Brown replaced Yardley in that game, only to perform with about the same impact. England played in the five Tests with 10 top cricketers and a skipper each time with doubts over whether he had earned his place.

The English team stumbled down to Australia for the 1950–51 Ashes under Brown once more and was given a 4–1 hiding. Hutton was dropped down the order for the First Test at Brisbane and in the second innings made 62 not out from 122 on a rain-affected pitch. *Wisden* did not understate this innings by calling it 'one of the most remarkable in Test cricket'. Some observers argued it was Hutton's best effort ever. He played with dead bat and soft hands, the ball often ending close to his feet. England went down by 70 runs, and then by just 28 in the Second Test at Melbourne. Hutton, still down the order, made 12 and 40. He was restored to opening at Sydney where he made 62 and 9, while England went down by an innings and 13 runs. Jack Iverson's variety of spinners tantalised and bamboozled the tourists, allowing him to take six for 27 in England's second innings. At Adelaide, Hutton 156 not out (carrying his bat through the first innings of 272) and 45 was the only tourist to consistently defy the powerful bowling line-up of Lindwall, Miller, Johnson, Iverson and Bill Johnston. In the Fifth Test at Melbourne, which England won well by eight wickets, Hutton again led from the front with 79. When the game had to be won in a small chase of 95 in the final innings, he had made an 'in control' 60 not out.

This victory made the England team members ecstatic. They had beaten Australia in a Test for the first time since The Oval victory in 1938 – a break of nearly 13 years. It may have been a dead rubber, but it didn't matter to England. The psychological boost to the team's morale as it headed for two Tests in New Zealand (won 1–0 by England) was huge.

Yet still the selectors buried their heads in the sand, and

kept on with robust Brown, now 41, as skipper rather than blooding Hutton, 34, for the 1951 home series against South Africa. Hutton was less inspired than in Australia, scoring one century. In his last innings of the series, he was out in a most unusual way: obstructing the ball. In defending his wicket from a ball he had hit, which may have deflected onto the stumps, he accidentally prevented the keeper from taking a catch.

England's 3–1 series win saw Brown bow out as somewhat of a hero. Hutton and other top English players did not tour India, Pakistan and Ceylon in 1951–52, deciding to rest from those arduous tours. Amateurs Nigel Howard (four Tests) and Donald Carr (one Test) led the side. But when it came to the home season of 1952, selectors Norman Yardley, Freddie Brown, Bob Wyatt (all amateurs who led England) and Leslie Ames, the former champion keeper/batsman, chose Hutton to lead his country for the first time, against India. He would turn 36 during the season. The decision was six years late, but better late than never.

Captain of England

Hutton had no choice, or desire, but to stay a professional, an act that would change the attitude to leadership in England forever, and for the better. No longer would a captain need to have the right pedigree, and come from the South of England and Oxbridge. Nor would he need to be out of the MCC, which barred professionals. Class as a performer, not class in the societal sense, would be the key determinant in selecting an England skipper. It was the first big step in the quest to win back the Ashes.

Hutton scored only 10 and 10 in his first Test, at

Headingley, as leader but had at his command an impressive-looking team. Fred Trueman, the son of a Yorkshire miner, on debut took three for 89 and four for 27, and put fear into the Indians with his quick bowling. Jim Laker, the off-spinner, was now a world-class performer. Alec Bedser could still deliver. The batting line-up of Hutton, Reg Simpson, Peter May, Denis Compton, Tom Graveney and Allan Watkins was strong and of high calibre. Evans was by now the world's best keeper, ahead of Don Tallon, whose skills were fluctuating.

It took Hutton that one Test to adjust to the captaincy. In the next three Tests of a series of four, he scored 150, 39 not out at Lord's, 104 at Old Trafford and 86 at The Oval. England won the series comfortably: 3–0. The country was now brimming with confidence that the new-look, classy line-up would rock the Australians in 1953. Certainly, Hutton was now king of English cricket.

There was no away tour in the winter of 1952–53, which was the perfect preparation for the coming tough Ashes battle. It allowed players to be fresh for the big challenge. Australia still looked strong, even without Bradman in an Ashes competition in England for the first time since 1930. The series was marred by poor weather which helped, along with unenterprising leadership by both Hutton and his counterpart Lindsay Hassett, four games to end in draws. Nevertheless, the crowds – a record 549,650 – flocked to the grim matches. In the Fourth Test at Headingley, all-rounder Trevor Bailey became a hero of sorts by batting 262 minutes for 38 runs in England's second innings. This knock shortened the time for Australia to win. Bailey then bowled leg theory under Hutton's direction – on or outside leg-stump to a packed leg-side field. This slowed Australia to such an extent that a draw was forced, with the tourists 30 short with six wickets in hand. The competition drew out the Yorkshireman in Hutton. He made it tougher for himself by losing the toss in all five Tests. Yet Hutton performed well and dourly to suit the mood of the contest, scoring 43, 60 not out, 145 (at Lord's, his only century and hampered by an attack of fibrositis), 5, 66, 0, 25, 82 and 17 run out. This gave him 443 at 55.38, easily the highest aggregate and best average – the only one of more than 50 – in the series.

Hutton requested that Freddie Brown (then chairman of selectors) play in the Second Test at Lord's because the skipper thought his leg-spin would be useful and add balance to the attack of Brian Statham, Bedser, Bailey and the variety of left-arm spinner Johnny Wardle. Brown played and bowled well and then dropped himself to make way for Laker at Old Trafford. Hutton's request for Brown to play had another dimension. The skipper was being appointed one Test at a time, as if the selectors were uncertain of his ability to take on the Australians. This was not the kind of endorsement, or lack thereof, he needed for such tough competition. Brown's inclusion allowed the key selector to see at first-hand how Hutton was coping. He must have approved. After two successive draws Hutton was selected again to lead. Some critics found him overcautious. They maintained that had he been more aggressive in the first two games he may have rammed home wins. But, by the Third Test, no one was calling for his head. Hutton kept his. England went into the final Test at The Oval with a chance to win the Ashes for the first time since the infamous 1932–33 Bodyline series in Australia.

After the wars of attrition of the first four games, Hutton knew he had to win to retain the leadership. A loss would surely see a reversion to England's system of choosing a rank amateur, even if highly ranked, to captain the team. There was terrific pressure coming into the match. The Second

World War was now eight years past and the nation was yearning for a big victory over the Australians, especially in the year of the Queen's Coronation. A loss would simply not do. England had the best-looking attack in decades – Trueman, Bedser, Laker and left-arm spinner Tony Lock (like Laker, also from Surrey). Trueman was back in the squad after his national service, and Hutton hoped he would wreak havoc. It was retribution time for the Australians after their years of intimidation by Miller and Lindwall. Trueman played his part, taking the figures with four for 86 in Australia's first innings of 275. Only Hassett (53) at the top of the order, and Lindwall (62) near the bottom of it, reached 50.

England replied with 306 (Hutton top score with 82) – these scores typical of the tight series. The lead was just 31. There was televised coverage of the game as the wonderful Day Three for England unfolded, with Laker and Lock taking nine wickets. Australia was dismissed for 162. England had 132 to get to win, which it did easily, losing just two wickets. Hutton was run out for 17.

'The nation was riveted by the series and by this game in particular,' Bradman said. 'A kind of fever gripped England. Then with victory, delirium followed.'

Hutton, immortalised for his 364 in 1938, had risen among the gods of English cricket once more at The Oval, this time with an Ashes win after a long time in the wilderness.

Caribbean Capers

Hutton's next mission was an equally tough one – a tour of the Caribbean in 1953–54. He was given the strongest possible team except that Bedser opted out in order to rest for the next winter tour to Australia in 1954–55. After England's thrashings at the hands of the West Indies six years earlier, and again in 1950, the Caribbean cricketers would never be taken lightly again.

But even with a strong team, England went down in the First Test at Sabina Park by 140 runs. Hutton warmed up with 24 and 56, but he and the other bats struggled with the spin of Ramadhin and Valentine, who had troubled them in 1950 (taking 59 out of 77 wickets to fall in the Tests). The game was notable for two incidents. Tony Lock became the second player after Australia's Ernie Jones to be called for throwing. And when umpire Perry Burke gave local player John Holt out lbw six short of his century, the umpire's wife and child were later physically assaulted in the street outside their home. Riots were always a potential problem.

Hutton stepped up a notch in the Second Test at Bridgetown, scoring a fine double, 72 and 77, but England went down again, this time by 181 runs. He led a fightback in the Third Test at Georgetown, making a fine, battling 169 in 480 minutes in England's nine-wicket win. Hutton showed his cool in a real crisis in this game when, after a clear run-out of West Indian C.A. McWatt, the crowd rioted and threw bottles and other missiles onto the field. The main problem was not so much the rum consumed, but the bets placed on McWatt making a century-stand with John Holt for the eighth wicket. Hutton would not leave the pitch, despite officials pleading with him to do so.

'I want a couple of wickets before the close of play tonight,' were his immortal words in the face of danger.

The game went on. Hutton got his wickets and eventual victory. He drew high praise for his classic batting and the courageous way he faced the ugly situation. The game did much to enhance him as a leader. The players were more united than ever behind him.

In the Fourth Test at Port of Spain high scores were assured on a jute-matting pitch. Hutton managed a modest 44 and 30 not out, while the West Indies big guns – Worrell (167), Weekes (206) and Walcott (124) – all got going. The game was drawn, leaving the need for a face-saving effort by the tourists in the final Test at Sabina Park. Hutton led the way, making 205 and becoming the first England captain to score a double century in an overseas Test. England won by nine wickets again, thus levelling the series at 2–2. Hutton sailed away from the Caribbean with an aggregate of 677 and an average of 96.7. Just as important to him was the prestige of a much-heralded revival by England after the 1953 Ashes triumph. The prestige was still intact.

Hutton was mentally and physically exhausted on return to England and, on the advice of his doctor, opted out of the Second and Third of four Tests against Pakistan. In his place the selectors chose the Rev. David Sheppard as skipper, another amateur who captained Cambridge and Sussex. Hutton's health brought media speculation that Sheppard should be chosen to lead England down-under in 1954–55. The spectre of amateurs being chosen over professionals to captain England emerged again. After much back-room caballing, the MCC chose Hutton for the Australian tour to defend the Ashes.

Final Triumph

Hutton had a strong squad but his 'team within a team' of Frank Tyson and Brian Statham was his strongest asset. He erred in Brisbane in the First Test by putting Australia in when he won the toss. The response was 601 with Neil Harvey and Arthur Morris scoring big hundreds. Hutton's old foes Lindwall and Miller had him cheaply in both innings and England went under by an innings and 154.

Hutton scored 30 and 28 in the Second Test at Sydney, with only Peter May (104) in the second innings putting up strong resistance as England recorded 154 and 296. Tyson made up for the batting failures by taking four for 45 and then in a devastating spell, six for 85. Hutton put down Tyson's fire to the fact that Lindwall had knocked him out with a bouncer. England won in a tight game by 38 runs.

The blow apparently still riled Tyson less than two weeks later in Melbourne in the Third Test when he took seven for 27. Most observers thought that he bowled as fast as anyone had ever done in a Test. It was enough to give England another win, by 128 runs. Hutton struggled with 12 and 42, the latter innings taking 146 minutes. Despite its tardiness incurring the wrath of the Melbourne crowd, the knock was invaluable. Hutton proved to be unperturbed by this and the continual criticism of his slow rate of overs. England was delivering at the miserable rate of 11.5 overs an hour (69 overs a day – 21 overs less than must be delivered now, since in those days overs were eight balls, rather than six) compared with Australia's 14. Hutton had a habit of changing the field when the bowler was at the top of his mark. He admitted it was a tactic particularly directed at Harvey, who liked to get on with the game.

England now led 2–1 with two Tests to play. Australia had to win both to win back the Ashes. In Adelaide, Hutton struck better form with a top score of 80 in the first innings, which gave England a narrow 18-run lead. Then Tyson, Statham and Bob Appleyard (bowling medium-pace off-spinners) each took three wickets and reduced Australia to 111. England had 94 to make for victory. It lost five wickets doing it. The win gave England the Ashes (the final game at Sydney was hampered by rain and a draw).

Hutton, at 38 years of age, had triumphed. He had done what no other English captain in the twentieth century had done by being on the field for every Test in two winning series against Australia. He skippered on for two Tests in New Zealand and made 53 in his last Test innings – not far short of his Test average 56.67. He made 6971 runs in 79 Tests and included 19 centuries.

He seemed set to go on for a series at home against South Africa, but illness (severe lumbago) and a lack of enthusiasm for the demands of another season as skipper saw him retire. Hutton was just short of his thirty-ninth birthday. He continued on in the 1955 season spasmodically for Yorkshire and ended his first-class career with 40,140 runs at 55.51, including 129 centuries. Hutton's bowling returns of 173 wickets at 29.42 suggested he may have been underbowled through his long career.

Hutton wrote for the London *Evening News* until 1963. In 1960 he began a 25-year career as a promotions man at J.H. Fenner and Co, a power transmission engineering group.

In many ways, Hutton's career paralleled Bradman's. They both held the world-record score for Test cricket and were their country's leading batsman over two decades. Both men proved successful captains and led their teams to convincing Ashes victories before retiring.

Len Hutton was knighted for his services to cricket in 1956. He was a fitting choice to open England's best-ever team. Bradman recognised him for his technical skills, courage and leadership. These qualities made him a suitable choice to join Sir Jack Hobbs in taking on a strong Australian bowling line-up.

CHAPTER 15

CRICKET'S CAVALIER

DENIS COMPTON

3

(England)

23 May 1918–23 April 1997

Denis Compton joined fellow batsman Bill Edrich
with England's score at two for 28 on the first day
of the Third Ashes Test at Manchester. It was 8 July
1948, a day that Compton and all who witnessed events
would never forget. Ray Lindwall was bowling at his most
hostile and was supported by Bill Johnston who was using
the humid conditions well. Compton began confidently.
This partnership could be dangerous to the Australians. So
Lindwall put the pressure on with a series of bumpers. The
brilliant paceman, who had modelled his rhythmic run-up
and smooth unwind on the approach of England's Harold
Larwood, whistled one past Edrich's head. A few balls later
he hit Compton on the forearm.

The scoring slowed to a trickle. In Lindwall's next over,
he dragged his back leg on delivery. Umpire Dai Davis,
yelled 'no ball'. Compton, already on the back foot ready to
defend against a short-pitcher at throat level, changed his
mind in a split second. He tried to smash the ball on the on-
side. The shot was late. He got a top edge. The ball struck
him just above the eye and bounced high down towards fine
leg. Compton dropped his bat, held his head and reeled
towards the off. Bradman, Sid Barnes and keeper Don
Tallon rushed to him. Compton was bleeding and had to
retire hurt on 4. The packed Manchester crowd, aware that
Lindwall and Miller had been using aggressive bumper
tactics, particularly in the Tests, was restless. In the dressing room, former Test player and selector, Sir Pelham

Warner, who had been at the centre of the Bodyline controversy in 1932–33, was disquieted. In the press box, Bill O'Reilly opined that it was Bodyline without the field placements on the leg-side. This qualification, of course, was crucial. The packed leg-side field and precision, intimidatory bowling on leg-stump was uniquely Bodyline. Lindwall's method relied on 'softening up', with bouncers, then pace and swing for the dismissal. He was well within the rules in his approach. It had bluffed England's selectors into dropping their star bat, Len Hutton, for this Test. Now Lindwall was in the process of securing the Ashes. Australia was 2–0 up. A win here would give the tourists a series victory. With Hutton not selected and Compton now dealt with, all seemed lost for England, which was effectively three for 33. It was believed that the Middlesex champion right-hander had been effectively knocked out of the contest.

The in-form Gloucestershire left-hander, Jack Crapp, in his first-ever Test innings, joined Edrich, and the two withstood Lindwall's continual barrage to still be there at lunch with the score at two for 57. It was grim stuff. Edrich's 14 had taken 90 minutes.

Lunch had been on for a half-hour when the ground announcer told the crowd: 'Denis Compton has had stitches inserted in his head and is resting. He will bat again if required.'

This resulted in a murmur from the crowd. Most were astonished that his return was contemplated. Everyone knew he would be 'required'. But was he fit to bat?

After lunch, Bradman was forced to rest Lindwall. Crapp went after Ian Johnson's off-spinners. It was a relief not to have to face such hostility, and to move the score along. It reached 87. Fifty-five overs were up, and Bradman called for the new ball under a new law. Before the Second World War he would have been forced to wait until the score was 200. A rested Lindwall returned.

Back in the pavilion, Compton was assuring everyone, including his skipper, Norman Yardley, that he was fit to bat. Yardley told him he should practise in the nets to test his condition. He obliged, taking with him England pace-man Dick Pollard and left-arm orthodox spinner Jack Young. He missed several quicker deliveries from Pollard, but then his confidence returned. He thought he was seeing them well enough. After 15 minutes he was ready to face Lindwall again. Compton walked back to the pavilion and looked up at the scoreboard. England's tally had crept up to 96. Yardley suggested he go in at the fall of the fifth wicket.

On the field, Crapp let go two fast deliveries that veered towards slips (the in-swinger to a right-hander). Then Lindwall hurled down a very quick ball that swung the other way – an in-swinger to the left-hander. Crapp, expect-ing a third away-swinger, didn't offer a shot. The ball cannoned into his pads. He was plumb in front. England was three for 96. Tom Dollery was then yorked by Johnston. England was four for 97. Edrich (32) was next to go, caught by Tallon off Lindwall, making the score five for 119.

Compton came through the gate, his forehead bearing a white plaster. The crowd erupted. He received an ovation as many stood to salute his courage. He showed no sign of hesitation and, if anything, seemed more self-assured than in the short stanza before he was hit. He and Yardley were workmanlike until tea, with the score at five for 141. Compton received applause for his courage.

Yardley (22) was caught soon after the break. Godfrey Evans came to the wicket. He proceeded to entertain the crowd with his 'lucky dip' batting mix of snicks and drives. This took the pressure off Compton, who, while relying on defence, was edging the score along. He reached 50. The crowd stood to him again. It was already deemed a heroic effort and would be remembered for its intestinal fortitude if he were removed at this point. The partnership reached 75 in as many minutes. Compton gave two hard, low chances to Tallon, off Lindwall and Johnston. Any other keeper would not have got a glove to them. But Tallon, in a league of his own, was miffed that they had not stuck.

At 216, Evans became the seventh wicket to fall when he swung at Lindwall and was caught for 34 – an innings that delighted onlookers and counterbalanced Compton's fighting batsmanship.

At stumps on Day One, England was seven for 231, Compton on 64 not out and Bedser on 4.

Compton had a severe headache that night, but managed to sleep well. He woke still feeling poorly, and with a black right eye that was half-closed. He was bandaged again as he strode to the middle, galvanised to continue on England's fight.

Bradman used the third new ball first thing next morning under overcast skies and in front of 30,000 spectators, who had been queuing for hours. He put the field back to allow Compton singles, which put Bedser on strike against Lindwall. Runs came at a crawl. On 73, Compton gave his third chance that perhaps again only Tallon could have taken. It went to the keeper's left glove as he dived full stretch and deflected the ball to fine leg.

England reached 250 in 400 minutes. It appeared slow on paper, but was the most absorbing Test cricket fight imaginable. Bradman replaced Lindwall with Ernie Toshack, but Compton took 10 off his first over. Lindwall came back on. Compton steered himself into the nineties and then a century with an on-drive for a four off Toshack. It had taken him 237 minutes. Only three false strokes – those 'chances' to Tallon – marred an otherwise near-faultless performance. The crowd rose to Compton, a cricketer of exceptional fight and class.

Bradman had Lindwall, his main strike weapon, on in bursts. Lindwall's last over before lunch was at maximum speed. Although he thrice beat Compton's bat, he could not remove him. The Middlesex star trotted off, still undefeated. England looked certain to reach 350. A run-out broke the partnership of 121 in 150 minutes. Bedser was on his way for 37.

Compton hogged the strike from the tail-enders and pushed his score up to 145 not out with 16 fours in 327 minutes. England reached a strong 363. With Australia to bat last, the home team was in the box seat. England had not been there since The Oval victory in 1938.

Australia, without Barnes, who had been struck a fierce blow in the stomach while fielding close to the bat, cobbled together 221. England replied with three for 174 declared. Weather intervened and Australia at one for 92 in its second innings forced a draw.

Compton's innings was the finest he ever played, given the opposition, his injury and his fightback against the odds. His powers under such adverse circumstances defined him as one of England's finest batsmen

Early Recognition

Denis Compton was the mid-twentieth century's great cavalier of sport, who although professional at both soccer and cricket, always gave the impression of being carefree in his performances. Sport seemed to be fun to him. This does not mean he didn't play it hard. He was one of England's greatest competitors, especially against Australia, which drew the best from him. Compton always competed with finesse and good humour. A lifetime of companionship came from the friends he made in the games he played.

The son of a lorry driver, Denis was brought up in Hendon, Middlesex, a number-13 bus ride from Lord's, which was to become his other home. He had a poor but happy childhood in the 1920s. Boys swarmed in the street outside his home playing cricket. School matches were competitive events played in the evening and watched by hundreds from the neighbourhood. Such a competitive, popular cauldron, missing now in suburban England, was bound to produce talent. Compton excelled at games, particularly cricket and soccer, and at 12, in 1930, he played in his father Harry's team, Stamford Hill. At 14, in 1932, he played for an Elementary Schools team against a side of public schoolboys from a more privileged background. He was the most successful player in the game, scoring a stylish 114 and taking two wickets for 5 runs. It won him a cricket bat from the *Star* newspaper and some publicity. It was the first recognition on a national level for Compton, a sporting prodigy. More important still was the impression made on Sir Pelham ('Plum') Warner, the former England and Middlesex cricketer. Young Compton had just finished school and Warner, who was an excellent judge of a cricketer, asked him to join the ground-staff at Lord's. That took care of employment for half the year. A few months later Compton was picked to play soccer for England schoolboys against Wales. His brilliant play was reported to Arsenal. He was offered work with the ground-staff at Arsenal's Highbury North London home. Now the teenager had income all year round in a fairy-tale beginning to a career that would span another generation. It was a case of merit spotted early and rewarded.

This progress fitted well with Compton's demeanour. He always looked the part of the debonair sportsman, right down to his neat attire and parted hair, and played his roles with flair and dash. Here was a sporting hero in the making.

Compton's individual style was not tampered with but he was shown a few things by those more experienced in the game. He had been a left-arm purveyor of orthodox off-spin, but was introduced by Jack Walsh, the Leicester spinner, to leg- or wrist-spinning. Compton liked the trickery he could indulge in with his Chinaman. It suited the more aggressive side of his character.

In batting, he was a natural at all the strokes, but the one he loved most and developed in this early period was the sweep. It became a Compton signature. His trick was not to brush the ball square. Instead, he used timing to help it along behind square or fine. It became an enormous source of runs for him. But so did his cover drive and cut. He was a fearless hooker and liked to pull. Perhaps only the true straight drive eluded him, but this was because Compton didn't consider it as productive as his other drives.

He was 16 in 1934 when Woodfull's Australian tourists were fighting to take back the Ashes after they had been so rudely removed from the southern hemisphere by Douglas Jardine. Compton blossomed in his limited chances for the MCC, scoring 222 at 44.40. A year later, he managed 16 matches, scoring 690 at 46. At 18 years of age, in 1936, he came in last for Middlesex, led by Walter Robins (and including Gubby Allen). He batted well enough in scoring 20 to suggest he should have been at least five places up the order. Compton's next match was against Nottinghamshire, and the combination of Harold Larwood and Bill Voce – the most feared duo in cricket. Compton drove Larwood for four in the first innings. Larwood responded with his trademark accurate bouncer, which was hooked for four. Scores of 26 and 14 appear modest, but his attitude in handling pace said much more about his potential. This was demonstrated further in the next game against Northamptonshire, when he made 87. The *Times*' cricket writer noted: 'He has style, he has discretion, and he has the strokes.'

Progress continued and in the return match against Northants he hit his initial first-class century – an even 100 not out. Of this, *Wisden* said:

'By perfect timing, Compton drove, pulled and cut with remarkable power, and took out his bat, with 14 fours as his best strokes, in one and three-quarter hours . . .'

It wasn't just the batting that impressed the correspondent from cricket's bible. Compton showed fight with the tail, a pugnacity that England could well employ on its coming tour to Australia for the 1936–37 Ashes contest. There was criticism from cricket purists. It had to do with his unorthodoxy, born of a free spirit and attitude. But Compton was a superior talent because of his natural flamboyance, which dictated his capacity to take to bowlers and win the battle.

Compton's development, now acknowledged at first-hand by *The Times*, *Wisden*, Warner, Robins, Allen, and all the other scribes who saw him, was a fraction late to include him on tour. His first-class season ended with an aggregate of 1004 runs at 34.62 with just that one hundred against Northants and eight fifties. It was not enough to cause selectors to take a punt with such precocious talent.

This non-selection left Compton with the wonderful option of playing football on the wing for Arsenal. The confidence gained from playing first-class cricket was transferred to the football pitch. His first game was against Glasgow Rangers, who were so impressed they offered to poach him for 2000 pounds. Compton rejected the offer. Arsenal had nurtured him. The young man had his loyalties. Besides, his natural environment was North

London, not Glasgow, which would have been a world away from his comfort zone.

Compton was rewarded straightaway by selection in Arsenal's next home game played in front of a crowd of 68,000. In turn, he rewarded the club with the first goal after a sprint down the wing, a pass, a receive and a cool guide into the net in front of ecstatic fans.

He developed into a fine soccer player – an outside left – with an outstanding temperament. One fault was a tendency to hold on to the ball too long. Compton loved to dribble and baulk around an opponent. It wasn't because he was a showman. It was just that this was a one-on-one aspect of combat that he had performed in the streets of Hendon practically ever since he was upright.

At Home in Test Cricket

With this breakthrough football season behind him, Compton turned up at Lord's in April 1937 with renewed zest for a big cricket season, which it proved to be. His total of 1980 runs was nearly double his aggregate in 1936. He scored three centuries, with a top score of 177 at Lord's against Gloucestershire, and averaged 47.14. Compton was aided by mentor Patsy Hendren, then 48 years old and in his last season. Perhaps it was Hendren's Irish background that ensured he played for enjoyment and he imparted this to the 19-year-old up-and-comer. Hendren's attitude of always letting the opposition think you were relaxed and on top of things fitted with Compton's natural demeanour. England selectors noted Compton's manner, acknowledged he had runs on the board, and picked him for the Third Test of a three-match series versus New Zealand. He was then the youngest player ever selected for England – an enormous act of faith and contrary to a cricketing tradition known more for bringing back veterans than blooding its youth. Len Hutton made his debut in this series too. But his typically serious Northern mien and capabilities made him appear like someone much older than his 21 years. Compton's selection at just 19 was an inspired choice in recognition of potential brilliance. He didn't let anyone down with his 65 run-out in his only innings in The Oval Test. Compton already had a poor reputation as a caller for a run. His cry of 'yes', it was joked, was merely an opening bid. But in his first Test knock, the ball was deflected onto the stumps after the other batsman had hit it straight back. He was left out of his ground. The innings itself was praised for Compton's judgment of which deliveries to hit hard.

His 1938 first-class figures remained similar to the previous season, except that he hit five hundreds rather than three. One of those centuries came in the opening Test against Bradman's Australian team at Trent Bridge. His 102 made him the youngest centurion – at 20 years and 19 days – for England in an Ashes competition. He hit 15 fours and figured in a record fifth-wicket stand with Eddie Paynter (216 not out) of 206 in just 138 minutes, including 141 in the last 90 minutes of the first day's play. This innings was the first where Compton was noted as 'cavalier'. *The Times* reporter liked his range of shots, particularly his cuts and drives. His on-side play was described as 'aggressive'.

Nevertheless, he was admonished by his grim skipper Wally Hammond for not going on to a double, especially against the Australians. *Wisden*, however, was kinder, naming him as one of its five cricketers of 1938.

Compton managed 76 not out at Lord's in the second innings of the Test. It was a further brilliant knock of another variety on a rain-affected wicket. In the Fifth Test at The Oval, he grew restless waiting for Len Hutton to wade his way towards a triple century. When Compton finally came in at four for 547, he was bowled for just 1. It was not a situation to inspire a fighting innings. His 1938 series aggregate was 214 at an average of 42.80.

Compton was chosen to tour South Africa for the 1938–39 season, but he remained loyal to his winter sport, and played for Arsenal. Yet he could not find a regular spot in the football team. Nevertheless, he was now an early pick for England's cricket XI, and he showed why in the first of three Tests versus the West Indies during the 1939 season. Compton cracked a stylish 120. A slashing 181 against Essex even surpassed this innings. The last 131 came in just 100 minutes. His dominance only just failed to give Middlesex the County Championship. Through no fault of Compton, who had a fine season scoring 2468 runs, including eight centuries, at 56.09, Middlesex finished second to Yorkshire for the third year in succession.

War Intervention

Compton was 21 and reaching a playing peak just when war broke and suspended first-class cricket for six years. Compton was called up into an anti-aircraft regiment of the Royal Artillery not far from London, then moved to Aldershot in Hampshire where he completed a Physical Training Instructors Course. By all accounts, Sergeant-Major Compton was not well suited to his rank and army work. He had always been averse to rigorous exercise, except in competition on the pitch.

Compton was able to keep up his soccer, playing 127 games (many with brother Leslie) for Arsenal and scoring 72 goals. He also played for England against Scotland and

Wales in a team that was considered not far below the best that could be produced in peacetime.

Compton surfaced again in pads here and there in armed forces games until 1945 and played in the 'Victory Tests' between British and Commonwealth forces. He encountered Australians Keith Miller and Lindsay Hassett in these contests. They were later rivals in Ashes combat and became lifelong friends.

County cricket revived in 1946, and Compton, now 28, began a horror stretch that continued until he was bowled first ball at Lord's in the first of three Tests against India. It took him until the end of June to find form when he hit 122 versus Warwickshire at Lord's. Inside two months, he was back to his 1939 best. He ended the season with figures that were similar to his final pre-war efforts in scoring a Test century against the West Indies, and his great 181 against Essex. Compton scored 2403, with 10 centuries, at 61.61. His four Test innings against India registered 0, 51, 71 not out and 24 not out.

Compton could have played with Arsenal again in 1946–47, but this time he answered the MCC's call to join the England team for the Ashes in Australia. It was not a happy tour on the field. Hammond's leadership was uninspired as opposed to Bradman's, which was always inspired. England didn't win a Test. Compton's series got off to a slow start with scores of 17, 15 and 5. But in the second innings of the Second Test at Sydney he fought well for 54.

During the Melbourne Test and after Compton had failed with a score of 11 in the first innings, Bradman, in keeping with his longtime bonhomie towards opposing international players off the field, invited him to dine at the Windsor Hotel. Bradman spoke of the importance of self-confidence, no matter what the circumstances. It had resonance for Compton, who had suffered at the beginning of the 1946 season and was in trouble again at that moment. Bradman was reassuring, saying that once his confidence returned, Compton would get runs. The two got on well, and Compton was relieved that off the field Bradman was congenial company. His on-field intensity often made opposing players feel he was a cold and distant character.

Compton was run out for 14 in the second innings at Melbourne, but his confidence returned in Adelaide and he scored 147 in the first innings against the exceptional pace duo of Ray Lindwall and Miller, who had troubled him before.

In the second innings, Compton again played well, but was intent on keeping England in the middle long enough to ensure a draw, and to even give themselves a semblance of a chance of victory with Australia having to bat last. He figured in a bizarre but effective stand with keeper Godfrey Evans, where Compton hogged the strike and refused to take singles offered by Bradman's field placings. Bradman, ever conscious of the paying public as this tedious stand developed, complained that this was not the way cricket should be played. Compton suggested he bring his fielders in to normal positions. Bradman obliged. Compton promptly belted a four. A peeved Bradman put his fielders out again and the farce resumed. The atmosphere of their convivial dinner in Melbourne had evaporated. Compton went on to 103 not out, and the usually rare double in a Test – a century in each innings. Australia's Arthur Morris did the same in this game, making it a unique batting event.

The game fizzled to a draw. Compton made 17 and a strong 76 in the final Test at Melbourne and so went home with the impressive series figures of 459 runs at 51.00. Only his main rival as England's best bat, Hutton, did as well for the tourists with 417 at 52.13.

That Year: 1947

Compton returned to England a more rounded and hardened cricketer, his sense of competitive spirit up a few notches after taking on the Australians and succeeding. The touring South Africans were a far less daunting prospect and he played a big part in the 3–0 thrashing England handed out to the tourists in the five-Test series. Compton hit 65, 163, 208, 115, 6 (hit wicket), 30, 53, and 113 for an aggregate of 750 runs at 93.75.

His 163 in 286 minutes at Trent Bridge was out of a team score of 291 in a chanceless effort, which was more defensive, as the situation demanded. His 208 came at Lord's in a 370 third wicket with Bill Edrich (189). It was then a world-record score.

By the end of the series, Compton had bowled far more than normal, and this, coupled with his huge run production, put enormous strain on an injured knee sustained in a soccer game. If stress on it was to come it had to be in 1947, a year in which he had an overload of batting. Compton had 50 innings for eight not outs. He scored a record 3816 runs, including a record 18 centuries (taking Hobbs' 1925 tally of 16 hundreds), with a highest score of 246 in the last innings of the season for Middlesex, the champion county, against the Rest of England. His 1947 season average was 90.85. He bowled 635.4 overs and took 73 wickets at a cost of 28.12. His batting was the most dominant since Bradman rocked England in 1930 for figures of 2960 runs at 98.66.

Like Bradman, Compton's intent was always to entertain. If there was a chance to be adventurous he would take it. His uncanny eye and placement were seen at their best in that glorious summer of 1947.

Against the Invincibles

On paper it seemed that Compton never reached such dizzy heights again, but his 1948 season returns and the opposition he faced tell a different story. In first-class cricket he tallied 2451 runs in 47 innings at 61.27, with 10 centuries. These figures were remarkably similar to those of the 1946 season. But, in 1948, Compton had a fine Ashes series against Bradman's Invincibles, which, regardless of other assessments, was the strongest team in the world at the time and was the best Australian combination ever to tour England.

Compton performed at his best against the world's most lethal and greatest fast-bowling combination, at the time, of Lindwall and Miller, scoring 562 runs at 62.44. These figures were considerably better than any other English batsmen, including Cyril Washbrook, Hutton and Edrich. Only Australia's Arthur Morris with 696 (at 87.00) had a higher aggregate.

Compton played one of the finest knocks of his Test career at Trent Bridge in the First Test with 184 in the second innings (after Miller dismissed him for 19 in the first). The innings was slow, but still important in the context of an uphill fightback. England made just 165 in the first dig. Australia's reply was 509. Compton's second effort was aided by a groin injury to Lindwall, which left Miller as his chief combatant. Compton's innings ended when he stumbled under a Miller bouncer and trod on his wicket – an unsuitable way for him to go after a long struggle. It left England with little resistance and eventually a lead of 97, which the Australians polished off easily, losing two wickets.

Compton struggled with 53 and 29 at Lord's (both times falling to Bill Johnston caught by Miller in slips), but came back in the Third Test at Old Trafford with his finest Test innings, making 145 not out (and a duck caught off Ernie Toshack in the second). His battles with Lindwall, Australia's best bowler in the 1948 Ashes, were titanic. Miller was less effective because of a back injury, but he could still back up Lindwall on occasions with a burst of belligerence. Bill Johnston's left-arm medium-pace swingers also afforded unsettling variety.

At Headingley, Compton was dismissed by Lindwall for 23 in the first innings, then by Johnston for 66 – England's highest score – in the second. Set 404 for victory on the last day, Australia seemed doomed to fail. England skipper Norman Yardley expected a spinner's wicket. Jim Laker with his off-breaks, Hutton with leg-spin, and Compton, with his left-arm wrist-turners, were the keys against Bradman and Morris. Compton, in one remarkable early over to Bradman, had the twentieth century's master batsman misread his wrong'uns twice in one over. The first time the ball flew past first slipper Jack Crapp. Yardley brought in a second slip. Three deliveries later, the edged ball went to Crapp's left hand and he dropped it. Compton would dine out on this, albeit ruefully, for the rest of his life. Bradman rarely gave chances. You had to take them or suffer, which usually meant your team lost. Bradman went on to a fine 173 not out, while Morris, the best batsman of the series, hit a great 182. Australia got the runs, the most ever recorded, at that time, in a last-innings Test win. Compton's figures of 15 overs, three maidens, one for 82, looked woeful, especially as he conceded 5.5 runs an over. But had the chance from Bradman been taken by Crapp, and a stumping opportunity (from Morris on 32) grabbed by the normally reliable Evans, Compton would have been the hero. An England win would have meant it could still level with a win at The Oval in the final Test. Instead,

Australia won by seven wickets with 15 minutes to spare in one of the great wins in history.

As it turned out, no one had an answer to the lethal pace of Lindwall at The Oval, who delivered one of the fastest spells of bowling ever seen. In England's first-innings debacle of 52 Lindwall took six for 20 off 16.1 overs of unplayable fury. Compton was among his victims, caught by Morris for 4. He fought it out for 39 in the second innings before Johnston had him caught. England went down by an innings and 149 runs, giving Australia the series 4–0. Yet Compton could hold his head high. His performances were gallant. His presence often meant the England team would fight rather than capitulate.

Brylcreem and Other Bonanzas

In late 1948, Compton became one of the first-ever sports stars to use an agent, Bagenal Harvey, who did a deal between Brylcreem and his client. From then on, Compton was known as 'the Brylcreem boy', featuring in advertisements for the hair product. It fitted his image as a dasher — a batsman who always went for his shots — which was enhanced by the fastest recorded first-class triple century. It was belted against North Eastern Transvaal at the town of Benoni on the England tour of South Africa in 1948–49. The first hundred took 66 minutes, the second 78 minutes and the third a whirlwind 37 minutes, making a minute over three hours of controlled mayhem.

His Test series against South Africa was less spectacular but he still managed strong contributions in four of the five Tests. Compton was the key player in the First Test at Durban. His bowling for England's thin attack was important. In South Africa's second innings he sent down 16 overs for 11 maidens and took one for 11, thus restricting the opposition, and helping Alec Bedser and leg-spinner Doug Wright to take wickets. Compton hit a second-top score of 72 in the first innings and a top score of 28 in the second innings, which saw England scrape home by two wickets on the last ball of the match. He was dismissed before the winning bye was scored, and could not bear to watch. Instead, he locked himself in a toilet, unable to avoid the unfolding drama any other way. No one appeared to have more nerve and verve than Denis Compton. He usually conveyed a sense that he was enjoying himself. Batting seemed pleasurable, not a graft or a chore. Bowling, too, when he got the chance, for him was something to enthuse about. Slip fielding was a joy. But, off the field, as a spectator, he was a nervous wreck.

Yet he recovered by the Second Test at Johannesburg, where he hit 114 in England's massive 608 in a drawn match. At Cape Town, he contributed 51 in England's second innings and also took five for 70 off 25.2 overs with three maidens – his only five-wicket haul in his 78 Tests. At Port Elizabeth in the Fifth and final Test he made 49 in the first innings. His top score of 42 in the second innings was the highest contribution in England's second narrow win in the series, this time by three wickets.

Compton played a big part in England's 2–0 close series victory. His magnificent form of 1947 and 1948 on England's green fields flowed on across the browner pastures of South Africa through to February 1949. He cracked eight centuries in an aggregate of 1781 runs at an average of 84.80. He took 30 wickets at more than 30, but was more than useful in the Tests with the ball.

Off the field too, Compton was having a momentous time. It was at this time that he met his second wife, Valerie (his first marriage during the war to Doris had failed).

Valerie and Denis Compton had two sons, but this marriage, too, did not last. Denis, the cavalier on the field, seemed to have a similar attitude to matrimony, and in those heady days when he was a household name in England, good times with the lads took precedence over domestic bliss.

1949 was Compton's benefit year (where matches played in his honour netted him 12,200 pounds), and there was a falling away of the incredible two-year run as a player in the very top bracket of world batsmen. Yet he still managed impressive Test centuries against a battling New Zealand team at Headingley and Lord's. For the entire 1949 season, he scored 2530 at 48.65, with another fine collection of nine centuries. At 31 years of age, and with nagging soccer injuries, especially his right knee, he had peaked. There would be many more triumphs but Compton had 'been there, done that' before. On occasions now, he gave the impression of being a bit jaded. His football career was even more in jeopardy because of his wonky knee. The wing dash didn't have quite the same acceleration seen in his 14 capped games during the war. He spoke about retirement. But, in a last spark, he performed well in early 1950 for Arsenal. The team scraped into the FA Cup final against Liverpool and won 4–1. Compton scored a goal and admitted to being pepped up in the second half after being given a liberal shot of brandy. He was a very lucky footballer, who finished on the highest note possible with a cup-winner's medal. But that was it for Compton and soccer. His injuries had made a crock of him, and he retired before he was pushed. From the 1950 summer on, cricket was his only professional sport.

Not Quite the End Run

Injury and poor form kept Compton out of the England team until the Fourth and final Test versus the West Indies at The Oval in 1950, where he was run out for 44 and hit just 11 in the second innings. The West Indies, with Frank Worrell, Everton Weekes and Clyde Walcott dominant with the bat, and its spin twins Sonny Ramadhin and Alf Valentine in control, crushed England 3–1. Compton's form in Australia in 1950–51 was again dismal and he failed to get going in any of eight innings, returning a paltry 53 at 7.57. He had a great time with his mate Miller off the field and renewed a good acquaintance with Bradman. But it was depressing for fans to see Compton struggle because of his damaged knee. He couldn't move with alacrity to spinners or swivel against the quicks. Courage, it seemed to Australian fans, was all he was left with. Yet it was far from the end of his career.

Compton battled on, making a better fist of easier attacks in the domestic England summer of 1951, where he scored 909 in May, his best effort yet in that first full month of cricket. Despite his handicap, he made 2193 at 64.50, which was a better return than his mighty summer of 1948. His appointment as joint captain of Middlesex with Bill Edrich was another achievement, and he began the Test series against South Africa with a century at Trent Bridge. England lost the game by 71 runs.

At Lord's, Compton made 79 in a Test won by England by 10 wickets. An infected toe kept him out of the Third Test but he returned for scores of 25, 73 and 18 in the final two Tests. His series figures of 312 at 52.00 were strong.

After a luxurious first-ever winter off from 'work', he found it difficult to become enthusiastic about the 1952 cricket season. He was 34 and appeared stale. It reflected in his figures – just 1880 runs at 39.16. He did worse in the Tests against the Indian tourists, scoring 59 runs at 29.50 in four innings. Feeling out of sorts, he dropped out of the last two Tests.

Compton fired up for the next season in 1953 against the Australians and was part of England's 1–0 series win and the return of the Ashes for the first time in two decades. But there was no century contribution from this great player of yesteryear. Scores of 0, 57, 33, 45, 0, 61, 16 and 22 not out produced a yeoman-like 234 at 33.43. His most brilliant and aggressive foe, Ray Lindwall, had him four times out of the seven he was dismissed. It was not the performance of the 1948-vintage Compton.

Yet, still he was always an early pick for England, and he was taken on tour to the West Indies.

Riots and Rum

England ran into wild crowds in the Caribbean and two Test losses in succession at Jamaica – where there were riots by the drunken crowd – and Bridgetown. Compton checked a run of low scores with a fighting top score of 93 in England's second innings in the Second Test, but his team was thrashed by 181 runs. In the first innings of the Third Test at Georgetown, he continued his return to form with a 64. He followed this at Port of Spain with 133 in a high-scoring draw. Hutton used him as a bowler and he took two for 40 in the West Indies' first innings. Compton and the other England players thought it should have been three when a slips catch was adjudged not out. It was a bump ball, the umpire said. Compton remonstrated with the decision and made a sarcastic remark about rule interpretation being different in the West Indies. The umpire made a formal complaint.

The game was drawn. In the final Test at Sabina Park, he was out hit wicket for 31 in England's heroic win, which levelled the series at 2–2 under Len Hutton's leadership. Compton's figures of 348 at 49.71 were strong enough to suggest that he could still mix it with the best.

Revival Against Pakistan

The next home season, 1954, brought abundant proof that he really could still mix it with the best. Compton managed 453 at 90.60 in England against Pakistan. The series was dominated by his highest Test innings of 278 at Trent Bridge in the Second Test. His 200 took just 245 minutes and his innings, in all, took just 290 minutes, making it one of the fastest big Test performances ever recorded. He showed remarkable stamina and fought his knee pain.

Wisden observed the innings as: 'a torrent of strokes, orthodox and improvised, crashing and delicate . . .'

Compton had two further fine innings in the series: a top score of 93 at Old Trafford, and a gutsy 53 at The Oval.

He felt in good form for the tour to Australia for the 1954–55 series and, despite a delayed start because of his injury, ended as an important player in the series won by England 3–1. He scored 201 at 40.2, which was second in the averages for England behind Tom Graveney.

At home, he had a good Test series against South Africa, notching 492 at 54.66, with a top score of 158 at Old Trafford in the Third Test. No one else reached fifty against the pace of Peter Heine and Neil Adcock. He followed that up with 71 in the second innings, an even more polished knock, but still England lost by three wickets. The thrilling series went to England 3–2.

A few months after the season in November 1955, Compton had his right kneecap removed. It was placed in a biscuit tin at Lord's for posterity. Compton rehabilitated himself quickly and turned out for Middlesex against Australia well into the season. He scored a sparkling 61 in 106 minutes. It was enough, along with some other useful county form, for selectors to bring him back for the final Test of the Ashes at The Oval. He struggled against the fire of Miller and the spin of Richie Benaud, but went on to play a beautiful innings of 94 with all his favourite strokes – the sweep, the late-cut and the cover drive. In the second innings there was more of the same with 35 not out. It gave him enormous satisfaction to withstand and come out on top against Lindwall's and Miller's assault, one last time. Sadly, the commentators would never again say, 'Compton waits as Lindwall comes in and bowls . . .'

Compton toured for the final time to South Africa and managed 242 from 10 innings at an average of 24.20 with a top score of 64.

His Test career figures were 5807 runs with 17 hundreds, at an average of 50.06. Compton's full-time first-class career finished after the 1957 series. His aggregate was 38,942 runs, with 123 centuries, at an average of 51.85. As a bowler, he took 622 wickets at 32.27. He took 415 catches, mainly at slip.

Compton married for the third time in 1972 to Christine and they had two daughters. Compton's career, after cricket, involved public relations consultancy work. He also performed BBC commentary work and was a long-term correspondent for the *Sunday Express*. In addition, he worked hard for his beloved Middlesex county club, putting in a five-year stint as president in the 1990s.

He remained a close friend of Keith Miller and kept up

good relations with Bradman, even turning up in Australia for his eighty-fifth birthday party in 1993. Compton's death in 1997 – just short of his seventy-ninth birthday – brought a flood of effusive eulogies for a fun and flamboyant character and cricketer.

Denis Compton was one of the finest artists and characters cricket has known. His warm-hearted, carefree approach made him an unusual champion. He was a worthy choice as the batsman at number three – the prime batting position – in Bradman's best-ever England team. In effect, Bradman, who was at three in the Australian team, was naming him as his counterpart in the opposition. There could be no one more worthy in England's ranks.

CHAPTER 16

ENGLAND'S
MOST ELEGANT

PETER MAY

(England)

31 December 1929–27 December 1994

> *'May was the finest batsman in arguably the best and most balanced line-up England ever put in the field.'*
>
> DON BRADMAN

Peter May didn't hesitate to bat when he won the toss at Melbourne in the Second Test of the 1958–59 Ashes series. The wicket was a green top, just right for his pacemen Peter Loader and Brian Statham. May, 6 ft (183 cm), strong and broad-shouldered, was buoyant despite being under pressure because of England's loss in the First Test at Brisbane. The date was 31 December 1958. It was his twenty-ninth birthday. What better way to celebrate it than with a big innings in a Test against Australia? He had received plenty of birthday salutations from home and he was ready for a special effort at the wicket. Among the England team there was a slight worry about the overcast skies, but it was over-ridden by the need to bat first, post a big score and turn the pressure back onto Australian captain Richie Benaud and his men.

May had good reason to be confident. He was leading the world's premier team and he was England's best bat. Some English critics even rated him as England's best post-war bat ahead of Len Hutton and Denis Compton. May's captaincy record at that point – 14 wins from 25 matches – was not far behind that of Don Bradman (15 wins from 24), who had, until the year 2000, the best win rate of all captains.

A first-day crowd of more than 40,000 – high considering it was New Year's Eve – was settled into the vast MCG stadium. Left-hander Peter Richardson opened with the experienced Trevor Bailey, who had bored everyone to distraction with his slow batting at Brisbane. May, batting at five, a position which many thought was too low in the order, was sitting in front of the dressing room with friends. Alan Davidson began his second over – the third of the match – from the outer end, aided by the humid, heavy atmosphere. His first ball moved away from the left-hander and he nicked it to keeper Wally Grout. England was one for 7. May stood up and went into the dressing room to pad up. He hadn't even put on one pad before there was a tremendous roar. Willie Watson, another left-hander, played all over a Davidson yorker that scattered his stumps. England was two for 7. May had his pads on as Tom Graveney took block. Davidson, making use of a cross-breeze, bowled an in-swinger to the right-hander. It swung in so late that it was unplayable. Graveney didn't offer a shot and was out first ball lbw for a duck. England was now three for 7. May had just completed his preparation and was on his way to the wicket. He was facing a hat trick. Davidson delivered a wide one and he didn't have to play at it.

May looked scratchy, playing and missing at Davidson and the fast, erratic left-armer Ian Meckiff in the next few overs. Bailey surprised all onlookers by going for his strokes and the partnership consolidated.

Benaud came on to bowl his leg-spinners in the last over before lunch. May popped back a 'sitter' first ball. Benaud was not expecting such an easy chance. He took a step forward and fumbled it. England went to the break on three for 52.

Mid-afternoon, Meckiff removed Bailey for 48. May struggled and was slow, as the circumstances dictated. He was textbook straight in defence, showing the maker's name to all bowlers. Yet as the afternoon and final session wore on, he showed glimpses of his brilliance with superb drives straight or wide of mid-on. Benaud moved his field accordingly, placing his two best fielders, Norman O'Neill and Neil Harvey, where they could be most effective in cutting off May's run supply. By close of play, his timing was not consistently effortless, as it had been in other more attacking innings, but he was disciplined all the way through to stumps on 89 not out. It was not a productive return for a few overs short of a full day's play (300 minutes in these games played over six days), yet it was vital for England in the context of the awful start. England was four for 173 at stumps with Colin Cowdrey on 28 in 142 minutes. May had engineered a fine recovery.

The next morning he sailed through a hundred with drives between cover and mid-wicket, and became the first England captain to score a century in Australia since Archie MacLaren in 1901–02. May reached 113 and was set for a much bigger score. Then Meckiff produced – according to May in his autobiography *A Game Enjoyed* – an 'absolute thunderbolt'. 'My bat was still in the air,' May said, 'when it shattered the wicket.'

There was something more behind the England captain's words. He and other members of the touring team had complained in private that Meckiff was a thrower, or in Australian parlance, 'a chucker'. There was some debate over his naturally bent elbow (similar to the perception of Sri Lankan spinner Muttiah Muralitharan in the 1990s), thin wrists and double-jointedness. Benaud considered his action fair, after viewing it from all positions on the ground. No one had 'called' Meckiff in New Zealand, Australia or South Africa. But now, under English media, management and player scrutiny, Meckiff was perceived as suspect. The English were most vocal about his quicker ball – that thunderbolt from nowhere.

England reached 259, thanks to May, in one of his most gallant performances for his country. Australia replied with 308, mainly because of a great 167 by Neil Harvey. But it was Meckiff, with more lightning and spectacular catching by his fielders, who destroyed England in the second innings when it registered just 87. He took six for 38. Australia won by eight wickets.

There was disappointment and disquiet in the England camp. Yet May waited until he returned home to complain. He didn't wish to create another situation similar to the one that ensued during the Bodyline series of 1932–33. In this Test, he was given the highest marks for his fighting century, captaincy and diplomacy.

Dream Beginning

The son of a Reading wholesale ironmonger and builder, Peter May was a prodigy at his exclusive public school, Charterhouse, and was coached there in cricket by former England fast-medium bowler George Geary. Geary saw him, even at 14 in 1944, as a future Test player. May was a versatile sport, captaining the school team in soccer, fives, hockey and cricket. By the time he left Charterhouse, all of these sports became leisure pursuits except cricket. May moved easily from school to playing cricket for the Royal Navy and Combined Services team at first-class level, then on to Cambridge University where, in between scoring centuries, he managed an honours degree in Economics and History. He was in good company in Cambridge's team, which included batsmen Raman Subba Row, David Sheppard and paceman John Warr, who all went on to play for England, and also the talented off-spinner, Robin Marlar. Two other bats of real class were Hubert Doggart and John Dewes. Playing amidst such skill lifted May's general standard of play another notch as he developed, again with ease and modesty, into the best batsman of his generation.

May's outstanding ability was clear to most seasoned observers in 1950 during his first full County Championship season when he hit 1187 at 33.91, including two centuries and four fifties. In 1951, he scored 2339 at 68.79 with nine centuries. He not only looked the part with his upright driving and attacking manner, but he was also putting scores on the board. It was enough for national selectors. They chose him for his First Test against the touring South Africa at Headingley. The visitors scored 538, thanks to a fine start by opener Eric Rowan (236). May came in at one for 99. On paper, this looked an ideal set-up on a batsman's wicket. But without a sightscreen, he was distracted by the shimmering white shirts and dresses directly behind the bowler as he delivered. After an anxious, streaky start, his defence was immaculate. His confidence grew and he began to drive with his classic trademark elegance on either side of the wicket from wide mid-on to wide mid-off. As the innings built, he widened the arc. May reached 92 and then unleashed two magnificent straight drives to the fence to become the tenth Englishman to score a century in his first Test. The Yorkshire crowd, who, as writer R.C. Robertson-Glasgow observed, 'tend to believe only what they see', rose to their feet in rapturous applause. May was, after all, a 'southerner' and a student. He had to prove himself in front of the northern crowd. Yet apart from their 'eyes-on' appreciation, no supporter group in the country was more finely tuned to ability, or lack of it. May won their approval. It touched him in a way never to be repeated in his illustrious career. Buoyed, he went on to the top score of 138 in England's 505 in a game that fell away to a draw.

May had arrived at the highest level with style at age 21.

In the Fifth Test he made 33 and 0. His studies caused him to miss the 1951–52 tour of India. He came back to Cambridge for his last term in 1952, having been named one of *Wisden*'s five cricketers of the year (for his 1951 season). When the students were on vacation, May played with Surrey and his combined first-class season saw him accumulate 2498 runs at 62.45, which placed him second only to David Sheppard in the national averages. May's Test progress was steady without being spectacular against the touring Indians. In a four-Test series won by England 3–0, he posted scores of 16, 4, 74, 26, 69 and 17 – 206 runs at a modest average of 34.33.

Lindwall – First Nightmare

The touring Australians under Lindsay Hassett in 1953 were well primed for their encounter with Surrey at The Oval. Their main target for early demoralisation was England's rising young star Peter May, just 23. The aim was for Ray Lindwall to unsettle him early and get him out as cheaply as possible in both innings. This, it was hoped, would cause him self-doubt and sow seeds of uncertainty among the selectors. Lindwall had him caught by keeper Don Tallon for a duck in the first innings. The second innings then became the key event. Even a 35 or 40 in goodish style would be enough for May to proceed against the Australians in the Tests. Hassett employed the arrogant-looking so-called Carmody field of a ring of slips and gullies to Lindwall, who wheeled in against May. The most out-standing paceman in the world at the time sent down five out-swingers and one in-swinger. May played at and missed each ball. By a miracle he survived. He was rattled. Not even tail-enders were so humiliated. His confidence gone, he played over a yorker from Ron Archer and was bowled for 1.

Hassett and Co. considered they had won a small battle in the ongoing Ashes war. They won another at Lord's playing the MCC. May was again Lindwall's victim, cheaply, in the second innings. In the first, leggie Doug Ring also had him before he settled in. He was saved by an imperious 136 against Northamptonshire. Its attack included Freddie Brown, chairman of selectors, who bowled 34 overs of medium pace at him. May was picked for the First Test.

But the selectors' attitude to him did not engender confidence in the young man. He was dropped down the order from mainly number three in his previous six Tests to number six. This was a clear message from selectors: 'fail and you're out'.

May batted in failing light and was caught behind off leg-spinner Jack Hill for nine. The harsh reality of Ashes competition struck home. May was dumped, unfairly, given his talent. He battled on during the season and made a fifty against Australia in the second Surrey game before Lindwall again dismissed him. This time, May looked more assured. He was selected for the Fifth and deciding Test at The Oval. What's more, he was placed in the hot-seat number-three spot. In a low-scoring contest (Hutton's 82 was the highest score in the game's four innings), May took on Lindwall, saw him off and contributed important knocks of 39 (caught off Bill Johnston) and 37 (caught off Keith Miller). England won by eight wickets and took back the Ashes for the first time since Douglas Jardine's team won in Australia in 1932–33.

May was pleased to be part of such an historic win, especially since it was in the 1953 Coronation year. But he would not be satisfied until he faced Australia again and lived up to his potential.

Toughening Curve

May was taken on the tour of the West Indies for Tests early in 1954. He was given a lesson at close quarters in courage and determination from his captain Len Hutton. After being soundly beaten in the first two Tests at Sabina Park, Kingston, and at Kensington Oval, Bridgetown, England had to lift in the Third at Bourda, Georgetown, in British Guiana, to have any chance of squaring or winning the series.

After a slow start to the tour and trouble with out-swingers, May was taking block on leg-stump. This followed Hutton's advice that this would allow him 'to know where his stumps were'. It seemed to work. May scored 31, 69, 7 and 62 in the first two Tests. But he, like most of the team, had shown patchy form. A more cohesive, fighting effort was needed. May was having trouble with the diminutive spinner Sonny Ramadhin. His quick arm action, accentuated by loose wrists covered by rolled-down sleeves, resulted in fast, low deliveries. He was predominantly an off-spinner, but he had a surprise leg-break, which none of the English bats could pick. The best way to play him, the consensus of batsmen suggested, was to move forward to counter the off-break and hope that the shock leg-turner, that he slipped in now and again, missed everything. It wasn't exactly a scientific approach, but nothing else worked anyway. Ramadhin caused all the batsmen concern and dismissed May three times. Ramadhin was twinned with orthodox left-armer Alf Valentine for the first three Tests of the series.

Some steel was needed at Bourda, British Guiana, which was pushing for independence (as Guyana) and had recently experienced political turmoil. Hutton provided some backbone with a typically gritty, yet ever-polished 169 from 435, while May failed with 12 (and 12 again in the second innings). In the West Indies first innings, a brilliant pickup and throw by May ran out Clifford McWatt. The crowd rioted. Hutton's stoic decision to stay on the field made a big impression on May, who thought the skipper's courage way beyond normal bounds. May, with others in the team, was concerned that they would be injured by the angry, alcohol-fuelled rioters. Despite the unruly crowd, England went on to win by eight wickets. May and his team-mates left Georgetown relieved, and hopeful that the series was not lost.

May hit good form and top-scored for England with 135 – his second Test century – at Queen's Park, Trinidad, in a high-scoring draw. May contributed well with 30 and 40 not out – the latter being a bright knock against the clock to finish the match. England won by nine wickets and squared the series.

May sailed away from the West Indies much tougher and wiser for the experience. He had also seen what it took to be a strong and successful skipper under dangerous and testing conditions. Hutton had shown the way with the bat, never capitulating no matter what the pressures. A high standard had been set for all captains to follow. Peter May, a possible successor, took note.

Plunder Down-Under

May's series versus Pakistan at home in a wet 1954 was ordinary, with just one fifty, but it mattered little. He was chosen as vice-captain under Hutton to defend the Ashes in Australia in 1954–55. Much was expected of him and of the rest of the England team. Injuries to Compton cut his performances drastically and he was ineffective. Hutton, burdened by the pressure of leadership, and lacking form, was half the player he was in the West Indies. It meant the younger players had to lift their rating with the bat, or England would fail.

May began shakily at Brisbane, dismissed by his nemesis Lindwall, bowled for 1 and lbw for 44, and England went down by an innings and 154 in a disastrous beginning to the Ashes series. At Sydney in the Second Test, England failed again with bat, scoring a meagre 154 (May 5). Tyson's speed reduced Australia to 228. Something special was needed, and May, in his biggest test, came through with a controlled, defensive, yet vital 104 in 298 minutes, giving England a lead of 222. With Tyson in a pugnacious mood, it was enough. England won by 38 runs and launched on to Melbourne as a united, fired-up group.

May was in terrific form, hitting centuries in four successive matches leading up to the Third Test. But he ran out of luck on 31 December, Day One of the MCG Test, when he received a lifter from Lindwall that was gloved to Benaud in the gully. May left the wicket in a whirl of disappointment, having made a duck on his twenty-fifth birthday. He was so preoccupied with his head down that he walked ten metres wide of the players' gate. The crowd laughed as May groped for the non-existent gate, only to be waved to the right place by an official. Yet it said much about May's emotional state. He hated failing when England was now back in the series. He wasn't alone as the restored Lindwall–Miller combination reduced England to four for 41. But another newer member of England's line-up, Colin Cowdrey, who had partnered May well at Sydney, came through with a timely 102, a feature being his textbook-perfect stroke-play against Australia's speedmen. England scrambled to 191. Brian Statham, with five for 60, this time held Australia to 231.

May then played a brilliant innings of 91, with great driving in the arc between mid-wicket and cover, and especially mid-on and mid-off. His innings saved and then set up England for a win as the tourists reached 279 – a lead of 239. Tyson again ripped through the opposition. The tourists won by 128 runs.

England, 3–1 up after winning the Fourth Test at Adelaide by five wickets, could not be beaten. In the drawn Fifth Test formality, May cracked 79, to end his series with an aggregate of 351 (the highest for England) at 39.00 (only Tom Graveney and Denis Compton averaged more).

May had stood up to the demands and matured into a seasoned Test bat on this tour. The batons of champion batsmanship and leadership had passed from Hutton and Compton to the new stars of the post-war generation, May and Cowdrey.

Captain in the Golden Years: 1955–1958

Hutton was chosen to lead England at home in 1955 in all five Tests against South Africa but his fitness fell away and he was replaced by May, who was 25 years of age. The new skipper eased into the position, with two successive wins at Trent Bridge by an innings and 71 runs at Lord's. His own form – 83, 0, 112 – demonstrated that he was ready and able to lead and keep making runs as the country's number-one bat. He was ably backed up by Tyson (match figures of eight for 79) at Trent Bridge, and then Statham at Lord's (nine for 88). But matters became more problematic at Old Trafford in the Third Test, when South Africa, chasing 145 in 135 minutes, got home by three wickets. May again proved in fine touch, scoring 34 and a fighting 117. His runs had come against a top-class attack including speedsters Neil Adcock and Peter Heine, off-spinner Hugh Tayfield, and medium-pacer Trevor Goddard. May again performed well at Headingley, scoring 47 and a captain's knock of 97 (top score), before falling lbw to Tayfield – the wicket that effectively gave South Africa the Test by 224 runs.

So, once more The Oval was the setting for a deciding Test. A winning result would mean it was the first five-Test series in England that featured no draws. With the teams poised 2–2, it promised to be tight. England chose the spin twins from Surrey, Jim Laker and Tony Lock, playing on their county home turf, for the first time in combination in the series. The turning wicket helped make the selection decisive for England in a low-scoring affair. England notched just 151 first up (Goddard: five for 31, and May: 3), but South Africa, in reply, could muster just 112. Lock took four for 39, and Laker two for 28. May once more responded to the challenge, as he had all series, with a gutsy and defensive match top score of 89 not out. This allowed England to crawl to 204. Laker and Lock (five for 56 and four for 62 respectively) rolled up the Springboks for 151 – giving England a 92-run win and the series 3–2. Thus May, with a lot of help from his spinners, had won the contest and retained the leadership. Had he lost, England's selectors may well have opted for their long-term bridesmaid favourite, the Right Reverend David Sheppard, the future Bishop of Liverpool, to replace May. Sheppard had captained Cambridge, winning the ballot over May by just one vote, mainly because he was considered a more charismatic figure.

Yet May was the better bat. England was tempted to pop Sheppard in as captain ahead of Hutton, then May, but in the end the selectors opted for the Australian approach that was to choose the best 11 players and then select the skipper from among them. By the end of that 1955 summer, May's natural ascendancy to the leadership, without fanfare, had proved right for England.

Defending the Ashes: 1956

May's first-class season figures for 1956 were deceptive. He had 50 innings, with just three centuries, and had scored 1631, at the modest average of 37.93. These scores did not reflect his dominance in the Tests. He had the highest aggregate – 453 runs – in seven innings at the best average by far of 90.60. Consistency was the key word. Batting at number four every time, May did not fail in a single innings, scoring 73 in the Trent Bridge draw; 63 and 53 in a game England lost at Lord's; 101 at Headingley; 43 at Old Trafford; and 83 not out and 37 not out in the final drawn game at The Oval.

His cause was helped by Lindwall being unfit and below his best, and by Australia's attack in general appearing particularly weak, except for the veteran Miller, who took 21 wickets at 22.24. But in a series on poor wickets when the highest score was 113 by Sheppard, May was the standout cricketer of the series, out-batting everyone and out-generalling his opposite number Ian Johnson. Laker (46 wickets at 9.61) and Lock (15 wickets at 22.47) allowed May to keep control throughout the series, except for the Lord's Test where the wicket was true.

The series gave May his most satisfaction so far in big cricket. He led one of the best outfits ever in world cricket, with batting and bowling depth of the highest order. Alongside May variously throughout the series were batsmen of high calibre including Colin Cowdrey, Peter Richardson, Tom Graveney, Cyril Washbrook, David Sheppard and Denis Compton. England gambled on bringing in Washbrook (98), Sheppard (113) and Compton (94) in the Third, Fourth and Fifth Tests, and won each time. The selectors were able to bask in the glory of their apparent wisdom, although it could easily have gone awry when Washbrook on just 1 survived a vigorous and confident lbw appeal.

Bradman, who covered the series as a journalist for the London *Mail*, noted: 'Had the ball been just perhaps a centimetre to left or right, and Washbrook had been adjudged out, there would have been such a blast for the selectors (of whom Washbrook was one) for bringing back a player of 42, that it is doubtful whether they would have risked Sheppard, and maybe Compton as well.'

Such are the vicissitudes of cricket. England, the far superior team, had the luck running with it. All its hunches and gambles paid off.

In the bowling department, backing up Laker and Lock were Statham, Fred Trueman, Tyson, all-rounder Bailey (medium pace), Bob Appleyard (off-spin) and Johnny Wardle (left-arm spin, both varieties). Behind the stumps was Bradman's choice for the title of England's finest-ever keeper, Godfrey Evans.

Bradman said that the Test team May presided over at The Oval in 1956 went very close to his 'Ideal XI' in terms of the specifications he set down for an ideal team, based on a balance of left- and right-hand batsmen and bowlers. It read in batting order: Richardson (left-hander), Cowdrey, May, Compton, Sheppard, Washbrook, Evans, Statham, Tyson, Lock (left-hand orthodox spinner) and Laker. He would have preferred another left-hand specialist bat and an all-rounder, but apart from that it was Bradman's on-paper perfect combination.

May had now been in three successive Ashes wins against Australia, a record rarely matched in history. He took the nucleus of this strong side to South Africa and had to be content with a 2–2 drawn series. Yet May was far from happy with his own form. After the high of the English summer, he came down to earth on the South African veldt, scoring just 153 for an average of 15.3 It was a curious dip in form. In the other games on tour he was in fine touch. He became the first player to score four successive hundreds in South Africa.

But before he could ponder his series failure, he was head-long into another home season in 1957 and five Tests against the touring West Indians, as well as taking over from Stuart Surridge as skipper at Surrey. Under his command in the bowling department of the county side were Peter Loader, Alec and Eric Bedser, Jim Laker and Tony Lock. With bowling strength like these players to call on, May continued Surrey's great run under Surridge with another championship win.

Batsman Alive with 285

May was nervous going into the First Test at Edgbaston after his woeful Test efforts in South Africa and his first-innings score of 30, cut short by more deceptive spin from Ramadhin, who had bamboozled him in the West Indies three years earlier. The offie/leggie took seven for 49 and England was rolled for 186. The West Indies replied with 474, a lead of 288, with the quick-footed and aggressive Collie Smith making 164.

England had attacked Ramadhin in the first innings. That tactic failed. Plan B was a war of attrition. No one would take risks. They would attempt to wear him down. This strategy looked like working early in England's second innings, but the spinner struck on 65 and removed two batsmen. May came to the wicket at two for 65. At the end of Day Three, Saturday, May was still there and the score had inched up to two for 102. He had Sunday to cogitate on his situation. He blamed himself for not winning the South African series. Another batting failure here and a loss would put his captaincy and Test place in jeopardy. May needed to make amends with a really big score. Nothing short of a double century would do if England were to get out of this predicament in the next two days. May set his mind on something special like never before. He lost partner Brian Close to the quick but spasmodic Roy 'Gilly' Gilchrist, but then the speedster limped off with an injury. The attack was thin, apart from Ramadhin, the medium pace of Frank Worrell, and the variety of pace and spin from Garry Sobers.

May was fortunate to have his good friend Cowdrey at the other end. Cowdrey urged May to put his head down at fifty. May tried to push a standard Ramadhin wide of mid-on and missed. The West Indians appealed for lbw. The umpire thought it was drifting to leg. But it was a near thing. May asked Cowdrey to remind him not to be naughty enough to play that shot again. He told Cowdrey not to play it either. When May reached a century, Cowdrey strolled up the pitch and said: 'Now come on Peter, we're not out of this yet.' He added with a grin, 'Just think of the veldt. Keep your mind on the veldt.'

The horrors of his South African scores and paltry average were a continuing spur for May. Cowdrey was committed, against instinct, to pure technical defence. Nobody did it better than Colin. May's inclination to go after Ramadhin was curbed just by watching his talented batting partner. At 289, England was in the lead. May and Cowdrey had another mid-pitch chat, asking each other for further application to the task. They made it through to stumps, May on 193 not out, Cowdrey, 78. England was three for 378. The score had moved along 276 in a day, which was at a fair, if disciplined, clip.

May eased through 200 on the final morning and the batting partnership continued on with the same strictures until Cowdrey reached his century a half-hour before lunch. Then both began to play more freely, Cowdrey opening up all round the wicket before he was dismissed 45 minutes into the second session for 154. The partnership was 411, the then highest-ever Test fourth-wicket partnership, and England's best for any wicket. The lead was then 236 with about 185 minutes batting time left. May wondered about declaring, but feared the West Indies' batting strength – which included Garry Sobers, Clyde Walcott, Everton Weekes, Frank Worrell and Collie Smith – might just get the runs. He decided to bat on for another 50 minutes, thus killing the game. During this time Ramadhin nearly reached his century, not in runs against him, but in overs. For the innings he sent down an incredible 98 overs, 35 of them maidens, for a return of two for 179. His 588 deliveries were the most ever bowled in a first-class innings. May and Cowdrey had turned this brilliant West Indies 'strike' spinner into a stock bowler.

May reached 285 not out and declared at four for 583 – a lead of 295 – leaving 140 minutes to dismiss the West Indies. The West Indies collapsed to the old firm of Laker and Lock and was seven for 72 at stumps. Those 50 minutes may well have given England the game. But May preferred discretion rather than a dash for valour. Had his captaincy and place not been on the line, he may have been more adventurous. As it was, he had pulled England out of a huge hole in one of the best fightbacks in Test history. And the innings was May's finest and biggest ever.

It was followed a few weeks later by a May duck in the Second Test at Lord's, won handsomely by England, thanks to the swing of Trevor Bailey, whose match figures were eleven for 98, a record against the West Indies. May hit 104 in the drawn Third Test at Trent Bridge – in a game dominated by Tom Graveney, who scored a magnificent 258 and 28 not out. The game was drawn, but not before Collie Smith again demonstrated his prowess by smashing 168. At a low-scoring Headingley game in the Fourth Test, May's 69 was the highest score in the match. He was well served again by his bowlers: Trueman, Loader, Laker and Lock. England won by an innings, as it did the Fifth Test at The Oval. May scored just 1, but Graveney dominated again with a dashing 164, while Peter Richardson stroked his second century of the series.

May's series aggregate was 489 runs at a 97.80 average. The years of 1956 and 1957 were the pinnacle of his career.

The crushing 3–0 series win restored England to its top-of-the-world status after the shaky series in South Africa. If anything, the 1957 Oval team was even better balanced than the one that had so enchanted Bradman in the corresponding game a year earlier against the Australians. It was made up of Richardson, Sheppard, Graveney, May, Cowdrey, Bailey, Evans, Lock, Trueman, Laker and Loader. Bailey was the all-rounder who had been missing in the 1956 line-up. The team looked impressive on paper and performed accordingly on the field. May could never complain about the talent at his disposal. England's cricket pool was teeming with at least as much ability as at any time in its history. It was apparent once more in 1958 at home when England thrashed a weak New

Zealand team 4–0, with three more wins by an innings.

May had another bumper series, scoring 84, 11, 19, 113 not out, 101 and 9, giving him a tally of 337 at 67.40. For the third successive English summer, he and his team had dominated the opposition, losing just one Test in 15. With a pre-eminent place at the top of world cricket, May led his team to Australia for the 1958–59 season and what was expected to be another big Ashes victory.

The England team ran into a controversy waiting to happen. It centred around throwing by some of its players. Every country had its share of 'chuckers', but so far the issue hadn't become an issue in cricket. May noted in *A Game Enjoyed*: 'Those of suspect action had been nearly all spinners and no one had done much more than raise eyebrows.' Umpires who called bowlers for throwing were viewed as stirrers or publicity seekers, he said. The tendency was to sweep such 'unpleasantness', as May called it, under the carpet.

During the 1953 Ashes, Tony Lock had more than raised eyebrows in the final Ashes Test at The Oval. Australian captain Lindsay Hassett was certain Lock threw his fast delivery and complained in private. It caused grumbling in the Australian camp, especially as Lock had been a match-winner in a deciding Test, taking five for 45 in Australia's second innings. Now the boot was on the other foot. May's team ran into Ian Meckiff in the Test team. Almost every Australian State team seemed to have at least one player with a suspect action. (There was the added problem of fast bowlers who dragged the trailing foot over the line.)

It wasn't much of an issue until the Second Test at Melbourne when Meckiff bowled May on 113 in the first innings and then crashed through England in the second innings, taking six for 38. England had been the top cricketing nation over the five years 1953 to 1958.

Suddenly the team was down 0–2 and facing an unexpected thrashing in an Ashes series after winning three on end. This exacerbated the attitude towards Meckiff. The throwing situation had been left to drift through the 1950s. Now it was an issue. And the supremacy of May's team was in jeopardy. In the Third Test at Sydney in January 1959, much interest now centred on Meckiff's action. Most judged it passable, except when he whipped in his faster one. That flicking double-jointed left wrist, along with what was generally perceived as a lower, bent-elbow delivery, gave the media something to stir up. As it turned out, Meckiff was not effective, taking just one for 45 in the first innings and breaking down with a strained Achilles tendon within a few overs into the second. The game was drawn. The issue of throwing died a little. Meanwhile, May batted at four and made 42 until he fell to a tremendous catch by Ken Mackay off Keith Slater. In the second innings May seemed off the boil until joined by Cowdrey at three for 64. Once more, Cowdrey's calming, quietly inspiring manner lifted May. They embarked on a determined partnership and were still there at stumps on the fifth day, with one day to play. May was 63 not out and Cowdrey 50 not out, having endured negative tactics by Benaud in the field. England was three for 178 – 40 runs ahead. Benaud changed his approach on the morning of Day Six, but May and Cowdrey resisted until lunch, when both were on 82 not out. England then led by 93. May was out, bowled at 92, from a faster, suspect off-spin delivery from Jimmy Burke. Cowdrey remained not out 100 when May declared at seven for 287 and the game fizzled to a draw.

Twice now in the series, May felt he was thrown out. But a draw, and not a loss, kept the problem under the carpet for the moment.

May won the toss at Adelaide in the Fourth Test

beginning 30 January and did the near unthinkable on that batsman's paradise by deciding to bowl first. But his thinking was logical. He had to win here and in the Fifth Test at Melbourne to level the series and retain the Ashes. Benaud's negative bowling tactics during England's second innings showed he would prefer to draw rather than risk defeat. Taking note of this, May had to gamble on rolling Australia in a day or less, then batting for two days in compiling a big lead that would put Australia under pressure in its second innings.

As they left the field after the toss, May said to Benaud: 'Will you take strike?'

'What did you say, Peter?' Benaud asked.

'I want you to bat first.'

'Thank you,' Benaud said, with eyebrows raised incredulously. 'You have given us the game.'

The Australian skipper's intemperate remark proved prescient. Australia compiled 476 (Colin McDonald 170). May demonstrated his particularly sporting nature during McDonald's innings. The Victorian had been plagued by knee problems and during one lunch break – on 149 not out – asked if he could retire hurt. May did not hesitate to allow it, perhaps thinking of a chance to make inroads into Australia's tail. Yet it was still a generous act. He could have said 'no, but you can have a runner'.

When England batted it ran into another problem in the form of the big New South Wales speedster Gordon Rorke. May and his fellow tourists thought his faster ball was also suspect. But his drag made him frightening. Instead of delivering over 22 yards, it appeared like 18.

'He seemed right under your nose on delivery,' Cowdrey noted. 'Only [Jeff] Thomson and [Wesley] Hall were as terrifying in my experience.'

May, who was in terrific touch, launched into Ray

Lindwall. The veteran speedster had fought his way back into the Test side after being discarded on Australia's Test tour of South Africa the season before. He trapped Richardson lbw for 4, but May, intent on squaring off for their very early encounters when he had been a tyro and Lindwall the world champ, thrashed 11 off one over from him. Benaud came on. The week before, May had clobbered the leggie in the game against New South Wales. He tried to do it again and was bowled for 37. England made 240. Benaud, now showing his more natural positive side, enforced the follow-on. May kept his dash, and for a while in a link with Graveney, it looked as if England could fight its way out of the predicament. But Rorke rapped May on the pad with a ball that kept low. May, ever the sportsman, 'walked'. It is now rare in twenty-first century cricket ever to see someone give themselves out. Even in the 1950s, this was remarkable.

England was beaten by eight wickets.

The loss meant the Ashes went back to Australia. It was a shock, but one that had been coming since the First Test. May's heart was now elsewhere and he only made 4 in the first innings of the Fifth Test, this time caught by Benaud in the gully off Meckiff, a dismissal that would have irked the batsman. The ball seemed to jump off a good length. May committed to the shot, got an edge. He only managed 11 in the second innings, this time caught in slips off Lindwall. Thus the duel between these two truly great cricketers ended the way it began, with Lindwall dismissing May cheaply.

Overall, despite the 4–0 thrashing, May was effective with the bat, scoring 405 at 40.50. His aggregate was second only to McDonald (519).

After the turmoil of Australia, May relaxed in New Zealand on the way home, scoring 71 and 124 not out in the two Tests – one of which was won by England at Lancaster Park, Christchurch, and the other drawn at Eden Park, Auckland. This improved his figures for the Antipodean tour to an aggregate of exactly 600 at 54.55. May was happy with his returns but not with the Australian results.

Yet once more he found himself headlong into an English summer, this time entertaining India in five Tests. Before the season was fully underway he married Virginia Gilligan, the daughter of the former England and Sussex captain Arthur Gilligan. (Peter and Virginia ultimately had four daughters.)

May began well in the First Test of the 1959 summer at Trent Bridge, scoring 106 – the only century of the match – and leading his team to an innings win. May now had scored three centuries in seven Tests. His aggregate since the beginning of the Tests in Australia in November 1958 was 706, and he was averaging just short of 60 an innings. His form dropped off a fraction in the next two Tests, but his playing at Headingley in the Third equalled F.E. Woolley's record of 52 consecutive appearances.

Soon after, he fell ill with an ischiorectal abscess. He missed the next two Tests yet felt fit enough to tour in the West Indies in 1959–60. But he fell ill once more with the same problem after another three Tests, which included two draws and a troublesome game at Port of Spain, Trinidad. It was also the scene of a riot, which reminded May of the trouble in Georgetown six years earlier. A commotion was again caused by a legitimate run-out of a West Indian. Missiles and bottles were hurled onto the pitch by sections of the record 30,000 crowd. This time, spectators invaded the playing area. Fred Trueman grabbed a stump and acted as bodyguard for May. The England players were forced to retreat to the pavilion. Play was abandoned for the day. As luck would have it, the next day was Sunday, and when play resumed on Monday, the game went on as if nothing had happened. England ran out easy winners by 256 runs, the only result of the series.

May's wound opened again, and he was flown home to hospital and another operation. This time his convalescence was longer. He missed the entire 1960 season and was only fit enough to return for the Second Test of the 1961 Ashes series at Lord's. May, batting at five, made 17 and 22. England lost and this put Australia up 1–0. In the Third Test at Headingley, May hit 26 and 8 not out in a game that was a triumph for Fred Trueman, who took eleven for 88. England won by eight wickets. May's return had solidified an already strong batting line-up that included Geoff Pullar, Raman Subba Row, Ted Dexter, Colin Cowdrey and Ken Barrington.

In the Fourth Test, Australia managed just 190 and, in reply, England made 367, May hitting an impressive top score of 95. Despite the debilitating illness and a second-ball duck in the second innings, May seemed to have lost none of his ability and was still the best bat in the game. Thanks to Bill Lawry and Alan Davidson with the bat and Benaud with the ball, Australia came back from the dead to win by 54 runs.

May made 71 and 33 in the drawn Fifth Test at The Oval, which was dominated by Australia's Peter Burge hitting 181. Australia won the 1961 series 2–1.

May was not enjoying the game any more. He was only 31, but the recent illness, the need to move on in his business with an insurance broker, and the desire to spend more time with his family, saw him retire early from Test cricket. He played a nearly full season for Surrey in 1962, maintaining more or less the same high standard (1352 runs at 52.00) he had since his first full season in 1950.

May played in 66 Tests, accumulating 4537 runs, with 13 hundreds and 22 fifties, at an average of 46.77. He played 388 first-class games, scoring 27,592 runs, with 85 centuries and 127 fifties, at an average of 51.00. He captained England 41 times for 20 wins, 11 draws and 10 losses – a 48.78 per cent win ratio.

Yet, upon retiring as a player, May was not lost to the game. He went on in the following decades to become chairman of England's Test selectors and MCC president. In late 1994, May fell ill with a brain tumour and died four days short of his sixty-fifth birthday.

In the 40 years since he stopped playing at the highest level, no England player has been ranked above him. Peter May was one of the greats of world cricket and a fitting choice to bat at number four in Bradman's best-ever England team. Bradman was thinking not just of May's outstanding technique though. In selecting him in the important position of number four in the team – a place usually reserved for the second-best and best batsmen – he was making his choice on May's temperament which gave him the ability to bat well in a crisis and thereby lead from the front.

CHAPTER 17

WALTER THE GRAND

WALLY
HAMMOND

(England)

19 June 1903–2 July 1965

'Hammond was one of cricket's aristocrats.'

A.G. Moyes

Walter Hammond was 25 before he made his first Test century, but once he had broken through the barrier, he exploded in an unprecedented burst of run-making. He went on to 251 in that first big innings at the Sydney Cricket Ground in the Second Test of the 1928–29 Ashes. That series established Hammond as the best batsman in the world. He took over from Jack Hobbs, who was then 46 years and still great in the true sense, but not the attacking star of former years. Hammond had been in blistering big-scoring form before the Tests on the Australian tour, along with Douglas Jardine, but could only manage 44 and 28 in the First Test at Brisbane. Yet he found the best sustained touch of his career for the next three Tests – 251 at Sydney, then 200 and 32 run out at Melbourne, followed by 119 not out and 177 at Adelaide. He failed in the final Test at Melbourne with 38 and 16 after that most purple of patches in the middle three Tests, which yielded 779 runs. He occupied the crease for 27 hours – a run rate of something under 50 runs per hundred minutes. He was not quick, but he was steady, combining attacking strokes with mundane periods that bordered on boring. He was just about immovable. In compiling this amazing aggregate, the bowlers could only get rid of him thrice.

When the boat sailed back to England, Hammond, with 905 runs at 113.13, had more than doubled Hobbs' very good figures of 451 at 50.11. It was early in 1929. The baton bearing the title 'world's finest' had been passed on. Walter Hammond, it seemed, was unassailable at the top of cricket.

House Match Marvel

Young Wally had a happy enough childhood except for not seeing much of his peripatetic army career father William, who was later killed in action at the end of the First World War. Wally boarded at Cirencester Grammar School from the age of six, and was always the quiet type who excelled at games but not academically. A score of 365 not out in a house match made the local papers in Gloucestershire. A decade later, the county tried him out. He did little in his first three county appearances in 1920, but in 1921 was in the team that played against Warwick Armstrong's Australians. Mid-season, he was nearly 18 and had been coached by two of the best players who never made the England XI – John Tunnicliffe and George Dennett. But it was one brilliant unofficial lesson from Australia's dancing aggressor, Charlie Macartney, that shaped the Hammond who would dominate an Ashes in Australia seven years later. Hammond made a duck, took 0 for plenty and chased a lot of leather. Like all champions, he learned from such experiences. In this case he studied Macartney's foot movements. Charlie was a solid 5 ft 6 in (168 cm), and had to use his feet to get to the ball, whereas, the tall (6 ft – 183 cm), athletic Hammond liked to anchor at the crease. Macartney's twinkle-toes, that reminded spectators of a dancing boxer, demonstrated what could be done with full use of the crease and beyond. Hammond copied him, and worked on his feet movement until, by the end of 1921, it was a feature of his play. He had all the strokes, power and now footwork. All he needed was the temperament – the concentration – and he would be top of his profession. Yet taking on that final characteristic was the toughest. The youthful Hammond was inclined to be impetuous. He didn't keep his head still when he got excited by a couple of big hits. Hammond was impatient.

There were other setbacks en route to the greatness of his 1928–29 Ashes performances. He was born in Dover, Kent and the county challenged his right to play for Gloucestershire. He was forced to sit out one-and-a-half seasons before he qualified. Once settled, Hammond built his reputation as an all-rounder, who bowled medium-fast, in 1923 and 1924. He made selectors sit up in August 1925 when he played against Lancashire (which included the Australian speedster Ted McDonald) and made a scorching 250 not out. This, plus a batting average in the mid-30s and a bowling average under 30 for the season, caused him to be chosen early in 1926 on a tour of the West Indies, which was then a tour just short of Test status. He cracked 238 not out in an unofficial Test, but was cut down by a mystery illness, rumoured to be a venereal disease, that saw him close to death in mid-1926. If fit that season, he would have been tackling the Australians in his first Ashes series. It was his most serious setback. Hammond recovered but seemed to come away from the experience more moody, and determined. A characteristic lack of concentration, which had hindered his progress with the bat, was not there. The darker, leaner version of Hammond was now a run-hungry machine. He thumped 1000 runs in May 1927, and gave Ted McDonald another thrashing in an innings of 187 in three hours of controlled mayhem at Old Trafford. While he brutalised with drives on the off and back-foot brilliance, onlookers noticed a tighter defence. The hook was rarely on show. The upshot of this advance was a 1927 season aggregate of 2825 and an average of 65. Hobbs and all the other county batsmen looked over their shoulders. Hammond was not there. He was in front of them.

He was first pick for the 1927–28 tour of South Africa. Injuries to England's top bowlers saw the burden falling on Hammond. His batting suffered. He did manage an impressive 51 in his first Test, but could follow this with just 90 and 66 among other mediocre performances. That Hammond spring had been pushed back again. He produced a similar set of Test figures in 1928 against the West Indies touring England as an official Test side for the first time. His county batting effort was just up on 1927 and he took 84 wickets at 23.11. Critics asked if he was capable of repeating his county performances at the international level. This made Hammond an even more dour, laconic figure as he sailed off to Australia in September 1928 with the powerful England team under Percy Chapman, hell-bent on big scores on the faster, harder Australian pitches.

The long boat ride refreshed him. He had a phenomenal 1928–29 season down-under, scoring 1553 runs from 18 innings at an average of 91.35. While tripping round the vast brown land, he notched three double centuries, four centuries and one fifty. Even in a mighty batting side, perhaps the best England ever sent abroad, he overshadowed all others. England thrashed Australia, which had its weakest bowling side since the inception of Test cricket, 4–1.

Bradman: First Encounter

Hammond's first double hundred of the season came at Sydney in November 1928 in England's game against New South Wales. He was run out by a young colt by the name of Bradman. Hammond, on first sighting of the

19-year-old, recalled in his autobiography, *Cricket My Destiny*, that Bradman 'was a slim, shortish boy with a grim, nervous face . . . He looked . . . not very formidable'.

It was an honest underestimation by Hammond, who had a penchant for writing about the physique of others, presumably because he was such a fine specimen himself. Few by comparison were as impressive as he was. Yet there was a portent in the scores in that tour match against New South Wales that gave him a clue of what was to come. Bradman scored 219 in two innings for once out, six runs less than Hammond, who dominated the game. Even as a callow youth, Bradman managed to match it with his far more illustrious rival.

Hammond only delivered 119 eight-ball overs in the Test series, and was not needed as a front-line bowler. England had a good attack, led by John White, George Geary, Maurice Tate and Harold Larwood. Hammond could concentrate on his batting. He returned to England in triumph. It was the moment to move on in life and he married Dorothy Lister, the daughter of a rich Yorkshire textile merchant, in April 1929.

There was now more pressure on him to perform. Fans around England now flocked to see him bat. He began 1929 where he had left off in Australia, scoring 238 not out against Warwickshire early in May. Hammond dipped at the end of the year but still finished second in the averages – only just – to Hobbs, who hit 2263 at 66.55. In 47 innings he accumulated 2456 runs at 64.63, with 10 centuries and eight fifties. He did well in eight innings against South Africa in the Tests of 1929 without setting the standards of his massive knocks in Australia, scoring 352 at 58.67, with two centuries.

Hammond was still king of cricket in 1929. Yet his reign, like that of Edward VIII, was spectacular but short.

Hammond's abdication by the end of the 1930 season was unpalatable for English supporters and Hammond alike. The youthful Don Bradman amassed 974 runs at 139.14. This was more than treble Hammond's 306 runs at 34.00.

To put in historical perspective the enormity of this run-making by Hammond in 1928–29 and Bradman in 1930, no batsman for the rest of the twentieth century would again score 900 or more in any Test series.

In 1930, Hammond struggled against Clarrie Grimmett, then the best leg-spinner ever to play Test cricket. Grimmett rocked him in the first three Tests, dismissing him in five out of six innings. In the other innings – in the Third Test at Headingley – Hammond batted dourly for 113 in over five hours, to help save a game affected by the weather. This was after Bradman had scored 334 – 309 not out in a day.

Hammond grew to loathe Bradman, or at least his name, which cropped up everywhere in the news and in conversation. It was not an unnatural reaction for a superstar who had reached the heights in his sport, only to see his records and performances eclipsed while he was still in the game. Hammond gained some compensation when Gloucestershire was runner-up to Lancashire in the 1930 County Championship by a very close margin. His county also nearly toppled the Australians in a match after the final Test of the series (won 2–1 by Australia). The match was tied. Hammond got 17 and 89, and it would have given him some satisfaction that Bradman only managed 42 and 14, and that Grimmett, who took three for 28, didn't get his wicket.

Bodyline Leveller

Hammond's next encounter with Bradman and Australia was in the 1932–33 Bodyline season. He scored four centuries on tour and two in the Tests, and his performances in the Tests were more or less on par with those of Bradman. Hammond hit 440 at 55.00, which was just under his career Test average; Bradman scored 396 at 56.57. This was a little over half of Bradman's career average. Hammond was thankful that Jardine's tactics in the series had brought Bradman back to him in performance. Hammond was also buoyed by scoring 336 not out against New Zealand in a Test on the way home to England. This topped Bradman's world record of 334. It was another little victory in the ongoing rivalry between the two greatest batsmen of the era.

Yet Hammond was also uneasy with Jardine's method of using the Lancashire speed duo of Harold Larwood and Bill Voce to bowl at the body to intimidate Australian batsmen and limit their scoring capacity. In private, he and others, such as England bowler Gubby Allen, were against Bodyline. As a tactic, it brought the Ashes back to England, but in 1933 the West Indies speedmen Learie Constantine and 'Manny' Martindale employed Bodyline in the Tests against England just as effectively. In the Second Test at Old Trafford, Martindale took five for 73 and split Hammond's chin with a bouncer. Hammond made 34 before Constantine had him caught in the leg-trap. Hammond came out publicly against Bodyline and said he would bow out of the game if it continued. Others also complained. Pressures built on the MCC to outlaw the tactic. It had nearly vanished from first-class cricket in England in 1934 when the Australians turned up again under Bill Woodfull. Larwood and Voce delivered hints of it in county games, much to the displeasure of the opposing batsmen, but that was the last of it.

In the Tests, Bradman and Hammond resumed their rivalry. Once more, the heavyweight championship went to Bradman. Hammond failed, scoring a miserable 162 at just 20.25. He didn't even reach 50. Bradman, even when well below his normal fitness level, accumulated 758 at 94.75 with a triple and double century in the series-deciding final two Tests.

In contrast to his Test form, Hammond's county season was sensational. His batting average of 126.25 was a record for any batsman, exceeding 1000 runs in a season. His plundering reached a peak mid-season when he gathered 1293 runs in just seven knocks. He hit eight hundreds, including scores of 290 versus Kent, 217 versus Nottingham, 265 versus Worcester and then the big score for the season: 302 against Glamorgan at Bristol in early August. These scores were compensation for the disappointment of his efforts in the big games. Even in the Players versus Gentlemen match he made just 5 and 0.

Again, the mention of his Australian tormentor brought a response of 'bloody Bradman' from him, as it did in 1930. Bradman sensed the hostility and remained reserved. He had friends in the England squad but Hammond could not be one of them. In later encounters, when Bradman was captain of Australia, he tried to humour him. He told him jokes and made an effort to draw him out of his enigmatic shell. It didn't work. Hammond didn't seem to have the inclination, or perhaps the capacity, to meet the Don halfway. He had an obsession with Bradman that he could not discard. Yet even without his Australian nemesis, Hammond was a detached figure in cricket circles.

Their rivalry was extended in the 1936–37 Ashes series encounter in Australia. Bradman was now captain and

Gubby Allen was leading England. The series began poorly for both men at Brisbane in the First Test. Hammond scored 0 and 25. Bradman hit 38 and 0 and Australia lost. In the Second Test at Sydney, Hammond streaked ahead in the battle within an Ashes battle by hitting a magnificent 231 not out. It was an awesome performance of power and patience as O'Reilly pegged away at leg-stump and Hammond waited for something he could drive off front or back foot.

Hammond loved Sydney. On four tours he would average 110 at the SCG. Bradman failed by comparison with 0 and 82. England won again, and Bradman nearly lost the leadership when some players caballed against him. The story of this Ashes seemed to be following a new pattern when both teams were caught on a sticky at Melbourne in the Third Test. Bradman once more failed – caught off left-hand orthodox spinner Hedley Verity for 13 – in the first innings. England got the worst of the wicket when it batted, but Hammond played what he considered was his finest-ever Test knock. He made 32 out of England's nine for 76. Bradman then sent his tail-enders in on the dog of a wicket so that he could preserve himself and the top order in better conditions. The tactic worked. Bradman at last struck his true form with 270. Australia won.

Hammond fell cheaply to spin in both innings at Adelaide in the Fourth Test but was very much in the game with two for 30 in Australia's first innings and five for 57 – his best figures ever against Australia – in the second innings. He even snared Bradman caught and bowled, but not before he had hit 212 to win the Test.

In the Fifth Test at Melbourne Hammond battled hard for his 14 and 56 before O'Reilly removed him both times. He was forced to look on with remorse when Bradman led the way with an innings of 169 that was the key factor in

Australia's innings win. It was the biggest comeback in Ashes history. Australia won the series 3–2.

After a misleading first half, the respective final 1936–37 Ashes figures of Hammond and Bradman had a familiar ring about them. Hammond hit 468 at 58.50, which was very much his career average and outstanding in comparison with all who had performed before or after, except for Bradman. He scored 810 at 90.00, an average a little below his career average statistic.

Hammond, on the surface, put the loss behind him. He, after all, could not be blamed. Even his bowling was serviceable. He took 12 wickets at 25.00. England was a superior team player for player, if Bradman was not included. He was the difference between the two teams.

Motoring On

Hammond loved motor cars and drove a sponsored vehicle from 1933 to 1937 when he went a step further and joined the Board of the Marsham Tyre Company. His main job was to meet potential customers, making him a glorified front-of-shop salesman. It was not demanding work. Many wanted to meet Walter Hammond in the 1930s. The company let him have as much time off to play cricket as he liked. In effect, he was now financially independent of the game and could afford to claim amateur status. This qualified him for the England captaincy, a position he coveted.

Hammond made the rare move of being a 'Player' – a professional paid for services – who became a 'Gentleman' – an unpaid performer. His conduct on and off the field was impeccable and soon important amateurs supported him. The press, reflecting public opinion and admiration, ran campaigns in his favour.

Most importantly, Hammond's form held. He went on to a fine 1937 at home, passing 3000 runs for the second time and equalling his best of 13 centuries in a season in 1933. He twice hit centuries in four successive matches. The Third Test, at The Oval against New Zealand, was his sixty-fifth cap for England, surpassing Frank Woolley's 64. Hammond may not have been the world's top cricketer any more, but he was certainly king of English cricket. He had worn the crown now for a decade and it sat easily with him again in 1938.

After a Test trial against Bradman's Australians, he was appointed captain of England. Hammond's first-class season was even better than in 1937. In just 26 innings he topped 3000 for the summer – a tally that included 15 centuries – for the third and last time.

Yet the truer gauge of his skills was still the Tests against the visiting Australians. This time in the First Test at Trent Bridge, he made 26, and took a back seat to Eddie Paynter (216 not out) and Stan McCabe (a brilliant 232). He also watched Bradman fight to save Australia with 51 and 144 not out in a drawn game.

At Lord's, Hammond came to the wicket with England in trouble at three for 31 on the first morning of the Second Test and proceeded to play the best innings of his career, given the state of play and the opposition. He was in touch from the moment he reached the crease. At lunch he was 70 not out. At tea, he was 140, and at stumps was 210 not out. He went on to 240 on Day Two as England compiled 494. Hammond batted 367 minutes and hit 32 fours in a chance-less knock. Bradman couldn't get going in Australia's first innings, but again saved his team with a not-out century in the second as the game ended in the second successive draw. The Third Test was washed out without a ball being bowled. In the Fourth, O'Reilly (five for 66) removed

Hammond for 76, after a fine innings on a difficult wicket, and 0. Bradman scored another century to set up a five-wicket win for Australia.

In the Fifth Test Hammond scored 59 as England batted on and on with Len Hutton (364) in outstanding touch. Fearing reprisal from Bradman on a perfect, easy wicket, Hammond let England's score go on through 600 to 700, then 800. He only declared at seven for 903 when he had verifiable word from the dressing room that Bradman, who had injured his ankle while bowling, would take no further part in the match.

Australia lost by the biggest winning margin ever but still retained the Ashes after a drawn series. Hammond's series figures of 403 at 67.17 were his best against Australia since 1928–29. Bradman maintained his personal ascendancy with 434 runs at 108.50.

Hammond's resurgence as skipper continued on tour in South Africa when in the Tests he scored 24, 58, 181, 120, 1, 61 not out, 24 and 140. His aggregate was 609 at 87.00. England won a tough five-Test contest 1–0 and secured the same result in a three-Test series against the West Indies in England in 1939. Hammond had not lost a series as leader when war broke out and shut down international cricket.

He enlisted as a pilot officer and was first posted at an initial training wing at Torquay, England. He was tough on recruits and this made him unpopular. Hammond was posted to Egypt in charge of arranging sports and entertainment, then was sent to South Africa. He returned to England in 1944 and in 1945 played in the Victory Tests. He made a fine century on a wet wicket against the Australians at Sheffield in the second of these contests. At Lord's in August playing against the Dominions – a combined non-English forces side – he hit 121 and 120. Hammond, at 42 years of age, seemed to have lost nothing of his excellent stroke-play and power.

He led in England again in 1946 in the first post-war series against India. Crowds flocked to the games despite India providing weak opposition. It ended in another 1–0 victory for England, thus maintaining Hammond's unbeaten record as captain in four successive series. At age 43, he led England to Australia in 1946–47 on his fourth and last tour down-under. It was perhaps a series too much. Hammond had a woeful time in the first four Tests, scoring just 168 at 21.00. He was so displeased with his form that he dropped himself from the final Test at Sydney.

Matters were made worse for Hammond by the resurgence of Bradman who had suffered five years of debilitating fibrositis. When England first played against South Australia early in the 1946–47 series, Bradman struggled and seemed but a shadow of the player of the 1930s. But a disputed umpire's decision in the First Test at Brisbane went Bradman's way when he was on 28. England appealed for a catch at second slip, which was adjudged a bump ball. Hammond was furious. He saw the chance to remove Bradman slip away. His comment to Bradman soon after the incident – 'fine way to start a bloody series' – betrayed his frustration with his long-term adversary. Those feelings became more bitter as Bradman went on to 187 at Brisbane. Then he topped that at Sydney with 234 while Hammond, at his favourite ground, managed only 1 and 37.

England lost the series 0–3, and Hammond retired from Test cricket.

In 85 Tests he scored 7249 runs at 58.46. He hit 22 centuries and 24 fifties, while snaring 110 catches. Hammond also took 83 wickets at 37.81.

In 1947, after divorcing his first wife Dorothy, Hammond married a former South African beauty queen,

Sybil Ness-Harvey. They had three children, Roger, Carolyn and Valerie.

Hammond played in another couple of first-class games in 1950 and 1951 to end an outstanding career of 634 matches in which he scored 50,551 runs at 56.11. He hit 167 centuries – 36 of them doubles – and 183 fifties. Hammond also took 732 wickets at 30.59.

In 1951 he resigned from Marsham Tyres and under wife Sybil's influence emigrated to South Africa where he took a job in a car dealership, Denham Motors. Recession hit and the company closed. In 1959, Hammond took a job at Natal University as a cricket groundsman and coach. This was an enjoyable time for him, but in 1960 he was badly injured in a car accident. He resumed work but never fully recovered. Hammond died of a heart attack at just 62 in 1965.

He would have been a champion cricketer in any era, and was England's finest batsman between the wars. He proved himself also to be a good bowler in any company and a sure slipper.

Wally Hammond's record ranks him among the greatest English batsmen of the twentieth century alongside Hobbs, Hutton, May and Compton. By placing him at five, Bradman ranked him ahead of W.G. Grace as an all-rounder. He also had high regard for Hammond as a leader. In 1938, his first Ashes series as captain of England, Hammond performed better than any other skipper in Tests in a decade, except for Jardine in the 1932–33 Bodyline series against Australia. Bradman found Hammond a 'tough and uncompromising' rival, and a captain who could also lead by example with a big, match-winning score.

CHAPTER 18

THE NINTEENTH CENTURY'S GREATEST

W. G. GRACE

(England)

18 July 1848–23 October 1915

'One day I hope to meet W.G. in Elysian Fields and as I reach up and touch his shaggy beard recount that I proudly walked through the Grace Gates at Lord's many times and tried to live up to his image.'

DON BRADMAN IN A LETTER TO AUSTRALIAN
BROADCASTER ALAN JONES

William Gilbert Grace, when he was just nine years old, first played in the West Gloucestershire club – a club created in part by his father, Dr Henry Mills Grace. Some historians ranked the team as near first class, although such rankings were not clearly delineated in mid-nineteenth century England. When W.G. began playing it was more like second class with pretensions for a higher rating on occasions. Cricket developed with a rush in the last half of the century and Grace himself would be the most powerful force in the growth of the game's popularity in England. Certainly, a high early standard was set by West Gloucestershire and invitation games were played against a touring All-England XI, which was regarded as the team setting the standard of play for the entire century.

W.G.'s maternal uncle, George Pocock, was his early coach. He was disciplined into the drills of sound batting orthodoxy: *left elbow up; left shoulder well forward; body over the ball*. He was steeped in the game's thinking and skills before he was 10. His father had carved a cricket pitch and oval out of an apple orchard on his property. The pitch was said to be of top quality, which meant that W.G. was schooled in the ways of good curators long before it was an important aspect of top cricket. (Nearly two decades later in Australia, he would put this knowledge to good use by helping a curator prepare a pitch for a game against Victoria.)

W.G. practised and played each day with his father and four brothers (there were four sisters as well in the family), including his talented elder brother E.M., thus gaining a competitive edge at a high standard from his early days. Nothing in those premature years suggested greatness in the making. It wasn't until he was nearly 12, in a game against Clifton in 1860, that W.G. showed something of what was to come for almost another five decades. He made a patient and correct 35 not out on Day One. On the second day he added 16 to be out for 51. Later in his life when looking back on his career, W.G. said in his biography (called W.G.) that that knock gave him his greatest satisfaction and was his first serious inspiration. He felt then, he said, that cricket would be his life. It sustained him through 1861 when he had 10 innings and averaged less than five. In 1862 he scored 298 at less than 20, but began to be thrown the ball occasionally for his round-arm deliveries (overarm was then banned) which netted him 22 wickets. At 14, his development accelerated as he was exposed to competition for other local clubs, and at his local private schools at Downend, near Bristol. A year later, he made an excellent 32 playing at Durdham Down for the 22 of Bristol against the All-England XI.

Distinguishing Lines

W.G.'s knock featured aspects of batsmanship that would distinguish him above nearly all others for the rest of the century. The 15-year-old demonstrated a sound defence mixed with an attacking flair that saw him hit a terrific straight six into the ground's tent. He also played forward or back, depending on the ball received. This, in itself, was a rarity. Most batsmen were known as either back- or front-foot players, with no mixing of styles. It meant that bowlers for the first time ever were confronted with a player to whom they could not bowl a particular line for very long. He would use any method to hit them off it. W.G., who had learned much about the psychology of the game from his father and three elder brothers, was neither a slogger nor a stonewaller. His approach fell in between, although from the age of 15 he was a batsman whose natural inclination was to attack and dominate. This innings against the illustrious All-England squad was an example to W.G. of how he should better calibrate and discipline his dominant tendencies. He was bowled going for another six.

His precocious capabilities were noted by selectors and he was invited to play for All-England a year later in 1864. He also played for South Wales, which his brothers had supported and represented, and it was by playing for this side that he made his first impression nationally. In two innings in his first game at The Oval against the strong Surrey club, he made 5 and 38. Then, as a replacement for E.M., who was just off the boat from an Australian tour and not quite ready to play, W.G. came in at first wicket against Sussex at Hove and compiled a masterly century – his first ever. The fact that he did not let reaching this milestone in good company go to his head said much about his mentality, self-discipline, powers of concentration and inner expectations. He moved on relentlessly to 170, then followed this up with 56 not out in the second innings. He continued on to further worthy scores in 1864 and by the end of the season had hit 1189 runs and taken 122 wickets.

At just 16, young W.G., now a little over 6 ft (183 cm), lean at 11 stone (70 kg) and broad-shouldered, was firmly placed on the national map of cricket. Yet appreciation for his potential was discreetly understated. The top professional John Lillywhite wrote in his cricket review of the year, *Companion*, that 'Mr W.G. Grace promises to be a good bat; bowls fairly well'.

The next year saw W.G. blossom as a fast fieldsman with a strong arm. Gloucestershire wasn't considered worthy of ranking for the early version of the championship of counties, made up in 1865 of Notts, Surrey, Middlesex, Kent, Sussex, Yorkshire and Cambridgeshire. So W.G. made the long train trips around the country to play as an amateur for the Gentlemen against the Players, the Gentlemen of the South and once for England against Surrey. As a result, at 17 he had reached the highest representative honours open to him. His bowling and fielding kept him afloat at the top of the game, although he also showed glimpses of form with the bat, opening with E.M.

Hunger for the Big One

In 1866, playing for England against Surrey again, he batted in a manner rarely seen before, scoring his first century (and double) in first-class cricket. The desire to go on beyond the 100, as if he was making up for failures on other occasions, distinguished him again from other players of the time, who were inclined to hit at everything once that tantalising milestone was attained. W.G. showed a merciless streak that fans throughout England came to love. He was out at 224. He got leave on the last day of the match from his skipper to compete at Crystal Palace in a hurdle race which he won. (In his youth, W.G. was a superb sprinter and hurdler.)

Three weeks later he smashed 173 not out for the Gentlemen of the South versus the Players of the South at The Oval and then took seven wickets bowling through an innings without a break. The poor wickets around the country worked against him with the bat and for him with the ball, and W.G. in 1867 had to be content with outstanding bowling figures in what he later remembered in his biography as his 'best bowling year'. He took 131 wickets at 13.12 runs per wicket. He was now sporting a beard, perhaps to give him a more fearsome and mature appearance, in keeping with his performances.

1868 was an historic year, marking the first tour by a visiting Australian team made up entirely of indigenous players, except for its skipper, Charles Lawrence. W.G., turning 20, competed in ball-throwing competitions against them at The Oval when the tourists played Surrey. He made some appreciative remarks about the Australians in *W.G.* saying that they 'acquitted themselves very well. The best all-rounder of the team was Mullagh'.

In writing this, W.G. was mindful of his own good all-round season in 1868, when he scored 1825 runs in mainly minor cricket, that is, below first-class, but also first-class games at an average of around 48, while taking 143 wickets at about 14, which was much the same as his penetration in the previous year. (Mullagh's efforts saw him collect 1698 runs at just under 24, and take 245 wickets at 10, suggesting that the naturally talented Aborigine, who was a fine attacking bat with weakness against spin, could be compared with Grace in bowling.)

In 1869 he became a member of the MCC all of whose members were unpaid amateurs or 'gentlemen'. W.G. was still playing as an amateur although he was actually getting paid. W.G. would remain officially outside professional ranks. His father had set a tone for the sons to follow and they would remain 'gentlemen'. The contradiction in England's quaint class system was that the rustic W.G., although middle class, would often have more in common with the professional cricketers from working-class backgrounds than members and patronisers of Lord's.

1869 also saw him begin an amazing run of 33 seasons in which he would reach at least 1000 runs on all but a handful of occasions. This year marked the coming of age for the 21-year-old, who hit nine centuries, six of them first class. He also stamped his authority at both ends of the cricketing compass when he went to Sheffield to play for the South against the North. He crafted an accomplished 122 out of 173 against a fine northern trio of bowlers, George Freeman, George Wootton and Thomas Emmett.

In his biography, W.G. rated 1870 a 'good year' but regarded 1871 as his 'most successful'. The figures were remarkable. He made 10 centuries in all cricket, collecting 2739 first-class runs at 78.25 – which was twice that of the best of the rest. W.G. this year took batting into a new dimension of big scoring that would set a standard and trend forever. No longer would averages in the twenties and thirties be considered outstanding. He also had his best first-class return with the ball, taking 79 wickets at just over 17.

There was an inevitable dip in his returns in 1872, but his average was still a healthy 53.82 from an aggregate of 1561 runs. He took 62 wickets. W.G. and his younger brother Fred played for the United South Eleven, who were otherwise all professionals. W.G. was instrumental in organising matches for the team and he took a sizeable cut of the proceeds. Some saw him as obsessed with money, but by playing cricket he felt he was sacrificing much in his professional life and progress to become a future country doctor (he was still studying intermittently). It was his right, W.G.

thought not unjustly, to make the most of his skills outside the surgery. And, in his mid-twenties, he was well aware of his enormous attraction to spectators. The full import of the 'Grace Gates' was appreciated a half-century before they were erected at Lord's in his name – games always had good 'gates' when Grace was playing.

Weight & Grace

W.G. turned 25 in 1873 and ballooned up to 95.5 kg (15 stone). His athleticism had dropped away. No longer would he hurdle or sprint at every chance in London or at meets anywhere. His paunch of prosperity, nevertheless, did not stop him from being a fine field and throw, or diminish his exceptional stamina that often saw him bowl long stints and then open the batting for an innings lasting several hours. 1873 was the year he married Agnes Day and combined a honeymoon after the English season with a tour of Australia for which he was to be paid 1500 pounds plus all expenses for him and his new bride. These tours, begun in the early 1860s, were becoming regular for English cricketers. Grace was paid a hefty fee, more than 10 times that of the professionals he mustered to come with them. The discrepancy of the Graces and the other amateurs travelling first class while the professionals went below deck to second-class cabins caused some friction. Yet it was not directed at W.G. but the Australian promoters of the tour who provided inducements to tour and made the travel arrangements.

The tour was a huge trial and test of endurance for all concerned. Having survived the long boat trip, the team encountered dust storms in Ballarat, extreme heat, rough coach rides, ghastly sea voyages from port to port in Australia, hair-raising train rides in the Blue Mountains, poor hotel living conditions, a critical press, and competitive teams in Victoria and New South Wales. Some of W.G.'s true character traits – dominance, obduracy, gamesmanship that often spilled into poor sportsmanship, and a mercenary approach – were drawn out and put on show through the testing tour. His manner of playing was often dictated by the betting he placed on a match, and while there is no hard evidence to suggest he threw games and had umpires in his pocket, he certainly stretched the boundaries to make sure he won games, and accompanying wagers, for instance, by shortening the tea break if he was batting and chasing victory. Through all this, he strode on in his own impeccable style on and off the field, a leader, manipulator and organiser not given to reflection. Attacks, verbal and in the press, washed off him, even if on more than one occasion he was close to fisticuffs with Australian journalists who dared to question his tactics. Late in the tour, in a fourth game against Victoria – the first in which the local side fielded just 11 players instead of 15, 18 or 22 as they had done in the past – he smote a century in 58 minutes just to show how good he was. This innings gave him much satisfaction, although perhaps not as much as shooting a kangaroo, which he did after many forays into the bush. He had not been content at bagging smaller game and slaughtering quail and so much wanted to return home boasting that he had obliterated a big marsupial. Often on the long trips on horse-drawn coaches, he and others rode shotgun and used their weapons to attack anything moving in the bush or anything flying.

The trip revitalised W.G., who, on return, scored 1664 runs (including his usual century for the Gentlemen against the hapless Players) and took 140 wickets during the 1874 England season. He spent half his time in minor, second-class matches, where he notched another 1187 and took an extra 130 wickets. Cricket this year for W.G. was non-stop and only interrupted by the time taken to travel between matches, and the birth of his son, William Gilbert, who would be known as Bertie to distinguish him from W.G. senior.

Rotten weather in 1875 reduced him to 1498 runs – not a serious reduction in any sense of the word – and seventh in the first-class averages, but he was supreme with the ball, taking a whopping 192 wickets at 12. As with all tall poppies, W.G. came in for criticism from commentators quick to predict his demise when he faltered at the beginning of 1876 with a trickle of 163 runs in eight innings in May. But as with all champions in their prime, W.G. silenced his tormentors by smacking 1278 runs in 10 innings in August – including 344 for the MCC versus Kent and 318 not out against Yorkshire. This allowed him to rack up 2622 runs at an average of 62 for the season. In a minor game for the United South against 22 (Players) of Grimsby he celebrated the birth of his second son (Henry Edgar) by scoring 313 not out. He went on the next day and was not out at the end of the innings.

Grace came off the ground and popped into the scorer's box to see how many he had made. His score was 399.

'Oh, make it 400,' W.G. suggested.

One run was added and his score was set down as 400 not out, leaving the question of whether or not W.G. Grace ever truly made a quadruple century a good one for trivia buffs.

The Players were not forgotten either in W.G.'s 1876 onslaught. They suffered to the tune of 169 and, as in previous years, were none too pleased at their annual humiliation.

At 29 years of age, he showed he could still deliver with the ball too, taking 129 wickets.

New Inspiration

In 1878, W.G. would turn 30, and there seemed little left to keep him in the game. His family life beckoned, and he was close to finally qualifying as a doctor. But the tour of a powerful Australian team, described by English writer Bernard Darwin 'as rugged, hirsute and serious', galvanised W.G. for an extended cricket life. In the historic MCC versus Australia game at Lord's, W.G. opened in the first innings and promptly smacked Henry Boyle for four. He hooked at the second, top-edged it and was caught at square leg. The MCC made just 33. Spofforth took six wickets for 4, including a hat trick. The small crowd that had turned up was stunned. The colonials could play after all. Then the might of England fought back, dismissing Australia for 41, with Alfred Shaw and Fred Morley taking five wickets each. The crowd at Lord's grew from 1000 to 10,000 in the afternoon as word swept through London that a terrific fight was on. England saddled up again without much confidence against the unprecedented speed and ability of Boyle and Spofforth. Spofforth, who claimed to have bowled W.G. in a net in Melbourne in 1873, had him dropped first ball by Will Murdoch behind the stumps. He bowled him next ball with one that broke in sharply from the off. W.G.'s duck set a pattern as the MCC collapsed again, this time for 19. Australia lost one wicket in mopping up the 12 needed for victory.

England, the seat of the Empire, was stunned. It was as if it had lost a war against France. Many historians actually traced the beginning of Great Britain's decline – at least in symbolic terms – as the most dominant nation on earth, to that incredible day at Lord's. That a group of colonials, who were not even from a nation as such, could rock England in such a devastating manner, was a blow to the collective ego

of a country's people accustomed to dominance in everything from business and technological achievement, to
territorial and sporting battles. Reflecting this attitude,
Bernard Darwin wrote in his 1934 biography of W.G.,
W.G. Grace: 'Of all the shocks that a complacent England
has had to suffer, in all manner of fields, in the last hundred
years, this, the first of them, must have been the most
sudden and appalling.'

No doubt Darwin was a little tongue-in-cheek when he
penned those words. Yet the events at Lord's on 27 May
1878 were the wake-up call for English cricket and for
W.G. From that time on, the Australians would be taken
seriously. England would never be complacent again. That
game led to the beginning of one of the longest-running
international team sport contests in history. The intense
rivalry that had now been sparked was maintained when a
few weeks later Gloucestershire played Surrey at The Oval.
W.G. was incensed that Billy Midwinter – who was the first
international cricketer to split his year between Victoria and
Gloucester – was set to play that day for the Australians
against Middlesex at Lord's. He took a carriage with James
Bush to Lord's, abused the Australian manager, John
Conway, and bullied Midwinter into coming back to The
Oval with him. Conway reported the incident to Australian
skipper Dave Gregory, who immediately grabbed another
carriage and gave chase across London, only to just miss
stopping W.G. from bundling Midwinter through The
Oval gates. A bitter verbal altercation ensued. W.G., in his
squeaky voice, delivered a schoolboyish parting taunt to
Gregory and Conway:

'You haven't a ghost of a chance against Middlesex.'

W.G. was wrong. Australia won at Lord's and Gloucestershire was beaten, even with the dithering Midwinter, at The
Oval. The Australians demanded an apology from W.G. for

his 'kidnapping' and for his abuse or else they wouldn't play against Gloucestershire. At the beginning of the tour, this would have been laughed off. But the Australians had taken England by storm and were attracting big crowds after beating the MCC. The gates were rich. Money talked, and did so with a clear, loud voice to England's foremost sportsman. In a rare backdown, W.G. penned a suitable apology.

On the field, there were fewer beg-your-pardons as W.G. compiled his usual fine double – 1151 runs and 152 wickets. The birth of a daughter, Agnes Bessie, capped off his big year.

Good *Dr* Grace

W.G., at 30, at last became a doctor and it led to more time spent at his Bristol practice, and less at cricket practice. The figures of the next few years reflected this as he made less than 1000 runs and took less than 100 wickets. He was still top of the batting averages in 1880 – a position he held in all but three years between 1866 and 1879. Once again, the Australians turned up on England's shores and in September 1880, England at last deigned to play a true international contest – a Test – at home, with the best of each nation's cricketers pitted against each other. Until this time, the game's controllers in England had not regarded the challengers from down-under as worthy competitors.

Lord Harris captained the home team, won the toss and batted. E.M. and W.G. opened with a stand of 91 and W.G. went on to a superb 152 in his first Test innings. Ever up for a bet, especially with the colonials for which it was a way of life, he wagered a sovereign that the Australian captain, Will Murdoch, could not beat his score. Murdoch was out for a duck in the first innings, but batted beautifully in his second knock to make 153 not out after a thrilling ride with the tail-enders. W.G., in particular, hurled his best deliveries at his opponent, who was to become a great friend.

Murdoch won the sovereign, but England took the game by five wickets. The honour of England and W.G., inextricably bound in that era, and so emphatically taken away by Australia two years earlier at Lord's, was intact once more. Notably though, Australia was without Spofforth, who thought he had W.G.'s measure.

During the season, Fred Grace, W.G.'s fit and talented younger brother, died at 29 after a cold developed into lung congestion. It was a blow for W.G. who was closest to Fred out of all his family.

Time off for the Test

The following years of 1881 and 1882 (in which W.G.'s fourth and last child, Charles Butler, was born) were lean times in terms of runs and matches but W.G. took time off from his medical practice to prepare for the only Test in 1882 at The Oval, late in August. The match began well for England in front of a sell-out crowd, when Albert 'Monkey' Hornby lost the toss to Will Murdoch, who judged that the wet wicket would get worse and decided to bat first. This was a strategic error and Australia was bundled out for 63. Spofforth became W.G.'s nemesis when he bowled him for 4 in England's total of 101. Australia's Hugh Massie played the innings of his life when Australia batted. He opened with a thumping 55 in quick time, forcing the score up to 122. Late in the innings, W.G., always the gamesman, ran out Sam Jones after he had completed a run and was patting down the wicket, thinking the ball was dead. This

unsporting act fired up the Australians, particularly
Spofforth, who bowled at his most fierce in England's
second innings. W.G. held things together for some time in
a fighting knock, but when he was 32, Harry Boyle had him
caught by Alick Bannerman. Thereafter, England collapsed
under the pressure applied by Spofforth who took seven for
44, giving him fourteen for 90 for the match. England lost
by seven runs in front of another sell-out crowd. The tension
was so high it caused one man to die of a heart attack while
another chewed through his umbrella. The *Sporting Times*
carried a mock obituary notice, stating that the body of
English cricket would be cremated and the ashes taken to
Australia. And so began 'the Ashes', born out of a Test
thriller that attracted nearly 40,000 fans in two days. W.G.
could take some credit for generating more than a century
of hard-fought competition. His own desire to win exceeded
the spirit of fair sportsmanship and created fire and aggra-
vation beyond that of normal competition.

If anything, England's harrowing rather than humiliating loss caused W.G. to bat and bowl on. The Empire now
had a more than worthy modern-day opponent comparable
to threats of the Spanish Armada and Napoleon to its
might. This new opponent had to be met head-on by
England's finest. And while W.G. was hardly 'fine' in his
physical stature any more, having beefed up as he
approached his mid-thirties, he was still his nation's most
formidable cricketer and notable sportsman. He would lead
from the front, but his medical practice kept him from
another tour down-under in 1882–83, when four Tests were
played where each team won two games. This only fuelled
interest and competitive spirit between England and its
roughest, wildest colonies.

Meeting Murdoch

W.G.'s work as a doctor even kept him from his annual centurion act against the hapless Players in 1883, but he returned with a career-prolonging vengeance in three Tests at home in 1884 against the new enemy that was led by his good mate Murdoch. He scored two centuries against them in the lead-up games but struggled in the Tests. In the First Test at Old Trafford, he withstood Spofforth but was dismissed by Boyle for 8 and George Palmer for 31 in England's two innings of 95 and 180, as opposed to Australia's one innings of 182 in a drawn game shortened by bad weather. In the next Test, the first ever at Lord's, Palmer got him for 14, while the outstanding all-round amateur Allan Steel hit 148 and led England to a win by an innings and five runs. In the Third Test at The Oval, W.G. was run out for 19 in another draw in which he and his team-mates chased a lot of leather as Murdoch (211), Percy McDonnell (103) and Henry Scott (102) pushed Australia's score up to 551. W.G. sent down 24 (four-ball) overs and took one for 13, demonstrating an impressive economy but little penetration. For the first time, his mighty image was dented. The big bearded one at 36 years of age was 'past it', many thought and his critics claimed.

As if to answer them, W.G.'s batting rating lifted in 1885 with hundreds against the Players (they suffered no matter what W.G.'s state of mind), Yorkshire and Surrey, and 221 out of 348 plundered from Middlesex – a demonstration that he was still strong enough for the big gesture. It was a build-up for the return of the Australians in 1886, this time led by Henry Scott. Once more, W.G. gained a psychological advantage with a century against the tourists before the Tests but, in the first two, couldn't repeat his form. England knocked the visitors over by four wickets in the First Test at Old Trafford, but W.G. only contributed 8 before Spofforth snared him, and 4 before George Giffen did the same in the second innings. W.G. only got warmed up again with 18 in the Second Test at Lord's, which was another big innings win for England thanks to Arthur Shrewsbury's 164 and the bowling of Johnny Briggs who took eleven for 74 for the match.

The pent-up passion to do well must have been profound but, as ever, was well hidden behind the granite Grace façade when he strode out to open again at The Oval on 12 August. Not only had the Australians limited him while his team-mates were winning, Arthur Shrewsbury, the Notts champion, had taken W.G.'s highest Test score record for England, making 164 at Lord's in 1886 versus the Australians. He was as determined as he had ever been when he and the ultra-cautious William Scotton built a then record opening stand of 170. W.G. went on to a century and was well on his way to another before Spofforth had him caught behind by Jack Blackham. His score of 170 restored his personal record and his reputation at 38 years of age as England's premier batsman.

He carried this touch into the 1887 season with a 2062 first-class batting aggregate, and although his best days of penetration with the ball may have been behind him, he still managed to capture 97 first-class wickets. In 1888, he collected 93 wickets, a remarkable performance for a 40-year-old. A paunch, a dodgy knee and the passing years had not dulled his enthusiasm for running in and attempting to outwit a batsman. When asked about this by the *Sporting Times*, W.G. remarked:

'It helps to be able to think like a batsman when bowling and vice versa.'

This indicated he was using all his experience, particularly with the ball, when the zip had gone out of his deliveries. W.G. was rarely tossed the ball by his skipper against the Australians in 1886 and, when they returned in 1888 under Percy McDonnell for three Tests, he didn't deliver one over. The tourists always seemed to come up with a good opening bowling pair to throw at him when he batted. In the past, Spofforth and Boyle had troubled him. Now they had J.J. Ferris and Charlie 'Terror' Turner to test him. A wet wicket at Lord's in mid-July didn't help. W.G., with 10 in the first innings of 53, was one of two English batsmen to reach double figures. In the second, it was the same, with W.G. top scoring with 24 out of 62 in a defiant knock. England lost by 61 runs. The home powers-that-be – in this case the Surrey committee – made several changes, selected five Surrey players and made W.G. captain for the next Test at The Oval.

It was the first time he led England in a Test. He began by losing the toss, but it was providential. Australia was routed for 80 with Briggs' (five for 25) guileful, slow left-armers puzzling the Australians. W.G. was disappointed to be caught off Turner for 1, but pleased that England hoisted a winning score of 317. Australia only managed 100 in the second innings, thanks to William Barnes (five for 29) and Bobby Peel (four for 49), and England had a big innings win.

In the Third Test at Manchester in late August, W.G. won the toss and showed courage in deciding to bat on a wet wicket after heavy rain overnight and into the morning. Yet his thinking was pragmatic. When the pitch dried out later it could turn into a sticky. Better to struggle first before the wicket deteriorated. W.G. batted with the skill and the experience of 30 summers on such strips, top scoring with 38 in an excellent tally of 172 under the conditions. According to *Wisden* a 'hot, drying sun on day two' made the pitch 'vicious'. Eighteen wickets fell before lunch, a record for all Tests. The follow-on margin in 1888 was just 80 runs and Australia recorded 81 and 70, the latter innings taking just 69 minutes. Peel was the key destroyer for England with seven for 31 and four for 37.

W.G. strode away from the series a proud man, having batted well and led his country to an Ashes victory. The experience was a spur as any thoughts of retirement were supplanted by the inspiration to continue playing as long as he could. W.G. had his medical practice operating well in Bristol and his family life with a wife and four children was busy yet settled. He now had a different perspective on his life. Why retire from his main love if he could still manage it, his work and the rest of his private affairs?

The years of 1889 and 1890 were ho-hum for him as he continued to score 1000-plus runs – enough to justify being a first-class batsman but not near the top. He was now no longer a bowler because of a knee problem. Yet he was still capable of holding up an end with steady trundling and still able to take his share of wickets. There were not the 100-wicket first-class hauls that marked most of his seasons in the 1870s and 1880s, but he still managed solid performances of half that.

Down-Under Again

In 1891, at 43, he was motivated for another Ashes tour down-under – his first for 18 years despite many overtures in that time from promoters. This time he was captain of a side sponsored by Lord Sheffield. W.G.'s fee was 3000 pounds (twice that for 1873–74), with all expenses paid, which was far too much for him to refuse despite many thinking his reputation as England's greatest cricketer would be diminished by such a gruelling venture. The long, tough sea voyage and the arduous touring of Australia were demanding and it was feared his performance might suffer as a result.

On his first trip he was still a young man, headstrong and incompletely shaped. At 43, in a strong marriage of 18 years and with four children, he was surer of himself, and maturer, although no one could be sure if he would behave better. He had a cantankerous nature and, at times, a confrontational style. He was not above questioning umpiring decisions, and local umpires were invariably affronted by him. Agnes and their two youngest children, Bessie (13) and Charles (9), went with him on tour. There was grumbling again about the size of W.G.'s fee, which was 10 times that of the professionals – the players from working-class backgrounds – again, making a mockery of the class-driven distinction between them and W.G. and his fellow 'amateurs'. Lord Sheffield was warned that W.G. alone would consume enough wine to 'sink a ship'. But Sheffield knew what a drawcard W.G. would be, even if some Australians, who recalled the previous tour vividly, would just turn up to see W.G. humiliated. This never quite occurred, although his team lost the Ashes 1–2 to Jack Blackham's Australians. The tour started with good-will, but W.G.'s insistence on confrontation, insults, abuse of umpires, arrogance and gamesmanship that, as ever, often seemed unsporting to everyone else, meant that by the end of the tour, W.G. was bid good riddance, rather than farewell.

He had a fair tour himself, scoring 164 Test runs in five innings at 32.80, and taking nine catches, but too many controversial encounters with umpires, opponents and the press made him unpopular. He insulted Blackham's Victorians in an early game by batting on through tea himself, instead of taking the time-honoured break, presumably because he was in good touch (he made 159 not out). This was tolerated by Blackham, but resented by the toiling fielders. W.G.'s bullying gamesmanship began in earnest at the MCG on New Year's Day 1892, when Blackham produced an old penny to toss in the First Test. He called heads and won. W.G. objected to it, suggesting it was loaded – designed to come down heads. Blackham let him toss it six times – it came down tails on four occasions – to disprove W.G.'s silly suspicion, and then decided to bat. Australia won by 54 runs. W.G. acquitted himself making 50 and 25 and retained his humour, despite the incessant barracking from a section of spectators, by 'walking' when a ball whistled over his middle stump. The crowd roared, fooled into thinking the great man was on his way. When he returned to his crease, the spectators were hushed for some time before catcalling began again. It was W.G.'s way of giving the 'fingers up' to the crowd that had been at various times amusing or abusive. It demonstrated he was in charge, if not of the match then of himself at the crease in the face of hostility.

He later challenged Australia's William Bruce, who had taken a diving catch in the outfield, saying that the ball had bounced first, when even the batsman, George Bean, had thought himself out. This was vintage double-standard W.G. Eighteen years earlier he had not been outraged when his brother Fred seemed to all onlookers not to have saved a boundary in a game at the MCG but was taken at his word that he had saved it. Or was it just W.G. being perverse and making a point about that earlier incident? In the Second Test at the SCG, which Australia won by 72 runs, he angered onlookers again by wringing his left glove as if it had been hit when a loud lbw appeal was made. W.G.'s worst behaviour was, as ever, reserved for umpires, although it could not be said he discriminated against anyone in particular. Everyone was open to a serve from the mouth behind the bushy beard. In the New South Wales match between the Second and Third Tests, he led several vociferous appeals that irritated umpire E.J. Briscoe. At one point when W.G. went up for a caught behind, and the appeal was rejected, he remarked loudly 'it is unpardonable, you must be blind'. Briscoe walked off later and did not umpire the rest of the game. The New South Wales Cricket Association demanded an apology from W.G. but he declined, denying that he questioned the umpire's sight. With that controversy still simmering around him, W.G. became more capricious. According to Australian ex-batsman and skipper, Tom Horan, writing as 'Felix' in the *Australasian*, W.G. delivered a 'gratuitous insult' for not allowing umpire Flynn to stand the Third Test at Adelaide, which England won by an innings and 230 runs. The rejection of Flynn had come about when W.G. was refused another umpire, Philips. Flynn was highly reputed and respected in Australia.

Horan, the most fair-minded of observers, summed up W.G. by writing that he was: 'a bad loser, and when he lost two of the Test matches in succession he lost his temper too, and kept on losing it right to the finish . . . Grace seems to have developed a condition of captiousness, fussiness and nastiness . . .'

Despite, or more likely because of W.G.'s style and manner, the attendances were high. Many flocked to see him for his performances, but the crowd also wallowed in his high minded, dictatorial manner. He was the first 'foreign' star to visit Australian shores who the locals loved to hate. The crowd's response to Grace was akin to what would befall English Test captain Douglas Jardine forty years later, and fifty years further on again, John McEnroe, the tantrum-prone American tennis player. W.G. gave the perception of lording it over the colonials, which touched on long-held sensitivities concerning the not-so-distant penal past. (The last convict ships reached Perth in 1868. Many former convicts would have been spectators when W.G. played.)

Lord Sheffield's tour was judged a success and he generously split his tour profits with the professionals who ended up with more than their guaranteed 300 pounds each. And because money was not lost, W.G.'s whims were tolerated. His reputation as a drawcard remained, despite rumblings after he lost the Ashes.

Knee Deep in Trouble

W.G. somehow managed to struggle through the Australian season with his wonky knee, strapped and with an ointment of his own prescription rubbed on it. But it deteriorated more in the 1892 season, and his bowling suffered most. He only managed to capture 31 wickets – his lowest return in England since his second first-class year at home in 1866. His batting held up and he cleared 1000 runs at an average of 31, still an impressive effort for a 45-year-old.

In 1893, he was galvanised once more by a tour by Jack Blackham's Australians, who were divided along colonial lines – the Victorian and NSW cliques – more than any team from England to tour down-under. W.G. wanted revenge again, and got it. He didn't play in the First Test at Lord's, which was drawn, but replaced Andrew Stoddart as skipper for the Second at The Oval. W.G. won the toss and led from the front as usual, scoring 68 in an opening stand with Stoddart (83) of 151 that set England up for a big innings win. In the Third Test – also drawn – at Old

Trafford, he notched 40 and 45, giving him 153 runs at 51.00 for the series. The Ashes win gratified him. All of England placed him on a pedestal once more. At 45, he was still very much the king of cricket.

Indian Summers

W.G. may well have been expected to retire after that 1893 triumph but he battled on through a mediocre 1894, declining the chance for a third tour of Australia. Instead Stoddart led a team to an historic 3–2 victory – in a great series decided in a titanic last-Test struggle at Melbourne, won by England. The England team were fêted when they returned, but their glory was short-lived as W.G., as if determined to return the spotlight to himself, contrived the most unlikely season for a 47-year-old, which he called 'the crowning point' of his career. He crashed 1000 runs in May 1895, scored his hundredth hundred, reached 2346 runs for the season, and experienced the glory and satisfaction from several testimonial matches that generated more than 9000 pounds of which Grace took a large share. The hundredth was scored against Somerset and once through the nervous nineties he went on for a big one – 288 – to mark the occasion. He also made 257 and 73 not out against Kent. An innings of 169 against Middlesex secured his 1000 in May and, by this time, there were musings about W.G. taking a youth potion. But it apparently only worked with his batting and not his fielding and bowling, where he was down to an occasional trundle. He took 16 wickets for the season. Bad weather reduced his run production in June and July but he still managed to humble the Players with a century against them – something he had managed almost every season since 1876.

W.G. maintained this display of rejuvenation through 1896, perhaps to accommodate the Australians who were led by the tactically astute and unassuming postman, captain Harry Trott.

W.G. wanted to size them up and was selected to play in Lord Sheffield's XI at Sheffield Park in the first game of the tour. He was surprised at the pace delivered by an ex-miner, Australian player Ernie Jones, who whistled them off a rough wicket. One went through W.G.'s beard and sailed to the boundary.

An agitated W.G. was halfway down the wicket when a four was registered. 'What! What! What!' he 'did rumble out' in a 'falsetto', according to writer and England Test player C.B. Fry, who was playing in the game.

Trott, standing close to the two men, said to Jones: 'Steady Jonah.'

This caused the fast bowler to say: 'Sorry Doctor, she slipped.'

His sorrow was not heartfelt. W.G. received a few welts to remember the game by for some time. In the same innings Jones cracked England player F.S. Jackson's rib. It set the tone for a hard-fought Test series.

Trott won the toss at the First Test at Lord's and batted. Speedster Tom Richardson ran through the Australians, taking six for 39 and they were all out for 53. This collapse caused the crowd to grow to 30,000, most of them there to see W.G. He didn't let them down. Seizing the chance to crush the great foe, he set about scoring more than them in total himself. Some historians thought that early in the innings Jones bowled a bumper through W.G.'s beard for the second time in the season.

'Whatever are ye at?' W.G. protested this time, according to Lord Harris, who saw the incident. Despite the big man's discomfort, the wicket was far better than at Sheffield

Park and he went on to 66 before Giffen had him caught. Robert Abel also weathered the bowling and drove the advantage home with 94. England made 292. Australia showed truer form in its second innings, with Harry Trott (143) and Syd Gregory (103) leading the way to 347. England lost four wickets, including W.G.'s for 7 caught off off-spinner Hugh Trumble, in reaching the 111 target for a six-wicket victory.

This was a triumph for W.G. but a month later Australia won the Second Test at Old Trafford by three wickets. W.G. was outplayed by Trott. When England batted in pursuit of 412, Trott, mindful that the pitch seemed to be turning, made a surprise tactical move by opening the bowling himself with his slow, lobbed leg-breaks. W.G. (2) and Stoddart (15) thought they would counter his bowling by going down the pitch and attacking him. They were both stumped by J.J. Kelly. W.G. was caught by Trott off paceman Ernie Jones for 11 in England's second innings.

England was unsettled by a dispute over match fees, but still W.G. led the team in a rain-affected game in the deciding Test at The Oval. W.G. won the toss, batted and got England off to a fair start with F.S. Jackson (45) in an opening stand of 54. Giffen got him caught by Trott again, for 24. In the second innings, Trumble (six for 30) bowled him for 9. Australia was set 111 to win but collapsed for 44 (Peel six for 23). England won by 66 and took the Ashes 2–1.

W.G. celebrated by completing another Indian summer, notching 2135 and remaining fifth in the averages. Whatever type of youth potion he was taking for this revival at 48 years, it kicked in for his bowling and he took 52 wickets. This form was maintained in the 1897 season when he scored 1532 runs at just under 40 and took 56 wickets. In 1898 he turned 50, and the Gentlemen were pitted against the Players on his birthday at Lord's. W.G.

would dearly have loved a century and a win, but had to be content with a fine 43 in 90 minutes, and a loss. If ever there was a sign that he was nearing the end, it was not being able to harvest a hundred at will against the Players.

One Last Hurrah at the Top

Nevertheless, W.G. rumbled on in 1899, unable to resist the challenge of the Joe Darling-led touring Australians, for whom, a colleague noted, 'he always pulled his beard'. There was even more incentive since they had thrashed Andrew Stoddart's team 4–1 in Australia in 1897–98 a few months earlier.

After a dispute and misunderstanding with Gloucestershire, W.G. sadly resigned from the club after 30 years of service and had to settle with playing for London County – a team of his own creation.

He took it seriously enough and in playing for the new side was as competitive as ever. Simon Wilde in his book, *Number One: the world's best batsmen and bowlers*, noted that when a bowler (F.B. Wilson) once appealed for his wicket leg before, W.G., who had missed the ball, ran down the wicket shouting: 'Out if I hadn't hit it, well bowled, out if I hadn't hit it.'

The umpire's finger was up, but W.G.'s outburst caused him to drop his hand and signal not out.

Gamesmanship aside, he could still deliver, as he demonstrated with a score of 175 against Worcestershire. It was enough to ensure his selection at Trent Bridge in the First Test in early June.

Australia chose the dashing Victor Trumper for his first Test. Darling won the toss and batted, and Australia recorded a slow 252. Grace opened with Fry and they withstood an onslaught by Jones. It began with a brutal head-high bouncer that W.G. just managed to evade. He batted on, seeing Jones off, until he relaxed facing Monty Noble's gentle off-spin and was caught behind for 28. He made just 1 in the second innings before Bill Howell bowled him with a brilliant 'break-back' delivery, similar to one from Jack Hearne that removed Trumper for a duck in Australia's first innings. England on seven for 155 was lucky to force a draw in pursuit of 290.

W.G. still showed he had what it took to play at the top for the MCC versus the Australians at Lord's with a good 50 and the wickets of stars Clem Hill and Trumper. But behind that stern face and beard was a pragmatist. W.G. knew he was no longer the batsman of 1896, three years earlier. He was an embarrassment on the field and was catcalled at Trent Bridge for his ineffectiveness if the ball went other than straight to him. His experience and competitive spirit still made him worthy enough to make England's side, but he decided enough was enough. He retired from Test cricket. It was a shock to selectors, who tried to persuade him to continue his playing career.

W.G.'s retirement from international cricket was big news in England in 1899. Without warning, the British Empire realised that one of its pillars – a figure who gave it a sense of superiority – would never again have the impact he'd had for 30 years. No W.G. Grace playing for England and Gloucestershire would leave a void that would never be filled again.

Nevertheless, there were a few encores from Crystal Palace, the home of the London County side, and elsewhere as Grace batted on. Despite his age (52) and troublesome knee, he was still a drawcard. Amazingly, he could still provide the force for the powerful hundred as he did for London County versus the MCC and Worcestershire, and for the

South versus the North. A year later, and a few months after the death of that other pillar of the nineteenth century, Queen Victoria, England was in need of a gesture from W.G., now regarded as the senior 'eminent person' of the nation. Perhaps aided by an improved ointment or strap for his knee, he provided it by wheeling in for two big wicket hauls (seven for 30 and six for 80) for London County against the MCC at Lord's. W.G. still lifted for the big occasion and Joe Darling's Australians provided him with one in 1902, when he took five for 29 for London County. In that same wet season he had a lean trot with the bat but still managed some entertaining opening stands, notably one of 120 with Australian Will Murdoch, then aged 47 (who was living and playing in England), for the MCC. W.G. motivated himself for the game against the Players, and a first encounter with the great fast-medium bowler, S.F. Barnes. From all accounts it was a good tussle. W.G. thumped his way to 82. Barnes had him dropped once. The old stager could still match it with the very best of the era.

In 1904, he began with 52 for London County against Surrey, then his batting fell away in May until the end of the month when he cracked 45 against Cambridge University. On 30 May he made his final first-class performance at Lord's and it was a big game – the MCC versus South Africa. The tourists included the renowned speedster J.J. Kotze. W.G. played him without any apparent difficulty until nicking one behind at 27.

By 1906, W.G. was fading slowly but had the odd flash of distant youth, as if not to alarm the Empire that a day would come when he would not be seen somewhere in the summer playing the national game. He had one last hurrah versus the Players when he hit 74. He was now down to a trickle of first-class games. His last big game was in 1908, a few months short of his sixtieth birthday. W.G. prepared for it in a way he had for nearly half a century, with several diligent practice sessions in the coldness of March. The match was the Gentlemen versus Surrey in the first round of the season. He made 15 and 25, both in good style. Still, W.G. was not done. Such was his love of the game, he fronted for the odd minor match until 1914, not long before the beginning of the First World War. On 25 July, a week after his sixty-sixth birthday he played for Eltham against Grove Park in London for his last innings. He carried his bat for 69 and also took four for 48.

A year later he had a stroke, which forced him to bed. He told H.D.G. Leveson-Gower – one of the great personalities and long-serving player/administrators of the game – that the German Zeppelin bombing raids on London bothered him. Some explosions occurred near his home. Leveson-Gower tried to lightly disabuse him of his fear, citing the fast bowlers, 'like Ernie Jones', as being more frightening.

'I could see them,' W.G. noted mournfully.

Soon after this, he died of a heart attack.

W.G. played 878 first-class matches, over 43 years, scoring 54,896 runs at an average of 39.55, with 126 hundreds and 254 fifties. W.G. also took 2876 wickets at 17.92, with 246 five-wicket hauls and 126 match figures of 10 wickets or more. W.G. had 22 Tests, scoring 1098 runs at 32.29, including two centuries. He took nine wickets at 26.22, and 39 catches.

W.G. Grace was the greatest England all-rounder before the First World War, and it would take the career of Ian Botham in the 1980s to challenge him – a century after W.G.'s peak. His impact on cricket in the nineteenth century was only matched by Bradman's in the twentieth century. By choosing Grace in his all-time Ashes team for England, Bradman was acknowledging one of the great creators of the modern game and a towering figure in cricket history. Perhaps the biggest compliment from Bradman was to choose Grace for his ideal Ashes team for England, even though he never saw him play.

CHAPTER 19

ENGLAND'S CHAMPAGNE KEEPER

GODFREY
EVANS

7

(England)

18 August 1920–3 May 1999

*'He was on his toes throughout our long
innings and never lost his zest or good
humour. He kept his fielders at it under
trying conditions. He was an outstanding
keeper.'*

DON BRADMAN, ON EVANS KEEPING WHEN AUSTRALIA
AMASSED 659, AT THE SECOND TEST IN SYDNEY,
DECEMBER 1946

odfrey Evans' indefatigable spirit and skill behind
the stumps were his greatest contributions to
English cricket, especially in the golden years of the
1950s, when the Test team was the best in the world. No
matter whether the opposition was eight for 80, or two for
400, Evans' enthusiasm and drive lifted English spirits like
no other. It was his personality as much as his diving for
miraculous leg-side catches or brilliant stumpings that
made him such an important part of a winning team.
Spectators loved him too. His theatrics, smiles and
boundless energy made him worth watching. He loved his
cricket and it loved him. His batting too had a certain
attraction and was never dull except for the odd occasion
when he had to play defensively for the team.

Keepers have always been characters, but most liked to
go about their work unobtrusively. Evans was too fun loving
and extroverted not to be noticed at every chance. And there
were plenty of opportunities in his position on the field. If
he kept to the menacing spin of Jim Laker and Tony Lock,
his very presence was intimidating to batsmen, who knew

that the merest slip forward of the crease would invite a swift dismissal. Evans would affect an exaggerated twist of his broad shoulders and upper body towards the square-leg umpire. The gloves would be swept and the pose held until the umpire either agreed with the appeal or turned it down. Evans was daring too. He quite often kept up to the stumps to medium pacers, which took both lightning reflexes and courage. The stocky and muscular Evans (5ft 9 in/174 cm; 74 kg/11 stone 9 lb) loved being up at the stumps, not the least reason being his ability to dive forward of the wicket for a catch or to stop a run. Yet he was equally adept at standing back to Frank Tyson when he bowled faster than anyone ever had in Australia. Then, in 1954–55 Evans was seen diving like a soccer goalie leg-side, off-side and high.

Aiming at Ames

The young Godfrey was brought up in Kent at the family's property Lords, Sheldwich, near Faversham, the 100-acre farm home of his once rich stockbroker grandfather. Evans' mother died when he was three. His father, an electrical engineer, was often abroad. Evans boarded at Kent College from age eight to 16 and at 14 made a quickfire 101 not out for his school in an evening match against Choir School Canterbury. It was his good fortune that the game was witnessed by a member of the Kent County staff at the St Lawrence Ground, Canterbury. It led to his own appointment on the staff at Kent at the beginning of the 1937 season. He decided to become a keeper like his hero, Les Ames, who was also at Kent, along with another former Test champion all-rounder, Frank Woolley. The ground became Evans' cricket headquarters for the next 22 years.

That first season saw him working the scoreboard at

Dover when Kent scored 219 in 71 minutes and managed a memorable victory against Gloucestershire. His efforts that day, he said later, were more a test of agility – and mathematics – than coping later in his career with Alec Bedser's late swingers.

In his second year at the ground, 1938, he was assigned to pavilion duties, which included whitening the boots of the visitors, Bradman's Australians.

'I didn't miss a ball,' Evans recalled about watching the game that day. 'All the Australians batted well. Bradman hit a fifty in no time. Les Ames made a century in our second innings and Frank Woolley belted 80 in an hour.'

Kent was beaten by 10 wickets, but the game was an early inspiration for Evans to play Test cricket. Over the winter of 1937–38, he took up boxing to earn extra money – 30 shillings a fight – and knocked out two opponents in three fights. But Kent was not happy with his off-season activity. He was advised that eye injuries could cause his cricket some problems. He gave away boxing and instead took up hockey and squash to keep fit in the winter.

Ames blocked his way as a keeper for Kent so Evans was initially chosen in July 1939 as a batsman. He appeared in another four games, in which Ames stepped aside and fielded at first slip while Evans, now 18, kept. The youth was most grateful to the older man for his advice and encouragement, even though Ames knew that Evans was being groomed to take his place.

Ames told him not to worry about missed chances. Everyone made them. He was advised to keep battling on, especially after poor performances.

War intervened. Evans joined the army. He married Jean at Maidstone, Kent in January 1941 (and later had one son, Howard Leslie, named after Howard Levett and Leslie Ames, both Kent keepers and mentors of Evans). While stationed at Aldershot during his time in the army, he was seen keeping in 1943 by former Test skipper Arthur Gilligan. Within weeks he was playing for an England XI against the Dominions at Lord's. Evans, by now, had adopted his unique style of acrobatics behind the stumps, which included much diving and confident appealing.

He admitted in his 1960-published autobiography, *The Gloves are Off*, that these antics were all calculated to attract notice for himself, first for Kent and later, England. It worked. His stance was also notably different from the conventional approach of sitting back on one's heels. Evans rocked forward on his toes, allowing himself to press his knuckles into the ground, exposing the red underside of his gloves – another factor that made him stand out.

Soon after the war ceased he was back playing for Kent as its number-one keeper.

Test Break

In 1946, in the first post-war Test series, versus India in England, at the age of 25 he was chosen to guard wickets for England in the Third Test at The Oval. It was a forgettable start. The game was almost washed out, with India making 331 and England three for 95 in reply. Evans didn't make a dismissal or have a bat. The game fizzled to a draw and was notable only for Wally Hammond being the first player to make 7000 in Tests, and also for a run-out by Denis Compton, an England soccer star, when he kicked the ball onto the stumps.

Evans was chosen to tour Australia for the 1946–47 series, but was kept out of the First Test at the Gabba. Evans blamed his omission on captain Wally Hammond's great rivalry with Bradman. Bradman had played for South Australia against England early in the season. Evans had dropped a tough chance at the wicket when Bradman was 2, then again when he was 50. Had Bradman been dismissed for 2, he may not have battled on after his severe fibrositis illness during the war. As it was, he had scored 76 and his confidence had been restored. Evans felt that Hammond left him out of the First Test at Brisbane for those two lapses against Bradman. Cambridge University and Yorkshire amateur Paul Gibb was chosen instead.

However, Evans was a better keeper. Gibb was not as efficient as Evans at handling the spin of leg-spinner Doug Wright, Evans' Kent team-mate. This influenced the recall of Evans for the Second Test at Sydney in mid-December 1946 and it was there that he set a standard that future keepers would find hard to emulate. During the game, Bradman made a point of telling Evans that he had kept magnificently and that the Australians were most impressed with his form. According to Evans in his biography, Bradman added:

'You gave the English boys all the encouragement possible by the way you kept wicket. Carry on doing it.'

Bradman played hard and shrewdly, Evans noted, but this sort of remark showed his dedication to good sportsmanship and his devotion to what was best for the game and competition.

In that Sydney Test, Bradman (234) and Sid Barnes (234) set a fifth-wicket world record of 405 in 393 minutes as Australia amassed 659. Evans did not concede a bye. He took part in his first Test dismissal, catching Keith Miller (40) off leg-break bowler Peter Smith. It was still a lean experience for Evans with the bat. In his first Test innings he was bowled for 5 by Ian Johnson. In the second he was stumped by Don Tallon off Colin McCool for 9. Yet it was his keeping in this match in the face of adversity that left a lasting impression on Bradman.

'He was on his toes throughout our long innings and never lost his zest or good humour,' Bradman noted. 'He kept his fielders at it under trying conditions. He was an outstanding keeper.'

Evans didn't concede a bye in Australia's first innings of the drawn Third Test at Melbourne. It wasn't until well into the second innings of that Test that he let some through, but not before 1054 runs – including those in the only Australian Second Test innings of 659 – had been scored. Yet there were blemishes on his performance record. Like all keepers, he had his off days, and for Evans they were extreme. In this Test he missed four catches, including one off Arthur Morris on the first ball of an innings and later, one off Bradman.

In the Fourth Test at Adelaide, his performance was noteworthy again, this time for failing to score until he had been at the wicket for 97 minutes. This was a world record in first-class cricket. Evans was normally an attacking bat, but he became defensive to help England avoid defeat. His defiance (he remained 10 not out in 133 minutes) with Denis Compton (103 not out) didn't allow Australia enough time for victory. In these Tests, Evans amazed onlookers by standing up to medium pacer Alec Bedser, which added to the bowler's menace but proved effective. Evans hardly let anything through, relying on his eye, balance, quick footwork and fitness. It prompted former Australian great leg-spinner turned journalist Bill O'Reilly to compare Evans favourably with Don Tallon. Evans was delighted. He regarded Tallon as the best keeper he had ever seen.

The tour ended with four matches in New Zealand. In the only Test, Evans took two catches at the wicket off Bedser and demonstrated that his standing up was not just for show or to pressure batsmen. He finished the long Antipodean tour with 33 dismissals (28 catches and five stumpings) from the 39 games in which he played. Evans' success convinced him that standing up to pace, if possible, was the best way. He claimed that by standing back, a keeper missed chances that fell short. Standing up, he felt, compensated for catches he might miss by being so close. Evans also pointed out that by standing up there were chances for stumpings too. He had amazed onlookers in a match against Victoria when he stumped Ken Meuleman off a quick ball down the leg-side from Dick Pollard.

Bradman thought Evans performed 'wonderfully' and marvelled at his exceptional agility and hard hands that took some tough knocks.

Evans' worth with the bat was further in evidence at home in 1947 when he scored 74 against South Africa in the First Test at Trent Bridge. In the Fifth Test he made 45 run out and 39 not out. He scored more than 1000 runs for the season and made 95 dismissals, the nearest he was ever to come to the double of 1000 runs and 100 wickets in a first-class season.

Evans toured the West Indies in 1947–48 and then played in the 1948 Ashes series in England.

He began well against the Australians at Trent Bridge, taking a spectacular catch off Laker to dismiss the dangerous Sid Barnes for 62. Barnes chopped a ball onto Evans' right leg. The ball bounced up and over the keeper's right shoulder. Evans, on instinct, dived backwards and grabbed the ball as he hit the ground.

He was involved in a century-stand with Compton in England's second innings. He made 50, while Compton played one of his great innings, scoring 184. It wasn't enough to stop Australia winning comfortably by eight wickets. Evans took two catches at the wicket to the spinners.

In the Fourth Test at Leeds, he helped England into a strong position by scoring 47 not out in the second innings, allowing skipper Norman Yardley to bat on into the last day and declare at eight for 365. This left Australia with 404 to make for victory in 344 minutes on a wicket that was taking spin. Evans had his worst day in Tests behind the stumps, missing three stumping chances. One was from Arthur Morris off Jim Laker. According to Bradman, Morris obscured the keeper's view as he hit over a ball that spun away from the left-hander outside off-stump. The other misses appeared hard – one skidded through low, another spun unexpectedly high – but opportunities that Evans would normally have taken. For once, the spring-heeled keeper looked down. He said little in the field. The Australians had never seen him more dispirited as they scored the runs (Bradman 173 not out, Morris 182) with 15 minutes to spare in the most remarkable last-innings' performance ever seen in Test cricket.

Les Ames' advice on fighting on after a poor performance was never more pertinent. Evans understood it now and appreciated his mentor's words. Despite Evans' lapses, Bradman still thought him to be the best keeper in England.

Evans bounced back in the next series against South Africa in 1948–49, taking three fine catches in the first innings of the First Test at Durban. In the only completed South African innings of the Second Test he made another three dismissals, one catch and two stumpings. His confidence had returned and the black day at Leeds, while not forgotten, was seen as an anomaly. His form continued in the Third Test at Cape Town where he pulled off three stumpings and a catch. In the following series against New Zealand in 1949, his batting was unimpressive but his displays behind the stumps ensured his place. He capped off the series in the Fourth and final Test at The Oval with four catches and a stumping, his best effort yet.

Evans Above All Others

Evans had no peer in England by 1950 when he reached his peak at age 29 and played in the shock series against the touring West Indians, who won 3–1. He, and England, began poorly at Old Trafford in the First Test against the fine left-arm spin of Alf Valentine. Evans came to the wicket at five for 88 and turned the match around by unleashing a flurry of cuts and front-foot drives. He belted 104 in 140 minutes, which included 17 fours. His innings was the only century of the game. It was his maiden first-class and Test hundred. He swung, hit and occasionally missed, but still gave no chance. It was one of those fortunate days for a batsman whose hit-and-miss style often saw him dismissed early.

Evans also effected three stumpings, took a catch and let through only four byes in two innings. He was easily the player of the match in England's 202-run win. Despite Evans performing brilliantly behind the stumps again in the next two Tests, England was comfortably beaten in both games. Evans took four dismissals (two stumpings and two catches) in the Second Test at Lord's and scored 32 and 63, favouring attack again against the spin twins Alf Valentine and Sonny Ramadhin at Trent Bridge. A damaged thumb kept him out of the final Test – won again by the West Indies – and the rest of the season.

Evans toured Australia for the second time in 1950–51 and judged the Second Test at Melbourne as his best ever behind the stumps. He took two catches in each innings and revelled in the hot, humid conditions over Christmas. Just like a batsman in form, he saw the ball as big as a pumpkin as it sailed cleanly into the gloves. He also made 49, second-top score over England's two innings in a low-scoring thriller.

After losing the First Test by 70 runs, England fell just 28 short in this Second Test. Evans felt the Australians were not the 'Invincibles' of 1946–47 and 1948. He was confident of a breakthrough win in the series. It came in the Fifth Test at Melbourne.

Evans and his fellow team-mates, under the captaincy of the rotund and popular Freddie Brown, returned home with their first post-war victory against Australia. It was 12 years since England had savoured success against the old enemy. Evans was thrilled with his form and fitness, especially standing up to Bedser. He had successfully copied Tallon's method of taking down the leg-side on the right side of his body. His powers of concentration, alertness and agility had peaked on the 1950–51 tour. Evans returned to England for the 1951 season full of confidence, but had not allowed for mental fatigue. His enthusiasm for the game suddenly waned. He lost form and was dropped after the Third Test at home against South Africa and replaced by Yorkshire's Don Brennan.

Evans, now 30, had to rekindle his passion for playing. He decided against an invitation to tour India with the MCC 'A' team during England's winter of 1951–52, and was again in good touch when India came to England for the 1952 season. His batting against the battling Indians was also outstanding. He hit second-top score of 66 in the First Test at Leeds (Tom Graveney made 71). It earned him a bottle of champagne, promised by his skipper Len Hutton if he managed a fifty.

Evans followed this up in the Second Test at Lord's with a blistering 98 before lunch on Day Three. No Englishman had ever hit a century before lunch in a Test and, with two minutes to go before the break, he had every chance to join the magnificent company of Bradman, Charlie Macartney and Victor Trumper, who had all managed the feat. But the Indian skipper, Vijay Hazare, took his time setting the field. Umpire Frank Chester, in an uncharitable act, called lunch. Evans trailed off the ground disappointed. He did, however, get his century after lunch before being caught and bowled by Ghulam Ahmed for 104.

It was Evans' match. He claimed his hundredth victim — S.G. Shinde stumped Evans bowled Allan Watkins — and then signalled the dressing room to break open the champagne. The keeper was now legendary for his off-field exploits as much as his exploits on the field. It was the way he played cricket and life.

He surprised even himself by finishing third in the batting averages with 60.5, behind Hutton and David Sheppard, but did not get carried away with his success. India had fielded a weak side.

For the entire 1952 first-class season, Evans scored more than 1600 runs and collected 70 victims. He had come back to form with character and flair at just the right moment. The Australians were due in 1953 so, if there was a chance to defeat them for the first time since the Bodyline series of 1932–33, this would be it. Evans kept fit over the winter by playing hockey and squash. He needed to be in shape. The Ashes series turned out to be hard-fought and tense, and Evans performed at his best. In the drawn Third Test at Old Trafford, he scored third-top score of 44 not out and made six dismissals, but personally didn't rank his effort highly after dropping a tough chance from Neil Harvey early in his innings. Harvey went on to 122. The Fourth Test was drawn, but England won the final Test by eight wickets to give it the Ashes for the first time in more than 20 years.

Evans and England celebrated long and hard. It was his benefit year and 5000 pounds was raised for him from gate attendances during a game against the Australians that ended on 1 September.

Keeper of the Golden 1950s Era

The 1953–54 tour of the West Indies was incident packed, with a riot in Georgetown and a fightback by England, led by its skipper Hutton, that resulted in a level 2–2 series. This was followed in the 1954 home season by a 1–1 draw with Pakistan in a four-Test series. Evans caught captain A.H. Kardar off Brian Statham, his 131st victim, in the final Test at The Oval. This broke the record set by Australia's Bert Oldfield in the 1930s. Evans signalled the dressing room. It was a good excuse to break open the champagne, yet again.

Evans was impressed with first-gamer paceman Peter Loader, yet even more pleased with the debut in this game of Northamptonshire speedman Frank Tyson who played for the first time in the final Test at The Oval. He took four for 35 and one for 22. Tyson was the fastest bowler to whom Evans ever kept. The keeper rubbed his gloves together with glee at the thought of what Tyson would do on the next tour down-under for the 1954–55 Ashes contest.

Neil Harvey was England's prime target. In the vital Third Test at Melbourne, when the series was 1–1, Evans took one of the great leg-side diving catches to dismiss the Australian champion left-hander off Tyson. The pace bowler ran through the Australians taking seven for 27. This gave him nine for the match following a haul of 10 at Sydney in the previous Test. Evans took five catches off Tyson and the accurate speedster Brian Statham, and three in the Second

Test. Tyson proved the difference and England won the series comfortably: 3–1. Tyson and Statham were also effective in two further Tests in New Zealand that were both won by England, giving it a most successful five-wins, one-loss, two-draws tour.

This consolidated England as the world's leading team. Len Hutton retired as captain and the more serious Peter May took over. Evans, who enjoyed his cricket and knew how to relax on and off the field, found himself a tad in-hibited. He didn't feel inclined to whistle between overs or joke as he had under the less strict Len Hutton.

May inherited a fine squad and at home led England against South Africa. And he had Tyson on the team, the most exciting cricketer in the world after his devastation of Australia. Wherever he turned up, the grounds were packed with spectators, crowds that brought back memories of the glory days of Nottingham's Harold Larwood and Bill Voce in the 1920s and 1930s. Evans loved keeping to him, not the least reason was the fear he instilled in batsmen, which led to edged strokes, sometimes behind. There was no keep-ing up to the stumps to Tyson, and Evans found himself looking for a new position, further back from the stumps than ever before.

Tyson took eight wickets and was again the decisive player in the First Test at Trent Bridge, a Test that England won easily. But injury plagued him and he played only one more Test in the series. Evans, and indeed England, were fortunate to have replacements such as Fred Trueman and Peter Loader to partner Statham, who was a permanent fixture in the side. At Lord's, in the Second Test, Evans had the unusual distinction of taking a catch off the first ball by Statham. Tyson was back for the Third Test at Manchester, and Evans became a victim of his express pace when he chipped a bone in a finger and missed the last two Tests.

England scraped in with a 3–2 series win, after winning the first two Tests.

During the 1955–56 off-season, Evans worked hard on his finger with specific exercises, and increased his fitness with hockey and squash. At 35, he wanted to be extra-fit for the coming 1956 season against Ian Johnson's Australians. Evans, who liked a bet and drink, mixed well with the visitors, particularly Keith Miller. They bet on the outcome of the Lord's Second Test, which happened to be the only Test Australia won. At Leeds, in the Third Test, Evans backed up May (101) and Cyril Washbrook (98) with a bright 40, which he put down to Johnson's mistake of using the spinners against him. Lindwall bowled him soon after coming on.

Something similar happened at Leeds in the Fourth Test. After Peter Richardson (104) and David Sheppard (113) had set England up for a big score, Evans came in and belted 47 in 29 balls, and just missed scoring the then fastest fifty in Test cricket. England made 459.

Oddly, Evans was involved in just one dismissal in Jim Laker's off-spinning rampage when he stumped Ron Archer in Australia's first innings. Most of Laker's 19 wickets for the match fell to catches close to the wicket as the Australians fumbled and stumbled. Laker kept the ball up and spinning in, forcing the batsmen to play. Evans regarded it as the most brilliant, sustained display of spin bowling he ever saw. England won by an innings and 170, and retained the Ashes. The team remained on top in the drawn Fifth Test, giving England a 2–1 victory, its third successive Ashes win.

Evans next toured South Africa for a five-Test series over the 1956–57 season. He began well with the bat, making 20 and 30, and effecting four dismissals in a win at Johannesburg. He then followed this up with a smashing 62 in 50 minutes at Cape Town. He also made five dismissals and England won again. Evans finished well in the final Test at Port Elizabeth, with six dismissals. England lost the game despite a fine eight-wicket haul by Tyson and, in a slight dent to its sense of world superiority, could only manage a 2–2 drawn series. Evans' form, however, at 36, was as good as ever. *Wisden* made special note of his keeping on an atrocious pitch that made batting and keeping particularly difficult. Despite the *Wisden* scorecard showing 13 byes, its reporter noted: 'He allowed only one bye, an extraordinary performance by an extraordinary man.'

With such praise from the normally critical journal, Evans' place as king of keepers in England was assured. He continued on during the home season of 1957 against the West Indies. Even his batting was more reliable with scores of 14, 29 not out, 26 not out, 10, 40 and 82 at Lord's, a happy hunting ground for him. It was made in a stand of 174 with Colin Cowdrey, a seventh-wicket record versus the West Indies. Evans' runs came in 115 minutes. It was a smack-bang-wallop innings in which he was dropped five times. Yet, as he said himself, 'it was not elegant but it was effective'. It was the true Evans method with the bat. The ball was there to be hit hard and as often as possible. If he connected, it usually reached the boundary. Given England's batting power above him, including Peter Richardson, Tom Graveney, Peter May, Colin Cowdrey and David Sheppard, he was a useful man to come in at seven.

In the Fourth Test at Leeds, Evans became the first keeper to take 200 Test wickets when he caught Collie Smith. As soon as the catch was taken, Evans outlined the shape of a champagne bottle to the dressing room once more.

England won 3–0, and maintained its top-of-the-world-table ranking. The English were far too strong in 1958 at home for New Zealand, winning the first four Tests – three of them by an innings. Then came the unexpected shock of a 4–0 loss to Australia in 1958–59. Evans' form with the bat fell away and a finger injury caused him to miss half the series behind the stumps. The team was unsettled before the series began by the prospect of facing several Australian pace bowlers suspected of throwing. But, this aside, Benaud's Australians outplayed them. The wheel had finally turned for Australia after five years of England dominance. Heads were sure to roll. Evans felt he had kept his standards up at Trent Bridge in the First Test of the 1959 series against India. He had also made a handy 73. But rumours abounded that at 38 years of age he was tired after batting and that this affected his keeping. It was a rumour at which Evans scoffed. He remained his ebullient self, on and off the field.

At Lord's, in the Second Test, the rumour was given substance for those wanting to dump him when he missed four stumpings off Tommy Greenhough inside a session. Evans was dropped after 91 Tests. He had been dumped before. Yet there was a finality about this non-selection that shook him. He was disappointed. His form, in general, had been good for Kent in 1959 but selectors were looking for younger players. Those supporting Evans' inclusion argued that the best players of the moment should be chosen for 'now'. He could and would have carried on longer. He loved the game and playing for his country. His Test omission dispirited him and caused him to retire from first-class cricket at the end of 1959.

Evans scored 2439 runs at 20.49, and hit two Test centuries. He held 173 catches and made 46 stumpings. In first-class cricket he scored 14,882 runs from 1939 to 1969 at 21.22

and made seven centuries. He took 816 catches and stumped 250 batsmen.

Evans, who received a CBE in 1960, tried many areas of work after retirement. He was twice a publican and ran a jewellery business. He attempted running a farm of battery hens and a sportsmen's club. He invested in a leisure complex, a dice game and a pitch drier. When cricket tours became popular in the 1980s, he ran overseas package tours. Evans put his love for a bet to good use for 20 years by advising the Ladbrokes agency on what odds to lay at big cricket matches. His later appearance featured greying mutton-chop whiskers, which seemed to be modelled upon the look of his stockbroker grandfather who influenced his early life so much.

Evans married three times and had another child, a daughter, by his third wife Angela.

Bradman's choice of Godfrey Evans to keep wickets for England was based on his outstanding ability. But his exceptional character, which was in keeping with the true spirit of the game, was certainly a significant factor in Bradman's selection of Evans for his all-time best-ever Ashes team at number seven. 'Godfrey, by word and deed, from his pivotal position behind the stumps, was a wonderful inspiration to his fielders,' Bradman told me. 'Always encouraging, never scathing, he kept the team together even when the opposition amassed big scores. He was always capable of the spectacular catch or stumping, which was also inspirational.'

CHAPTER 20

WHERE THERE'S FRED, THERE'S FIRE

FRED
TRUEMAN

(England)

6 February 1931–

*'He was England's bowler with the lot —
fire, courage, guile, pace, line, length,
swing and cut. I don't think any batsman I
saw was comfortable against him in his
prime.'*

DON BRADMAN

The son of a Yorkshire coal miner at Maltby Main, Fred Trueman always had to be challenged by someone to beat, whether it was another bowler, a batsman, the Yorkshire committee, the English establishment or any Australian cricketer. He didn't always come out on top, but he was never truly defeated. His background — he worked at the pit himself — was his motivation to achieve and do better for himself. It was also the root of his exceptional mental and physical strength. His family — he was the fourth of seven children — was close and Trueman has fond memories of his upbringing. His dad, Alan, was a tough, god-fearing man, and the only one to whom Trueman ever deferred. Fred was driven to prove that he was the best at whatever he did. This developed a perfectionist's mentality towards everything he was passionate about, from bowling to his later television and radio commentating. His manner could be perceived as brusque and rude, as well as friendly, funny and warm. People either rolled with Fred's personality and enjoyed most of it, whether on the field or off it, or they were offended by it. Fred left such extremes in reactions in his considerable wake, wherever he travelled around Yorkshire, England or the rest of the cricket world.

Most English supporters willed him on, despite his indiscretions, real or imagined. Trueman, from 1946, was a counter-force for which every English cricket supporter prayed, after Australia's speed pair – Keith Miller and Ray Lindwall – harassed and humiliated England's batsmen in the era immediately following the Second World War. England had little answer to the Australian speedsters in three successive Ashes contests – 1946–47, 1948 and 1950–51 – and some of the 1953 series. Alec Bedser was a medium pacer of the highest order, but it was speed in their team that was craved by all of England. The nation wanted a character who could put the wind up Aussie kilts in a way no one had done since Harold Larwood in the Bodyline series of 1932–33.

Rough But Ready

In the late 1940s, any raw kid who showed a modicum of promise was noted, analysed and nurtured. Trueman was one such junior. At 12, while playing for Maltby School, his career and future were all but obliterated when he was hit in the groin by a fast delivery that left him in need of a walking stick for most of the next two years. He never forgot to wear a protector after that. At 14, about the time he recovered from the injury, he left school and took on labouring jobs while continuing on with his cricket. At 16, he was coached by Cyril Turner at Sheffield, and a year later, in 1948, he tried out in the nets for Yorkshire County at Headingley, while his father looked on. It was Trueman's first trip to Leeds. He delivered just 11 balls, bowling his batting opponent, young Brian Close, who would later play for England. The legendary fighting Test all-rounder and Yorkshire coach George Hirst was impressed enough to

send him on a tour of England in Yorkshire's under-18 team
– his first trip away from home. Fred enjoyed the
team camaraderie. It marked the beginning of two decades
on the road and of overseas travel to play cricket.

Trueman was just 5 ft 4 in (160 cm), but already had
broad shoulders and hips and also strong legs, the right
physical attributes for a fast bowler who wanted to last more
than a few seasons before experiencing injury. Then, the
teenage Fred was hell-bent on speed above all, and accuracy
and swing were afterthoughts. But coaching at this time
made his grip improve. He soon had a good late out-
swinger, the hardest fast delivery for a right-hand batsman
to play.

Meanwhile, in Test cricket, Bradman's Australians routed
England 4–0 in the 1948 Ashes. Australia's main bowling
weapon was Ray Lindwall who was at the peak of his awesome powers. There was also Keith Miller, who opened with
him and who could intimidate batsmen with a proficient,
provocative bouncer. England had no paceman to reply to
Lindwall and Miller and make the Australians wary. The
Australian bowlers set about nullifying England's greatest
batsman, Len Hutton, and succeeded. He struggled at the
top of the batting order and was dropped mid-series. To
counter Australia's dominance, England's search for speed
was stepped up. The hint given to young Trueman that he
possessed the rare commodity of pace that was in such fever-
ish demand in his homeland came in a speech in 1948 by
another Yorkshire legend, Herbert Sutcliffe, a prodigious
Test opening batsman. He, like all openers, had a special
sensitivity to the merits, or otherwise, of fast bowlers.

Sutcliffe predicted that a young fast bowler named
Freddie Trueman would play for Yorkshire before he was 19,
and England before he was 21. The comment, reported in
the *Sheffield Telegraph*, buoyed Trueman and was a catalyst

for a self-fulfilling prophecy. In his inexperience and youth-ful brashness, Fred believed that Sutcliffe had simply articulated something that Fred knew, within himself, already. Yet even he had not quite divined the years of success to follow like the canny Sutcliffe had. As it was, Sutcliffe's crystal ball gazing was impressive.

Trueman worked at the Maltby pit and was coached by former Test bowler Bill Bowes and batsman Arthur Mitchell during the winter of 1948–49. In May 1949, Trueman, at 18, was selected for the first time to play for Yorkshire, against Cambridge University. Alan, his father, was as chuffed as any Yorkshireman could be with his son playing for the county, but he said 'nowt'. Instead, he made sure his son had the right cricket equipment for his move into first-class cricket. The pipe-smoking tyro was on his way. He got a wicket – a catch to short-leg – with his first bouncer at first-class level. Trueman did well in this match, taking three wickets, and did even better against Oxford, taking four. Then he was dropped for the first time in a career that would experience sometimes unfair, often unjustified, dumpings from the Yorkshire and England teams.

In 1950, without doing anything to suggest he had serious class as a bowler, Trueman was picked in a trial game for Test selection, such was the desperation in England to bring on a speed merchant to counter Lindwall and Miller. Trueman was the hope of the nation long before he was worthy of this position. The focus was increasingly on him and he revelled in the attention. Lesser men would have collapsed under the weight of such expectation. He didn't get much of a go in the trial match – just nine overs – but in 54 deliveries he managed to bowl future England captain and its most celebrated batsman, Len Hutton, with a prodigious in-swinger. He also had former skipper Norman

Yardley caught. His two victims were both from Yorkshire. He didn't take a swag of wickets, but he had taken those with most influence. Trueman's capacities under pressure were noted. His temperament was fine, but he sprayed the ball too much in trying to live up to a reputation as a tearaway. If he could tighten his performance, and display more discipline and technical skill, his place in an England XI was assured. But he was dumped again for six weeks and not even chosen to play in the county's second XI. Trueman had to cool his heels back at Maltby. He was supported by his father, Alan, who advised him not to do anything precipitate, such as leave the Yorkshire club because of his non-selection.

Trueman thought long and hard about this drastic act. He was uncapped and struggling financially. He had no contract, as was his county's way, and no one was communicating with him about his present or his future. Nor did he feel popular in the club of professionals and amateurs, seniors and juniors, and its jumbled mix of class backgrounds. Some disliked him and he knew it. He was too rough for some and confrontational by nature. Trueman had no time for ex-public school or Oxbridge pretensions and airs. Others saw him as a loose cannon. He didn't mind letting go a very quick delivery at club batsmen in the nets, and for this alone he wouldn't be missed by a few if he left.

When Trueman came back the next season, 1951, bitter from his omission, he bowled better and even managed to reach eighth in the county bowling averages with 31 wickets at 28.25 runs per wicket, despite being five runs more expensive than in 1949 when he also took 31 wickets. Pertinent to his development was a growth spurt over the 1950–51 winter lay-off which took him to 5 ft 8 in (170.5 cm). He also filled out more to around 12 stone (76 kg). Trueman's chest and hip measurements were both widening, which gave him a bull-like body atop tree-trunk legs. He was now beginning to at least look the part of the much prayed-for speed champion, just at a time when Freddie Brown's team limped back from a 4–1 Ashes thrashing in Australia. Lindwall and Miller had once more been prominent in bruising English pride.

There was no thought by selectors of Trueman being rushed in for the five-Test series at home against South Africa. Besides, he was having enough trouble finding a permanent spot in his county team, with competition from up-and-coming stars such as speedster John Whitehead, medium-paced off-spinner Bob Appleyard, and others. Trueman was still in and out of the county team, but his bowling had tightened up. There was a little more sense in his technique. More importantly, he was taking big bags of wickets such as eight for 68 versus Nottingham, Larwood's old county club. Onlookers dubbed him 'the new Larwood', something even then, at 20 years of age, Trueman didn't appreciate. He was nobody's Second Coming. He saw himself as unique. His ambition was to be the greatest paceman England ever produced, nothing less. He found comparisons not just odious, but insulting.

Capped

Bolstered by success and the need to make more money, he apparently went to Yorkshire skipper Yardley, mid-season, and threatened to leave the club unless he was 'capped' – given a county cap, which signified two pounds a week extra, plus a monthly retainer. It was promptly given to him. The county cap was just as valuable, in terms of prestige, to a Yorkshireman as his England cap. Trueman rushed home to find his father waiting expectantly for him.

Alan had heard the news of his son's capping and had missed the night shift at the coalface to greet him. According to Trueman in his autobiography, *Ball of Fire*, the rugged old boy nearly broke down when Fred handed the cap to him and told him it was his. Fred never wore it again and proud Alan would later go to his grave with it.

That night, Fred promised his mother she could have his first England cap, and she shed tears of pride. It wasn't long in coming. Trueman took 90 wickets at 20.57 during 1951. Further self-development came for him doing national service in the RAF, and Yorkshire paid him five pounds a week while he was enlisted. It enabled him to quit mining, he hoped, for good. It was further motivation for the young battler.

During his comparatively undemanding days in the RAF based at Hemswell in Lincolnshire, just 32 miles (about 50 km) from his home, he had a further late growth spurt to reach his full height of 5 ft 10 in (176 cm) and a weight of 13.5 stone (85 kg). His chest and hips now measured 46 inches (115 cm) and he had a large derrière – a most useful asset for fast bowlers – along with 19 inch (48 cm) thighs. Such dimensions all contributed to an image of indestructibility and considerable force. There would be no back problems or leg strains for F.S. Trueman throughout a two-decade span that took him half a dozen years beyond the life of the average first-class paceman.

Four for None, Having Fun

At 21, in 1952, nearly on time for Herbert Sutcliffe's prophecy, Trueman was picked for his first Test – against India at Headingley. It was also Hutton's first Test as captain, and he made his first mistake, in Trueman's mind, by asking Alec Bedser to bowl from the Kirkstall Lane end, which has a downhill run. Trueman, who was faster, had to run up the hill from the other end.

India then had to face what Bradman saw as England's best opening bowling combination. Neither Trueman nor Bedser was at his peak, yet they still made a formidable duo of class, speed and swing. Trueman was on view at the national level for the first time. The crowd saw his attention to his unravelling left sleeve as he stalked back to the mark of a long run – more with the gait of an athletic rugby player than a cricketer – then they saw the wheel around and the curved run up, which would bring him centimetres close to the umpire. The run began as a paddle then accelerated at a controlled rate. Trueman, his black hair flopping, would twist his body so much for the delivery that the batsman could see his left shoulder-blade as he poised his left foot before thumping it down. This was followed by the mighty swing of the ball-propelling right arm that carried his body well forward after it. All through that last delivery propulsion, Trueman kept his head steady and his eyes glaring at the batsman, who had to contend with the speeding ball, the aggressive stare and the body force coming at him. He was no sight for the faint-hearted batsman.

His first wicket was number three for India, Polly Umrigar, caught behind by Godfrey Evans and beaten by sheer pace. Trueman took two more wickets and had to be content with three for 89 off 26 overs, a good first-up effort. Yet he was never really content with such returns.

It was different in India's second innings. Hutton let Trueman bowl down the hill. He had Pankaj Roy out, caught second ball by Denis Compton at slip. Bedser promptly had D.K. Gaekwad caught in the gully. India was two wickets for 0. It was soon three for 0 as Trueman

Straight with Drive. Jack Hobbs straight drives in the nets. Bradman considered him the most technically skilled batsman he ever saw.

Happy Hobbs. Jack Hobbs was a happy, successful man on and off the field as this relaxed shot, taken in 1929, indicates. He was later knighted for his services to cricket.

Skipper with Strike. Captain Len Hutton (left) and strike bowler Alec Bedser lead England onto the field in the Fifth and deciding Ashes Test at The Oval in 1953. England won. Both players were later knighted for their services to cricket.

One Knight to Another. Len Hutton, then captain of England, and Sir Donald Bradman (then retired and covering the Tests as a journalist), together during the 1953 Ashes. Hutton said that Bradman's articles in the London *Daily Mail* helped him tactically in the series.

Lofty Ambitions. Len Hutton on the attack as he lofts one over mid-wicket.

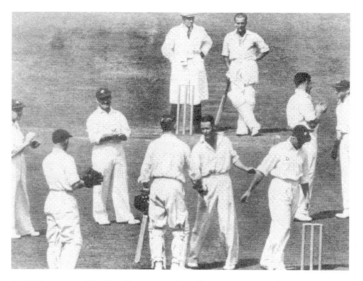

355 Reasons To Be Congratulated. Len Hutton being congratulated at The Oval in 1938 after he had made the run that beat Don Bradman's record of 334 in Tests. Hutton went on to score 364. It is still the highest score in Ashes Tests.

Ashes Victorious. Len Hutton lets his bowler, Tony Lock, lead the team off The Oval after spinning England to victory on the last day of the Fifth and deciding Ashes Test in 1953. Behind Lock are Peter May and keeper Godfrey Evans.

The Brylcreem Kid. Denis Compton looked and played the part of the dashing cricketer. He attracted endorsement from Brylcreem hair products.

He Also Spun. Denis Compton was an attacking batsman who also delivered handy left-arm spinners.

May the Style Be With You. Peter May, a graceful driver, hits one through the off-side. Bradman regarded him as England's best bat in its golden era of the 1950s.

Balance and Belligerence. Wally Hammond drives with balance and force. Bradman considered him the best cover drive he had seen.

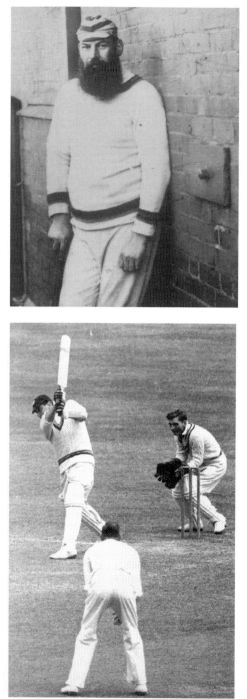

On Top of Lord's. Dr W.G. Grace on the roof of the Old Pavilion at Lord's cricket ground. He dominated cricket in England during the last third of the nineteenth century.

On the Front Foot. Wally Hammond drives straight.

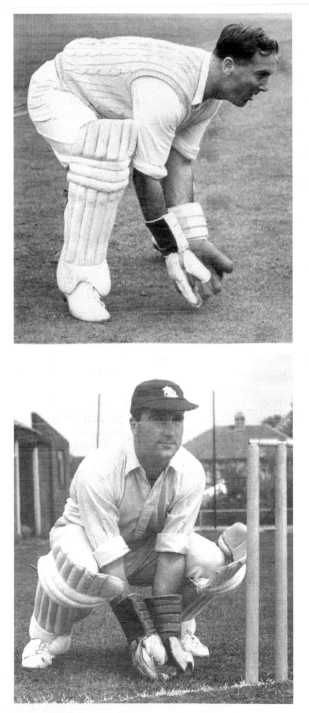

Gloves Ready.
Godfrey Evans, behind
the stumps, bends to
take a low delivery.
He was a brilliant,
inspiring keeper.

Eyes Steady. Godfrey
Evans, eyes steady,
waits for a delivery.

Great Fast Hope. Fred Trueman (front left) with Yorkshire skipper and former England captain Norman Yardley (right) in May 1953. Trueman was regarded as the great hope for England in countering Australia's pacemen.

High Arm Action. Fred Trueman, judged by Bradman as England's best-ever fast bowler, poses for the camera in May 1949.

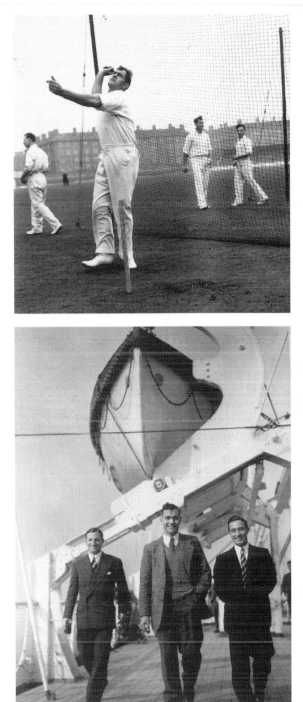

Mainstay. Alec Bedser, mainstay of the post-war attacks of England and Surrey, practises in the nets in May 1952.

Sailing to Victory. (l-r) Len Hutton, Alec Bedser and Denis Compton on the deck of the *Durban Castle*, prior to sailing to South Africa in October 1948.

That Lethal Right Arm. S.F. Barnes demonstrates his bowling action in 1920. He was one of the great bowlers of all time.

Verity with the Bat. Hedley Verity was Bradman's choice as England's spinner. He was also a useful batsman who, at times, filled in as opener in Tests.

Spin King. Hedley Verity pushes down one of his orthodox left-arm spinners.

Youthful Bladesman. A teenage Ian Botham taking a swing in a match for Somerset. He always went for his shots and displayed a perpetual belligerence that could turn a game in a matter of overs.

Wicket Delight. Ian Botham celebrates after taking a Test wicket. He was England's best all-rounder of the twentieth century.

Having a Fling. Ian Botham prepares to let the ball go.

Gower Power.
England's David Gower displays his timing and grace with the bat. Bradman delighted in watching him. He considered Gower's 123 at Sydney in the Third Test of the 1990-91 series as the best Ashes innings he ever saw in Australia in 80 years.

Laker Breaker.
England's off-spinner Jim Laker in action. He took nineteen wickets for 90 in the Manchester Test of 1956. Bradman ranked this as one of the best bowling performances he saw in Ashes Tests.

bowled the keeper, M.K. Mantri, with a slower ball that pitched on middle and uprooted off-stump. Then Trueman bowled V.L. Manjrekar next ball. India was four for 0 in the most sensational start ever to a Test, and Trueman was on a hat trick. The packed Headingley crowd of 30,000 was in raptures and England thrilled to the reality of a talented, intimidating paceman for the first time in two decades.

Trueman just missed the hat trick but not the celebrity that came with his debut. His second-innings figures of four for 27 were maintained at Lord's, where he met Queen Elizabeth II in the first summer of her reign. Trueman took four for 72 and four for 110. In the Third Test at Old Trafford he snared eight for 31 in nine overs, the best-ever figures secured in an India versus England Test and, as it transpired, Trueman's best-ever bowling feat. He added another five for 48 in the Fourth and final Test to give him 29 wickets at an average of only 13.31. *Wisden* made him one of its five cricketers of the year.

Young Fred from Maltby had arrived with a bang.

He was a sudden hero of the people, but an appealing character with it. Tall stories were going to be attached to him, whether they happened or not. Some did. Trueman himself tells in his autobiography how he knocked out an Irishman after an altercation at a cabaret show. The beginning of his reputation as an uncouth, wild character began at a dinner given by the Indian High Commissioner in London for the India and England teams. Trueman, in honour of his outstanding debut series, was placed at the head of the table next to a senior figure in the Indian government. To get this senior government figure's attention, Trueman, so the fable recounts, is alleged to have said: 'Hey, Gunga Din, pass t'salt.' Trueman denied this story long and hard but it was too much an apocryphal tale not to pass into legend.

His explosive entry to the highest level of the game was not sustained in 1953 when England fought Australia for the Ashes. National service held up Trueman's preparation and he didn't play until late May. Wet pitches, illness, injury, his own ordinary form and Hutton's reluctance to play him in front of more economical performers (such as Brian Statham and the fast-medium precision of Alec Bedser, Trevor Bailey and the spinners) combined to keep him out of the Tests until the vital final game at The Oval. Belatedly, Trueman made his mark against the old enemy, removing the dangerous Neil Harvey who couldn't resist hooking and was caught. He then dispensed with Graeme Hole, Jim de Courcy, and Ray Lindwall (62) after he had salvaged Australia's first innings, giving Trueman four for 86, the best figures for England. He had just two overs in Australia's second innings before Surrey spin twins Jim Laker and Tony Lock took over and ran through the tourists to deliver England a 1–0 series win.

Unhappy with Hutton

Trueman was selected for a tour of the West Indies under Hutton in 1953–54 and endured an unhappy time. He had a disagreement with the captain over whether Hutton should be addressed as 'skipper'. Trueman, who could call Hutton 'Len' in Yorkshire matches, wanted to keep using the more familiar address. It was trivial to Trueman but important to Hutton, who wanted his troops fairly, but not overly, disciplined. This disagreement was compounded by allegations against Trueman on and off the field for indiscretions that were not always perpetrated by him. Such attribution of blame was a continuation – in part – of the myths already abroad about this larger-than-life individual.

On the other hand, Fred was no angel. His rugged good looks were attractive to the opposite sex. Some women put up with his antics and loved him for them. Others loathed him. A classic story arose in Barbados when a snobbish English woman complained to Hutton that two MCC cricketers had jostled her in a hotel lift on a Saturday night after the celebration of Trueman's twenty-third birthday. She named Trueman and Lock as the jostlers. Hutton ordered them to apologise to her. The woman, from a services background who seemed to be a strict disciplinarian, dressed them down for 15 minutes. Afterwards, Hutton commended the players, telling them that he thought 'they took that very well'.

'So do I,' Trueman replied, 'since it weren't us.'

There were other unfortunate encounters with umpires on the West Indies tour and Trueman was unfairly blamed again for things he had not done. His bad boy image was working against him. It didn't help that he refused to attend a cocktail party given by a local dignitary who had described his bowling action as a throw. Trueman was justified in his loud complaint and boycott. But he proved to be a headache for the diplomatic, public relations-conscious and conservative Hutton, who was under undue pressure to prove that a professional player – and a Northerner outside the MCC establishment – could handle a team and a tough tour as well as any amateur ever did. He totted up his young charge's alleged misdemeanours, indiscretions and confrontations, and did not allow Trueman his good conduct bonus at the end of the tour. Trueman was the only player to miss out. This rankled with the aggrieved speedster. He felt he was the scapegoat for a tour that nearly went off the rails with riots and disputed umpiring decisions. Only Hutton's single-minded dedication and power as a great cricketer enabled England to come back to draw the series after being 2–0 down at the end of the Second Test. Considering the batting and spin capacities of the West Indies team, and the demands of the tour, this was one of the finest fightbacks in cricket history. Hutton's position of power in English cricket, while not unassailable, was as near to supreme as any professional would get. His influence was strong. If he used this with subtlety he could usually work through what he wanted. Selection was part of this. He respected Trueman and reckoned he would be as good as Lindwall, eventually. But he didn't want any mavericks in the build-up to the biggest challenge of his entire cricket life – a defence of the Ashes in Australia. Trueman, whether it was justified or not, was rumoured by some to be too hot to handle.

Tyson's Challenge

Whether this was the reason for his non-selection for England during the 1954 summer versus Pakistan may never be known. The selectors had an excuse. England had a surfeit of outstanding fast bowlers, including the quickest Englishman ever – Frank Tyson. (Bradman thought Tyson, from 1954 to 1956, was the fastest bowler he ever saw. Godfrey Evans, behind the stumps, thought Tyson at least the fastest he ever kept to or witnessed. But both these expert observers agreed that Trueman was the better bowler overall.) There were also Statham, Peter Loader, and the still top-line medium pacers, Bedser and Bailey, to back them up.

Trueman, the mighty competitor, was affronted by comparisons with Tyson, who could also lift for the big occasion. Their battles in the Yorkshire–Northants county games of the mid-1950s are part of the folklore of English cricket at its peak. Trueman would try to top Tyson for sheer pace and wicket-taking ability and vice versa. Pity the poor batsmen from either county facing and caught in the middle of such controlled hostility.

Despite not playing in a Test, Trueman had his best haul of wickets so far in 1954, his sixth county championship season. He topped 100 wickets for the first time, taking 134 at the outstanding average of 15.55 runs per wicket. Trueman had expected to be chosen by Hutton and the selectors for the Australian tour and was shocked when omitted. He was confident he was a big-occasion player – one who could lift his performance under the pressure of an Ashes fight. Yet this was ignored in the one small era in English cricket history when such a champion performer might not be sorely missed. As it turned out, Tyson, at the peak of his capacities, was enough to win the series for England 3–1 and keep the Ashes.

Trueman spent the off-season working as a furniture salesman and took the opportunity of the break from cricket to marry Enid Chapman. They made a home in Scarborough.

Hutton, overcome by the strain of leadership, retired from Test cricket during the 1955 season. If Trueman wished to keep playing for England, he had to keep mopping up bags of county wickets and hope that he would be reconsidered for selection to the national team. He wasn't over-confident, given the selectors' behaviour towards him so far in his career, and they remained inconsistent in their attitude. Yet there was a consolation. He was chosen for one Test against the touring South Africans – at Lord's – where he took two for 73 and none for 39 in a game England won by 71 runs. His selection reassured him that he was not on a banned list. There would always be hurdles for Northerner Freddie, but with persistence he could overcome them. He was still only 24 and, in his mind, the best speed purveyor in England. He wasn't alone in thinking this, but it counted most that he thought it himself. Now he had to prove it.

Trueman did much to support his self-belief at county level by taking 153 wickets at 16.03. During the season he took another hat trick against Nottingham. He had done it before playing the same county in 1951. He began the 1956 season full of hope that he would be selected against the visiting Australians. However, he suffered from a strained left side and this hampered his early progress. But he was selected for the Second Test at Lord's, taking two for 54 and five for 90. However, Richie Benaud with 97 before lunch in Australia's second innings, and Keith Miller, with match figures of ten for 152, stole the show and gave Australia its only victory of the series. Trueman was retained for the Third Test at Leeds, where Laker and Lock destroyed Australia. He took one for 19 and one for 21, getting rid of Colin McDonald cheaply each time. During this game, England's chairman of selectors, Gubby Allen, took Trueman into the nets and told him to bowl at a handkerchief on a good length to see if he could hit it. Allen, in a patronising way, was making the point that Trueman needed to bowl a fuller length to the Australians. This condescending lesson, in front of a crowd, demonstrated at least some of the attitude at the selection table towards Trueman. After that Test, he was dumped again. Yet he walked away with the second-best figures of the series for England, taking nine at 20.44, in an Ashes contest that had been dominated by Jim Laker.

Trueman still performed outside the Tests, especially for Yorkshire against the Australians. Despite his frustration, he never lost his humour. In one of his famous retorts, after being edged several times by Northampton's tail-ender Keith Andrew, Trueman stood hands on hips after following through and remarked pithily: 'You've got more bloody edges than a broken pisspot!'

1957: Year of Maturation

He hadn't performed well or often enough to tour South Africa in 1956–57 but came back for a full five Tests at home in 1957 against the West Indies, taking 22 wickets at 20.58. At Trent Bridge he put in a sustained spell of sheer brilliance, taking five for 20 in one 10-over session with six maidens. It was his best Test of the series and he ended with match figures of nine for 143. At the age of 26, Trueman had matured into the best fastman in the land. Tyson was troubled by injury and the only real rival was Statham, often his opening partner. 1958 saw Trueman retained in the Test team for a further five Tests against New Zealand – giving him 10 in a row. His development was also partly attributed to his skipper at Yorkshire, Ronnie Burnet, a perceptive leader, who read Trueman's moods well, and knew how to direct and encourage him. He was just the kind of captain Trueman needed at this time as he reached his career performance peak. His 15 wickets at 17.06 against New Zealand in 1958 and 106 first-class wickets at just 13.33 – the most economical returns of his career – presaged the speedster's great leap to a higher plateau reached a year later in 1959.

Australia for the First Time

First there was the unhappy tour of Australia in 1958–59 when England's golden years of the mid-1950s collapsed. Trueman was ignored for the first two Tests but came back to take nine wickets at 30.66 and a further five at 21.00 in New Zealand. The Australian crowds loved him as they always do a character. He commanded respect, while not taking himself too seriously. Cricket fans voiced admiration for a man who could sprint 13 eight-ball overs – a courageous performance – in a match against Victoria, played in January 1959 in 44-degree (109 Fahrenheit) heat, deplorable conditions. He took five for 42 in Victoria's 286. The spectators – especially in the MCG outer of the old Bay 13 – felt comfortable with a sportsperson prepared to be the showman, even in a Test. At Melbourne, in the final Test, the crowd roared their appreciation when he lobbed the ball in from third man with his left arm. It seemed to earn a frown of disapproval from skipper Peter May. Perhaps the crowd was not aware that Fred was a proficient thrower with either hand. But they loved his cheek and the interplay with May, who, as Godfrey Evans observed, was not into 'fun' on the cricket field.

From that 1958–59 tour on, for the next six years, regardless of how England stood Trueman was the world's best speed merchant and a huge drawcard in the game, wherever he played. Yet he was unavailable to tour to India–Pakistan in 1961–62, and was still left out of tours to India in 1963–64 and South Africa again in 1964–65.

In 1959, at 28 years of age, he was no longer concerned just with speed. His trademark was the bouncer, which some criticised him for over-using. But when his bouncer got a wicket, usually when a happy hooker tried one too many, attitudes changed. Trueman had never been afraid to 'buy' a wicket – that is, give away a few runs to tempt a batsman into error. This, however, was against the Yorkshire tradition of economy at all costs.

He was one of the best-ever purveyors of the two-card trick, the bouncer to force a batsman back, followed by the controlled yorker to uproot middle- or off-stump, or both. Many a county or Test batsman slumped back to the pavilion after having fallen for that trick from Fred. He had one of the best natural out-swinging deliveries of all time, but he could also bring the ball back. When he cut his pace in this period of dominance, he could deliver a deadly off-cutter. He copied Lindwall's method of banging the ball in short to get lift, and also get movement off the seam.

Trueman was a cunning assessor of his opponents' strengths and weaknesses. Like all great bowlers, he could recall detail about every relevant first-class batsman he ever bowled to. If they were timid against pace, he used it. If they were brilliant hookers, like Garry Sobers, he found out quickly and put away the bouncer against such batting mastery. If they liked to play back, he kept the ball up. If they were forward pushers, he bowled short. No shrewder bowler ever charged an opponent. Trueman used the menace in his run and in his expression to fool a batsman with a slower delivery.

Match-Winner

Trueman had waited eight years to show the Australians just what a match-winner he could be. With his adoring home crowd at Headingley urging and willing him on during the Third Test of 1961, in the first innings he sent back a terrific line-up of Neil Harvey, Norm O'Neill, Bob Simpson and Richie Benaud – all easily capable of turning a game in their own right. His figures were five for 58. Australia made 237. England replied with 299.

Trueman's grit and nous, in equal proportions, were evident in Australia's second innings. He had had a marital row on the Friday evening and had left his Scarborough home to spend the night in his car in a Leeds car park. He arrived at the ground early so he could have a wash and shave. This depressing distraction did not affect his on-field performance, for he was determined to clean up in an Ashes contest after his long wait to do so. A Harvey–O'Neill stand of 50 took the tourists to two for 99. Australia was well in the lead on a dusty pitch that seemed set to crumble. May turned to Trueman, who had spoken to him about cutting down his run and his pace in order to bowl off-cutters. Given permission to use this ploy, Trueman had Harvey playing too soon and caught in the covers. He then had O'Neill caught. Subsequently, he clean-bowled Simpson and Benaud. Ken Mackay was next, caught behind. Trueman had claimed one of the best bags of five in history for no runs. Australia was reduced to eight for 109. Not even Bradman after his triple centuries in 1930 and 1934 received a more thunderous applause than Trueman that afternoon. No one had ever delivered a more brilliant spell in a Test against such class. The Yorkshire crowd was ecstatic. Trueman ended with six for 30 and England won comfortably. His match figures were eleven for 88.

Trueman continued his outstanding form against the Australians in 1962–63 taking 20 wickets at an average of 26.05. He seemed to save his best for the Melbourne crowd, who cheered as if he were one of their own in the Second Test. Trueman won it for England in Australia's second innings when he took five for 60. Back home in England, a half-year later in the 1963 season, he repeated his 1961 Headingley devastation, this time in the Edgbaston Test of the series versus the West Indies. England skipper Ted Dexter won the toss, batted and made the side just 216. Charlie Griffith and Wesley Hall – two big fast bowlers with matching reputations – between them could only snare four wickets. Trueman looked on, eager to top these two, simply because they were so highly regarded. He was fired up, as ever, by personal competition. Rivalry brought out the best in him as it had done in the mid-1950s when Tyson's shooting star lit up cricket skies. Now he wished to show who was top dog once more. Fred had spring in his step. He was aggressive and, at times, positively belligerent. He willed results and in the West Indies' first innings found life in a dull pitch that had disdained the thumps into it from Hall and Griffith. Trueman sent back openers Conrad Hunte and Joey Carew, then later bowled Garry Sobers with a beauty. His figures read five for 75 off 26 overs.

England did better second time around and skipper Ted Dexter was able to declare at nine for 278 with a lead of 308. He had to go for a win. England was one down in the third of a five-Test series. Dexter gave quiet encouragement to Trueman. He responded with a tidal wave of bowling that left nothing standing, taking seven for 44. This included a spell of six wickets while conceding one scoring stroke in 24 balls. For the second time in a Test he took five wickets for 0 – on this occasion in just 19 balls (compared with 26 against Australia in 1961). The seven victims in that haul were Hunte, Rohan Kanhai, Joe Solomon, Frank Worrell, Deryck Murray (once more, a fine bag of accomplished bats, by any standard), with bunnies Wesley Hall and Charlie Griffith dismissed for the hell of it. Trueman's match figures were twelve for 119 – the first time a player had taken 12 wickets in an Edgbaston Test or against the West Indies in England.

Trueman had now been seen at his blistering best.

There were still great moments to be savoured against the Australians. In the final Ashes Test of 1964 at The Oval Trueman took four for 87. (This was after being dropped earlier in the series for over-feeding Peter Burge with bouncers. Burge had dispatched them to the fence en route to 160 and a Test win for Australia.) Neil Hawke, caught by Colin Cowdrey (so often a fine catcher for Trueman) in slip, was Trueman's three-hundredth Test victim. It was cricket's bowling equivalent to putting a human on the moon.

His Test career ended in 1965. In 67 Tests he took 307 Test wickets at 21.57, while scoring 981 runs at 13.81. He was also an outstanding catch, taking 64 – nearly one a Test. Trueman's marriage to Enid, which produced a daughter and twins (a son and another daughter), ended in the late 1960s. He went on playing for Yorkshire until 1968, a year that saw him produce – as a stand-in captain – one more big performance against the Australians, not for England but his county. Yorkshire, under Trueman's strong direction, won easily by an innings.

He was told by some at the club that he might captain the county in 1969. But it was too late. He had already told key Yorkshire officials he would retire.

In first-class cricket, Trueman took 2304 wickets at 18.29. He made 9231 runs at 15.56, scoring three centuries. He managed 438 catches.

After resigning from Yorkshire at age 37, he went home to Maltby to tell his dad. Alan was moved but content to have seen his son play from the start to the finish of his two-decade career. Trueman senior, according to Fred, said he could die happy and that he would never watch Yorkshire again. Alan died two years later, in 1970.

Trueman trod the boards as a nightclub comedian in 1969, married a second time (Veronica) in the early 1970s and pursued a career in the media as a journalist for the *Sunday People* newspaper. He became a popular television and radio commentator for the BBC.

Don Bradman regarded Fred Trueman as the greatest England speedster of all time. He was his first bowling choice to be part of Bradman's best-ever England XI.

CHAPTER 21

BATSMAN BEDEVILLER

ALEC
BEDSER

(England)

4 July 1918–

'Bedser's strength allowed him to bowl for long periods without sacrificing length or accuracy that would wear a batsman down.'

DON BRADMAN

When chosen in Bradman's dream world team published in *Bradman's Best* in 2001, Bedser said he felt 'honoured and privileged' to be included. He thought that if anyone was in a position to compose a world team from all those who had played the game it was the Don. Bedser was surprised that anyone could possibly compare so many great players from different eras, but acknowledged that Bradman had seen 'a hell of a lot of cricket over several decades'. In an August 2001 interview with Martin Rogers of Britain's *Daily Mirror* newspaper, following his selection in Bradman's world team, Bedser said that cricket in his day was not all 'cheerful chaps, chocolate cakes, three cheers, jolly good fellows and flannelled fools'. He was scathing about modern players' complaints that they played too much cricket and needed a rest.

'I bowled more than 3200 overs between April 1950 and August 1951,' he noted. This was 10 times the number of overs sent down over a similar stretch of time by England's modern fast bowlers, who are now not required to play for their counties during seasons when contracted to play international games.

Bedser and twin brother Eric, a successful off-spinning all-rounder for Surrey, were sceptical about modern fitness methods and athletic training. They believed that solid work on the field was the only true way to be fit for cricket. During his career, Alec Bedser was always the workhorse. His captains – Wally Hammond, Len Hutton, Peter May (England and Surrey) and others – could rely on him day in and day out to deliver. He and Eric put their immense strength and capacity for labour down to the physical work they engaged in from the age of 10. They made Pythonesque joint declarations – with one starting a sentence and the other, thinking identically, finishing it – about their early years helping their father – a brick-layer – digging ditches, working in gardens, chopping wood and so on. Yet their records of endurance on the cricket field, that would not be countenanced today by any professionals, were testimony to their decades of genuine toil.

Winning Twins

Alec was born at Reading, Berkshire, within minutes of his identical twin brother Eric, who was a talented county bowling all-rounder. They were raised in Woking. They assisted their father in building their Woking home in 1953, where they have lived as inseparable twins ever since.

They were ground-staff bowlers at The Oval in their late teenage years. The Bedsers joined the RAF in 1939 at 20, when the Second World War began and were 27 in 1946 on returning to civilian life. They missed prime years of cricket development but claimed that the war experience toughened them mentally and physically.

'They talk about tension today in cricket,' Sir Alec remarked, 'but after experiencing the war years, tension on the cricket field was nothing.'

The fates of the Bedser twins were perhaps sealed when,

as 16-year-olds, they tossed a coin to see who would bowl pace or spin. Alec won the toss and chose pace. Eric was one of the finest off-spinners not to play Test cricket. They both began their working lives in the city as clerks in lawyers' offices, but they only ever dreamed of playing cricket, particularly for Surrey. They both attained their dreams, and their skills as professional cricketers played a huge part in the county's golden years of seven successive championships between 1952 and 1958. In each of the first six years of this amazing run, Alec took more than 80 wickets at less than 19 runs per wicket. It was a sustained stretch of brilliance, rarely matched in the history of first-class cricket.

Alec's Test career began in an illustrious manner, post-war in 1946, when he collected 11 Indian scalps in each of his first two Tests. To his surprise, it was enough to ensure a trip to Australia under Wally Hammond in 1946–47. It wasn't an entirely happy time, with Hammond an aloof, unhelpful leader, who travelled separately from the team. Bedser got no advice from him and found England's greatest bat of the 1920s and 1930s uninspiring. It didn't help that the tourists failed to win a Test or even challenge the Australians. Bedser returned home with unflattering figures and a sense that he had been fortunate to start against the weak Indian line-up of 1946. Australia was a different proposition, with its power-hitting batting line-up of Barnes, Morris, Bradman, Harvey, Hassett and Miller. The Australian team also had a tail that included handy hitters such as Lindwall and Tallon. They rarely seemed to be completely dismissed, and even more rarely dismissed twice in one match. This unconquerable image was sustained in 1948 when Australia rolled England 4–0. Bedser's figures were once again unimpressive. Yet the wheel was to turn by 1950–51 when he starred down-under and established himself as one of the game's best-ever bowlers. He became a key to England winning the Ashes in 1953 under Hutton, an achievement that paved the way for its world dominance for the next years.

By the standards of the 1940s and 1950s, Bedser was regarded as a fitness fanatic and his inspiration came in part from his wartime RAF physical training. A large-framed man of more than 6 ft 3 in (191 cm), Bedser would be seen in the dressing room stretching, doing knee bends, sit-ups, side bends and running on the spot before taking the field. His aim was to be loose and ready to bowl as fast as he could, even inside his first over. Bedser would curl his large right hand over the ball for the in-swinger, the away-swinger or his specialty, the leg-cutter.

Bedser demonstrated his leg-break grip by placing his large right hand across the seam. Only someone with such a huge paw, and strong fingers, could exact the cut or spin he managed.

He had nowhere near the bowling speed of his contemporaries – Statham, Trueman, Lindwall and Miller. The keeper – Godfrey Evans for the most part – would stand up to the wicket. It took nerve and skill for a bowler and keeper to succeed in such a difficult double act. The bowler had to be dead accurate. Nothing could stray down leg-side. Bedser could make the ball rear from his relatively short 10-pace run-up. He had one of the most deceptive in-swingers of all time. His delivery action suggested an away-swinger. If not bamboozled by Bedser's bowling action, a right-hand bat might well have trouble with the very late swing. The sight of a batsman squared up and jamming down far too late was a common experience across England from 1946 to 1960 whenever Bedser bowled for Surrey and England. It didn't matter if the batsman was prepared for this delivery. It fooled most first-class batsmen at least once in their careers. The same applied to the leg-cutter, which was usually employed on poor pitches. For the bowler, it was far tougher to get right. But when it worked, it was unplayable, even for the greatest batsmen. Lindsay Hassett joked of his experience of swatting at a Bedser leg-cutter three times and missing each – once as it swung in the air, a second time when it hit the deck and a third occasion when it whipped past the bat.

Sir Donald Bradman regarded Alec Bedser as the most difficult bowler he ever faced in conditions conducive to swing and cut. The bowler troubled him during the Ashes of 1948 with deliveries that dipped late in from the off and caused him to be caught three times at backward short-leg – a method that former Australian Test leg-spinner Bill O'Reilly claimed he advised Bedser to deliver.

Bedser disputed this, saying that he often had 'a beer with O'Reilly [during the 1948 Ashes], but I don't remember that advice specifically. We [England's bowlers] worked it out ourselves. After I had dismissed Don in Australia [during the 1946–47 Ashes] with a leg-cutter [fast leg-break] it was clear that if I was to get a delivery [in-swinger] in the right spot, he would be committed to play it in case it was the leg-cutter again.'

However, Bedser conceded that O'Reilly may have given him the same guidance that the English bowlers had given each other. Such was the rivalry of O'Reilly towards Bradman, the spinner was keen to help dismiss Bradman, his old team-mate, even against England.

Even though in 1948 Bradman was past his prime – at nearly 40 – his canniness had allowed him to adjust his play so that he was almost as difficult to dismiss as he had been in his prime in 1930. The range of shots and power had diminished here and there, and he was not as quick up and down the pitch, yet his post-war Test and first-class average still hovered on 100. His defence and capacity to penetrate the field still made him the most devastating bat in the world, especially in pressure situations. In 1948 it was still a huge moment to take his wicket, which he guarded as jealously as ever, so removing him from the arena was still any bowler's dream. Bedser did it six times in all and, remarkably, in five successive innings. Yet Bradman's scores in those five knocks were 63, 138, 0, 38 and 89, suggesting that honours between them in these clashes were about even.

Ball of the Century

Bradman's only real failure was a second-ball duck at Adelaide during the 1946–47 Ashes in Australia. Bradman regarded this Bedser delivery as the best ball that ever dismissed him. It headed a list of 547 balls that got him out in his entire career from country to club, through first-class and Test level.

According to Bradman, this golden delivery from Bedser swung and dipped to leg late, hit the deck outside leg-stump and cut past the bat to crash into the off-stump.

'It was a fast leg-break,' Sir Alec told me in an interview at his Woking home near London. 'I very nearly got him with the same kind of delivery before he had scored in the second innings [of that Adelaide Test]. It missed the off-stump by a whisker.'

Had Bedser removed Bradman for a pair, it would have been one of the most remarkable bowling feats in history. No other player got remotely close to it, whereas the proverbial coat of varnish separated Bedser from immortality.

Imagine Shane Warne's delivery that removed Mike Gatting in the First Test of the 1993 Ashes. Add another 30 km/h (19 mph) and have it break a few centimetres less, and you have the Bedser ball in the first innings of that Adelaide Test. It would be a toss-up which was the better delivery. But given the batsmen dismissed, Bedser's delivery might just pip Warne's.

The Barnes–Tate Hybrid

'I never saw [Sydney Francis] Barnes play,' Bradman told me, 'but from what I understand, Bedser was similar to him in his nagging accuracy, which would wear batsmen down. Not allowing runs could ruin an opponent's concentration. Like Barnes, Bedser's strength also allowed him to bowl for long periods without sacrificing length or accuracy. This again tested a batsman's temperament and ingenuity. How to score off Bedser and Barnes was a constant test for batsmen.

'Bedser was like another outstanding medium-pacer – Maurice Tate. They both used swing, seam and pace off the pitch to tie up and dismiss batsmen. Alec's freakish stamina, like Tate's, enabled them to carry or, at times, bolster ordinary attacks.'

Big Alec had a lot of fun bowling to left-handers. Bedser dismissed Australia's Arthur Morris 18 times in 21 Tests. Admittedly, Morris's average was outstanding – more than 60 – throughout these contests. Yet Bedser would claim him, if not as his bunny, then as a great bat he could get through more often than not at some time in an innings. Bedser also checked the aggressive Neil Harvey, who was capable of taking a game by force, in much the manner of Bradman. Bedser considered that all left-handers were vulnerable to the ball that moved in quickly to them from their off. He would bowl his in-swinger or the off-cutter (the fast leg-break) to trouble the lefties.

The All-Seeing Selector

Sir Alec felt that Bradman would have been influenced to pick him in his best-ever world and England teams because he had seen so much of him, and had faced him as a batsman when Bedser was at his peak.

'He saw every ball I bowled in Ashes Tests,' Bedser noted. 'We played against each other in 1946–47, and in 1948. He was a selector in 1950–51 and also wrote for the *Daily Mail* when Australia toured England in 1953.'

Bradman witnessed many of Bedser's sustained bowling performances at Test level from 1950 to 1954 when he was the best bowler in the world. During the 1950–51 Ashes, at which time Bradman was now a selector, having retired from first-class cricket at the beginning of 1949, the bowler took 30 wickets at just 16.06, and this in a losing team beaten 4–1. Ten of these wickets were secured in the final Test at Melbourne. Bedser was easily player of the match. The Melbourne supporters saluted him and he was confirmed as the best bowler of the series. *Wisden* acknowledged his dominance too. It was a momentous time for him. He had at last been in a team that had beaten Australia in a Test. Bedser's influence made it all the more worth savouring.

He followed this up with a performance against South Africa in England in 1951 that Bradman did not see, when another 30 wickets were claimed at a miserly 17.23. Nor did Bradman witness Bedser's 20 wickets at 13.95 at home against India in 1952. But Bradman was in England for Bedser's most triumphant series – the Ashes of 1953. This time he was the decisive bowler in an Ashes victory – the first time England had conquered the Australians since the Bodyline series in Australia in 1932–33. Bedser had reached performance nirvana. There was no other pinnacle as high as this. He took 39 wickets at 17.48 and broke Maurice Tate's record for an Ashes series. The highlight was Bedser's fourteen for 99 at Trent Bridge in the First Test.

'This effort must surely be bracketed in the top few bowling performances of all time,' Bradman told me. 'It was certainly in the top two or three I ever saw against Australia.'

He also admired the swing bowler for his enormous capacity for hard work in the field, his never-say-die spirit, and his determination, even when carrying an injury. Bedser was never forced from the field through a breakdown. About as far as he got to the fence was at Adelaide when he succumbed to the fierce heat and was forced to the boundary to vomit. But he was back bowling in the middle minutes later. Bedser was a fighter, the type of warrior and aggressive character that Bradman loved on his team. The Englishman was very much in the Bradman mould – fiercely competitive but a performer within the rules, who loved the game and was a guardian of its values.

Bedser was vice-captain to Peter May at Surrey in 1957 when the county won the sixth of their straight titles and vice-captain again in 1958, 1959 and 1960. It was at a time when a professional was not permitted to captain Surrey. Had this arcane rule not been in vogue, Bedser, one of the most acute thinkers on the game, would certainly have led his county. Bedser would have collected 300 Test wickets had he not looked after himself by avoiding gruelling tours of the Caribbean in 1947–48, and 1953–54, and India in 1951–52. Yet he still passed Clarrie Grimmett's world record and ended his career with 236 wickets from 51 Tests at an average of 24.89 runs a wicket. This was a laudable effort, considering his late start in Test cricket at 27 years of age, a start delayed by the Second World War. His Test career ended without fanfare in 1954–55 in Australia.

Hutton preferred the speed of tearaway bowler Frank Tyson, and the steady Brian Statham. Injury in the form of debilitating shingles lessened Bedser's powers early in the tour and allowed the others to make their marks. He played just one more Test in 1955 against South Africa, replacing the injured Statham.

His first-class career continued until 1960. In 485 matches he took 1924 wickets at 20.41. He hit 5735 runs at 14.51. In 51 Tests he captured 236 wickets at 24.89 and made 714 at 12.75.

Continued Contribution

Like Bradman, Bedser put an enormous amount back into the game for little or no reward financially. He was an England selector for a record 23 years, starting as a member of the Test selection committee in 1962, and acting as chairman for 13 years from 1969 to 1981 inclusive. In that time, England played seven Ashes series and lost just two of them. This record, and his own playing performances, have given more than usual credence to the cliché, 'in my day', when uttered by Bedser. He was a key to England's superiority in world cricket in the early 1950s and had experienced success against the Australians.

He was a popular assistant manager to the Duke of Norfolk during the England tour of Australia in 1962–63. England, led by Ted Dexter, forced a 1–1 series against Richie Benaud's Australians. Bedser managed the England tours of Australia, led by Mike Denness in 1974–75, and by Mike Brearley in 1979–80.

The Bedser twins invested the proceeds of their cricket salaries from their days at Surrey and ran a successful office equipment company for some time. Alec was awarded an

OBE in 1964 and a CBE in 1982 for his services to cricket and was made president of Surrey in 1987, an honour that meant much to him. He served on both the Surrey and MCC committees. On 1 January 1997, Bedser became only the third bowler – after Sir George ('Gubby') Allen and Sir Richard Hadlee – to be knighted.

Bedser is one of three knights selected by Bradman in his best-ever England line-up (the others being Hutton and Hobbs). Bedser was pleased to have been chosen by Bradman in both the world and England teams but, surprisingly, wasn't sure he would be picked at the highest level if he were playing in the modern game. He felt that selectors today look for bowlers who deliver 'up around the batsman's ears'. Good, thinking swing bowlers might just be overlooked. Bradman, however, felt he had the perfect fast striker bowler in Fred Trueman, who was as canny as the next man. With him in the team, Bradman felt comfortable in choosing champions who were not speed merchants. Hence, Bradman's innovative selections of S.F. Barnes, Bedser and Hedley Verity. Bradman felt that this quartet of players together would form a formidable England bowling line-up, with Grace and Hammond to fill in as more than handy medium-pacers. Significantly, Bradman chose two bowlers – Bedser and Verity – who had been more successful than any others against him. Even in these team concoctions and well-honed flights of selectorial fancy, Bradman imagined the toughest challenges. Bedser got him six times, and Verity dismissed him a record eight in Tests. Certainly, Bradman was not looking for an easy time when facing the traditional sporting enemy. Yet that is not surprising. Bradman thrived on a challenge from the finest and fairest bowlers in history. Alec Victor Bedser was one of the very best.

CHAPTER 22

THE MAVERICK MAGICIAN

S. F.
BARNES

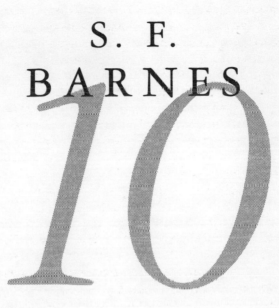

(England)

19 April 1873–26 December 1967

*'Barnes and O'Reilly were the two greatest
bowlers who ever lived.
Each was undoubtedly the greatest
of his time.'*

DON BRADMAN

Sydney Francis Barnes was one of only two selections (W.G. Grace being the other) in Bradman's Ashes teams that the selector never personally witnessed. But such was Barnes' reputation and record that Bradman was convinced as early as 1930, on his first tour of England, of the fast-medium bowler's place as one of the immortals of cricket.

Bradman met Barnes on subsequent tours, but they never faced each other on a cricket field. There was much talk in the English press in 1930 that Barnes would have been the only bowler who could have stopped Bradman on his rampage through England against the counties and in the Tests. But it was pure conjecture. Barnes was 57 in 1930 and, although still a respected bowler, would have been no match for Bradman, then 21, and in his prime.

Bradman was impressed by Barnes' Ashes record. Bowling his fast leg-breaks and off-breaks, and in- and out-swingers, he took 106 wickets at 21.58. Bill O'Reilly, with whom Barnes is often compared, took 102 England wickets at 25.64.

'From all accounts, they were similar in style. Barnes was faster, but he didn't have the googly [wrong'un],' Bradman noted. 'They were both aggressive and could deliver perhaps the hardest of all deliveries to keep out – the very quick leg-break. O'Reilly was relentless and unforgiving if you managed to strike him to the boundary. Reports suggest Barnes was in some ways similar in character. He may have had more variety in his deliveries than O'Reilly. Barnes bowled fast off-breaks, out-swingers and in-swingers. Like O'Reilly, he would have been more than a handful for the best batsmen of any era.'

Barnes, the Working Cricketer

Barnes was born in Smethwick, Staffordshire, and brought up as the second of five children. His father, Richard, worked for the Birmingham Muntz Metal Company, and encouraged his son's cricket career, but with the proviso that he always have a trade to fall back on. Professional cricket was acceptable to the working-class patriarch, but it was not to be relied upon because of the game's relatively brief earning time. Richard expected his son to last a decade as a professional cricketer, and Sydney found work as a clerk in a Staffordshire colliery – a solid back-up for his cricketing wages.

Barnes grew into a robust, powerful man of 6 ft 1 in (186 cm). He bowled off a shortish run, but made full use of his height by hooking the ball down from a high right hand. He extracted bounce and imparted spin using his strong hands and fingers, without seeming to use his wrists. This allowed him greater deception. Batsmen found it difficult to pick which way his fingers were propelling the ball, as opposed to watching the more obvious conventional break of the wrist. He was unerringly accurate and had the uncanny capacity to drop the ball on a length from his first delivery and maintain it there for long spells – much like Shane Warne in the modern era.

Barnes claimed to always 'bowl at the batsman's stroke', in order to create a false move. But the record is more ambiguous. He clean-bowled and captured lbw a fair proportion of his victims, suggesting that he delivered at the stumps just as much as at the batsman's stroke. More pertinent perhaps was his capacity to bowl at the batsman's weakness. If the batsman seemed unsure of the lifting ball, Barnes would use it. If he fidgeted outside off, Barnes employed the out-swinger. If he was a back-foot player, Barnes loved ripping a fast off-spinner or in-swinger at him. He boasted that he could deliver a distinctively different delivery for every ball in an over. No one dared doubt him. He was a master bowler, whether at league, county or Test level.

Barnes had an unconventional career, playing mainly league and minor county rather than county cricket except for two successful county seasons. He made his debut for Warwickshire (against Leicestershire) at the age of 20 in 1893, but it was not yet a first-class county. In 1894 he slipped back to Lancashire League playing for Rishton, and only performed in a couple of county games. Barnes preferred the security of the league, with its steady wage and hypocrisy-free atmosphere, over the uncertainty of county cricket, which offered him less and was complicated by the rankings of amateurs and professionals, who were looked down on for playing for money. Rishton paid him three pounds and ten shillings a week, which was well over three times the average skilled worker's wage, and substantially more than he would have been paid in county cricket at Warwickshire, which entered the County Championship in 1895 and was not rich enough to pay top salaries. The other advantage of league cricket in the eyes of Barnes and his father was that it was played on weekends, which allowed Sydney to maintain a steady job.

Barnes was well aware of the problems encountered by professionals and he noted that 'after fleeting years as famous cricketers, fêted and fussed, they dropped out, returned to the mine or factory, or, at best, a fourth-rate beerhouse, trading as best they could upon their faded glories'.

This mindset of what to avoid in English cricket dictated Barnes' approach to the game throughout his long, illustrious career. He would be hard to sway from his rock-solid path of steady income. This fitted with his somewhat dour character. There was little flamboyance in Barnes' make-up, although as he mellowed later in his career, a dry wit surfaced here and there. Cricket, essentially, was still a sport to be played part time, not a life in itself.

Nevertheless, pressure was put on Barnes to change his attitude. Archie MacLaren, captain of Lancashire and England, found a way to seduce Barnes to break his set pattern of play and work. MacLaren first asked him to play for Lancashire against Leicestershire in the final county game of 1901. Barnes adapted easily to the first-class contest, and bowled magnificently. He impressed with his easy, high action, control and menace. He took six for 70 in Leicestershire's first innings. MacLaren then realised that the description of 'fast-medium' was about one-tenth of the story when it came to S.F. Barnes.

He wanted to persuade Barnes to play for Lancashire in 1902. He found a sweetener to the deal that would be tough for Barnes to refuse: the trip of a lifetime down-under for a Test tour in 1901–02. Barnes was 28 in 1901 when he was asked by MacLaren, who wanted players to replace Yorkshire's Wilfred Rhodes and George Hirst, both star bowlers. Yorkshire's Lord Hawke, the county team's supremo who put county before country, would not allow his star bowlers to tour because it might harm Yorkshire's chances of victory in the 1902 championship. This left openings for the Australian trip. Barnes agreed to go.

MacLaren, who had toured Australia twice, was making the biggest selectional gamble in cricket. He was backing his judgment on one county game and his experience of facing Barnes in the nets.

MacLaren was criticised. He had failed to win back the Ashes from the Australians in 1899, which had been relinquished by England in 1897–98. The press questioned who Barnes was, beyond a league cricketer approaching 30 who had only had moderate success in half a dozen county games.

Barnes Storming

In the lead-up games to the Tests, Australian cricket followers were in no doubt about Barnes and his capacities. He took twelve for 99 against Victoria and his determined demeanour gained respect from opposition, spectators and the press. They liked his aggressive approach. He took four for 32 and one for 34 against South Australia at Adelaide, and two for 83 and three for 105 against the powerful New South Wales team. MacLaren had no hesitation in choosing Barnes for the First Test at Sydney beginning 13 December 1901, but then again he had few options. Gloucestershire's skipper, Gilbert Jessop, a fast bowler who was more renowned for his big-hitting, had played just one Test. Somerset's Len Braund, who bowled medium pace and leg-spin, and Colin 'Charlie' Blythe, a slow left-armer from Kent, were also both on debut at Brisbane. It was a thin attack. The Australians, with their powerful batting line-up – including Syd Gregory, Victor Trumper, Clem Hill, Monty Noble and Joe Darling – were confident of victory.

MacLaren won the toss, batted and scored 116, becoming the first batsman to score four centuries in Tests. England, with Tom Hayward (69) and keeper Lilley (84) also in touch, reached eight for 405. Barnes came in, scored 26 not out and added to the demoralisation of the home team. England's score was pushed up to 464.

When Australia was just 3 in reply, Barnes deceived Trumper with a slower one. The greatest batsman of the era pushed too early and sent back a return catch. Barnes took it one-handed. The casual method of the catch saw Barnes receive a reprimand from MacLaren.

'Well I caught it, didn't I?' Barnes retorted. He may have been a professional with less status than the unpaid amateurs who came from more privileged backgrounds but he would stand his ground against anyone, anywhere. MacLaren, an amateur, was one of the few men in the cricket establishment who knew how to handle this dark, brooding figure. There would be no forelock-tugging or 'sorry sir' from this straight-backed Staffordshirian.

MacLaren was jubilant to see the back of Trumper, who, with his brilliant 135 not out at Lord's in 1899, had been a key to Australia winning the Ashes 1–0. But Hill and Gregory formed a good link of 86 before Barnes was brought back into the attack. He bowled Hill for 46. Barnes and Braund rampaged on, with only Joe Darling (39), batting at number eight, resisting until Barnes induced a simple catch from him. Australia staggered to 168. Barnes took five for 65 off 39.1 overs. It was a sensational debut by an Englishman in Australia. MacLaren enforced the follow-on and a shell-shocked Australia was rolled for 172. England won by an innings and 124 runs.

There was more to come in Melbourne. There had been rain overnight and the pitch was rain-affected on Day One – New Year's Day, 1902. MacLaren won the toss again and this time sent the Australians in. Barnes stunned the big crowd by having Trumper out caught by Tyldesley for 0 off his second ball. Barnes again repeated his Brisbane act by bowling Hill, this time for 15. Australia was two for 32. It never recovered and was sent back for 112. Barnes took six for 42 off 16.1 overs bowling unchanged with Braund (four for 64) throughout the innings. But if Australia's effort was meagre, England's was wafer-thin, thanks to rangy Monty Noble who took seven for 17 with his off-spinners. The tourists could only manage 61 in 15.4 overs.

It was still only Day One when Australia batted again. The Australian skipper, Joe Darling, switched the batting order around after losing early wickets. Australia went to stumps five for 48. Twenty-five wickets had fallen in the day. Spectators weren't likely to forget the entry into the year 1902 in a hurry. On Day Two, and in better conditions, Clem Hill led a fightback with 99, while Reg Duff, batting at number 10, scored 104. Barnes was always dangerous and managed to dismiss Trumper cheaply for the third time in four innings. He finished with seven for 121 off 64 overs. Yet Australia compiled 353, giving it a lead of 404. England fell for 175 (Noble six for 60) and lost the Test by 229 runs. Both Barnes and Noble (they got on well but didn't start an American bookstore chain) took 13 wickets for the game.

Barnes had 19 wickets (at 17) for the series, but that was to be his final tally (with another 22 wickets on the first-class tour). He broke down with a knee injury at Adelaide in the Third Test and the playing side of the tour was over for him. Without him, England didn't have enough answers to Australia's long batting line-up. It lost the series 1–4. Had Barnes been fit, England would have achieved a much closer result. Instead, they lost the Ashes for the third successive series.

Yet Barnes sailed home with an enhanced reputation and an improved bowling repertoire, including an off-cutter taught to him by Monty Noble.

Barnes' knee kept him out of the 1902 Ashes until the Third Test at Bramall Lane, Sheffield, the one and only Test there. The first two Tests had been washed out. Barnes was not selected in the original XII, but when MacLaren woke to an overcast sky he made a snap decision to cable Barnes, asking him to make his way to the ground. MacLaren won the toss and sent Australia in. Just before going onto the field he informed Yorkshire fast-medium bowler Schofield Haigh he would be 12th man. But Barnes was running late. Haigh moved out onto the field with the team. Lord Hawke – who had personally picked Haigh – and his fellow selectors looked on and thought all was in order. They had no idea that Barnes had been selected and Haigh had been given drinks duties. Barnes arrived five minutes later and was immediately summoned onto the field, replacing Haigh.

This was a brave move by MacLaren, given that Haigh was in front of a home crowd and, more poignantly, that he was Hawke's choice. It was a coup, albeit a temporary and risky one. If Barnes flopped, MacLaren's leadership position would have been in jeopardy.

As soon as Barnes appeared, MacLaren threw the ball to him, thus thwarting any possible counter-move by Hawke, who was watching, flabbergasted. Once Barnes delivered a ball, there could be no doubt in the minds of the umpires or onlookers that Barnes was in the XI and not Haigh.

Barnes had only arrived just a little too late on the field to dismiss Trumper (bowled Braund for 1), who was having a bumper season. But he proceeded to dismiss Duff, Hill, Darling and Syd Gregory cheaply, leaving Australia, at one point, five for 73 and in disarray. They recovered, thanks to a brave 47 from Monty Noble, and reached 194. Barnes walked away with the handsome figures of six for 49 off 20 overs. Rarely had a player in either Australia or England made such an impact on debut. Now his home country understood the reason for the fuss over Barnes after his Australian tour. He had, inside four appearances for England, established himself as a truly great bowler against one of the best batting line-ups in the history of cricket.

Yet even he was unable to circumvent Australia winning by a healthy 143 runs, thanks to a blinding second innings start by Trumper (62) – his 50 coming up in 40 minutes, and a fine 119 by Hill. Trumper exacted some revenge for his drubbings at the hands of Barnes so far, and the big bowler took a thumping. He ended with one for 50 off 12 overs, four of them maidens, after Trumper had done his worst. Barnes was not happy, but gained no small measure of satisfaction in bowling Darling for a duck. Noble once more proved the difference in a Test result, taking five for 51 and six for 52.

Then came the shock of Lord Hawke's revenge. Barnes was dropped inexplicably from the last two Tests. Had this type of incredible and seemingly unjustified selection decision occurred in isolation and never happened before it may have caused public outcry. But English cricket was used to such moves where Lord Hawke was involved. The decision passed by with not much more than a ripple in the press. Some who a year earlier questioned Barnes' selection now queried his omission. But it was too late. Australia had won another series 2–1 – making it four Ashes victories on end. Again, had Barnes been playing, England may well have won.

Not in his League

Barnes, now 29 years old, had to make do with playing for Lancashire for 1902, and then once more in 1903. He was the first bowler in the country to take 100 wickets in 1903 and managed 131 wickets at 17 runs per wicket for the season. Many of those wickets were due to a new style of delivery dubbed 'the Barnes Ball'. It was a leg-break that swung into the batsman then cut away and lifted with some pace. By the time his county contract was over he had taken 226 wickets at 19.41. Barnes always had the league to fall back upon and this available option seemed to dictate his sometimes too-direct airing of views on and off the field. He certainly aggravated his gentlemen amateur team-mates. He was scathing about them if they didn't play hard to win, and he resented the attitude towards him when he did play hard to win, which was most of the time. His irreverent mien didn't make him popular with his fellow professionals. Paradoxically, they couldn't cope with his behaviour towards the amateurs when they themselves were being deferential and subservient to their amateur colleagues.

Barnes' independence cost him further immediate Test selection. MacLaren was no longer in charge of the national team after the loss to Australia. His place had been taken by Pelham Warner, who was under the misapprehension that Barnes could not bowl an off-break. This alleged short-coming arose from a false story propagated by *Wisden*, the establishment mouthpiece, which had never favoured Barnes and his maverick, anti-authoritarian ways. Consequently, Warner didn't campaign for him to go on the 1903–04 tour and Barnes was left out. A few days after the team was announced, Barnes met Warner in a game at Lord's. Barnes delivered three leg-breaks. His fourth ball was a beautiful off-break that bounced back

Warner's middle stump. The point was made, but too late.

Near the end of the 1903 season Barnes tried to re-negotiate his contract for 1904, asking the Lancashire county management to find him employment during the winter and also to grant him a benefit match after his eight years of service to the club. This was instead of the miserly one pound a week during the winter offered by the county. Lancashire turned down his request so Barnes departed.

England's stunning 3–2 win under Warner in 1903–04 in Australia and the triumphant bringing home of the Ashes didn't help Barnes' cause.

MacLaren tried to patch it up with Barnes early in 1904, offering the bowler the same pay as the top professionals at the club. Barnes rejected his old skipper's offer and returned to the Lancashire League. This isolated him from first-class cricket and gave those who didn't like him an excuse for not selecting him at the national level.

Barnes was left out of the entire 1905 Ashes, despite many good judges, among them the Test cricketer and writer C.B. Fry, insisting he was England's best bowler that year (and, as it turned out, in other years that followed). But England won the series 2–0 without him, so there were no press or public pleas for his return. It was no surprise to see him omitted from the 1905–06 tour of South Africa. England was thrashed 4–1 and there was good reason to urge Barnes' return for the next series in England – also against South Africa in 1907. But, despite taking a record 119 wickets at a remarkable 7.83 for Staffordshire in the minor counties in 1906, with no exposure at the top county level he was rejected once more.

S. F. BARNES

The Long Overdue Return

While England struggled to win the 1907 three-Test series
1–0, Barnes claimed 112 wickets at a staggering 3.91 play-
ing for Porthill Park in the North Staffordshire League.
This included all 10 wickets for 26 against a strong
Yorkshire Second XI at Wakefield. News reached Lord
Hawke, still the country's key selector.

Barnes had now missed Test selection for five years. He
was 34 years old, but not forgotten. He had cut a swathe
through Lancashire League teams and minor county teams,
returning amazing hauls of wickets. His enormous talent
had a mystique about it. He played to packed houses in
Lancashire but the only thing the rest of England knew
about him was regular small press items that said 'Barnes
Takes Eight', or 'Barnes Breaks Record'.

A lack of talent willing or able to tour Australia in
1907–08 caused Barnes' name to float to the surface after
too long an absence. But first, he cut a good deal for himself: a 300-pound cash payment at the end of the tour, a
first-class return ticket, thirty shillings a week for the sea
voyage and forty shillings a week expenses in Australia.
With this agreement secured he was selected for his second
tour down-under. It was a big challenge for Barnes and he
relished the thought of doing battle with Australia's outstanding batting line-up again. Only another six of the
15-man squad had been to Australia previously – Arthur
Jones, Rhodes, Braund, Frederick Fane, 'Charlie' Blythe and
Arthur Fielder.

The First Test was a thriller. Barnes contributed, without
being penetrating, yet he had the satisfaction of bowling
Trumper for just 3 and Noble for 27 in Australia's second
innings. Australia seemed beaten when eight for 219 and
still 55 short of victory when ninth-wicket pair Hazlitt and

Cotter steered their team to a two-wicket victory. The Second Test at Melbourne beginning New Year's Day 1908 belonged to Barnes for a fine all-round effort. He bowled tightly in the first innings, taking none for 30 and then took five for 72 off 27.4 overs in Australia's second innings of 397. It was his fifth five-wicket haul in just six Tests.

England was left with 282 to make for victory. Barnes came to the wicket at seven for 198 with still 84 needed. At 209, Crawford was out. Barnes was joined by Humphries of Derbyshire. They added a spirited 34. Then big Warwick Armstrong, bowling his leg-spinners, trapped Humphries lbw for 16. The score was nine for 243. Kent's Arthur Fielder, who was not a complete bunny, came to the wicket. It was a tall order for England to win, although not an impossible one, considering Barnes' run-making for Staffordshire had been commendable if unscientific. They edged the score up until Barnes hit the winning run off Armstrong, who was particularly dejected in front of his adoring home crowd. England won by one wicket and Barnes was cheered from the ground after playing a big hand in the second thriller of the series.

Australia exacted revenge with a 245-run win at Adelaide in the Third Test, but again, Barnes was not disgraced. He turned stock bowler in the face of a Clem Hill (160) and Roger Hartigan (116) 243-partnership that set Australia up. Among his six victims for the match was Trumper once again, this time bowled for a duck in Australia's second innings.

Back at the MCG for the Fourth Test, Barnes struggled, taking one wicket in each innings. Australia won easily and took back the Ashes. Barnes rallied in the dead rubber at Sydney, taking seven for 60 off 22.4 overs. His grand haul of wickets included Trumper (10), Noble (35), Hill (12), Charlie Macartney (1) and Gregory (44). Unfortunately for

England, he could not repeat his performance in Australia's second innings, and a brilliant 166 by Trumper turned the tables and set Australia up for an eventual 49-run win.

Barnes would once more sail home in a soundly beaten squad. But again he was successful with Test figures of 24 wickets at the more than respectable rate of 26.08 runs per wicket against a powerful batting side. He had now taken 50 wickets at less than 21 in just nine Tests since his debut in Sydney in 1901.

The Australians returned to England in 1909 to defend the Ashes. Lord Hawke reinstated Archie MacLaren as England's skipper, but failed to select Barnes, now 36 years of age, until the Third Test. There were rumours that Barnes was not well, having caught whooping cough from his son, but he was playing at league level. The series was 1–1, and while the horse had not bolted, Barnes' presence at Lord's, where Australia won by nine wickets, may have made a huge difference. He did make a difference in the Third Test at Headingley, and it was not his fault that England failed by 126 runs. Barnes was economical in the first innings with one for 37 off 25 overs, and devastating in the second. He took five of the first six wickets to fall, reducing Australia to seven for 127. He finished with six for 63 off 35. His bag included Trumper, Noble, Warren Bardsley and Vic Ransford. England was set 214 for victory but collapsed for just 87. Macartney returned eleven for 85 to win the game for Australia.

Relishing his return to the international arena, Barnes continued on at Old Trafford in the Fourth Test where he had left off at Headingley, taking five for 56 – this time collecting Trumper, Bardsley, Ransford and Macartney. The Fifth Test at The Oval was drawn (giving Australia the series 2–1) and Barnes was more than serviceable, taking two wickets in each innings, including Trumper (73) as they continued their decade-old arm wrestle. In just three Tests, Barnes took 17 wickets at 20. He now had 67 Test wickets at 20.73.

Australia for the Third Time

Wisden, long a detractor of Barnes, finally faced the truth about his abilities and got on the Barnes bandwagon by naming him one of its five cricketers of the year for his efforts in 1909. He declined to go on the tour of South Africa in 1909–10, but was available for the next tour of Australia in 1911–12. Only Barnes, Warner, Rhodes, Hobbs and George Gunn had toured Australia before.

Olympics boxing gold medallist Johnny Douglas led England in the First Test at Sydney, in place of Pelham Warner who was ill. Douglas immediately made his presence felt by opening the bowling himself.

Barnes objected and said: 'That's all very well Mr Douglas, but what am I 'ere for.'

The skipper ignored him. Frank Foster, also an amateur but a good pace bowler, opened at the other end. Australia, pleasantly surprised at Douglas' shunning of Barnes, managed a fair start. Trumper, coming in down the order and relieved not to face his old nemesis, was well set when Barnes was belatedly summoned to bowl. Trumper went on to his sixth century against England and his eighth in Tests. Australia reached 447. Barnes managed three for 107 from 35 overs.

England replied with 318. Then Australia placed itself in an unassailable position by scoring 308 in its second innings, after Douglas had insisted on Foster and he again using the new ball first. Barnes returned just one for 72 from 30 overs. England fought hard to reach 291 but was never going to reach the target, falling 146 short. Australian leg-spinner Dr Herbert 'Ranji' Hordern (H.V. Hordern) took twelve for 175 on Ashes debut and was the match-winner with the ball. Had Douglas given Barnes the new ball in either innings, the result would have been much closer. But it was true 'amateur hour' and England, along with a disgruntled Barnes, suffered the consequences.

Douglas read the Australian press that mocked his arrogance in making Barnes a second stringer and took part in a heated argument with his senior players over his misjudgment. Douglas was no tactical genius but got the point. He took things more seriously in the Second Test at Melbourne. After losing the toss he threw the ball to Barnes, who, despite suffering from flu, opened from the members' end. His first ball was an in-swinger that bowled Bardsley off his pads. He went on to bowl Hill with an in-swinging yorker, trap Kelleway lbw and have Armstrong caught at the wicket. The Melbourne crowd, who had long admired Barnes' fierce competitive nature, applauded him as if he were one of their own – a rare accolade for an Englishman. These four wickets fell in five overs, while a solitary run was conceded. Barnes managed alarming lift off the wicket and hit every batsman. Australia did recover to reach 184 (Barnes five for 44), but the damage was done and England cruised to an eight-wicket win.

Barnes was revved up for Adelaide after his success in Melbourne and was instrumental in helping to win this Test too, taking three for 71 and yet another 'Michelle' or 'five-for' – five for 105. He produced another match-winning effort at the return Test at the MCG, his favourite wicket-hunting ground, taking five for 74 and two for 47. Barnes, Foster (seven for 115) and Douglas (five for 46 in the second innings) combined to remove Australia twice while Hobbs (178) and Rhodes (179) set England off with an opening stand of 323. This led to a big tally – 589 – enough to win comfortably by an innings and 225 runs.

A jubilant England now led 3–1 and had won back the Ashes. They rubbed the Australians' faces in it by winning again at Sydney in the Fifth Test. (This series debacle left Australia in total disarray and culminated in a boardroom fistfight between skipper Clem Hill and selector Peter McAlister.) Barnes was again the best bowler taking seven for 162 in the match. During the match he took his hundredth wicket – Warwick Armstrong. He had taken 77 wickets in Australia in only 13 appearances.

After watching Barnes throughout the series, Warner, the captain, told Australian journalists:

'He is, on all wickets, the finest bowler in the world today – that, at all events, is the opinion of the Australians.'

Barnes sailed for home much happier than on his two previous trips. He had been the dominant bowler of the series taking 34 wickets at 22.88 (in all 101 at 21.44) and now he was returning a hero in a team that had won back the Ashes.

Home Run

Barnes was 39 when he saddled up for another minor county season, but now not even his relative obscurity outside first-class cricket prevented him from being considered for Test selection. In fact, he was going to see more Tests than ever before, three against Australia and three against South Africa in the Triangular Tournament (where Australia, England and South Africa played Tests against each other) of 1912. The first two Tests against Australia were washouts and he had little impact. But he was devastating against the South Africans, taking five for 25 and six for 85 – eleven for

110 – at Lord's; six for 52 and four for 63 at Leeds; and five for 28 and a career-best, magnificent eight for 29 at The Oval.

His performance at The Oval was noted in *Wisden*: 'Barnes surpassed himself, bowling in even more deadly form than in the previous Test matches. He broke both ways and his length was irreproachable. The South Africans thought that they had never faced bowling quite so difficult.'

Barnes could have been back in a league fixture, such were his results. His 34 wickets at 8.28 represented a return unmatched in Tests for the rest of the twentieth century. The final game at The Oval – the Third Test against the Australians – was to be the decider of the tournament. Barnes, in his final contest with the Australians, fittingly took five for 30 in Australia's first innings bowling unchanged and sending down 27 overs. His dismissals included Syd Gregory, Charlie Macartney – who played him better than any other Australian in the era – and Warren Bardsley. Barnes therefore played a key part in England's 244-run win, which gave it victory in the tournament.

Wisden, now completely won over, praised Barnes by saying that he was 'the best bowler in the world'.

Veldt Victorious

With such success behind him, Barnes agreed, on good terms, to tour South Africa in 1913–14. He revelled in the warm, dry conditions taking 125 wickets at 9.64 – 104 in the first-class games at 10.74. He found the matting wickets very much to his liking. In the first four of the five Tests he took 49 at 10.93 – a world record that has lasted into the twenty-first century. He took 17 wickets in the

Second Test at Johannesburg. His stamina, for a 40-year-old, was astounding and he seemed as fit at the end of the tour as at the start. Only one or two blemishes spoiled his tour. A single batsman, Herbie Taylor, played him with relative ease on a few occasions and frustrated Barnes to the point where he once threw the ball down in disgust. Yet Barnes still dismissed him five times in eight innings. Only once – in the first innings of the series – did Taylor take control and score a century. But two other innings of 70 and 93 had Barnes in a quandary on how to get rid of him. The world's finest bowler had not been conquered, but it must be said that he had been countered on occasions.

Barnes was told to expect a special monetary reward for his performances, but when it was not forthcoming he refused to play in the final Test at Port Elizabeth. It was an unfortunate end to his Test career but in keeping with his mercurial nature.

Wisden overlooked his minor tantrum and waxed lyrical about his tour (perhaps inadvertently coining a future pop song title in the process), by saying he was 'simply irresistible'.

Wisden showed it truly couldn't resist him by using him in its advertisements for its own brand of cricket balls. The ad ran for the next 11 years.

War and After

Barnes, at 41, was too old for active service, but would have been fitter than half those who marched off to the various war fronts. His nine-season verbal contract with Porthill Park was terminated in 1914. He had collected 893 wickets at just 5, and surprised with the bat, scoring 5625 at the fine average of 42.61. Porthill had won the North

Staffordshire League championship six times and was runner-up on the other three times during Barnes' stay. Pre-Barnes, the club had won the title only once in 15 years. Now with a wife and child to support, he had to find 'real' work. He answered a newspaper advertisement for a 'left-arm bowler' to play with Saltaire in the Bradford League. Barnes cabled the club, asking, 'Will I do?' Saltaire didn't hesitate to sign him up. The association lasted from 1915 to 1923.

Looking ahead, Barnes, despite his fitness, knew that one day his cricket earning time would end. He decided to take a trade and engaged in an apprenticeship as a sign-writer and calligraphist. Once qualified, he found work inscribing illuminated scrolls in the legal department of Staffordshire County Council, a job that lasted another fifty years. Barnes developed outstanding skill as a calligrapher. His beautifully written letters became a prized possession of any recipient.

Barnes continued to ply his other trade for the Saltaire club during the war years until 1918, taking 404 wickets at 5.17. In 1918 he took all 10 wickets in an innings against Keighley, a team that included Test players Jack Hearne and Schofield Haigh. In the same year he smashed 168, his highest score ever, against Baildon Green in a Priestley Cup match.

In post-war 1920, Barnes was invited to tour Australia. There was no doubt that he was still good enough for the highest level of cricket, yet the demands of a fourth and very long Australian tour – they lasted for nine or ten months – were too much to be away from his family. He asked that his wife and child be taken on the trip and paid for. The MCC rejected his request. Barnes, as ever, was eighty years ahead in his thinking and demands as a player. England's loss was Australia's gain. The tourists, bereft of bowlers, lost 0–5 to Warwick Armstrong's team.

Barnes was not too old at 48 to return to Test cricket at home in 1921, but his disagreement over terms for the 1920–21 tour put him out of favour with the establishment once more. It was nothing unusual for Barnes. He continued to plunder the Bradford League while Armstrong's team thrashed England 3–0. Had he played, that scoreline again could have been different. His mere presence would have sent shudders through the Australian dressing room as it had since he first appeared two decades earlier.

Barnes, at 51 in 1924, returned to Staffordshire to compete again in the Minor Counties Championship. He began where he had left off a decade earlier and took 73 wickets at 7.17. He emulated these kinds of returns, along with good service with the bat, until 1933. Then, at age 60, a phenomenal age for a fast-medium bowler, he played in only three games for Staffordshire and concentrated on his performances for league team Rawtenstall. In 1935, aged 62, he retired after 22 seasons with Staffordshire, in which he took 1441 wickets at 8.15. He kept playing league cricket on weekends until 1940, when at age 67, with war consuming the game once more, he reluctantly retired. 1939 marked the first year of the Second World War, and the first year since 1895 that he did not have a contract to play professional cricket. For 44 years of his adult and working life Barnes was proud that a team or club had been prepared to pay him to play the game he loved.

In 1957, while still working for Staffordshire County Council as a calligrapher, it was another proud moment when he presented Queen Elizabeth II with a handwritten scroll he had produced describing a visit to Stafford four hundred years earlier by Queen Elizabeth I.

Barnes, by all accounts, mellowed in his old age, and was chuffed to learn in 1963 that esteemed English cricket writer Neville Cardus had selected him as one of 'six giants of the Wisden century', to mark 100 years of the publication. The other five cricketing greats were W.G. Grace, Bradman, Hobbs, Trumper and England fast bowler Tom Richardson.

Thirty-seven years later, Bradman revealed to me that Barnes had a place in his best England team of all time. Barnes' record speaks for itself. He took 189 Test wickets in only 27 Tests at 16.43, while making 242 runs at 8.06. In first-class cricket Barnes took 719 wickets at 17.09, and made 1573 runs at 12.78. Whether opening the bowling with Fred Trueman or first change, Sydney Francis Barnes would be a dominating force in any era. The weight of his record compelled Bradman to select him, despite never seeing him bowl a ball. 'I regret never facing him,' Bradman told me, 'even in 1930 when the press tried to force an encounter between us. I'm sure aged 50-plus he would still have been a challenge.'

CHAPTER 23

THE MAN WITH NO BREAKING POINT

HEDLEY
VERITY

(England)

18 May 1905–31 July 1943

'His ideal physique and his lovely,
economical, lazy run-up, were coordinated
to put him in a perfect delivery position
with a superb command of length and
direction.'

DON BRADMAN

D on Bradman was in terrific touch as he thrashed
three successive fours off England's slow left-arm
spinner, Hedley Verity, in his first over during
Australia's first innings of the 1934 Lord's Second Test. It
was 23 June, and a sunny Saturday. Australia, one up in the
series, reached one for 141 chasing England's 440. With
Bradman in such murderous touch in partnership with a set
Bill Brown, Australia looked likely to lead on the first
innings. Bradman had started the series poorly at
Nottingham scoring just 29 and 25. His steel-trap mind
was programmed to concentrate as only he could do for a
big score – something in the order of his last effort at Lord's
in the Second Test in 1930 when he made 254. Australian
skipper, Bill Woodfull, who had been dismissed for 22, was
in the dressing room fretting about Bradman's 'terrible
power and splendour', as writer Neville Cardus described it.
Woodfull was remembering Verity's dismissal of Bradman
at the notorious Adelaide Test in the 1932–33 Bodyline
series. It was in that Adelaide Test that Bradman, in a
similar mindset of unrelenting aggression and brilliance,
had seen off Harold Larwood and had celebrated by hitting
Verity for six. Bradman was going for another boundary

when he was caught-and-bowled for 66, just when an innings of 266 from him was needed. Woodfull was at the other end when it happened and annoyed at Bradman's rush of blood. Woodfull thought that it cost Australia a Test and never forgave his charge for it. Now he was having nervous premonitions of Bradman, who had already hit seven fours in an innings of 36, being again impetuous against Verity and getting himself out. He sent a message out to Bradman, imploring him to be less aggressive.

'He [Woodfull] thought I was going to throw my wicket away,' Bradman said, 'and I was under instructions to "calm down". It threw my concentration. The very next ball I restrained myself when my natural inclination was to keep attacking. In so doing, I checked a shot against my better judgment and was caught-and-bowled.'

Australia still had most of a final session to play in the sun on Saturday. Bradman felt that had he been allowed free rein, Australia would have saved the follow-on by reaching 290, despite the storm that hit London on the rest day, Sunday, and the subsequent rain into Monday morning. Bradman's disgruntlement had some merit, but it was merely conjecture. The scoreboard showed the hard fact that Verity had removed him again at a critical point in a Test. Australia was two for 192 at stumps on Day Two.

At the team's London hotel Verity awoke on Monday morning and was delighted when he looked through his window onto the street. It was bleak and damp, just the way he loved it. The pitch would be wet after being left uncovered (as they were then). He drove team-mate Charlie Barnett to Lord's at St John's Wood for the game and, on the way, had the misfortune to run over and kill a black cat. To Barnett's amazement, Verity parked the car and went knocking on doors on both sides of the street until he found the cat's owner and apologised.

'A couple of people recognised Hedley,' Barnett recalled, 'and they were stunned that a famous English cricketer should be so concerned moments before he was due at Lord's. But it was typical Hedley. He was humane and humble to the bootstraps.'

That dead black puss was an omen, not for Verity, but for the Australians. He was so confident of the conditions he was about to bowl in that he could let himself be distracted in such a bizarre way, moments before a big occasion.

When play resumed under overcast skies, Bill Bowes removed Bill Brown, caught at the wicket for 105 with the score at 203. Then Verity continued the rot by having the dangerous Stan McCabe (34) caught by Hammond at slip. Australia was four for 205. Len Darling didn't last long. He was caught by Sutcliffe off Verity for a duck. Five for 204. Australia, still 86 short of avoiding the follow-on, was in trouble. Verity picked up steady wickets to render Australia all out for 284 — seven runs short of the follow-on. Bradman's dismissal the day before now seemed like the game's turning point. Verity's figures were 36 overs, 15 maidens, seven wickets for 61 runs. He was known in England as a master of the sticky, or near-sticky, wicket. Debate ensued about how bad the Lord's wicket was, an indication that Verity conjured problems for the batsmen by playing mind games with them by using calibrated changes in pace, spin and direction, along with adjustments in the field. Verity played on the fact that most batsmen thought he was easy to hit because he was a slow bowler. He left gaps in the field, inviting them to take him on. The great and the not-so-great fell for this more often than not, and Verity walked away with wickets by the bucketful in first-class cricket.

Now, at Lord's at age 29 and near his peak, Verity had demonstrated his subtle skills against top international opposition. England skipper Bob Wyatt enforced the follow-on. Australia began its second innings just before 3 p.m. It soon lost Brown, caught for 2. In came Bradman at two for 43. Subdued again by his skipper, the state of the game and the wicket, Bradman was cautious. He took 30 minutes to score 13. He became restless. Verity cunningly left cover open and the deep behind it unoccupied. Bradman took the bait, jumped down the wicket and mishit. The ball flew very high, straight above the wicket. Seven players could have taken it. Bradman stepped aside. Keeper Les Ames moved under the ball and caught it. The Englishmen, particularly the old guard led by Hammond, were delighted. Bradman always stood between England and victory. Now it was victory and much sooner than anyone dared contemplate. By 6 p.m. Verity had obliterated the Australians (all out 118), taking eight for 43 off 22.3 overs with eight maidens. England had won an Ashes Test at Lord's (by an innings and 38) for the first time since 1896. Verity had taken fourteen for 80 on that historic third day, including six of them in the last hour. Later, when asked about the highlight of his fifteen for 104 match achievement, then the best for England against Australia, he had no hesitation in saying: 'Dismissing Don Bradman twice in the one match, of course.'

This performance was the best in Verity's career.

Verity versus Bradman

Bradman's selection of Verity in his ideal of the best-ever England team had much to do with his own experience of facing him. He made the observation: 'I could never claim to have completely fathomed Hedley's strategy, for it was never static or mechanical.'

Verity, Bradman added, 'did not have a breaking point' like other great bowlers had. This meant, no matter how much punishment Verity took, he still came back with line and length. His left-arm spinners were always a threat. The Don could not break him. In the mind games of cricket, where dominance of one champion over another is paramount, the world's greatest batsman ever was never confident that he had the Yorkshireman's measure. No finer compliment could ever have been paid to a bowler.

Verity delivered more balls in Tests to Bradman – 932 – than any other bowler. Bradman scored 401 runs against him. Verity dismissed him more times than any other Englishman ever had – 10 times in first-class cricket, including eight in Tests. Verity bowled to Bradman 28 times in 16 Tests and Bradman averaged 87.88 in these innings. Verity's nearest English rival in confrontations with Bradman was Alec Bedser, who got the Don eight times, including six times in Tests. Harold Larwood dismissed Bradman seven times, including five in Tests, as did Maurice Tate. Bill Bowes removed him five times, all in Tests.

Hedley from Headingley

Hedley Verity was born at Headingley, a boundary throw from the famous Leeds Test ground, a fact that had an influence on his early years. It may even have begun to leave the vaguest imprints on the mind of Hedley, less than two months after he was born, when an Ashes Test was played in 1905. There was a bustle about the house when Hedley senior took time away from his coal merchant business to watch an Ashes session here or there, slipping home for lunch and a cuppa at tea-time. The players causing the intermittent roar from the ground in that Third Test of the 1905 Ashes included Tom Hayward, C.B. Fry, Johnny Tyldesley, Bernard Bosanquet, Charlie Blythe and Yorkshire legend, George Hirst. For Australia, there were also well-known names such as Victor Trumper, Clem Hill, Warwick Armstrong, Monty Noble and Joe Darling.

Like most fathers in Leeds, Hedley senior would have had dreams of his son playing for Yorkshire. He was the average weekend cricketer who played for fun, without any particular ambition but to enjoy himself. Yet he guided Hedley junior with the intention of seeing him do better than himself. The boy was like his father, except for one hidden trait that came from his tiny mother, Edith: an unbending determination that was to be the feature of his career with the ball.

The first illumination of where this innate steel might be directed came from his sheer enjoyment at being taken to the Headingley ground at age eight to watch Yorkshire play. Verity was a left-armer. It was not surprising that those bowlers of the same persuasion, medium-fast, George Hirst and spinner Wilfred Rhodes, became his heroes. He saw as much big cricket as he could, often going on his own to games at Bradford and Scarborough. By age 14 his infatuation even extended to playing truant to see Yorkshire's Second XI when it performed near his school. This led to his headmaster banning him from involvement in any sport for the school, but this only led Hedley into playing for the Rawdon Second XI, instead of his school's team. When promoted as a replacement into the Firsts he took seven for 38 and made 47. Hedley senior was pleased, but concerned that his son, who had followed him into his coal business after finishing school, should have a profession. Hedley senior chose accounting for him. Despite an aptitude for figures, it was not an alluring enough occupation for Verity. He preferred creating figures on a cricket field. The game consumed him. He had the courage to tell his father he wanted to play professional cricket for Yorkshire as a medium-pace bowler cum batsman.

Verity senior believed his shy son would make it as a professional cricketer. He decided to back his decision to try, as did the feisty Edith. But young Hedley found that not everyone shared his parents' helpful optimism.

Hedley senior was concerned that he didn't have any influence at Yorkshire but by giving his son employment in his coal business he was offering much that facilitated young Hedley's cricketing skills. Verity worked hard in the office and at labouring tasks. This built strong legs and back, which were imperative for success at the crease. The job also provided security and time off for cricket practice. The boy was not made to feel that he either had to work or play cricket. He had a job and the accompanying security of employment until, if ever, he was capped at Yorkshire.

At 16, Verity began regular strong performances for Rawdon and gained press attention in the *Leeds Mercury* and the *Yorkshire Post*. This encouraged him. He felt that he might just realise his dream. But there followed another two years of uninspiring apprenticeship at Rawdon until 1923, when he was 18. At 19, when he thought he had reached a dead end, he switched to the Horsforth Hall Park team. Verity worked hard on his batting and claimed all-roundership at the age of 21 in 1926 when he scored 488 runs at an average of 30, and took 62 wickets at just nine apiece. He had done just enough with his medium-pace seamers to earn a place in Yorkshire's summer trial games under the watchful eye of his longtime hero, George Hirst. The legend praised him, but did not think enough of him to recommend him to a Yorkshire League team. Instead, he introduced Verity to Accrington in the Lancashire League, a

fine enough club in need of a good coach. The move was a
blow to his Yorkshire pride. But he knuckled down on his
eight pounds a week, worked at his professionalism and
coaching, and let it be known, albeit quietly, that his aim
would always be a Yorkshire cap. Many doubted he would
make it, despite his development with the bat, especially
with players such as the ageing Wilfred Rhodes holding
down the only spot that Verity could ever wish to take. The
first year at Accrington was not an outstanding one for him.
There were mutterings at the club, especially among the
older players, that the 21-year-old was not up to coaching.
Yet the club was prepared to keep him, on its terms, which
included not releasing him if Yorkshire picked him for
County Championship matches. Verity couldn't agree to
these terms. In 1928 he ditched Accrington for Middleton
in the Central Lancashire League for just five pounds a
week, but with a clause in his agreement that indicated he
would be released to play for Yorkshire, if chosen.

Yorkshire's Hirst and Rhodes advised him to turn his
attention to spin because of the plethora of seamers in the
county. Rhodes would retire sooner rather than later. There
would be a vacancy for a left-arm spinner. Verity didn't need
to be told twice. He recognised his main chance and became
a spinner. In this 1928 season he tried out at Edgbaston for
Warwickshire on invitation, but on a hard wicket failed to
impress and was rejected. His spinners were not turning
enough. It was a minor setback and, anyway, his heart was
set on Yorkshire. Verity worked at his craft, learning about
drift, spin, variation in flight and other intricacies of the
spinner's art.

In 1929, he reached a crossroad in his life and career. East
Lancashire club was offering him up to 20 pounds a week to
return to the Lancashire League. He was 24. He had been
married less than a year to a Headingley girl, Kathleen

Metcalfe, and was looking for more security. (They had two sons, Wilfred and Douglas.) But support from friends and mentors, including his father, bolstered him. They urged him to hang out for the main chance with Yorkshire. Verity rejected the league offer. In 1930 he returned to Headingley to take one last stab at establishing himself at Yorkshire.

The Break

1930 was Hedley Verity's make-or-break year. After a decade of toil, buffeting from league to league, pay cuts, self-doubt, and development, he now had his chance with the proposed retirement of Wilfred Rhodes who was 52. It was to be Rhodes' last season and he would play in about half the championship matches. Verity's first game was against Sussex. His first wicket was that of Test all-rounder Maurice Tate, caught in the deep by Arthur Mitchell. Verity took three for 96 and went on to play 12 games for Yorkshire in the season, taking 64 wickets at a cost of 12.42, including nine for 60 in an innings against Glamorgan. Wet tracks helped, but did not detract from his place right on top of the national averages. Verity was still a long way behind Kent's leg-spinner Tich Freeman (252 wickets) in terms of numbers. But it was still a fabulous place to be, especially as the batsman on top of the batting averages in 1930 was 21-year-old Don Bradman with 2960 runs at 98.66. Bradman and Verity never played against each other in 1930. Rhodes was not going to miss playing for Yorkshire against the Australians – twice – in his final season. This probably worked in Verity's favour, given that he would acquire more know-how against a big array of first-class cricketers before he had his first crack at the Don, Stan McCabe, Ponsford and co. The year also marked the start of a mightily productive association with speedster Bill Bowes (76 wickets at 18.16) that would continue for the rest of the decade.

After wallowing as a hopeful across the Pennines, Verity could not have wished for a more meteoric rise inside a season, except to be picked for England. If he continued at the rate he started though, selection for England would be forthcoming too. But his feet were kept on the ground by his father and Verity's Yorkshire mentors. They criticised him – constructively – especially when he did well, yet not when he was down. Verity was told, for instance, to vary his length for his different types of deliveries. His skills were now being honed in more exacting company. He could spin the ball away from the batsman or swing it in, all with little clue from his action, making him very hard to pick.

The tall (more than 6 ft), lean and fit Verity cut a swathe through the counties in 1931 as he established himself as one of the country's finest bowlers. His quiet dignity (even his appeals were hushed affairs) impressed everyone. He gained wide respect for his capacity for the kill. In the opening five county matches he took 35 wickets. Still uncapped – the only player in the Yorkshire team without a 'cap' – he took ten for 36 on 18 May, his twenty-sixth birthday, in a game at Headingley against Warwickshire. This was the club that three years earlier had taken one look at him bowling in the nets and had insulted him by telling him to not bother about having a hit. If he felt he'd avenged this slight it was not apparent. Verity was just so satisfied to have fulfilled his 10-year-old dream of playing regularly as a professional for Yorkshire, that little else in his working life mattered. Perhaps it would only be playing for his country that could mean as much to him.

A few days after his triumph against Warwickshire, he played in his first traditional Roses match (Yorkshire versus

Lancashire) at Old Trafford. He took five for 54 off 28 overs – and would take another 84 wickets in these fiercely fought contests over the rest of the 1930s.

Verity was capped for Yorkshire in mid-June in the proudest moment of his career to that date. He secured the honour in a year in which he had dismissed more than 100 wickets at about 13 runs each. He now had a retainer.

Verity's next significant achievement was to take 11 New Zealand wickets for Yorkshire at Harrogate. This, and his effort against Warwickshire, saw him chosen for his initial Test for England, versus New Zealand at The Oval. He was given a 20-pound match fee.

England made four for 416 declared and New Zealand was bundled out for 193 and 197. Verity performed steadily, taking two for 52 and two for 33. He was on his way, at the very highest level of the game. He was chosen again for the final Test of the three-match series at Old Trafford. However, it was washed out, without him getting a bat or bowl.

Verity took more wickets than anyone else in 1931 – 188 at 13.52. Only Nottingham and England champion speed merchant Harold Larwood with 129 wickets at 12.03 had a better average. Verity and Bowes were instrumental in winning the championship for Yorkshire (this season and for several others to come in a decade of dominance for the county). No longer did observers suggest that Rhodes' shoes were too big for the younger man. Verity was already bracketed with that brilliant performer. Some even suggested he was better. All of this within two amazing seasons. But Hedley kept his head, thanks to his strong family values and some honest criticism. His stern yet proud father, however, was not above honest praise. He once said that in Hedley junior had been 'born a better man than myself'. It was a proud admission that not every father would make.

Opponents in first-class cricket learned about his undemonstrative determination and his competitive cunning, while county team-mates got to appreciate his patience and a few of his quirks. He couldn't be cajoled into big performances. He had to be warned that his task in dismissing a team was impossible. Then he lifted. It was as if he would not give everything to a cause unless the challenge was worthy of him. And there were plenty of challenges to come.

Wisden set the right tone for Verity by naming him one of its five cricketers of the year (1931) along with Bowes.

In 1932, he tussled again for the top county bowling spot with Larwood (162 at 12.86), taking 162 wickets at 13.88. Verity took another bag of 10, this time against Nottinghamshire, for just 10 runs. The location was Headingley, the date 12 July. It was a world record in first-class cricket. He took seven wickets in 15 deliveries, secured one hat trick and just missed another. Verity was aided by a wet wicket drying out in the sun – the classic sticky, which allowed him to spin the ball quickly. In 65 minutes he controlled his spin and length to remove 10 batsmen, all of whom had scored a first-class century. Most played back. The right-handers all had trouble with the ball that pitched on leg, or middle and leg, and moved away. Eight batsmen were caught, one was trapped lbw and the other was stumped, which was the identical breakdown of Verity's 10 dismissals against Warwickshire in 1931.

While the Notts batsmen were perplexed and blamed the wicket, Yorkshire openers Herbert Sutcliffe and Percy Holmes, in just over 90 minutes, polished off the 139 runs needed for victory in the county's second innings. The wicket gave them no problems. Verity believed it would help him. He was galvanised by Yorkshire captain Brian Sellers who told him that victory depended on him. The

Notts batsmen were bluffed before they took block, especially knowing Verity's reputation on wet wickets. This had been magnified by his 10-wicket haul in similar conditions a season before, and his outstanding form through the wet months of May, June and the early days of July.

Verity's aim, as the season progressed, was to impress selectors enough to be chosen for the tour of Australia in 1932–33. After his demolition of Nottingham his selection was ensured, no matter what the MCC and its proposed skipper, Douglas Jardine, were cooking up to counter Bradman.

Bodyline Bounty

Verity was never central to Jardine's thinking on how to defeat Bradman. The England captain had Harold Larwood and Bill Voce, the Nottingham pair of speedsters, as his main strike weapons. They would employ fast leg theory – deliveries on or about leg-stump directed at the batsman's body, chest and head, with a cluster of leg-side catchers. It would be more of a shock than a stock tactic. In Jardine's mind, the other bowlers – Bill Bowes, Wally Hammond, Hedley Verity and Maurice Tate – were bit players in the Bodyline strategy. Fast bowler Gubby Allen was an important player, but not part of the main plan. He refused to bowl Bodyline and expressed his view of it in no uncertain terms to his skipper. Jardine accepted his criticism but it didn't change his mind. Larwood and Voce were the keys to his plan. They were only too willing to carry it out. Both had experienced the power of Bradman's performances in 1930 in England. Larwood, in particular, would not have toured had he not had a tactic with which to tackle Bradman. Larwood did not want a repeat of his shellacking by Bradman in England in 1930, when he took four wickets in three Tests at 73.00 runs per wicket, nor his figures (18 wickets at 40.22 in five Tests) on his last tour of Australia in 1928–29, when Bradman was a novice. Rather than as a strike bowler, Verity was to be the spinner in the mix, used to steady an end, unless the weather provided a wet wicket. Verity had no trouble with this. He was pleased to be a part of the campaign to bring back the Ashes and honoured to have even a supporting role in Jardine's grand plan. He had enormous respect for the iron-fisted skipper, as did all the squad, even Allen.

Jardine, shrewdly, did not play Larwood or Voce in the first game of the tour at Perth against an Australian XI, which included Bradman. MCC totted up 583. Australia was none for 59 at stumps on Day Two. Overnight rain created a wicket that would dry out to Verity's liking. He dismissed Jack Fingleton (29) in his first over. This brought Bradman to the wicket to prolonged cheering. Many in the 19,970-strong crowd – a huge turn-out for Perth – had come from remote parts of the Western Australian bush to see Bradman on one of his rare forays west. He was on 3 when Verity got one to spin sharply away. Bradman edged it short of the slips. Hammond, diving forward, got his fingers under it. The crowd was stunned. Bradman trotted back to the pavilion as an elated English group gathered around Verity, who allowed himself a fleeting smile. In his first-ever encounter with Bradman he had dismissed him cheaply. It gave him, and the fielders, extra pep in their steps. Verity went on to take seven for 37 in the XI's all-out 159. Australia followed on and scored four for 139, Bradman making just 10 – dismissed for the second time in a day, this time by Gubby Allen, who had him caught. The match was dominated by the second-wicket 283-run partnership between Herbert Sutcliffe (169) and the Nawab of Pataudi (129), and Verity's brilliant bowling.

Jardine was delighted. Bradman's double failure and the Verity wild card had been unexpected. The England skipper still had his Bodyline card to play. The initial success and Bradman's demeanour – he looked ill and out-of-sorts – caused Jardine to consider using it earlier, in games leading up to the Tests. He had the psychological advantage and wanted to keep it running until the First Test.

The team took the 3700-km, three-day train ride from Perth to Adelaide for the game against South Australia. MCC batted first again and amassed nine for 634. Verity dominated again in hot conditions, taking five for 42 in the second innings. The Australian press now began to look more closely at him. His brief history in first-class cricket – two-and-a-half seasons – was given publicity, especially his two 10-wicket hauls. He, not Larwood, who had yet to be prominent on the tour, was billed early as the bogeyman for Australian batsmen. Jardine kept this publicity running by telling journalists that the faster Australian wickets gave Verity a margin of 10 feet in which to vary the length of his deliveries rather than the five feet it took in England. Jardine made reference to John White (who followed Wilfred Rhodes and preceded Verity as a top-class slow left-armer), and his success on the 1928–29 Ashes tour in Australia suggesting that Verity would be even better than him. White was then the best of England's bowlers in the Tests, taking 25 wickets at 30.40. It was all distractingly useful propaganda for Jardine's cause.

He omitted himself and Verity from the game in Melbourne in mid-November against another 'Australian XI', again including Bradman. It was played in front of record crowds for a game that was not a Test. Larwood played. Acting skipper Bob Wyatt was instructed to let Larwood use Bodyline, if the occasion demanded it. MCC batted first and made 282. Bradman came in after Woodfull was dismissed for 18 and proceeded to attack. His shots were a strange mix of the rash and the brilliant, much to the crowd's pleasure. Larwood, sensing a repeat of his thrashings by Bradman on all of their previous encounters, could not resist the temptation to test the new adaptation of leg theory. He asked Wyatt if he could have the required field – the cluster of catchers on the leg-side. Bradman received several short balls at his head and ribcage. He counter-attacked, but was forced onto the back foot. A good length ball from Larwood trapped him lbw. The ball was going down leg and the dismissal a poor decision.

Verity, watching from the pavilion, thought Bradman seemed 'rattled'.

Jardine, who had gone fishing in northern Victoria, was told about the strike by phone. He told Wyatt to instruct Larwood to let loose with Bodyline again in the second innings. This time Bradman was bowled for 13. England's psychological grip on the Ashes tightened, even before a ball was delivered. First, Verity, a surprise packet, had created uncertainty. Now Larwood had confirmed it.

The weight of Verity's wicket-taking forced him into the First Test at Sydney, but he was only given 13 overs in Australia's first innings (none for 35), and just four in the second (none for 15). England, with Larwood (who had match figures of ten for 124) supreme, won by 10 wickets. Jardine dumped Verity for the Melbourne Second Test and brought in Bowes to give England an all-pace attack of Larwood, Voce, Bowes, Allen and Hammond. This was in expectation of Bradman's return after illness, but the Don countered Bodyline with some special tactics of his own and made a fine unbeaten 103. This, along with outstanding bowling from O'Reilly (match figures ten for 129) spoilt Jardine's plan. Australia won by 111 runs. The series was 1–1.

Jardine dumped Bowes and brought back Verity for the Third Test at Adelaide, which began in the heat of mid-January 1933. He was again used as a change or stock bowler for the main strike bowlers in this game: Larwood, using Bodyline, and Allen. Verity took none for 31, and with no wickets in three innings and the series half over, he needed to do something spectacular or expect to be dropped again. In Australia's second innings Bradman was in a belligerent, if erratic, mood. He saw off Larwood, Allen and Voce as he and Woodfull chased 532 for victory. Jardine was running out of options. He brought on Verity. At last the left-armer would confront Bradman in a Test.

Bradman relished facing spin. He swept past 50 with two terrific pulls for four and then pushed to 60 in just over an hour at the wicket. Bradman was alight. Verity pitched up. Bradman danced down to him and hoisted him over mid-on for six. This was a rare event, in fact, Bradman's first six in an Ashes Test. Verity dropped the next one a few inches shorter. Bradman danced again and smashed back a caught-and-bowled. Verity swallowed it. Jardine clapped his hands and patted Verity on the back as the England team crowded around him. Bradman was out for 66 and Australia's chances went with him. England won by 338 runs.

Verity batted sensibly and straight in his two innings, making 45 and 40 batting at nine and eight. He took just one wicket for 26, but because the victim was Bradman, Jardine retained him for the Fourth Test at Brisbane. He was again a stock bowler in Australia's first innings, taking none for 39 off an economical 27 overs with 12 maidens. He was able to bottle up one end, thus causing frustration for the batsmen against the strike bowlers. Several Australians were out to injudicious shots. In the second innings Verity was more effective, removing Vic Richardson and McCabe.

His figures were two for 30 off 19 overs with six maidens. Verity again batted well, making 23 not out in his only knock.

England won by six wickets, giving it a 3–1 unassailable lead in the series.

Verity was selected again for the final Test at Sydney. The wicket offered more for the spinners as the game progressed. Verity took three for 62 in Australia's first innings, including the wickets of McCabe and Len Darling. He came into his own in Australia's second innings, taking five for 33 off 19 overs, in a performance that was both economical and penetrating. He removed Bradman (71) again when he was set and had seen off the pacemen, this time sending down a faster swinging yorker that got under the Don's bat and bowled him. Verity's match figures of eight for 95 were the best for the game. England won by eight wickets and took the series 4–1.

Jardine's brutal but effective and expertly executed tactics had worked like no other campaign in Australia. Verity with 11 wickets at 24.64 and 114 runs at an average of 28.50 had played his part behind the main executors of the strategy against Australia. He topped the tour bowling averages with 44 wickets at 15.86, proving that he was almost as effective on Australia's hard first-class wickets as on England's softer ones. He was also useful with the bat, scoring 300 runs at 21.42.

Bigger and Better

Verity returned to England a hero and fought for his position in the England team in a three-Test series in 1933 against the West Indies, taking seven wickets at 21 in two Tests, with a best innings return of four for 45 at Lord's.

This was in the middle of a bumper first-class season in which he took 190 wickets at 13.43, making him the most successful bowler in the country. He consolidated his Test spot with a strong tour of India (the first by England) in 1933–34, in which he took 23 wickets at 16.82. In the Third Test at Madras in February 1934, he snared seven for 49 off 23.5 overs and then backed this up with four for 104 in the second innings of an England win. Jardine, leading England for the last time, was more than pleased with Verity's performances. He labelled him a 'match-winner' and predicted he would continue to be just as effective at Test level for England as he had been for Yorkshire in the County Championship. Verity was the dominant bowler for the tour, taking 72 wickets at 15.54.

His form continued into the 1934 season at home for Yorkshire and for his first Ashes series at home. He took 150 wickets in first-class cricket at 17.63, which placed him third in the County Championship bowling, just behind slow left-armer George Paine of Warwickshire (156 at 17.07) and old rival Larwood (82 at 17.25).

Verity revelled in his first Ashes series at home and continued his tussle with Bradman. After his 15-wicket triumph at Lord's and his nailing of the world's greatest batsman twice in the match, he discovered for himself in a five-week blitz why and how Bradman had gained his formidable reputation. This discovery began at Bramall Lane, Sheffield in mid-July. Bradman returned to form against Yorkshire after a run of 'outs' that had seen his average for the season at 53.05 – just over half his normal performance level. He didn't shovel, defend or feel his way out of the slump in performance, but hammered free with a blistering 140 in two hours – or the equivalent of one session. Verity, Bowes and a Test-standard Yorkshire bowling line-up were left gasping. Bradman was intent on getting on top by an all-out attack. Verity, with none for 33 off six overs, was blasted out of the firing line.

'I've never seen hitting like that,' Verity said after the game. 'Every shot, every aspect of the batsman's art was on display. Power was on equal terms with a master's technique.'

Less than a week later, Verity and all of the English bowlers suffered at the 1934 Headingley Test as Bradman continued the form he displayed at Bramall Lane with a magnificent 304 in 430 minutes with two sixes and 43 fours. Verity, with three for 113 off 46.5 overs, was England's most economical bowler in the onslaught, as Australia compiled 584. Rain saved England from certain defeat on the final day.

A month later, at The Oval in the Fifth Test, Bradman was once more in murderous form as he obliterated England with 244 in 316 minutes in the first innings in partnership with Bill Ponsford (266). This pair put on 451 in 316 minutes. Verity's none for 123 off 43 overs in that innings, and none for 43 in the second, produced his worst figures for a Test. Australia won by a massive 562 runs and took back the Ashes which had been so rudely grabbed from them during the Bodyline series. It was Verity's first feeling of a Test-series loss. It was a hard lesson, but when the dust had settled after the series, his figures still read 24 wickets at 24.00.

There was one more heavyweight contest for the season – at Scarborough in the 'Mr H.D.G. Leveson-Gower's XI versus Australians' match. It was billed as a festival match, but England selected a Test-standard team. Australia responded with their big guns, including Bradman. He crunched 132 before lunch, his innings lasting just 88 minutes. Verity incurred the wrath of his blade for the fourth successive match. Bradman had amassed 897 runs in those four games, but Verity gained some measure of satisfaction by having him stumped by former Test keeper George Duckworth. Verity had so far broken fairly evenly with Bradman in their encounters, taking into account the Bodyline series.

Wicket-Taking Wizard

Life, and cricket, went on. Verity, at 30, had matured as a spinner. After experiencing Bradman, no batsman in 1935 was as difficult. Verity became a wicket-snaring machine, taking his best first-class haul yet of 211 wickets at 14.36. This analysis included 12 wickets at 20.83 against South Africa in four Tests. No one in the county competition came near him. No batsman, however grand, felt 'in' when he was bowling. Verity's leap in effectiveness was displayed in his figures. He bowled less overs than in the 1934 season and took 61 more wickets. The devouring of batsmen rolled on for him into 1936 when he went five better and took 216 wickets at 13.18. Fifteen of these (at 15.20) were in three Tests against India in England. Only Larwood (119 at 12.97) returned a better average in his final first-class season.

Verity had now established himself as the most prolific English bowler of the 1930s, and ranked with Larwood as the country's most effective performer with the ball. Every so often he proved he was no batting bunny with a fine Test innings. In 1936, against India, he was unconquered on 66 at Old Trafford in the Second Test, a draw, which topped his 60 not out at the same ground in the Third Test of the 1934 Ashes series.

Verity toured Australia under Gubby Allen in 1936–37 in a season that he would rather forget. He took just 10 Test wickets at 45.50 and again suffered the unforgiving force of Bradman's bat as he ended the season with 270, 212 and 169 to win the series for Australia. Yet there were still some highs for Verity in that losing campaign. He dismissed Bradman twice (for 13 and 270) in a Test for a second time – at Melbourne in the Third Test. England's openers had trouble forming a partnership and in the Fourth Test Allen tried Verity with Charlie Barnett, his good friend. They put on 53 and 45 together, the best opening stands for England in the series. Observers dubbed Verity a poor man's Herbert Sutcliffe which was a fair compliment, given Sutcliffe's record. This was testimony to Verity's fighting spirit. No challenge was ever too big.

Verity's relative failure didn't upset his equilibrium in the 1937 County Championship. He returned to England as strong as ever, taking 202 wickets at 15.67 and improved his Ashes rating in 1938, taking 14 wickets at 25.29 in a drawn series. He maintained his first-class season rate of 15.67 runs per wicket, taking 158 wickets, and rolled on into the 1938–39 series in South Africa. Verity was consistent in the Tests, taking wickets in all five matches for a series return of 19 wickets at 29.05, which topped the averages.

For Yorkshire, King and Country

In his final season of 1939, at age 34, Verity took 191 wickets at 13.13. He was at his peak. In a quaint symmetry he headed the English averages as he had done in 1930 – his first season. He finished on a magnificent note, against Sussex at Hove, taking seven for 9 off just six overs on a sticky that was drying out.

Verity took 1956 first-class wickets at 14.90 and made

5605 runs at 18.08, with one century. In each of his nine full English seasons, Verity took at least 150 wickets. He averaged 185 wickets a season and three times topped 200 wickets to equal a record set by Wilfred Rhodes.

Verity's huge hauls of wickets occurred frequently. His best haul was seventeen for 91 for Yorkshire versus Essex at Leyton in 1933. He took 15 wickets four times, including the 1934 Lord's Test; 14 wickets six times; 13 wickets seven times; 12 wickets seven times; and 11 wickets 14 times. His single-innings' efforts were also notable: 10 wickets twice; nine wickets seven times; eight wickets 13 times; and seven wickets an incredible 34 times.

In 40 Tests he took 144 wickets at 24.37 and made 669 runs at 20.90.

Bradman had Verity in mind when he was formulating his best-ever combinations. In his book *The Art of Cricket*, a left-arm orthodox bowler of the Verity variety took up the spinner's spot in his ideal XI on paper. The extent to which Verity demonstrated his gifts influenced Bradman's assessments of the perfect players for his ideal England Ashes team.

Verity joined up to fight during the Second World War as a captain in the Green Howards and died as a POW in Italy after being wounded in a British 8th Army attack in Sicily. His last recorded words to his company were 'keep going'. This was characteristic of his courage and selflessness. As Bradman observed, Hedley Verity had no breaking point.

CHAPTER 24

ENGLAND'S GLADIATOR

IAN
BOTHAM

(England)

24 November 1955–

'He was England's best all-rounder of the twentieth century'

DON BRADMAN

Ian Botham approached the wicket in a relaxed mood with England five for 105. It was half an hour after lunch on Day Three of the Third Test of the 1981 Ashes series at Headingley, Leeds. England was all but beaten. Australia had made nine for 401 declared. England had made 174 in the first innings and was following on towards defeat. Botham had returned to form in this game with six for 95 and a blistering 50 in 54 minutes after a miserable start to the series. This, in addition to the fact that he had been relieved of the England captaincy after not recording a win in 12 games as leader, had unburdened the strongly built, 186 cm (6 ft 1 in), 15 stone (100 kg) all-rounder. He was resigned to defeat but would go down fighting. Botham began with a couple of slogs to the boundary. A cautionary comment by English umpire Barry Meyer, who indignantly asked him if he was going to play himself in, caused Botham to settle in with a touch more discretion. He was doing his bit, but England crumbled to seven for 135 – still 92 runs from making Australia bat again. If England lost it would put them down 0–2 with three Tests to play in the six-Test series. Botham continued to restrain himself until tea when he was 39 not out in 87 minutes. His partner, Graham Dilley, had been the more attacking of the two. After tea, they both decided that there was no point in trying to defend. They would have a bit of fun. Botham led the way with an assault on all the Australian bowlers – Dennis Lillee, Terry Alderman and Geoff Lawson. (Australian captain, Kim Hughes, held back spinner Ray Bright.) Botham moved from controlled power-hitting into something more murderous. He swung at everything and usually connected, sending the ball to all points of the compass on the field.

When Dilley (56) played on to Lawson, he and Botham had added 117 in 80 minutes. Since tea they had added 76 in 44 minutes. It was a period of devil-may-care slather and whack that had succeeded without any science or serious planning. They had transformed the game's mood but had yet to put England in a winning position. England was eight for 252, just 25 ahead, and effectively eight for 25.

Botham was joined by Chris Old and raced through his century. During this link the Australian wheels fell off. Hughes lost control of his troops. Old observed that the Australians began bitching at each other. Keeper Rod Marsh, paceman Lillee and medium pacer Trevor Chappell ignored Hughes' directives. He, in turn, still failed to use spinner Ray Bright, which the English players and skipper, Mike Brearley, thought was a tactical error, given Botham's rampage. Botham and Old, sensing the demoralisation of their opponents, continued to plunder the bowling, which became loose. At 319, Old (29) was bowled by Lawson. Their 67-run partnership had given England the lead by 92.

Bob Willis came to the wicket with 20 minutes to go. Botham had not thought of slowing down as stumps approached. There was no point. The Australians were down. Botham put the boot right in with some more swashbuckling while shielding bunny Willis from all but five balls. Another 31 runs were added. Botham galloped to 145 not out. The score as stumps were drawn was nine for 352. England's lead was 125. Botham, criticised for his weight, his form, his apparent lack of leadership skills and his attitude, was suddenly a national hero of an unparalleled dimension in English cricket in the 25 years since Jim Laker had taken nineteen for 90 at Manchester in the Fourth Test of the 1956 Ashes series. Botham's performance had even more impact than this. Laker's effort was against a weak Australian team down for the count and kept there on a spinner's dustbowl paradise. As exciting as falling wickets are for a fielding team and its supporters, there is nothing quite like a powerful batsman bludgeoning an opposition into submission. And Botham's performance came when England, not the Australians, had been all but counted out. His size – he was known as 'Guy Gorilla' and 'Beefy' – gave him a fighter's image and so he was just the sort of bloke the English loved to see knock the stuffing out of the Aussies. He was their gladiator, the toughest character playing for England since Fred Trueman terrorised opposing batsmen more than a decade earlier.

The morning after the mayhem, Botham (149 not out) crunched one more boundary before Alderman removed Willis. England had reached 356. Australia had 130 to make for victory.

Willis felt that unless he bowled exceptionally well he would be dropped. His Test career was on the line. Motivated by this fear and inspired by Botham's batting feat, Willis delivered a great performance, taking eight for 43 from 15.1 overs. He kept his place. England won by 18 runs in the most amazing turnaround in Ashes cricket history. Botham's attitude, and his preparedness to risk everything to gain all, triggered an unlikely win and boosted England's confidence. It went on to win the 1981 series 3–1, thanks largely to Ian Botham's force and exceptional skill.

The MCC 'Boy'

Cheshire-born Ian Botham was just six when he told his parents, Marie and Les, that he was going to be a professional sportsman. The Yorkshire couple didn't ever disabuse him of this ambition. They were both devotees of a variety of sports. Les, an engineer and former Navy man, was a good park cricketer, runner and football player. Marie liked cricket, badminton and hockey. They encouraged their physically precocious son to strive hard in all his sporting pursuits, and it happened that young Ian chose cricket – the sport common to both his parents – as his number-one summer interest. He saw his initial first-class game at Bradford at age eight. At nine he was playing with adults at the Milford Recreational Ground in Yeovil, Somerset where he was brought up. At 12, he made the Yeovil Second XI, and played in his father's team. A year later young Botham captained the under-16 team at Buckler's Mead Secondary School. He was soon picked up for the schools' team of his county, Somerset, and crashed 80 in his first-ever knock, but was unfairly ignored as a bowler.

At 15 he was showing equal promise at soccer. He supported the flamboyant good-time 'glamour' boys at Chelsea Football Club, who exhilarated the King's Road on Saturdays in the late 1960s and early 1970s. Crystal Palace wanted to sign him up. Botham was only in his mid-teens and already his prophecy that he would live by his sport seemed a likelihood. His lack of academic application began to be of less and less concern to his parents. This highly determined, talented youngster had the mindset to achieve his sporting dreams. His ultimate desire, with which his parents concurred, lay with cricket.

A big opportunity to demonstrate talent in England centred on the annual competition between England Schools – made up of boys from non-public institutions versus

Public Schools (boys from the more privileged fee-paying institutions). Important cricket figures, often including Test selectors looking for the new Hobbs, Compton, May or Cowdrey, watched the game. Botham did well in trial games for selection of the England Schools team, especially with the ball. He had been billed as a batsman, not a bowler or all-rounder. At the time, there just wasn't a Lord Hawke or a Pelham Warner with the cricketing nous to spot a future champion and Botham wasn't selected. He felt let down, but like other greats before him (Bradman being a notable example), and others after him (Steve Waugh being another) who had received selection setbacks in their teens, his talent had plenty of time to be acknowledged. His next step was to spend two seasons as a Lord's ground-staff boy – a job that included being a cricketing dogsbody on call for MCC members wanting a hit in the nets. Botham at 16 in 1971 was paid 12 pounds a week to survive in expensive London – a salary that had to be subsidised by his parents. He didn't impress his coaches. Yet his staggering self-belief, when no one else saw any greatness in him, was the key to his desire to continue. Despite building a reputation as being wild, Botham worked hard on his skills in the nets. He listened to the coaches he respected, especially those that took a more laidback, less dictatorial approach to their charges. The mentality at Lord's was diametrically opposed to his, whether it be from the members' attitude of superiority, or the coaching which mainly attempted to dis-abuse him of his natural aggression with the bat and, strangely, his capacity to swing the ball. He was a quick learner but his talent was ignored. He became frustrated, and his irritation from the stifling experience never left him. But he surmounted it, absorbed the positive side of the personal development he underwent at Lord's in the technical elements of the game, and moved on.

Ian Botham knew he was destined for far greater things, even if no one at Lord's did. His attitude was that he would show them how wrong they were in their attitude to him. It was the kind of incentive he would revel in for much of his career.

Sun Up at Somerset

Botham left Lord's with plenty of good mates – something that was important to the exuberant youth. He loved the game, the competition and the camaraderie.

At 17, in 1973, he played in Somerset's Seconds, along with a brilliant young West Indian bat, Vivian Richards. They became close mates. Both respected the other's toughness, brilliance and competitiveness. Botham was blooded in two Sunday league games for the county at the end of 1973. Then he made the big step up to first-class cricket at the age of 18 in 1974, under the expert guidance of coach Tom Cartwright, who helped develop Botham's bowling. Another strong influence on Botham was Somerset captain, Brian Close, a legend in post-war cricket for his fighting qualities in county and Test matches.

1974 was the year Botham emerged as a teenage force and hope for Somerset and England. He played in a Benson & Hedges one-day quarter-final against Hampshire. First he bowled the best bat in England at the time, Barry Richards of Hampshire, which restricted that county to just 182. When Someset batted, Botham came in at seven for 113, with just 15 overs to go and 70 to win. Andy Roberts, the fastest bowler in England that year, hit him with a bouncer that smashed into his mouth. The helmetless Botham spat out blood and teeth, continued, and dominated the final overs. He hit the winning run with seven balls to spare and was an instant hero. His courage impressed everyone but the old-timers at the club told him about being a rooster one day and a feather duster the next. They didn't want the super-confident youngster to get a swollen head. But the young Botham didn't change. He expected to always perform like this. It was an exhilarating experience, but no big deal for him. His attitude was that if he couldn't come in and take control of a game at a critical point, what was the point of playing? Botham wasn't in the game for averages or awards or draws or tactical defensive measures. He didn't engage in negative thoughts; he didn't believe in reverse gears or putting up the shutters. He visualised himself as a match-winner; someone for the extra-big occasion.

In Taunton, where he was based, he was becoming a legend for being a wild drinker, but meeting a young Yorkshire woman, Kathryn Waller, steadied him just enough at a critical time. Botham didn't transform into an angel, but his relationship with her matured him fast. They got engaged and now, at a young age, he faced responsibilities. His cricket benefited. Botham, like any professional sportsperson taking on marriage, had to succeed for reasons other than self-aggrandisement. Perhaps he tried too hard and was impatient. His second season, 1975, fell short of expectations. He did well enough with the ball, taking 62 wickets at 27.48, with a best return of five for 69. But he scored just 584 runs at 18.25. Somerset didn't cap him, and he was struggling financially. But he and Kathryn married in early 1976, pushing Botham to lift his rating. He did better early in 1976 and was capped. His salary increased. Over the summer he achieved almost identical bowling figures as in 1975, but his batting lifted a notch, helped by a dashing 167 not out against Nottinghamshire in August. It was his maiden first-class hundred, and a beauty. It allowed him to break the 1000-run barrier (1022 in all) at an average of 34.06.

His aggregate included a timely 97 off Sussex, led by England's skipper, Tony Greig. Greig pushed for his selection in the end of season one-day internationals against the West Indies. Botham played in two of them, but didn't shine. It was his slim chance to impress selectors but he gave them little to be excited about. He missed the 1976–77 tour of India and the Centenary Test in Melbourne that marked the hundred-year anniversary of the first international ever played.

Test Break

In 1977, Botham saw his main chance of playing Test cricket for England against the touring Australians. First, he took up a Whitbread scholarship – offered to promising young cricketers – to play club cricket in Melbourne early in 1977, yet did not distinguish himself on or off the field except for the notoriety he gained after he was involved in a pub altercation with former Australian captain Ian Chappell.

Unfazed by his apparent lack of progress, Botham returned to England for the 1977 season. He played well for Somerset against the Australian tourists but overdid the bouncer. He was selected in an MCC side to play the Australians, along with a few others close to Test selection. He again used the bouncer too much and paid for it in boundaries. Botham maintained his batting improvement with a century and several fifties and he tightened up his bowling. It was enough for him to be selected for his debut Test, the Third Test in the Ashes series that England led 1–0. The venue was Trent Bridge, Nottingham. It was a good situation for Botham, 21, in which to make his first big international appearance. Australia was on the run. Morale in the tourists' camp was low. England skipper Mike Brearley, who struggled with the bat at Test level, nevertheless was out-generalling his counterpart Greg Chappell. Furthermore, Yorkshire opener Geoffrey Boycott was set to return to Test cricket after a self-imposed exile of 30 matches. His, at times, painstaking but usually effective run-making technique was likely to put the tourists under more pressure.

The Australians couldn't blame their poor form on the looming Packer crisis, where the best world players had been contracted to play in a breakaway international competition. Both teams had defectors, who had signed to play in Packer's World Series, beginning later in 1977 in Australia. It affected team morale. Chappell was suddenly persona non grata with Australia's managers.

Australia batted first and Botham was on early. He bowled erratically, but settled down after he took his first wicket, Greg Chappell – one of the world's three top batsmen (the others at the time being Barry Richards and Viv Richards) – with a long-hop wide of off-stump. Chappell dragged it onto his stumps. Later, Botham gave left-hander Rod Marsh the old one-two: a bouncer, then a pitched-up in-swinger that trapped the vigorous Aussie keeper lbw. Botham ended with the fine figures of five for 74 off 20 overs. He was somewhat of a hero by the time he met the Queen and the Duke of Edinburgh during the last session of the day. It was a red-letter day for the novice and one he would remember.

Botham made 25 in his only innings, while Boycott returned as Australia's bête noir, making 107 and 80 not out. England went on to win comfortably by seven wickets. Boycott again dominated in the Fourth Test at his home ground of Headingley as he ground out 191 in England's 436. Botham made a duck but relished the cloudy atmosphere when he bowled. He was able to get his out-swinger going. This time he took an excellent five for 21 off 11 overs. Included in his bag were Doug Walters and left-handers David Hookes and Rod Marsh. England went on to win by an innings and 85 runs, and took the Ashes 3–0.

Botham broke a bone in his foot before the Fifth Test and missed selection. His 10 wickets were taken at 20.20 meaning he could be more than satisfied with his sensational entry to the international level. Early autumn was also a joyous occasion in the Botham household when Kathryn gave birth to a son, Liam. (They would later have two daughters, Sarah and Beccy.) When visiting his wife and new-born baby, he accidentally entered a hospital ward full of children with leukaemia. Thankful that his own son was healthy, the plight of these youngsters drew out a compassion in Botham that was largely unappreciated outside his friends and family. He arranged an anonymous regular donation to fund Christmas parties in that ward.

Botham's place as England's all-rounder was entrenched with the defection of Greig to Packer's World Series Cricket. But severe dysentery prevented him taking the opportunity of building his record on England's tour of Pakistan in 1977–78. He had to sit out the three Tests there and wait until the touring party moved on to less exacting accommodation in New Zealand which made touring more enjoyable. (Tour conditions often impacted on team morale and performance.) Botham, now 22, returned to the team and took two more five-wicket hauls against New Zealand, in addition to his first Test century – 103 at Christchurch in the Second Test. It was a responsible, patient knock of 312 minutes, made more laudable by his 'rope-a-dope' tactics against paceman Richard Hadlee, who tried to bounce him out. Botham waited until Hadlee had tired, then picked him off with ease, hitting several boundaries.

England scored 418. New Zealand replied with 235. England needed quick runs in its second innings. When Boycott, the acting captain in place of the injured Brearley, couldn't get them, Botham came in at number four and deliberately ran out his skipper to allow others in to score faster. Botham led the way by belting 30 not out off 36 balls. England went on to win by 174 runs. Botham became the second England player after Tony Greig to score a century and take five wickets in an innings in the same Test.

Botham finished the three-Test series with 17 wickets at 18.29, and a batting average of 53.00. He also took several splendid catches. These returns were those of a true all-round champion.

The lad from Yeovil had arrived as a top-line Test all-rounder.

Consolidation at the Top

Botham continued his strong, consistent Test batting into the 1978 season at home with a century in the First of the three-Test series against Pakistan. Then at Lord's in the Second Test he improved on his Christchurch effort by scoring 108. This second successive century took just 104 deliveries and was achieved under bizarre circumstances. Botham and Chris Old went out drinking after the first day, 15 June, was washed out. They thought that Day Two would also be wet. Instead, it was sunny. England captain Mike Brearley knew his opening bowlers had been out revelling until the early hours. He batted when he won the toss. Therefore, Botham's third Test century surprised Old and his skipper, coming as it did after a particularly convivial evening. It helped propel the Botham legend as an individual with the constitution and recuperative powers of an ox.

His performances didn't end there. In Pakistan's second innings he took eight for 34, including a final spell of six wickets for 8 in 53 deliveries. It was the best-ever analysis at Lord's. Botham was able to get the ball to swing late and at genuine pace. Some of the deliveries in his last spell were unplayable, even for a master batsman. Botham became the first player to score 100 and take eight wickets in an innings in a match. He joined Garry Sobers and Mushtaq Mohammad as the two other players until that time to take five or more wickets in an innings and make a century. At just 22 years of age, he was in serious company in the record books for great all-rounders. Again, his Test figures were outstanding. He averaged 70.66 with the bat and took 13 wickets at 16.07. He continued the devastation with the ball in three Tests against New Zealand later in the summer, taking 24 wickets at 14.04, including eleven for 140 at Lord's in late August. Botham gained enormous satisfaction with his outstanding displays twice in the one summer at the home of cricket. Five years earlier he had been just another lowly hopeful on the ground-staff. Now those members who had yelled 'boy!' when they wanted him to bowl to them were standing to applaud him. In the summer of 1978, Ian Botham was Lord of Lord's, and had no peer.

In his debut year he had taken five wickets or more eight times in just 11 Tests, and had scored three centuries. Botham also lifted his first-class rating, taking 100 wickets for the first and only time in a season, at 16.40, including 10 five-wicket hauls.

Down-Under Plunder

With this record behind him, Botham looked forward to touring Australia under Brearley and causing some devastation there, especially as he would be playing against Australia's Second XI. Its top 12 players had all gone over to Packer's WSC.

England won the series 5–1, with the inexperienced new Australian skipper, Graham Yallop, no match for the wily Brearley. Botham and off-spinner Geoff Miller took the most wickets for England – 23 apiece (Botham at 24.65 and Miller at a far more economical 15.04). Botham could not put Australia's bowlers to the sword as he hoped. He scored two fifties in an aggregate of 291 at 29.10 with a highest score of 74. Yet the WSC defections had already developed some other worthy Australian bowlers such as Rodney Hogg. This speedster was by far the most successful bowler in the six-Test series, taking 41 (a record aggregate in a series against England) at an amazing 12.85. Paceman Alan Hurst (25 at 23.08) and leg-spinner Jimmy Higgs (19 at 24.63) also helped ensure that Australia was not slaughtered. In fact, England failed to reach 400 runs in any innings. It was a bowlers' series. Australia's bats were the weak link that handed England the Ashes. Only left-handers Graham Yallop and Allan Border averaged more than 30.

Botham continued on his merry way in 1979 at home, this time against India. Now he seemed assured not to fail with bat and ball in any Test. If he didn't make a big score he took a 'five for'. If he didn't take a wicket, as in the drawn Third Test at Headingley, he made runs – 137 in this instance. This powerhouse knock included five sixes and 16 fours. It took only 152 balls. He was a 23-year-old in a hurry and preferred getting there with boundaries – 94 runs' worth. He averaged 48.80 in the Tests and took 20 wickets at 23.60. England won the four-Test series 1–0. Botham was at the peak of his powers with both bat and ball, and had proved to be a regular match-winner. At The Oval, in the final game of the series, India was set 438 to win and looked likely to do it when its score was one for 365. A few wickets fell but the runs kept coming. Brearley threw the ball to Botham with the score at three for 389 and eight overs to go. India had to make 49 off 48 balls – which was a tight but likely proposition. Botham's chest puffed out, as it seemed to in these moments. He roared in like a bull, putting pressure on the Indians, who faltered. Botham took three for 17, including Sunil Gavaskar caught for a magnificent 221, and also effected a brilliant stop and run-out of Venkat. India reached eight for 429, and fell 10 short of the target. The game was drawn.

Put Asunder, Down-Under

Botham travelled again to Australia for a three-Test series in 1979–80 against a side strengthened by the return of some of its best soldiers, after the ending of the Packer experiment. He couldn't prevent a 3–0 thrashing of England but performed admirably himself, especially with the ball, taking 19 at 19.52. He bowled outstandingly in the First Test at Perth, taking eleven for 176 for the match. Yet Botham struggled with the bat in the first five innings of the series, compiling just 68 runs. It prompted him to ask for help from former batting great Ken Barrington, the England team's assistant manager. Barrington suggested he was falling forward when playing a shot, rather than remaining still. Botham corrected the fault by taking guard on leg-stump. This meant he was not into the shot too quickly and therefore, in theory, less likely to topple forward after playing it. It worked. In the Third Test at Melbourne in February 1980 he made 119 not out in grand style off 188 balls in 199 minutes. This was against a rampant Lillee, bowling leg-cutters on a slow, low Melbourne wicket. It was Botham's first hundred against Australia.

With lessons learnt and reputation intact, he and the team moved on to Bombay in mid-February for the Golden Jubilee Test to mark the formation of India's cricket Board of Control. Botham continued his Melbourne form, coming in at four for 57 and scoring 114 in 206 minutes with 17 fours. He took six for 58 and seven for 48 – thirteen for 106. He strode like a colossus through this game and became the first player to score a century and take 10 wickets or more in a Test. England won by 10 wickets. He returned home for a challenging summer against the West Indies, which had established itself as the dominant world cricketing nation in the aftermath of WSC.

Captain Botham

Brearley, one of the more cerebral leaders England ever had, stepped aside to pursue a qualification in psychotherapy, and Botham was appointed captain in 1980. He had been given the toughest assignment in world cricket and was not able to force a win against the West Indies during the five-Test series, which England lost 0–1. England then drew with Australia in the Centenary Test. It marked the first Australia and England match ever played in England. Botham again battled to find touch with the bat. He began the 1980 season well enough, scoring 57 in the first innings of the First Test at Trent Bridge. But his batting form fell away against a bowling barrage from Andy Roberts,

Michael Holding, Joel Garner, Colin Croft and Malcolm Marshall — the most formidable speed force in cricket history. Botham could only average 16.90 for the six Tests, including the one against Australia. He was less penetrating with the ball, taking 14 Test wickets at 36.93 for the summer. A consolation was the three times he dismissed his close friend Viv Richards.

Botham's trials against the formidable Caribbean combination continued in another five-Test series from February to April 1981. The tour was calamitous, beginning with the cancellation of the Second Test at Georgetown, Guyana, when paceman Robin Jackman was deported from that country. This occurred after it was discovered he had played and coached in South Africa (then run by an apartheid regime) over the previous 11 years. Then Ken Barrington died after a heart attack in his hotel room during the second evening of the Barbados Third Test. Barrington had been a cricketing mentor for Botham and his death touched the England skipper deeply.

England was soundly beaten 2–0. Botham's form fell away further with the bat. He could manage just 73 runs at 10.42 with a top score of 26 from nine knocks. He had now gone 17 innings while scoring just one fifty. His bowling returns (15 at 32.80) were fair for him, but in 10 Tests now he had failed to take a 'five-for' in an innings.

Botham returned to England and was immediately into the 1981 season, which would feature six Tests against the Australians. There were calls for his sacking as leader, but fairer minds pointed out that he had to be given another chance, considering the difficult task of taking on the West Indies at their peak in his first two series.

Australia won the First Test at Trent Bridge and honours were even at Lord's in a drawn game. However, Botham's form with the bat – he managed a 'pair' at Lord's – and with the ball convinced selectors that he should be relieved of the leadership. After no wins, four losses and eight draws from 12 games, Botham's short tenure as England skipper was over. It was a miserable time for him. He was angered by the Lord's members' cold reaction to his second-innings duck, bowled around his legs first ball by spinner Ray Bright. Not one pair of hands were put together in a gesture of sympathy for one of the country's greatest-ever players down on his luck. Botham was bitter about this and concerned about his form. He accepted the sacking and was consoled by the return of Brearley to the helm. It meant Botham was free to be his flamboyant self as an all-round champion.

Sacked but Back

Instead of wallowing in self-pity, Botham was back in the fray nine days later in the Third Test at Headingley. He was now unfettered by the strictures and problems of leadership. His determination returned and he dominated this game as probably no player had done with bat and ball in any Test before him. He took six for 95 and one for 14, and made 50 and that thumping 149 not out. This, plus Willis's eight for 43 in Australia's second innings, won the game for England and levelled the series.

Botham's explosive return to form and confidence seemed to falter in the Fourth Test at Leeds when he scored 26 and 3 and took one for 64 in Australia's first innings. The tourists were four for 105 in their second innings, needing just 46 for victory when Brearley brought him on to keep the runs down in the hope that off-spinner John Emburey could pull off a near miracle at the other end. Emburey had the tenacious Allan Border caught off a difficult ball that bounced sharply. Australia was five for 105, and still needed 46.

Brearley's introduction of Botham, his jousting knight, did strange things to the Australian bats. The aggressive Marsh seemed intent on smashing him out of the firing line. He hit across the line of an ordinary ball and was bowled. Martin Kent did the same. Lillee wanted to hit him too, and went out of his way to snick a near wide to keeper Bob Taylor. Tail-ender Bright was beaten by a quicker one and trapped lbw. Finally, Terry Alderman only needed a straight one, which he duly got, and he was bowled for a duck. Botham had taken five wickets in 28 deliveries while conceding one run. Only one wicket – Bright's – was taken on merit. The other four were self-inflicted dismissals by the batsman. This was testimony to the psychological impact Botham had in the tight circumstances. Brearley's intuitive skills and the bowling prowess of Botham had won another Test for England. It now had a 2–1 grip on the series with two more to play. Gone were the horrors of Lord's for Botham. He had triumphed. But he had much more to prove in those final two games.

At Old Trafford in the Fifth Test, Lillee had him caught for a duck but he fought back with three for 28, including the prize Australian wicket of Border for 11. Botham came to the wicket in England's second innings at five for 104 – a lead of 205 with five wickets intact. The pitch was true. He began sedately, scoring three in singles. He stepped up his rating and reached 28 off 53 deliveries before the new ball was taken. Lillee steamed in and let go two bouncers. Botham smashed each of them over long leg for six and hooked another – all inside two overs. Soon the crowd was applauding his fifty. The mayhem didn't stop as he crunched the others – Alderman, Mike Whitney on debut, and Bright, en route to a century. He hooked and drove on the off, or hit straight drives over or past the bowler. It took just 86 balls. His last 72 had taken just 33 balls in only 37 minutes, which would be a terrific rate for two bats in a one-day rush for runs. But this was Botham on his own in a Test, and in a hurry. The hearts of fans were in their mouths on two occasions as he mishit high catches to mid-off and third man, only to see these possible chances grassed. Apart from these mishaps it was a top innings of that rare combination of power and class. Bradman observed – as he did with Sobers a decade earlier at the MCG in an Australia versus Rest of the World double century – that Botham's innings was a case of an awesome bludgeoning power in control of technique. This applied off the front or back foot. Bradman said the innings was 'enthralling'. He saw the difference between a batsman simply 'having a go', and Botham's approach of clinical execution.

Botham's innings ended on 118 when he was caught behind off Whitney. It took 123 minutes and 102 balls. He hit 13 fours and six sixes – then a record number of sixes for a match played in England and a record against Australia in a match played anywhere in the world.

Australia was left with a target of 506 for victory, about 100 more than any team had ever achieved to win in the final innings of a Test. Brave centuries from left-handers Yallop (114) and Border with a broken finger (123 not out) threatened England. But once Yallop was dismissed at 198 after a 79 stand, Australia's cause was lost. It went down by 103. England had won the Ashes. Botham, with three successive Player of the Match awards in the Third, Fourth and Fifth Tests, did more than anyone to achieve the series victory. He was the difference between a series being won and lost. Without his spirit, the result could easily have gone the other way.

He finished off the series with two failures with the bat and two fine bowling performances that netted him ten for 253. Only Lillee with eleven for 159 did better. It was

Botham's forty-first Test and he reached the 200-wicket milestone. He was only 25 years of age. He had been involved in Test cricket for just four years, although this larger-than-life figure seemed to have been around for a decade. His best performances were often devastating and when he failed it looked horrendous. So much was expected of him. Now, after his dramatic return to dominance, especially against Australia, he was billed as England's finest all-round cricketer of the twentieth century. Certainly no one since W.G. Grace in the nineteenth century seemed as forceful a character in the minds of English cricket historians.

Post-1981

When he toured India in 1981–82 Botham found it tough to maintain the form that had destroyed Australia. Yet with match figures of nine for 133 off 50 overs at Bombay in a losing First Test for England, and a dashing 142 in the final (Sixth) Test at Kanpur, he demonstrated the ability to deliver the grand performance when he put his body and mind to it. His bowling analysis of 17 wickets at 38.82 was not up to his usual high standard. But his batting was consistent and strong. He had an aggregate of 440 at an average of 55.00.

A few months later, the demanding grind continued through another summer. In 1982 England played three Tests each against both India and Pakistan. Botham faced challenges to his position as the world's leading all-rounder from India's Kapil Dev and Pakistan's Imran Khan. Once more he lifted his rating, first against India when he hit 67 and took five for 46 at Lord's, then with an innings of 128 at Old Trafford and his highest score in Tests – 208 – at The

Oval. The double came up in 220 balls and 268 minutes. Overall, his innings lasted 226 deliveries in 276 minutes. His 403 for the series was scored at an average of 134.33, while his nine wickets were at a less than economical 35.55. He was kept on his toes by Kapil Dev, who hit three fifties including a dashing 97 in 93 balls. Botham bowled better against Pakistan, taking 18 wickets at 26.55, and twice more passed 50. Imran Khan did better, taking 21 wickets at 18.57, and also cracked two fifties.

Botham also performed well for Somerset, smashing a century in just 52 minutes against Warwickshire. He was approaching 27 years of age, and feeling the pressure of non-stop touring and almost year-round playing at first-class and Test level. He was now a superstar, who had widened his circle of friends to include other superstars such as singer Elton John. Botham enjoyed these distractions of his social life perhaps too much to also live the more austere life of an international sportsman. He found it tough getting himself motivated for his third tour to Australia in four years. It showed in his analysis. His 18 wickets were at 40.50, and he only averaged 27.16 with the bat. After the heroics of 1981 England was beaten 1–2 and lost the Ashes.

For the next decade, from 1983 on, his outstanding performances were more sporadic but he could still do extraordinary things here and there, except with the ball against the strong West Indian line-ups of the 1980s. He met another challenge from New Zealand's Richard Hadlee, who outshone him over two series in England and New Zealand in three of the four sets of analysis. Hadlee won out in England in the four-Test series of 1983 with both bat and ball. In New Zealand, over 1983–84, Botham was superior with the bat, while Hadlee did better with the ball.

In 1984, Botham received a record benefit of 90,000 pounds from Somerset. In 1985, after bowing out of a tour of India and Sri Lanka to recuperate after eight years of non-stop travelling, he came back for a strong all-round effort against Australia. Botham took 31 wickets at 27.58, by far the best figures of any player for England, and it won back the Ashes by 3–1. At the end of the season – his last as Somerset captain – he had scored 1530 runs at 69.54, easily the best average of his first-class career. He hit five centuries and nine fifties, and lifted 80 sixes – yet another record.

Hannibal Botham

In 1986, Botham was suspended from cricket for admitting in a newspaper article that he had smoked marijuana. But this was overshadowed when Botham became a hero off the field in support of leukaemia research with an 874-mile (1398-km) walk from John o' Groats to Land's End. Botham had never lost his compassion for victims of this disease, ever since his first encounter with the sick children at a Taunton hospital a decade earlier. This charitable side to Botham, to some extent, countered the poor aspect of his media-generated image, over a decade, as a pot-smoking, hard-drinking lout, given to fits of violence. Botham set himself a gruelling schedule, walking 30 miles (48 km) a day. After this success, he involved himself in further challenging walks over the years and raised considerable amounts for leukaemia research. 1986 also marked a sad end in his long association with Somerset. The county sacked its West Indian pair Joel Garner and Viv Richards, and Botham walked out in sympathy. He joined Worcestershire.

On a fourth tour to Australia in 1986–87, he showed all his old touch with a dashing 138 at Brisbane in the First Test of the series and brought back plenty of 1981 night-mares for the Australians. But it was to be his last show of power against the old enemy. His other five innings saw him accumulate just 51 runs. He took only nine wickets at 32.89.

Botham enjoyed his visits to Australia. He decided to accept an offer to play for Queensland for three seasons. He had a moderate season with Queensland in 1987–88 but it was impaired by alcohol-fuelled loutish behaviour on a long plane trip from Melbourne to Perth in March 1988. This saw him charged with assault and offensive behaviour. Botham was bailed out of gaol by Dennis Lillee, who arrived with a crate of beer. Botham was fined $320 after pleading guilty. The incident resulted in him being sacked from his three-year contract with Queensland. Undeterred, Botham took off for another walking assignment, complete with accompanying elephants and a herd of media people, this time from Perpignan in the South of France across the Alps to Turin in Italy. It was a distance of 450 miles (720 km) over 21 days. This was an even more demanding effort than his mighty stroll from John o' Groats to Land's End. He was following the route taken by Hannibal, the Carthaginian general, in the spring of 218 BC.

Botham's courage was unmistakable, especially since he had suffered from a nagging and serious back injury for years. Not long after the walk he underwent surgery. His threatening days with the ball seemed to be over, mainly because of his back problem. Botham did play again in the 1989 Ashes but was ineffective. In 1992 he left Worcestershire to play for Durham for their inaugural year of first-class cricket and played his last Test. He retired halfway through the 1993 season.

In 102 Tests he scored 5200 runs at 33.54, including 14 centuries, and took a then world record of 383 wickets at 28.40. He was always an athletic catch, snaffling 120 victims. In first-class cricket he hit 19,399 runs at 33.97, including 38 centuries. His tally of wickets was 1172 at 27.22, and he took 354 catches.

After retirement, he became a regular television commentator and even performed in some pantomimes.

By selecting Ian Botham as 12th man in his all-time best England team, Bradman acknowledged him as England's finest all-rounder of the twentieth century.

Index

INDEX

Index

Index

Photo Credits

Player photographs

The author and publishers gratefully acknowledge Getty Images/Hulton Archive for permission to use the pictures of: Bradman (page 11); Ponsford (page 61); Morris (page 91); Harvey (page 131); Miller (page 163); Lindwall (page 207); Lillee (page 221); Grimmett (page 251); Benaud (page 267); Hobbs (page 307); Hutton (page 333); Compton (page 369); May (page 397); Grace (page 445); Evans (page 479); Bedser (page 525); Botham (page 595).

Picture section: Australia

Thanks to Getty Images/Hulton Archive for use of the pictures captioned: *Bill and Bertha; The Man and Stan; Mates and Masters; Boys' Own Hero; Driving Demonstration; On the Run at Leeds; Stand and Deliver; Miller Time; On Bended Knee; A Keeper of Prey; Lindwall, Windmill; Side On Power; What the Batsman Saw; 'Scarl'; Well Done Skipper; Spin King; Read All About It*. Thanks to Australian Picture Library for permission to use the pictures captioned *Atomic Ray* and *Ashes Heroes*, and Newspix for use of *Morris's Major Combatant* and *Head-Steady Hooker*.

Picture section: England

Thanks to Getty Images/Hulton Archive for use of the pictures captioned: *Straight with Drive; Happy Hobbs; Skipper with Strike; One Knight to Another; Lofty Ambitions; Ashes Victorious; The Brylcreem Kid; He Also Spun; May the Style Be With You; Balance and Belligerence; On Top of Lord's; On the Front Foot; Gloves Ready; Eyes Steady; Great Fast Hope; High Arm Action; Mainstay; Sailing to Victory; That Lethal Right Arm; Verity With the Bat; Spin King; Youthful Bladesman; Wicket Delight; Having a Fling; Gower Power; Laker Breaker*.